THE WORLD'S CLASSICS

# TRAVELS THROUGH FRANCE AND ITALY

TOBIAS SMOLLETT (1721–71), born in Dunbartonshire of a landed Scottish Presbyterian family, studied at Dumbarton Grammar School and Glasgow University. After an incomplete medical apprenticeship, he travelled to London and joined the Navy, serving as surgeon's mate on the expedition to Cartagena. The experiences of his early life provided graphic backing for his first novel, *Roderick Random* (1748), which established his reputation as a writer. This was followed by *Peregrine Pickle* (1751) and *Ferdinand Count Fathom* (1753). Living by his pen, Smollett was prolific and variously successful as an editor, translator, dramatist, political satirist, historian and poet. His remarkable powers of observation are most in evidence in the creative masterpieces of his later career, when, despite a constant struggle against ill health, he wrote the *Travels through France and Italy* (1766), describing his personal experiences on the Continent, and his brilliant last novel, *The Expedition of Humphry Clinker* (1771).

DR FRANK FELSENSTEIN taught at the University of Geneva, and is now a lecturer in the School of English, University of Leeds. As well as editing the *Travels*, he has published articles on Smollett, Fielding, Burke and Johnson.

THE WORLD'S CLASSICS

TOBIAS SMOLLETT
*Travels through
France and Italy*

EDITED BY
FRANK FELSENSTEIN

Oxford   New York
OXFORD UNIVERSITY PRESS

Oxford University Press, Walton Street, Oxford OX2 6DP

Oxford New York Toronto
Delhi Bombay Calcutta Madras Karachi
Petaling Jaya Singapore Hong Kong Tokyo
Nairobi Dar es Salaam Cape Town
Melbourne Auckland

and associated companies in
Berlin Ibadan

Oxford is a trade mark of Oxford University Press

First published 1979 by the Clarendon Press
First published as a World's Classics paperback 1981
Reprinted 1990, 1992

This edition © Frank Felsenstein 1979
Introduction and notes © Frank Felsenstein 1981

British Library Cataloguing in Publication Data

Smollett, Tobias
Travels through France and Italy, — (The World's classics)
1. France — Description and travel
2. Europe — Description and travel — 17th–18th centuries
3. Italy — Description and travel — 1501–1800
I. Title   II. Felsenstein, Frank
914.4'04'34   DC25

ISBN 0–19–281569–5

Printed in Great Britain by
BPCC Hazells Ltd
Aylesbury, Bucks.

For V.L.F.

# Contents

Introduction     ix

Note on the Text     xxi

Select Bibliography     xxii

A Chronology of Tobias Smollett     xxv

Map: Smollett's route through France and Italy     xxviii

TRAVELS THROUGH FRANCE AND ITALY     1

Notes     359

Appendix     417

Index     419

# Contents

Introductions

Note on the Text

Select Bibliography

A Chronology of Tobias Smollett

Map: Smollett's route through France and Italy

## TRAVELS THROUGH FRANCE AND ITALY

Notes

Appendix

Index

# Introduction

During his visit to Nice in 1789, the celebrated traveller and agronomist Arthur Young recalls being told by the British consul of the warning given to Smollett 'that if he were to go again thither the Nissards would certainly knock him on the head.'[1] When Young heard this, Smollett had already been dead for eighteen years. More than twenty years before, the historian and philosopher David Hume relates a similar story, that upon Smollett's appearance in Nice the 'People would rise upon him and stone him in the Streets.'[2] Nowadays, it appears wellnigh incredible that a work of travel could evoke such a physical response, but then few works have enjoyed — or perhaps suffered — the notoriety of the *Travels through France and Italy* (1766). In consequence of its publication, Tobias Smollett acquired the reputation of being possibly the most atrabilious, ill-humoured British traveller ever to venture over the Channel. In the popular imagination, the label pinned upon him by his contemporary traveller-novelist, Laurence Sterne, has stuck, for in the *Sentimental Journey*, published two years after in 1768 and written largely as a riposte to Smollett, the latter is portrayed in canker and spleen as 'the learned SMELFUNGUS', epitome of the worst kind of traveller, 'the man who can travel from *Dan* to *Beersheba*, and cry, 'Tis all barren —.'[3]

Indeed, the enormous popularity and frequent translation of the *Sentimental Journey*, which became the rage throughout Europe, almost overnight eclipsed whatever early success the *Travels through France and Italy* had enjoyed. Wherever Sterne's book was acclaimed, Smollett the traveller was

1. *Travels in France during the Years 1787, 1788, 1789*, ed. M. Betham-Edwards, 1913, p.276.
2. *New Letters of David Hume*, ed. R. Klibansky and E. C. Mossner, Oxford, 1954, p.173.
3. *A Sentimental Journey through France and Italy*, ed. Gardner D. Stout, Jr., Berkeley, California, 1967, pp.115–16.

vilified. An amusing anecdote by Voltaire, first published in his *Mensonges Imprimés* of 1750 and included in the first collected edition in English of *The Works of M. de Voltaire* which bears Smollett's name as co-translator, tells of 'the German, who happening to have a small difference with his landlady at Blois, whose hair was somewhat inclinable to the sandy, put down in his pocket-book, "*Nota bene*, All the women in Blois are red-haired and scolds."'[4] Curiously, after the publication of the *Travels*, a version of the story recurs with tedious predictability, the anonymous German traveller being transferred and replaced by Smollett himself.

Yet, despite the vagaries of its reputation, the *Travels* has qualities that belong to the best factual travel books, being highly readable, replete with fascinating perceptions, and (most importantly) infused with the individualistic person-ality of its author. Smollett's consummate ability as a racon-teur, which we associate most readily with his novels, is here translated into an autobiographical account, recording his experiences between June 1763 and June 1765 on a journey with his wife across the Continent in the pursuit of a climate more salutary to his failing health. The aggravation to his already weakened constitution caused by the death in April 1763 of his only child, Elizabeth, and by the political failure of *The Briton* which he edited, seems to have hastened his departure from England. His own medical knowledge must have given him a pretty clear idea as to the nature of his illness — 'in such a bad state of health, troubled with an asthmatic cough, spitting, slow fever, and restlessness, which demands a continual change of place, as well as free air, and room for motion' (p.64) — though the elusiveness of a cure prompted both his scepticism and speculation. At Montpellier, where that 'great lanthorn of medicine', Pro-fessor Fizes, correctly diagnosed his illness as a slow con-sumption, Smollett — as doctor turned patient — rejected the diagnosis as flagrantly absurd, savouring 'strongly of the old woman' (pp.88, 101). His anger at Fizes's albeit super-ficial examination of the case led him to accuse the rapacious specialist of being all too ready 'to scramble up two pair of

4. *The Works of M. de Voltaire*, translated by T. Smollett, M.D., T. Francklin, M.A. and Others, 36 vols., 1761–9, XIII, p.244.

stairs for a fee of six livres . . . [but] without a fee he will give his advice to no person whatsoever.' (p.89). Both here and elsewhere, the abrasiveness and bad temper which characterize many of Smollett's remarks seem to have had a more immediately therapeutic effect than the medicinal remedies proffered him. There is something positively curative to be found by venting his spleen, if only as a sign of his determination not to allow his ill health to get the better of him.

The lack of effective treatment for respiratory complaints leads Smollett to speculation and practical experiment. He can put to the test his own pet theory, expressed a number of years earlier in a curiously controversial pamphlet, *An Essay on the External Use of Water* (1752), that the exercise of bathing will have a recuperative effect upon the body. Though contrary to 'all the dogmata of physic' as then practised, and considered highly eccentric, its efficacy proves immediate when at Boulogne he tells us (with just a hint of self-mockery) that he 'hired a chaise, and going to the beach, about a league from the town, plunged into the sea without hesitation. By this desperate remedy, I got a fresh cold in my head: but my stitches and fever vanished the very first day; and by a daily repetition of the bath, I have diminished my cough, strengthened my body, and recovered my spirits' (p.13). It is characteristic of the enquiring mind that lies behind the *Travels* that Smollett should again repeat the experiment at Nice with some improvement to his health (p.185), and that later, in describing his visit to Rome, he gives us a detailed account of the bathing methods of the ancient Romans, a practice that 'was certainly necessary to health and cleanliness . . . [though] these purposes would have been much better answered by plunging into the Tyber, than by using the warm bath in the thermæ' (p.264). Even the valetudinarian details in the *Travels* are frequently informative and entertaining.[5]

5. An interesting parallel occurs in *Some Thoughts Concerning Education* (1693) in *The Educational Writings of John Locke*, ed. James L. Axtell, Cambridge, 1968, pp.120–1. Locke advocates a similar regimen for infants, who, 'tender as they are thought, may, without any Danger, endure Bathing, not only of their Feet, but of their whole Bodies in cold Water. And there are at this Day Ladies in the Highlands of *Scotland*, who use this Discipline to their Children in the midst of Winter; and find that cold Water does them no harm, even when there is Ice in it.' Cf. *Peregrine Pickle*, p.28.

But Smollett's concern for his physical state was considered obsessive by several contemporary critics. One of the most persistent, the malevolent Philip Thicknesse, quipped that the *Travels* should 'more properly . . . be intitled, "QUARRELS through France and Italy for the cure of a pulmonic disorder." '[6] Nevertheless, it should be remembered that for Smollett — and presumably for many other British tourists on the Continent during the eighteenth century — the experience of travel inevitably produced continual wrangles with landlords and cudgelling of post-boys, 'abundance of little vexations, which may be termed the Plagues of Posting' (p.327). Yet, where most travellers, however much they suffered in private, avoided publishing these uncomfortable details for fear of appearing indelicate or xenophobic, Smollett was far too honest an observer to shirk the truth. His *Travels* is a splendidly personal account, in which even the refusal to conceal his bad temper may be seen as a mark of his intellectual integrity and determination not to suppress or varnish the experience of the journey. Throughout the Letters, by astute combination of personal observation and anecdote, Smollett brings to life the very essence of travelling on the Continent in the century before the advent of the railway. Yet, without the acrimony and ill-humour, his everyday adventures on the road would be too mundane to deserve recounting. If there was ever an occasion when spleen was turned to literary advantage it is in the *Travels through France and Italy*.

Following Sterne and Thicknesse, it is perhaps a little too easy to emphasize the bad temper and to play down the incisiveness with which Smollett can pick upon certain traits of character which he deems peculiar to the French or the Italians, and magnify these until they verge upon caricature. The hostile reaction to the *Travels* in Nice must have been aggravated by the deliberately unflattering generalizations with which he depicts the Nissards, of whom we are told that the common people 'are all diminutive, meagre, withered, dirty, and half naked' (p.167); the artisans 'are very lazy, very needy, very aukward and void of all ingenuity' (ibid.); the

6. *Useful Hints to Those Who Make the Tour of France*, 1768, p.4.

shopkeepers 'are generally poor, greedy, and over-reaching' (p. 166); the merchants 'are in general such dirty knaves, that no foreigners will trust them in the way of trade' (p. 165); the gallantry of the noblesse is to be compared to 'dean Swift's description of the Yahoos' (p. 150); most of the women 'are pot-bellied' (p. 149); their churches are 'sanctuaries for all kinds of criminals . . . and the priests are extremely jealous of their privileges in this particular' (p. 147); 'the state of the arts and sciences at Nice . . . is almost a total blank . . . consecrated to the reign of dulness and superstition' (p. 174), etc., etc. In absolutely refusing to mince his words, Smollett makes no concession to delicacy of sentiment, insisting on the 'temperance and impartiality' of his remarks, while (in the same breath) bluntly confessing to owe the Nissards 'nothing on the score of civilities' (p. 150). More often than not, and particularly in Letters VI and VII in his extended diatribe against the manners of the French, Smollett's generalizations, however unfair, are memorable for their consummate cleverness rather than striking us as gross and blundering. As Hippolyte Taine shruggingly acknowledged, Smollett's remarkable eye for significant detail allows him to isolate 'a national prejudice or a professional trick until it absorbs the whole character'.[7]

But for many early readers, the *Travels* was not seen as vituperative merely for the sake of being vituperative. Rather, if we may judge by the favourable reviews that appeared during the two years before the damning of Smollett as Smelfungus, the work was lauded for its sturdy defence of British values over the foppish and effeminate habits that were likely to be imbibed by the traveller in France and Italy. Instead of criticizing the book for its trenchancy or for its bad temper, these early reviews emphasize in chauvinistic terms the extent to which the *Travels* could be considered as scoring a hit against our 'natural enemy', the French, with whom we had been at war until a few months before Smollett's departure for the Continent.[8] One review, having praised the intellectual and moral soundness of the *Travels*, concludes: 'This publication may be of infinite service to our country,

7. *History of English Literature*, 4 vols., Edinburgh, 1874, III, p. 305.
8. See I, n. 8.

by giving some check to the follies of our Apes, male and female, of French fashions and politeness, with whom we are over run';[9] while another, echoing a passage from Addison's *Spectator*, no. 45, strikes a very similar note: 'we hazard nothing in saying, that a work of this kind does more service to Great Britain than fifty acts of parliament for prohibiting French fripperies and foreign commodities, or even forbidding the exportation of fools, fops, and coxcombs.'[10]

Of course, the main object of these reviewers' scorn is not the French themselves, but the many rich young Englishmen, supposed representatives of their country — 'simple birds of passage' as Smollett calls them, that 'allow themselves to be plucked' (p.85) while abroad on the Grand Tour — who return to England having fallen victim to the exotic habits of fashion of the French *petits maîtres* and Italian Macaronis.[11] In the *Travels*, Smollett describes with vehement glee the gullibility of this kind of *milord* on the Grand Tour:

I have seen in different parts of Italy, a number of raw boys, whom Britain seemed to have poured forth on purpose to bring her national character into contempt: ignorant, petulant, rash, and profligate, without any knowledge or experience of their own, without any director to improve their understanding, or superintend their conduct. One engages in play with an infamous gamester, and is stripped perhaps in the very first partie: another is poxed and pillaged by an antiquated cantatrice: a third is bubbled by a knavish antiquarian; and a fourth is laid under contribution by a dealer in pictures. Some turn fiddlers, and pretend to compose: but all of them talk familiarly of the arts, and return finished connoisseurs and coxcombs, to their own country. (p.241)

Throughout the *Travels*, Smollett deliberately eschews the humbug and the charlatan, refusing to bow to the prescripts of contemporary fashion and artistic doctrine. His avowed contempt for ostentation and pretence becomes frequently an assertion of fundamental no-nonsense British values, which

9. *The London Magazine*, xxv, May 1766, p.234.
10. *The Critical Review*, xxi, May 1766, p.406. Smollett had been editor of this important journal from its inception in 1755 until shortly before his departure for the Continent in 1763.
11. See M. Dorothy George, *Hogarth to Cruikshank: Social Change in Graphic Satire*, 1967, pp.59–62.

appear threatened by false taste and looseness of principle. His particular eye for scrupulous detail will not allow him to blink before the truth, despite the fact that what is revealed may, like Swift's carcass of the beau, turn out to be unpleasant or nasty. Even at the risk of being ridiculed, Smollett is unashamedly honest in putting forward his views, however idiosyncratic or unfashionable they may be, and this honesty is reflected in the urge for accuracy that underlies so many of his remarks. The same determination to tell the truth — and it has been said of the *Travels* that 'there is not a more truthful book in the language'[12] — makes it both impossible to conceal his bad temper and imperative to voice his opinion.

But Smollett is far too skilful a writer to allow his reader to be overwhelmed or put off by the dogmatic bluntness of many of his assertions. There is little that is sententious in his remarks. On the contrary, a distinct trace of self-mockery and an engaging modesty are sufficient to counter any tendency towards priggishness or self-righteousness. More than once in his description of works of art and antiquities Smollett insists that his remarks are 'too superficial and capricious to belong to any other person' (p.279), and that they are very likely to 'incur the ridicule of the virtuosi' (p.231). Equally, he demurs at the dictates of received opinion, preferring to form his own judgement, even at the risk of appearing iconoclastic or unorthodox. Thus, it is Smollett who can complain of the Venus de Medicis — the Mona Lisa of the eighteenth century — that 'there is no beauty in [her] features . . . and . . . the attitude is aukward and out of character' (p.227); and of Raphael's painting of the *Transfiguration* at the church of S. Pietro in Montorio, the nether portion of which has often been attributed to Raphael's pupils, he insists that 'if it was mine, I would cut [it] in two parts' (p.277). Out of context, these remarks may appear deliberately provocative, even outrageous, but they are supported by detailed criticism that is both sensitive and sensible. Of the Venus, he recognizes that the statue con-

---

12. W. J. Prowse, 'Smollett at Nice', *Macmillan's Magazine*, XXI, Cambridge, 1870, p.530.

forms 'to the nicest rules of symmetry and proportion', but he manifestly refuses to allow himself to be duped into an 'enthusiastic admiration' for an artefact commonly considered to be above criticism. Nowadays, while the Venus de Medicis remains an object of prepossessive admiration, few would share the unthinking veneration accorded it by the majority of eighteenth-century visitors to the Uffizi Gallery.[13] The fickle index of artistic taste has come round to agree with Smollett.

Similarly, his account of Raphael's *Transfiguration*, which according to Edward Gibbon the historian was 'esteemed the first picture in Rome and perhaps in the world',[14] is assiduous in its avoidance of pretence and singular as a piece of art criticism. Having recognized that the two 'groupes seem to be intirely independent of each other', Smollett shows his instinctive gift for acute yet sympathetic judgement in suggesting that 'the extraordinary merit' of the painting 'consists, not only in the expression of divinity on the face of Christ; but also in the surprising lightness of the figure, that hovers like a beautiful exhalation in the air' (p.277). Significantly, the prurient Sterne makes capital of both these passages, writing of the Venus that 'in passing through Florence, I had heard he [Smelfungus] had fallen foul upon the goddess and used her worse than a common strumpet, without the least provocation in nature', and contending that he himself, far from attempting 'to swell the catalogues we have of pictures, statues, and churches . . . would rather enter in, and see the original drawings and loose sketches hung up' and exhibited in the female heart 'than the transfiguration of Raphael itself '.[15] Given the exceptional success of the *Sentimental Journey*, we can understand that the effect of such ridicule was severely to undercut and devalue the reputation of the *Travels*.

The urge for accuracy is also reflected in Smollett's use of a number of guidebooks which he employs as the source of much of his factual information. For passing reference, he makes use of several standard works of travel that were

13. See also XXVIII, n. 23.
14. *Gibbon's Journey from Geneva to Rome*, ed. Georges A. Bonnard, 1961, p.242.
15. op. cit., pp.118, 218–19.

available in English. Notable among these were Joseph Addison's *Remarks on Several Parts of Italy* (1705), which despite being dismissed by Johnson as 'observations . . . as might be supplied by a hasty view'[16] was requisite reading for the eighteenth-century English tourist in Italy, Thomas Nugent's *The Grand Tour* (1749), a vade-mecum much in vogue among travellers, and Johann Georg Keysler's *Travels through Germany, Bohemia, Hungary, Switzerland, Italy and Lorrain* (third edition, 1760), the four volumes of which Smollett calls 'so laboriously circumstantial . . . that I never could peruse them, without suffering the headach, and recollecting the old observation, That the German genius lies more in the back than in the brain' (p.230). More than half of Smollett's allusions to these works represent refinements or corrections of details, suggesting that he carried them with him on his tour or consulted them later specifically for purposes of reference.[17]

In addition to works in English, Smollett acquired *en route* particular French and Italian guidebooks to several of the places he visited, using them discriminately to amplify the factual details of his descriptions. At Nîmes, he was presented with a copy of Abbé Antoine Valette de Travessac's *Abrégé de l'Histoire de la Ville de Nismes* (fourth edition, Avignon, 1760), which he refers to several times (see Letter X, *passim*); at Florence, he made extensive use in his tour of the Uffizi Gallery of Giuseppe Bianchi's *Ragguaglio delle Antichità e Rarità che si Conservano nella Galleria Mediceo-Imperiale di Firenze* (Florence, 1759); and, in Rome, he refers to two guidebooks from which it is evident that he culled a great deal of information, namely Giuseppe Vasi's *Itinerario Istruttivo . . . di Roma* (Rome, 1763), and more particularly, the anonymous *Roma Antica, e Moderna* (3 vols., Rome, 1750), which Smollett found to be replete with 'many curious historical annotations' (p.240), some of which he

---

16. Samuel Johnson, 'Life of Addison', *Lives of the English Poets*, ed. G. B. Hill, 3 vols., 1905, II, p.87.

17. Smollett also made use of Bernard de Montfaucon's *Travels . . . from Paris thro' Italy* (1712) and Anton Friedrich Büsching's *A New System Of Geography* (1762). In describing the countryside between Florence and Rome, during his two month Italian excursion, he tells us that Nugent was 'the only directory I had along with me' (p.234).

reproduces in the *Travels*. If Smollett borrows with freedom from these source books, even resorting to wholesale translation of certain passages, he does so to give accuracy and colour to his descriptions, and not as a substitute for personal experience. The only source book to the *Travels* that he does not refer to by direct citation is an obscure Latin treatise, Pietro Gioffredo's *Nicaea Civitas* (Turin, 1658). From it, he appears to have transcribed certain relevant details during his eighteen-month stay at Nice, when for a time, he tells us, he had 'thoughts of writing a complete natural history of this town and county' (p.177), but the debt here is incidental. More pertinently, it should be mentioned that these source books were not available to the English reader and that Smollett shows considerable skill in selecting from them, and unobtrusively adapting the material to his own use. We are certainly never aware, unless Smollett specifically tells us, that passages of descriptive detail are often direct translations. His employment of these source books is a further mark of the copiousness with which the *Travels* was written.[18]

It is apparent that the preparation of the forty-one Letters that comprise the work was already well under way during Smollett's sojourn at Nice. It even seems likely that early drafts of the Letters were sent home to friends in Britain before being revised for publication on Smollett's return to London.[19] Certainly, the Letters (XXV–XXXV) describing his visit to Italy in the Autumn of 1764 are all dated from Nice, where Smollett had the leisure to peruse his travel notes and the various guidebooks. The use of the letter form, a convention practised by many eighteenth-century travel writers, gives intimacy to his remarks and prevents dryness in the mere listing of things seen. Smollett can impart to the reader of his Letters the sense of intellectual excitement that accompanies the first view of a famous object — witness his wonderful account of the Pont du Gard (pp.79–80) or his

18. For further discussion of Smollett's application of these source books, see L. L. Martz, *The Later Career of Tobias Smollett*, Yale Studies in English, 97, 1942 (reprinted by Archon Books, 1967), pp.67–89, and the Introduction to the Oxford edition of the *Travels*, ed. Frank Felsenstein, Oxford, 1979, pp.xli–xlviii.
19. A number of the Letters appear to have been addressed originally to Smollett's friend, Dr. George Macaulay (*c.* 1716–66). See the Oxford edition of the *Travels*, pp.xxxv–xli.

description of the entry into Rome (pp. 236–7). He can turn his attention to particular interests of his own, such as the state of hygiene (on which he is frequently most amusing) or the construction of bridges and aqueducts or the unjustified adulation accorded to certain historical personages. The flexibility of the form is also evident in the ease with which he can shift from the chronological account of his journey to satirical descriptions in the manner of the best periodical essays of the excesses of French fashion (Letter VII) and the practice of duelling (Letter XV). Elsewhere, in a Letter (XXXVI) on the state of France, he can anticipate with uncanny foresight the coming of the French Revolution some twenty-five years before 1789, while the description of his journey is enlivened by the frequent intrusion of anedcotal material, personal details and learned disquisition.

The cumulative effect of the epistolary form is particularly apparent in Smollett's account of Nice, which systematically deals over a number of Letters (XIII–XIV, XVI–XXIV, XXXVII) with the history, antiquities, government and institutions, living conditions, commerce, and climate of the town. The description owes far more to personal observation than to secondary sources, Smollett even going to the trouble of revisiting the arena at Cemenelion so as to measure it with packthread (p. 140), and keeping in minute detail a daily register of the weather during the whole eighteen months of his stay. It is significant that during the nineteenth century, when the reputation of the *Travels* was at its lowest ebb, the work was at least remembered as the first to make known to the British the merits of the Riviera as a wintering resort. The hostility that had made Smollett *persona non grata* in Nice during the latter years of the eighteenth century appears to have been forgotten, for one of the thoroughfares of the town was named (but surely unintentionally misspelled!) 'la rue Smolet'.[20]

There is no doubt that Smollett must have been aware of the adverse criticism that dogged the *Travels*, and it is intriguing to speculate whether he was affected or influenced

---

20. See Eugène Joliat, *Smollett et la France*, Bibliothèque de la Revue de Littérature Comparée, 105, Paris, 1935, p. 139, n. 1. The house in which the Smolletts lived was elsewhere in Nice; see XXXIX, n. 1.

by it. Certainly, there is no reference to it in his surviving personal correspondence, though in a letter dated 17 January 1767 Smollett applied to Elizabeth Gunning, Duchess of Hamilton, asking her to sue in his favour for the British consulship at Nice,[21] which suggests some apocryphal exaggeration in Hume's anecdote of the stoning of Smollett. But the application for the consulship was a year before Sterne's caricature of Smelfungus in the *Sentimental Journey*, and a year before Smollett's final departure to Italy, where he settled first at Pisa and then near Leghorn until his death in 1771. It is again characteristic of Smollett's diligence as an author that during these last years of his life, as well as writing his best novel, *The Expedition of Humphry Clinker*, he annotated the *Travels*, with the view to publishing a new edition of the work, a plan that was thwarted by his death. The revisions, which are in his personal copy of the *Travels*, now in the British Library, remained unknown until the beginning of this century. Several of the most detailed additions and emendations are to descriptions in Letters XXVII and XXVIII of Pisa and Florence, which Smollett revisited after his return to Italy. The nature of the revisions is a good indication of the emphasis throughout on eye-witness enquiry and accuracy of detail. In the first edition, for instance, he tells us that he knows of no commerce in Pisa except that 'occasioned by the emperor's gallies, which are built in this town' (p.214), a detail which he probably picked up from Keysler (I, pp.485–6). On closer inspection several years later, finding this to be incorrect, he adds a footnote: 'This is a mistake — no gallies have been built here for a great many years; and the dock is now converted into stables for the grand duke's horse guards' (p.214). Again, a change of circumstance in the intervening years causes him to amend his earlier encomium of the curator of the Uffizi Gallery, 'Signore Bianchi, . . . a learned and judicious antiquarian', replacing it with a curt footnote: 'This antiquarian is now imprisoned for life, for having robbed the gallery and then set it on fire' (p.228).[22] Smollett's revisions are for the most

21. *The Letters of Tobias Smollett*, ed. Lewis M. Knapp, Oxford, 1970, pp.128–9.
22. For further details of this bizarre episode, see *Gibbon's Journey from Geneva to Rome*, op. cit., pp.123–4.

part amplifications of detail, often in the form of illuminating footnotes, English translations of quotations and passages from the French, Italian and Latin, and correction of obvious textual errors. They do not display any tendency to rescind his viewpoint in the light of criticism: even here, Smollett remains totally impenitent in maintaining the independent stance that accounts for the uniqueness and particular excellence of the *Travels through France and Italy*.

FRANK FELSENSTEIN

## Note on the Text

The first edition of the *Travels* was published on 8 May 1766 by R. Baldwin in Paternoster Row, London, the two leather-bound octavo volumes costing 10s. The author's own copy of the book with his manuscript additions and emendations, intended for a revised edition, is now in the British Library (shelf mark: C.45.d.20,21.).

The present edition reproduces (with the correction of a few minor misprints) the text of the Oxford edition, published in November 1979. The copy-text is the first edition, which has been collated with two other early editions. All Smollett's MS revisions in his personal copy of the *Travels*, almost certainly made after his return to Italy in 1768, have been faithfully incorporated into the text. Quotations, particularly those from classical authors, have been left unchanged, unless one of the collated texts provided a better reading.

# Select Bibliography

The following list of books is deliberately selective; it has been considered neither practical nor useful to re-quote full titles of the large number of works referred to in the critical notes. The titles of certain key studies of outstanding importance and also other contemporary travel works from which I have quoted extensively are given in the list of abbreviations and short titles at the beginning of the notes.

## (A) SMOLLETT: CHIEFLY BIBLIOGRAPHICAL

Brander, L., *Tobias Smollett*, Writers and their Work, no. 11, 1951.

Cordasco, F., *Smollett Criticism, 1770–1924: a bibliography, enumerative and annotative*, Long Island, N.Y., 1948.

— *Smollett Criticism, 1925–1945: A compilation*, N.Y., 1947.

Korte, D., *An Annotated Bibliography of Smollett Scholarship 1946–1968*, University of Toronto Press, Ontario, 1969.

Norwood, L. F., "Tobias George Smollett", *Cambridge Bibliography of English Literature*, ed. F. W. Bateson, II, Cambridge, 1940, pp. 523–7.

—— "A Descriptive Bibliography with Notes Bibliographical and Biographical of the Creative Works of Tobias Smollett, M.D., 1746–1771", unpublished thesis, Yale, 1931 (University Microfilms, 70–5332).

Scott, W., "Smollett's Reputation and Influence in the Eighteenth Century, Chiefly as a Novelist", unpublished dissertation, Balliol College, Oxford, 1948.

Seccombe, T., article on Smollett in *Dictionary of National Biography*.

Whitridge, A., *Tobias Smollett: A Study of his Miscellaneous Works*, 1925.

*The Works of Tobias Smollett*, gen. ed. W. E. Henley, 12 vols., Westminster and New York, 1899–1901.

*Miscellaneous Works of Tobias Smollett*, ed. R. Anderson, 6th edn., 6 vols., 1820. (vol. I contains a "Life" of Smollett).

## (B) SMOLLETT'S *TRAVELS THROUGH FRANCE AND ITALY*

Biron, H. C., "Smelfungus", *National Review*, LXXV, 1920, pp. 344–53.

Burton, R., "The Vigorous Dr. Smollett", *Dial*, XXXII, 1902, pp. 81–3.

Chancellor, E. B., "Smollett as Traveller", *Fortnightly Review*, N.S. CVIII, 1921, pp. 478–88.

Cordasco, F., "Smollett's 'Register of the Weather'", *NQ*, CXCIV, 1949, p. 163.

## Select Bibliography

Doublet, G., *Les Anglais dans le Comté de Nice et en Provence Depuis le XVIII^me Siècle*, Musée Masséna, Nice, 1934.

Dutertre-Deléviéleuse, Em., *Boulogne en 1763: Lettres du Dr. T. Smollett*, Boulogne-sur-Mer, 1921.

Felsenstein, F., "A Note on Smollett's 'Travels'", *NQ*, CCXIII, 1968, pp. 452–3.

— "A Critical Edition of Smollett's *Travels through France and Italy* (1766)", Leeds University Ph.D. thesis, 1971.

Grant, D. J., "Unpublished Additions to Smollett's 'Travels'", *NQ*, CCXII, 1967, pp. 187–9.

Hunter, A. C., "Les Livres de Smollett détenus par la douane à Boulogne en 1763", *Revue de Littérature Comparée*, XI, Paris, 1931, pp. 736–7.

Joliat, E., "Millin's Use of Smollett's 'Travels'", *Revue de Littérature Comparée*, XVIII, Paris, 1938, pp. 510–14.

Milic, L. T., "Sterne and Smollett's 'Travels'", *NQ*, CCI, 1956, p. 80.

Pilatte, ed., *Lettres de Nice sur Nice et ses Environs (1763–1765)*, Nice, 1919.

Prowse, W. J., "Smollett at Nice", *Macmillan's Magazine*, XXI, Cambridge, 1870, pp. 527–33.

Rice, S. B., "Smollett's *Travels through France and Italy* and the Genre of Grand Tour Literature", unpublished dissertation, University of Arizona, 1968 (University Microfilms, 69–2018).

— "The Significance of Smollett's Weather Register", *NQ*, CCXV, 1970, pp. 94–5.

— "The Satiric Persona of Smollett's *Travels*", *Studies in Scottish Literature*, X, 1972–3, pp. 33–47.

— "Smollett's Seventh Travel Letter and the Design of Formal Verse Satire", *Studies in English Literature*, Rice University, XVI, 1976, pp. 491–503.

Rist, E., "Une Consultation Médicale au XVIII^e Siècle", *Revue de Paris*, 63, janvier 1956, pp. 112–24.

Schuyler, E. "Smollett in Search of Health", *The Nation*, XLVIII, New York, 1889, pp. 423–5, 444–5.

Seccombe, T., "Smelfungus Goes South", *Cornhill Magazine*, XI (N.S), 1901, pp. 192–210.

Sena, J. F., "Smollett's Persona and the Melancholic Traveler", *Eighteenth-Century Studies*, I, 1968, pp. 353–69.

"Smollett in Italy", *Anglo-Italian Review*, IV, 1919, pp. 31–45.

"Smollett in the South", *All the Year Round*, LXVIII, 1891, pp. 420–4.

Spector, Robert D., "Smollett's Traveler", *Tobias Smollett: Bicentennial Essays Presented to Lewis M. Knapp*, ed. G. S. Rousseau and P. G. Boucé, New York, 1971, pp. 231–46.

*Travels through France and Italy*, ed. Osbert Sitwell, The Chiltern Library, 1949.

*Travels through France and Italy*, ed. James Morris, The Centaur Press, Fontwell, Sussex, 1969.

*Travels through France and Italy*, ed. Frank Felsenstein, Oxford University Press, Oxford 1979.

*Select Bibliography*

## (C) GENERAL

Batten, C.L., Jr., *Pleasurable Instruction: Form and Convention in Eighteenth-Century Travel Literature*, Berkeley, 1978.

Carlyle, A., *Anecdotes and Characters of the Times*, ed. James Kinsley, Oxford English Memoirs and Travels, 1973.

Doran, J., *Mann and Manners at the Court of Florence, 1740–1786*, 2 vols., 1876.

George, M. D., *Hogarth to Cruikshank: Social Change in Graphic Satire*, 1967.

Hibbert, C. *The Grand Tour*, 1969.

Kirby, P. F., *The Grand Tour in Italy (1700–1800)*, New York, 1952.

*Grand Tour: A Journey in the Tracks of the Aristocracy*, ed. R. S. Lambert, 1935.

Latouche, R., *Histoire de Nice*, 2 vols., Nice, 1951.

Lewis, L., *Connoisseurs and Secret Agents*, 1961.

Maxwell, C. *The English Traveller in France, 1698–1815*, 1932.

Mead, W. E., *The Grand Tour in the Eighteenth Century*, Boston and New York, 1914.

Moloney, B., *Florence and England*, Biblioteca dell' "Archivum Romanicum", CIV, Florence, 1969.

Pine-Coffin, R. S., *Bibliography of British and American Travel in Italy to 1860*, Biblioteca di Bibliografia Italiana, LXXVI, Florence, 1974.

Trease, G., *The Grand Tour*, 1967.

# A Chronology of Tobias Smollett

| | |
|---|---|
| 1721 (19 March) | Baptized in the parish church of Cardross, Dunbartonshire, Scotland |
| Dates uncertain | Attends Dumbarton Grammar School, and Glasgow University |
| 1735 (c. November) | Works in a dispensary in Glasgow |
| 1736 (30 May) | Begins five years' apprenticeship to William Stirling and John Gordon, Glasgow surgeons |
| 1739 (after June) | Goes to London; passes his examination at Barber-Surgeons' Hall, 4 December |
| 1740 (10 March) | Receives his warrant as surgeon's second mate in the Navy; begins service in the *Chichester* (3 April); sails to Jamaica (26 Oct.–10 Jan. 1741) in the Cartagena expedition |
| 1741 (September) | Back in England |
| 1741–4 | Movements uncertain; may have returned to West Indies; marries Anne Lassells (probably c. 1743), heiress daughter of a Jamaica planter |
| 1744 (May) | Practises as a surgeon in London |
| 1746 | Writes 'The Tears of Scotland' |
| 1746 (September) | *Advice*, a verse satire |
| 1747 (January) | *Reproof*, a sequel to *Advice* |
| 1747–8 | Prepares translation of Lesage's *Gil Blas*, published Oct. 1748 |
| 1748 (c. 21 January) | *The Adventures of Roderick Random* |
| 1749 (June) | *The Regicide* published after nearly 10 years of frustrating struggles to get it produced on the stage |
| 1749 (c. September) | Tours Flanders, Holland, and part of France, Paris probably included |
| 1750 (Summer) | Visits Paris and the Low Countries |
| 1751 (February) | *The Adventures of Peregrine Pickle* |
| 1752 (January) | *Habbakkuk Hilding*, a virulent attack on Fielding, probably by Smollett |
| 1752 (March) | *An Essay on the External Use of Water* |
| 1753 (February) | *The Adventures of Ferdinand Count Fathom*; c. June–November, visits Scotland for the first time in 15 years |
| 1754 (August) | Fourth edition of *Roderick Random*, dated 1755, set up and printed, with 'Apologue' |
| 1755 (February) | *Don Quixote*, a translation begun c. 1748 |
| 1755–7 | Working on *A Complete History of England*, published 1757–8 |

| | |
|---|---|
| 1756 (March) | In collaboration with 3 others, launches the *Critical Review*, and serves as an editor and reviewer until 1763 |
| 1756 (April) | Edition of *A Compendium of Authentic and Entertaining Voyages* |
| 1757 (January, February, April, May) | *The Reprisal*, a farce in two acts, performed at the Theatre Royal in Drury Lane; published 1 Feb. 1757 |
| 1758 (March) | Second edition of *Peregrine Pickle*, revised and altered |
| 1758 (May) | Savage attack against Admiral Knowles in the *Critical Review* |
| 1760 ( January) | Begins publication of *The British Magazine*, where *The Adventures of Sir Launcelot Greaves* appear serially Jan. 1760 to Dec. 1761 |
| 1760 (November to late February 1761) | In the King's Bench Prison for libel of Admiral Knowles |
| 1760–5 | Writing the *Continuation of the Complete History of England* |
| 1761–5 | Joint editor of the *Works of Voltaire* |
| 1762 (29 May to 12 February 1763) | Edits the weekly *Briton* in support of Lord Bute |
| 1762 | Health deteriorates; seeks appointment abroad in a warm climate |
| 1763 (3 April) | Only child, Elizabeth, dies, aged 15 |
| 1763 ( June) | With wife and friends, leaves for France and Italy; resides in Nice from Nov. 1763 to April 1765 |
| 1765 ( July) | Returns to England |
| 1766 (May) | *Travels through France and Italy* |
| 1766 (May–August) | Travels to Scotland, then returns to Bath and London |
| 1768 | Completes *The Present State of All Nations* begun in 1760 |
| 1768 (Autumn) | Leaves for Italy. Finally settles near Leghorn |
| 1769 (April) | *The History and Adventures of an Atom*, a political satire, most probably by Smollett |
| 1771 ( June) | *The Expedition of Humphry Clinker* |
| 1771 (17 September) | Dies at Il Giardino, a villa on the side of Monte Nero in Antignano, near Leghorn. Buried in the English cemetery in Leghorn |
| 1773 | *Ode to Independence*, composed in 1766, published posthumously |
| 1776 | Translation of Fénélon's *Adventures of Telemachus* published posthumously |

MAP OF SMOLLETT'S ROUTE
THROUGH FRANCE AND ITALY
(JUNE 1763 – JULY 1765)

Main centres visited are marked in
capitals. Towns on the route enclosed
within brackets were passed by Smollett
and not visited. The short Italian tour
took place between September and
November 1764.

# TRAVELS

## THROUGH

# FRANCE AND ITALY.

#### CONTAINING OBSERVATIONS ON

| CHARACTER, | POLICE, |
|---|---|
| CUSTOMS, | COMMERCE, |
| RELIGION, | ARTS, AND |
| GOVERNMENT, | ANTIQUITIES. |

With a particular DESCRIPTION of the

## TOWN, TERRITORY, and CLIMATE of NICE:

To which is added,

A Register of the Weather, kept during a Residence
of Eighteen Months in that City.

## BY T. SMOLLETT, M.D.

Ut Homo qui erranti comiter monſtrat viam,
Quaſi lumen de ſuo lumine accendat, facit :
Nihilominus ipſi luceat, cum illi accenderit.    ENNIUS.

## IN TWO VOLUMES.

## VOL. I.

## LONDON,

Printed for R. BALDWIN, in Pater-noſter-Row.
MDCCLXVI.

Title-page of the first edition, 1766. The epigraph from the Latin
poet Quintus Ennius (239–169 B.C.) is drawn from Cicero's *De
Officiis*, I. xvi, translated in the Loeb edition as follows:
'Who kindly sets a wand'rer on his way
Does e'en as if he lit another's lamp by his:
No less shines his, when he his friend's hath lit.'

1

# LETTER I.

*Boulogne sur mer, June 23, 1763.*

DEAR SIR,

You laid your commands upon me at parting, to communicate from time to time the observations I should make in the course of my travels, and it was an injunction I received with pleasure. In gratifying your curiosity, I shall find some amusement to beguile the tedious hours, which, without some such employment, would be rendered insupportable by distemper and disquiet.

You knew, and pitied my situation, traduced by malice, persecuted by faction, abandoned by false patrons, and overwhelmed by the sense of a domestic calamity,[1] which it was not in the power of fortune to repair.

You know with what eagerness I fled from my country as a scene of illiberal dispute, and incredible infatuation, where a few worthless incendiaries had, by dint of perfidious calumnies and atrocious abuse, kindled up a flame which threatened all the horrors of civil dissension.[2]

I packed up my little family in a hired coach, and attended by my trusty servant, who had lived with me a dozen of years, and now refused to leave me, took the road to Dover, in my way to the South of France, where I hoped the mildness of the climate would prove favourable to the weak state of my lungs.

You advised me to have recourse again to the Bath waters, from the use of which I had received great benefit the preceding winter: but I had many inducements to leave England. My wife earnestly begged I would convey her from a country where every object served to nourish her grief: I was in hopes that a succession of new scenes would engage her attention, and gradually call off her mind from a series of painful reflections; and I imagined the change of air, and a journey of near a thousand miles, would have a happy effect upon my own constitution. But, as the summer was already advanced, and the heat too excessive for travelling in warm climates, I proposed staying at Boulogne till the beginning of autumn, and in the mean time to bathe in the sea, with a view to strengthen and prepare my body for the fatigues of such a long journey.

A man who travels with a family of five persons,[3] must lay his account with a number of mortifications; and some of these I have already happily overcome. Though I was well acquainted with the road to Dover, and made allowances accordingly, I could not help being chagrined at the bad accommodation and impudent imposition to which I was exposed. These I found the more disagreeable, as we were detained a day extraordinary on the road, in consequence of my wife's being indisposed.

I need not tell you this is the worst road in England, with respect to the conveniencies of travelling, and must certainly impress foreigners with an unfavourable opinion of the nation in general. The chambers are in general cold and comfortless, the beds paultry, the cookery execrable, the wine poison, the attendance bad, the publicans insolent, and the bills extortion; there is not a drop of tolerable malt liquor to be had from London to Dover.

Every landlord and every waiter harangued upon the knavery of a publican in Canterbury, who had charged the French ambassador forty pounds for a supper that was not worth forty shillings.[4] They talked much of honesty and conscience; but when they produced their own bills, they appeared to be all of the same family and complexion. If it was a reproach upon the English nation, that an innkeeper should pillage strangers at that rate; it is a greater scandal, that the same fellow should be able to keep his house still open. I own, I think it would be for the honour of the kingdom to reform the abuses of this road; and in particular to improve the avenue to London by the way of Kent-Street, which is a most disgraceful entrance to such an opulent city. A foreigner, in passing through this beggarly and ruinous suburb, conceives such an idea of misery and meanness, as all the wealth and magnificence of London and Westminster are afterwards unable to destroy. A friend of mine, who brought a Parisian from Dover in his own post-chaise, contrived to enter Southwark after it was dark, that his friend might not perceive the nakedness of this quarter. The stranger was much pleased with the great number of shops full of merchandize, lighted up to the best advantage. He was astonished

3

at the display of riches in Lombard-Street and Cheapside. The badness of the pavement made him find the streets twice as long as they were. They alighted in Upper Brook-Street by Grosvenor-Square; and when his conductor told him they were then about the middle of London, the Frenchman declared, with marks of infinite surprize, that London was very near as long as Paris.

On my arrival at Dover I payed off my coachman, who went away with a heavy heart. He wanted much to cross the sea, and endeavoured to persuade me to carry the coach and horses to the other side. If I had been resolved to set out immediately for the South, perhaps I should have taken his advice. If I had retained him at the rate of twenty guineas per month, which was the price he demanded, and begun my journey without hesitation, I should travel more agreeably than I can expect to do in the carriages of this country; and the difference of the expence would be a meer trifle. I would advise every man who travels through France to bring his own vehicle along with him, or at least to purchase one at Calais or Boulogne, where second-hand berlins[5] and chaises may be generally had at reasonable rates. I have been offered a very good berlin for thirty guineas: but before I make the purchase, I must be better informed touching the different methods of travelling in this country.

Dover is commonly termed a den of thieves;[6] and I am afraid it is not altogether without reason, it has acquired this appellation. The people are said to live by piracy in time of war; and by smuggling and fleecing strangers in time of peace: but I will do them the justice to say, they make no distinction between foreigners and natives. Without all doubt a man cannot be much worse lodged and worse treated in any part of Europe; nor will he in any other place meet with more flagrant instances of fraud, imposition, and brutality. One would imagine they had formed a general conspiracy against all those who either go to, or return from the continent. About five years ago, in my passage from Flushing to Dover,[7] the master of the packet-boat brought to all of a sudden off the South Foreland, although the wind was as favourable as it could blow. He was immediately boarded by a custom-house boat, the officer of which appeared to be his

4

friend. He then gave the passengers to understand, that as it was low water, the ship could not go into the harbour; but that the boat would carry them ashore with their baggage.

The custom-house officer demanded a guinea for this service, and the bargain was made. Before we quitted the ship, we were obliged to gratify the cabin-boy for his attendance, and to give drink-money to the sailors. The boat was run aground on the open beach; but we could not get ashore without the assistance of three or four fellows, who insisted upon being paid for their trouble. Every parcel and bundle, as it was landed, was snatched up by a separate porter: one ran away with a hat-box, another with a wig-box, a third with a couple of shirts tied up in a handkerchief, and two were employed in carrying a small portmanteau that did not weigh forty pounds. All our things were hurried to the custom-house to be searched, and the searcher was paid for disordering our cloaths: from thence they were removed to the inn, where the porters demanded half a crown each for their labour. It was in vain to expostulate; they surrounded the house like a pack of hungry hounds, and raised such a clamour, that we were fain to comply. After we had under-gone all this imposition, we were visited by the master of the packet, who, having taken our fares, and wished us joy of our happy arrival in England, expressed his hope that we would remember the poor master, whose wages were very small, and who chiefly depended upon the generosity of the passengers. I own I was shocked at his meanness, and could not help telling him so. I told him, I could not conceive what title he had to any such gratification: he had sixteen passengers, who paid a guinea each, on the supposition that every person should have a bed; but there were no more than eight beds in the cabin, and each of these was occupied before I came on board; so that if we had been detained at sea a whole week by contrary winds and bad weather, one half of the passengers must have slept upon the boards, howsoever their health might have suffered from this want of accommodation. Notwithstanding this check, he was so very abject and importunate, that we gave him a crown a piece, and he retired.

The first thing I did when I arrived at Dover this last time, was to send for the master of a packet-boat, and agree with him to carry us to Boulogne at once, by which means I saved the expence of travelling by land from Calais to this last place, a journey of four-and-twenty miles. The hire of a vessel from Dover to Boulogne is precisely the same as from Dover to Calais, five guineas; but this skipper demanded eight, and, as I did not know the fare, I agreed to give him six. We embarked between six and seven in the evening, and found ourselves in a most wretched hovel, on board what is called a Folkstone cutter. The cabin was so small that a dog could hardly turn in it, and the beds put me in mind of the holes described in some catacombs, in which the bodies of the dead were deposited, being thrust in with the feet foremost; there was no getting into them but end-ways, and indeed they seemed so dirty, that nothing but extreme necessity could have obliged me to use them. We sat up all night in a most uncomfortable situation, tossed about by the sea, cold, and cramped and weary, and languishing for want of sleep. At three in the morning the master came down, and told us we were just off the harbour of Boulogne; but the wind blowing off shore, he could not possibly enter, and therefore advised us to go ashore in the boat. I went upon deck to view the coast, when he pointed to the place where he said Boulogne stood, declaring at the same time we were within a short mile of the harbour's mouth. The morning was cold and raw, and I knew myself extremely subject to catch cold; nevertheless we were all so impatient to be ashore, that I resolved to take his advice. The boat was already hoisted out, and we went on board of it, after I had paid the captain and gratified his crew. We had scarce parted from the ship, when we perceived a boat coming towards us from the shore; and the master gave us to understand, it was coming to carry us into the harbour. When I objected to the trouble of shifting from one boat to another in the open sea, which (by the bye) was a little rough; he said it was a privilege which the watermen of Boulogne had, to carry all passengers ashore, and that this privilege he durst not venture to infringe. This was no time nor place to remonstrate. The French boat came alongside half filled with water, and we were handed from the one to the other. We were then obliged to lie upon our oars, till the captain's boat went on board and returned from the ship with a packet of letters. We were afterwards rowed a long league, in a rough sea, against wind and tide, before we reached the harbour, where we landed, benumbed with cold, and the women excessively sick: from our landing-place we were obliged to walk very near a mile to the inn where we purposed to lodge, attended by six or seven men and women, bare-legged, carrying our baggage. This boat cost me a guinea, besides paying exorbitantly the people who carried our things; so that the inhabitants of Dover and of Boulogne seem to be of the same kidney, and indeed they understand one another perfectly well. It was our honest captain who made the signal for the shore-boat before I went upon deck; by which means he not only gratified his friends, the watermen of Boulogne, but also saved about fifteen shillings portage, which he must have paid had he gone into the harbour; and thus he found himself at liberty to return to Dover, which he reached in four hours. I mention these circumstances as a warning to other passengers. When a man hires a packet-boat from Dover to Calais or Boulogne, let him remember that the stated price is five guineas; and let him insist upon being carried into the harbour in the ship, without paying the least regard to the representations of the master, who is generally a little dirty knave. When he tells you it is low water, or the wind is in your teeth, you may say you will stay on board till it is high water, or till the wind comes favourable. If he sees you are resolute, he will find means to bring his ship into the harbour, or at least to convince you, without a possibility of your being deceived, that it is not in his power. After all, the fellow himself was a loser by his finesse; if he had gone into the harbour, he would have had another fare immediately back to Dover, for there was a Scotch gentleman at the inn waiting for such an opportunity.

Knowing my own weak constitution, I took it for granted this morning's adventure would cost me a fit of illness; and what added to my chagrin, when we arrived at the inn, all the beds were occupied; so that we were obliged to sit in a cold kitchen above two hours, until some of the lodgers should get up. This was such a bad specimen of French accommodation, that my wife could not help regretting even the inns of Rochester, Sittingbourn, and Canterbury: bad as they are, they certainly have the advantage, when compared with the execrable auberges of this country, where one finds nothing but dirt and imposition. One would imagine the French were still at war with the English,[8] for they pillage them without mercy.

Among the strangers at this inn where we lodged, there was a gentleman of the faculty,[9] just returned from Italy. Understanding that I intended to winter in the South of France, on account of a pulmonic disorder, he strongly recommended the climate of Nice in Provence, which, indeed, I had often heard extolled; and I am almost resolved to go thither, not only for the sake of the air, but also for its situation on the Mediterranean, where I can have the benefit of bathing; and from whence there is a short cut by sea to Italy, should I find it necessary to try the air of Naples.

After having been ill accommodated three days at our inn, we have at last found commodious lodgings, by means of Mrs. B——,[10] a very agreeable French lady, to whom we were recommended by her husband, who is my countryman, and at present resident in London. For three guineas a month we have the greatest part of a house tolerably furnished; four bed-chambers on the first floor, a large parlour below, a kitchen, and the use of a cellar.

These, I own, are frivolous incidents, scarce worth committing to paper; but they may serve to introduce observations of more consequence; and in the mean time I know nothing will be indifferent to you, that concerns

Your humble servant.

# LETTER II.

DEAR SIR,

The custom-house officers at Boulogne, though as alert, are rather more civil than those on your side of the water. I brought no plate along with me, but a dozen and a half of spoons, and a dozen teaspoons: the first being found in one of our portmanteaus, when they were examined at the bureau, cost me seventeen livres *entrée*: the others being luckily in my servant's pocket, escaped duty free. All wrought silver imported into France, pays at the rate of so much per mark: therefore those who have any quantity of plate, will do well to leave it behind them, unless they can confide in the dexterity of the shipmasters; some of whom will undertake to land it without the ceremony of examination. The ordonnances of France are so unfavourable to strangers, that they oblige them to pay at the rate of five per cent. for all the bed and table linen which they bring into the kingdom, even though it has been used. When my trunks arrived in a ship from the river Thames, I underwent this ordeal: but what gives me more vexation, my books have been stopped at the bureau; and will be sent to Amiens at my expense, to be examined by the *chambre syndicale*;[1] lest they should contain something prejudicial to the state, or to the religion of the country. This is a species of oppression which one would not expect to meet with in France, which piques itself on its politeness and hospitality: but the truth is, I know no country in which strangers are worse treated, with respect to their essential concerns. If a foreigner dies in France, the king seizes all his effects, even though his heir should be upon the spot; and this tyranny is called the *droit d'aubaine*, founded at first upon the supposition, that all the estate of foreigners residing in France was acquired in that kingdom, and that, therefore, it would be unjust to convey it to another country. If an English protestant goes to France for the benefit of his health, attended by his wife or his son, or both, and dies with effects in the house to the amount of a thousand guineas, the king seizes the whole, the family is left destitute, and the body of the deceased is denied christian burial. The Swiss, by capitulation, are exempted from this despotism, and so are the Scots, in consequence of an ancient alliance between the two nations. The same *droit d'aubaine* is exacted by some of the princes in Germany: but it is a great discouragement to commerce, and prejudices every country where it is exercised, to ten times the value of what it brings into the coffers of the sovereign.

I am exceedingly mortified at the detention of my books, which not only deprives me of an amusement which I can very ill dispense with; but, in all probability, will expose me to sundry other inconveniencies. I must be at the expence of sending them sixty miles to be examined, and run the risque of their being condemned; and, in the mean time, I may lose the opportunity of sending them with my heavy baggage by sea to Bourdeaux, to be sent up the Garonne to Thoulouse, and from thence transmitted through the canal of Languedoc to Cette, which is a sea-port on the Mediterranean, about three or four leagues from Montpellier.

For the recovery of my books, I had recourse to the advice of my landlord, Mons. B—.[2] He is a handsome young fellow, about twenty-five years of age, and keeps house with two maiden sisters, who are professed devotees. The brother is a little libertine, good natured and obliging; but a true Frenchman in vanity, which is undoubtedly the ruling passion of this volatile people. He has an inconsiderable place under the government, in consequence of which he is permitted to wear a sword, a privilege which he does not fail to use. He is likewise receiver of the tythes of the clergy in this district, an office that gives him a command of money, and he, moreover, deals in the wine trade. When I came to his house, he made a parade of all these advantages: he displayed his bags of money, and some old gold which his father had left him. He described his chateau in the country; dropped hints of the fortunes that were settled upon mademoiselles his sisters; boasted of his connexions at court; and assured me it was not for my money that he let his lodgings, but altogether with a view to enjoy the pleasure of my company. The truth, when stript of all embellishments, is this: the sieur B— is the son of an honest bourgeois lately dead, who left him the house, with some stock in trade, a little money, and a paltry farm: his sisters have about three thousand livres (not quite 140 l.) a-piece; the brother's places are worth about fifty pounds a year, and his connexions at court are confined to a *commis*, or clerk in the secretary's office, with whom he corresponds by virtue of his employment. My landlord piques himself upon his gallantry and success with the fair-sex: he keeps a *fille de joye*, and makes no secret of his amours. He told miss C——[3] the other day, in broken English, that, in the course of the last year, he had made six bastards. He owned, at the same time, he had sent them all to the hospital; but, now his father is dead, he would himself take care of his future productions. This, however, was no better than a gasconade. — Yesterday the house was in a hot alarm, on account of a new windfall of this kind: the sisters were in tears; the brother was visited by the *curé* of the parish; the lady in the straw (a sempstress) sent him the bantling in a basket, and he transmitted it by the carriers to the *Enfans trouvés*[4] at Paris.

But to return from this digression: Mr. B—— advised me to send a *requête* or petition to the chancellor of France, that I might obtain an order to have my books examined on the spot, by the president of Boulogne, or the *procureur du roy*, or the subdelegate of the intendance.[5] He recommended an *avocat* of his acquaintance to draw up the *memoire*, and introduced him accordingly; telling me at the same time, in private, that if he was not a drunkard, he would be at the head of his profession. He had indeed all the outward signs of a sot; a sleepy eye, a rubicund face, and carbuncled nose. He seemed to be a little out at elbows, had marvellous foul linen, and his breeches were not very sound: but he assumed an air of importance, was very courteous, and very solemn. I asked him if he did not sometimes divert himself with the muse: he smiled, and promised, in a whisper, to shew me some *chansonettes de sa façon*. Meanwhile he composed the *requête* in my name, which was very pompous, very tedious, and very abject. Such a stile might perhaps be necessary in a native of France; but I did not think it was at all suitable to a subject of Great-Britain. I thanked him for the trouble he had taken, as he would receive no other gratification; but when my landlord proposed to send the *memoire* to his correspondent at Paris, to be delivered to the chancellor, I told him I had changed my mind, and would apply to the English ambassador. I have accordingly taken the liberty to address myself to the earl of H——;[6] and at the same time I have presumed to write to the duchess of D——,[7] who is now at Paris, to entreat her grace's advice and interposition. What effect these applications may have, I know not: but the sieur B—— shakes his head, and has told my servant, in confidence, that I am mistaken if I think the English ambassador is as great a man at Paris as the chancellor of France.

I ought to make an apology for troubling you with such an unentertaining detail, and consider that the detention of my books must be a matter of very little consequence to any body, but to

Your affectionate humble servant.

# LETTER III.

*Boulogne, August 15, 1763.*

SIR,

I am much obliged to you for your kind enquiries after my health, which has been lately in a very declining condition. In consequence of a cold, caught a few days after my arrival in France, I was seized with a violent cough, attended with a fever, and stitches in my breast, which tormented me all night long without ceasing. At the same time I had a great discharge by expectoration, and such a dejection of spirits as I never felt before. In this situation I took a step which may appear to have been desperate. I knew there was no impost-hume in my lungs, and I supposed the stitches were spasmodical. I was sensible that all my complaints were originally derived from relaxation. I therefore hired a chaise, and going to the beach, about a league from the town, plunged into the sea without hesitation. By this desperate remedy, I got a fresh cold in my head: but my stitches and fever vanished the very first day; and by a daily repetition of the bath, I have diminished my cough, strengthened my body, and recovered my spirits. I believe I should have tried the same experiment, even if there had been an abscess in my lungs, though such practice would have been contrary to all the rules of medicine: but I am not one of those who implicitly believe in all the dogmata of physic. I saw one of the guides at Bath, the stoutest fellow among them, who recovered from the last stage of a consumption, by going into the king's bath, contrary to the express injunction of his doctor. He said, if he must die, the sooner the better, as he had nothing left for his subsistence. Instead of immediate death, he found instant ease, and continued mending every day, till his health was entirely re-established. I myself drank the waters at Bath, and bathed, in diametrical opposition to the opinion of some physicians there settled, and found myself better every day, notwithstanding their unfavourable prognostic. If I had been of the rigid fibre, full of blood, subject to inflammation, I should have followed a different course. Our acquaintance, doctor C——,[1] while he actually spit up matter, and rode out every day for his life, led his horse to water, at the pond in

13

Hyde-Park, one cold frosty morning, and the beast, which happened to be of a hot constitution, plunged himself and his master over head and ears in the water. The poor doctor hastened home, half dead with fear, and was put to bed in the apprehension of a new imposthume; instead of which, he found himself exceedingly recruited in his spirits, and his appetite much mended. I advised him to take the hint, and go into the cold bath every morning: but he did not chuse to run any risque. How cold water comes to be such a bugbear, I know not: if I am not mistaken, Hippocrates recommends immersion in cold water for the gout;[2] and Celsus expressly says, *in omni tussi utilis est natatio:*[3] in every cough swimming is of service.

I have conversed with a physician of this place, a sensible man, who assured me he was reduced to meer skin and bone by a cough and hectic fever, when he ordered a bath to be made in his own house, and dipped himself in cold water every morning. He at the same time left off drinking and swallowing any liquid that was warm. He is now strong and lusty, and even in winter has no other cover than a single sheet. His notions about the warm drink were a little whimsical: he imagined it relaxed the tone of the stomach; and this would undoubtedly be the case if it was drank in large quantities, warmer than the natural temperature of the blood. He alledged the example of the inhabitants of the Ladrone islands,[4] who never taste any thing that is not cold, and are remarkably healthy. But to balance this argument I mentioned the Chinese, who scarce drink any thing but warm tea; and the Laplanders, who drink nothing but warm water; yet the people of both these nations are remarkably strong, healthy, and long-lived.

You desire to know the fate of my books. My lord H——d[5] is not yet come to France; but my letter was transmitted to him from Paris; and his lordship, with that generous humanity which is peculiar to his character, has done me the honour to assure me, under his own hand, that he has directed Mr. N——lle,[6] our resident at Paris, to apply for an order that my books may be restored.

I have met with another piece of good fortune, in being introduced to general Paterson[7] and his lady, in their way to

England from Nice, where the general has been many years commandant for the king of Sardinia. You must have heard of this gentleman, who has not only eminently distinguished himself, by his courage and conduct as an officer; but also by his probity and humanity in the exercise of his office, and by his remarkable hospitality to all strangers, especially the subjects of Great-Britain, whose occasions called them to the place where he commanded. Being pretty far advanced in years, he begged leave to resign, that he might spend the evening of his days in his own country; and his Sardinian majesty granted his request with regret, after having honoured him with very particular marks of approbation and esteem. The general talks so favourably of the climate of Nice, with respect to disorders of the breast, that I am now determined to go thither. It would have been happy for me had he continued in his government. I think myself still very fortunate, in having obtained of him a letter of recommendation to the English consul at Nice, together with directions how to travel through the South of France. I propose to begin my journey some time next month, when the weather will be temperate to the southward; and in the wine countries I shall have the pleasure of seeing the vintage, which is always a season of festivity among all ranks of people.

You have been very much mis-informed, by the person who compared Boulogne to Wapping: he did a manifest injustice to this place, which is a large agreeable town, with broad open streets, excellently paved; and the houses are of stone, well built and commodious. The number of inhabitants may amount to sixteen thousand. You know this was generally supposed to be the *portus Itius*, and *Gessoriacum* of the antients: though it is now believed that the *portus Itius*, from whence Cæsar sailed to Britain, is a place called *Whitsand*, about half way between this place and Calais. Boulogne is the capital of the Boulonnois, a district extending about twelve leagues, ruled by a governor independent of the governor of Picardy; of which province, however, this country forms a part. The present governor is the duc d'Aumont.[8] The town of Boulogne is the see of a bishop suffragan[9] of Rheims, whose revenue amounts to about four-and-twenty thousand livres, or one thousand pounds sterling. It is also the seat of a seneschal's court, from whence an appeal lies to the parliament of Paris; and thither all condemned criminals are sent, to have their sentence confirmed or reversed. Here is likewise a bailiwick,[10] and a court of admiralty. The military jurisdiction of the city belongs to a commandant appointed by the king, a sort of sinecure bestowed upon some old officer. His appointments are very inconsiderable: he resides in the Upper Town, and his garrison at present consists of a few hundreds of invalids.

Boulogne is divided into the Upper and Lower Towns. The former is a kind of citadel, about a short mile in circumference, situated on a rising ground, surrounded by a high wall and rampart, planted with rows of trees, which form a delightful walk. It commands a fine view of the country and Lower Town; and in clear weather the coast of England, from Dover to Folkstone, appears so plain, that one would imagine it was within four or five leagues of the French shore. The Upper Town was formerly fortified with outworks, which are now in ruins. Here is a square, a town-house, the cathedral, and two or three convents of nuns; in one of which there are several English girls, sent hither for their education. The smallness of the expence encourages parents to send their children abroad to these seminaries, where they learn scarce any thing that is useful, but the French language; but they never fail to imbibe prejudices against the protestant religion, and generally return enthusiastic converts to the religion of Rome. This conversion always generates a contempt for, and often an aversion to, their own country. Indeed it cannot reasonably be expected, that people of weak minds, addicted to superstitition, should either love or esteem those whom they are taught to consider as reprobated heretics. Ten pounds a year is the usual pension in these convents; but I have been informed by a French lady, who had her education in one of them, that nothing can be more wretched than their entertainment.

The civil magistracy of Boulogne consists of a mayor and echevins;[11] and this is the case in almost all the towns of France.

The Lower Town is continued from the gate of the Upper

Town, down the slope of a hill, as far as the harbour, stretching on both sides to a large extent, and is much more considerable than the Upper, with respect to the beauty of the streets, the convenience of the houses, and the number and wealth of the inhabitants. These, however, are all merchants, or bourgeois; for the noblesse or gentry live all together in the Upper Town, and never mix with the others. The harbour of Boulogne is at the mouth of the small river, or rather rivulet Liane, which is so shallow, that the children wade through it at low water. As the tide makes, the sea flows in, and forms a pretty extensive harbour, which, however, admits nothing but small vessels. It is contracted at the mouth by two stone *jetties* or piers, which seem to have been constructed by some engineer, very little acquainted with this branch of his profession; for they are carried out in such a manner, as to collect a bank of sand just at the entrance of the harbour. The road is very open and unsafe, and the surf very high when the wind blows from the sea. There is no fortification near the harbour, except a paltry fort mounting about twenty guns, built in the last war by the prince de Cruy,[12] upon a rock about a league to the eastward of Boulogne. It appears to be situated in such a manner, that it can neither offend, nor be offended. If the depth of water would admit a forty or fifty gun ship to lie within cannon-shot of it, I apprehend it might be silenced in half an hour; but, in all probability, there will be no vestiges of it at the next rupture between the two crowns. It is surrounded every day by the sea, at high water; and when it blows a fresh gale towards the shore, the waves break over the top of it, to the terror and astonishment of the garrison, who have been often heard crying piteously for assistance. I am persuaded, that it will one day disappear in the twinkling of an eye. The neighbourhood of this fort, which is a smooth sandy beach, I have chosen for my bathing place. The road to it is agreeable and romantic, lying through pleasant corn-fields, skirted by open downs, where there is a rabbit warren, and great plenty of the birds so much admired at Tunbridge under the name of *wheat-ears*. By the bye, this is a pleasant corruption of *white-a——se*, the translation of their French name *cul-blanc*, taken from their colour; for they are actually white towards the tail.

Upon the top of a high rock, which overlooks the harbour, are the remains of an old fortification, which is indiscriminately called, *Tour d'ordre*, and *Julius Cæsar's fort*. The original tower was a light-house built by *Claudius Cæsar*, denominated *Turris ardens*, from the fire burned in it; and this the French have corrupted into *Tour d'ordre*: but no vestiges of this Roman work remain; what we now see, are the ruins of a castle built by Charlemagne. I know of no other antiquity at Boulogne, except an old vault in the Upper Town, now used as a magazine, which is said to be part of an antient temple dedicated to Isis.

On the other side of the harbour, opposite to the Lower Town, there is a house built, at a considerable expence, by a general officer, who lost his life in the late war. Never was situation more inconvenient, unpleasant, and unhealthy. It stands on the edge of an ugly morass formed by the stagnant water left by the tide in its retreat: the very walks of the garden are so moist, that, in the driest weather, no person can make a tour of it, without danger of the rheumatism. Besides, the house is altogether inaccessible, except at low water, and even then the carriage must cross the harbour, the wheels up to the axle-tree in mud: nay, the tide rushes in so fast, that unless you seize the time to a minute, you will be in danger of perishing. The apartments of this house are elegantly fitted up, but very small; and the garden, notwithstanding its unfavourable situation, affords a great quantity of good fruit. The ooze, impregnated with sea salt, produces, on this side of the harbour, an incredible quantity of the finest *samphire* I ever saw. The French call it *passe-pierre*; and I suspect its English name is a corruption of *sang-pierre*. It is generally found on the faces of bare rocks that overhang the sea, by the spray of which it is nourished. As it grew upon a naked rock, without any appearance of soil, it might be naturally enough called *sang du pierre*, or *sang-pierre*, blood of the rock; and hence the name *samphire*. On the same side of the harbour there is another new house, neatly built, belonging to a gentleman who has obtained a grant from the king of some ground which was always overflowed at high water. He has raised dykes at a considerable expence, to exclude the tide, and if he can bring his project to bear, he will not only gain a good estate for himself, but also improve the harbour, by increasing the depth at high-water.

In the Lower Town of Boulogne there are several religious houses, particularly a seminary, a convent of Cordeliers, and another of Capuchins. This last, having fallen to decay, was some years ago repaired, chiefly by the charity of British travellers, collected by father Græme,[13] a native of North-Britain, who had been an officer in the army of king James II. and is said to have turned monk of this mendicant order, by way of voluntary penance, for having killed his friend in a duel. Be that as it may, he was a well-bred, sensible man, of a very exemplary life and conversation; and his memory is much revered in this place. Being superior of the convent, he caused the British arms to be put up in the church, as a mark of gratitude for the benefactions received from our nation. I often walk in the garden of the convent, the walls of which are washed by the sea at high-water. At the bottom of the garden is a little private grove, separated from it by a high wall, with a door of communication; and hither the Capuchins retire, when they are disposed for contemplation. About two years ago, this place was said to be converted to a very different use. There was among the monks one *pere Charles*,[14] a lusty friar, of whom the people tell strange stories. Some young women of the town were seen mounting over the wall, by a ladder of ropes, in the dusk of the evening; and there was an unusual crop of bastards that season. In short, *pere Charles* and his companions gave such scandal, that the whole fraternity was changed; and now the nest is occupied by another flight of these birds of passage. If one of our privateers had kidnapped a Capuchin during the war, and exhibited him, in his habit, as a shew in London, he would have proved a good prize to the captors; for I know not a more uncouth and grotesque animal, than an old Capuchin in the habit of his order. A friend of mine (a Swiss officer) told me, that a peasant in his country used to weep bitterly, whenever a certain Capuchin mounted the pulpit to hold forth to the people. The good father took notice of this man, and believed he was touched by the finger of the Lord. He exhorted him to encourage these accessions of grace, and at the same time to be of good comfort, as having received such marks of the divine favour. The man still continued to weep, as before, every time the monk preached; and at last the Capuchin insisted upon knowing what it was, in his discourse or appearance, that made such an impression upon his heart. — "Ah, father! (cried the peasant) I never see you but I think of a venerable goat, which I lost at Easter. We were bred up together in the same family. He was the very picture of your reverence – one would swear you were brothers. Poor *Baudouin!* he died of a fall — rest his soul! I would willingly pay for a couple of masses to pray him out of purgatory."

Among other public edifices at Boulogne, there is an hospital, or workhouse, which seems to be established upon a very good foundation. It maintains several hundreds of poor people, who are kept constantly at work, according to their age and abilities, in making thread, all sorts of lace, a kind of catgut, and in knitting stockings. It is under the direction of the bishop; and the see is at present filled by a prelate of great piety and benevolence, though a little inclining to bigotry and fanaticism. The churches in this town are but indifferently built, and poorly ornamented. There is not one picture in the place worth looking at, nor indeed does there seem to be the least taste for the liberal arts.

In my next, I shall endeavour to satisfy you in the other articles you desire to know. Mean-while, I am ever

Yours.

# LETTER IV.

*Boulogne, September* 1, 1763.

SIR,

I am infinitely obliged to D.H——[1] for the favourable manner in which he has mentioned me to the earl of H——.[2] I have at last recovered my books, by virtue of a particular order to the director of the douane, procured by the application of the English resident to the French ministry. I am now preparing for my long journey; but, before I leave this place, I shall send you the packet I mentioned, by Meriton.[3] Meanwhile I must fulfil my promise in communicating the observations I have had occasion to make upon this town and country.

The air of Boulogne is cold and moist, and, I believe, of consequence unhealthy. Last winter the frost, which continued six weeks in London, lasted here eight weeks without intermission; and the cold was so intense, that, in the garden of the Capuchins, it split the bark of several elms from top to bottom. On our arrival here we found all kinds of fruit more backward than in England. The frost, in its progress to Britain, is much weakened in crossing the sea. The atmosphere, impregnated with saline particles, resists the operation of freezing. Hence, in severe winters, all places near the sea-side are less cold than more inland districts. This is the reason why the winter is often more mild at Edinburgh than at London. A very great degree of cold is required to freeze salt water. Indeed it will not freeze at all, until it has deposited all its salt. It is now generally allowed among philosophers, that water is no more than ice thawed by heat, either solar, or subterranean, or both; and that this heat being expelled, it would return to its natural consistence. This being the case, nothing else is required for the freezing of water, than a certain degree of cold, which may be generated by the help of salt, or spirit of nitre, even under the line. I would propose, therefore, that an apparatus of this sort should be provided in every ship that goes to sea; and in case there should be a deficiency of fresh water on board, the sea-water may be rendered potable, by being first converted into ice.[4]

The air of Boulogne is not only loaded with a great

evaporation from the sea, increased by strong gales of wind from the West and South-West, which blow almost continually during the greatest part of the year; but it is also subject to putrid vapours, arising from the low marshy ground in the neighbourhood of the harbour, which is every tide overflowed with sea-water. This may be one cause of the scrofula and rickets, which are two prevailing disorders among the children in Boulogne. But I believe the former is more owing to the water used in the Lower Town, which is very hard and unwholesome. It curdles with soap, gives a red colour to the meat that is boiled in it, and, when drank by strangers, never fails to occasion pains in the stomach and bowels; nay, sometimes produces dysenteries. In all appearance it is impregnated with nitre, if not with something more mischievous: we know that mundic, or pyrites, very often contains a proportion of arsenic, mixed with sulphur, vitriol, and mercury. Perhaps it partakes of the acid of some coal mine; for there are coal works in this district. There is a well of purging water within a quarter of a mile of the Upper Town, to which the inhabitants resort in the morning, as the people of London go to the Dog-and-duck, in St. George's fields.[5] There is likewise a fountain of excellent water, hard by the cathedral, in the Upper Town, from whence I am daily supplied at a small expence. Some modern chemists affirm, that no saline chalybeate[6] waters can exist, except in the neighbourhood of coal damps; and that nothing can be more mild, and gentle, and friendly to the constitution, than the said damps: but I know that the place where I was bred stands upon a zonic[7] of coal; that the water which the inhabitants generally use is hard and brackish; and that the people are remarkably subject to the king's evil[8] and consumption. These I would impute to the bad water, impregnated with the vitriol and brine of coal, as there is nothing in the constitution of the air that should render such distempers endemial. That the air of Boulogne encourages putrefaction, appears from the effect it has upon butcher's meat, which, though the season is remarkably cold, we can hardly keep four-and-twenty hours in the coolest part of the house.

Living here is pretty reasonable; and the markets are tolerably supplied. The beef is neither fat nor firm; but very good for soup, which is the only use the French make of it. The veal is not so white, nor so well fed, as the English veal; but it is more juicy, and better tasted. The mutton and pork are very good. We buy our poultry alive, and fatten them at home. Here are excellent turkies, and no want of game: the hares, in particular, are very large, juicy, and high-flavoured. The best part of the fish caught on this coast is sent post to Paris, in chasse-marines, by a company of contractors, like those of Hastings in Sussex.[9] Nevertheless, we have excellent soles, skaite, flounders and whitings, and sometimes mackarel. The oysters are very large, coarse, and rank. There is very little fish caught on the French coast, because the shallows run a great way from the shore; and the fish live chiefly in deep water: for this reason the fishermen go a great way out to sea, sometimes even as far as the coast of England. Notwithstanding all the haste the contractors can make, their fish in the summer is very often spoiled before it arrives at Paris; and this is not to be wondered at, considering the length of the way, which is near one hundred and fifty miles. At best it must be in such a mortified condition, that no other people, except the negroes on the coast of Guinea, would feed upon it.

The wine commonly drank at Boulogne comes from Auxerre, is very small and meagre, and may be had from five to eight sols a bottle; that is, from two-pence halfpenny to four-pence. The French inhabitants drink no good wine; nor is there any to be had, unless you have recourse to the British wine-merchants here established, who deal in Bourdeaux wines, brought hither by sea for the London market. I have very good claret from a friend, at the rate of fifteen-pence sterling a bottle; and excellent small beer as reasonable as in England. I don't believe there is a drop of generous Burgundy in the place; and the aubergistes impose upon us shamefully, when they charge it at two livres a bottle. There is a small white wine, called *preniac*, which is very agreeable and very cheap. All the brandy which I have seen in Boulogne is new, fiery, and still-burnt. This is the trash which the smugglers import into England: they have it for about ten-pence a gallon. Butcher's meat is sold for five sols, or two-pence halfpenny a pound, and the pound here consists of eighteen ounces. I have a young turkey for thirty sols; a hare for four-and-twenty; a couple of chickens for twenty sols, and a couple of good soles for the same price. Before we left England, we were told that there was no fruit in Boulogne; but we have found ourselves agreeably disappointed in this particular. The place is well supplied with strawberries, cherries, gooseberries, corinths,[10] peaches, apricots, and excellent pears. I have eaten more fruit this season, than I have done for several years. There are many well-cultivated gardens in the skirts of the town; particularly one belonging to our friend Mrs. B——,[11] where we often drink tea in a charming summer-house built on a rising ground, which commands a delightful prospect of the sea. We have many obligations to this good lady, who is a kind neighbour, an obliging friend, and a most agreeable companion: she speaks English prettily, and is greatly attached to the people and the customs of our nation. They use wood for their common fewel, though, if I were to live at Boulogne, I would mix it with coal, which this country affords. Both the wood and the coal are reasonable enough. I am certain that a man may keep house in Boulogne for about one half of what it will cost him in London; and this is said to be one of the dearest places in France.

The adjacent country is very agreeable, diversified with hill and dale, corn-fields, woods, and meadows. There is a forest of a considerable extent, that begins about a short league from the Upper Town: it belongs to the king, and the wood is farmed to different individuals.

In point of agriculture, the people in this neighbourhood seem to have profited by the example of the English. Since I was last in France, fifteen years ago, a good number of inclosures and plantations have been made in the English fashion. There is a good many tolerable country-houses, within a few miles of Boulogne; but mostly empty. I was offered a compleat house, with a garden of four acres well laid out, and two fields for grass or hay, about a mile from the town, for four hundred livres, about seventeen pounds a year: it is partly furnished, stands in an agreeable situation, with a fine prospect of the sea, and was lately occupied by a Scotch nobleman, who is in the service of France.

To judge from appearance, the people of Boulogne are

descended from the Flemings, who formerly possessed this country; for, a great many of the present inhabitants have fine skins, fair hair, and florid complexions; very different from the natives of France in general, who are distinguished by black hair, brown skins, and swarthy faces. The people of the Boulonnois enjoy some extraordinary privileges, and, in particular, are exempted from the gabelle or duties upon salt: how they deserved this mark of favour, I do not know; but they seem to have a spirit of independence among them, are very ferocious, and much addicted to revenge. Many barbarous murders are committed, both in the town and country; and the peasants, from motives of envy and resentment, frequently set their neighbours houses on fire. Several instances of this kind have happened in the course of the last year. The interruption which is given, in arbitrary governments, to the administration of justice, by the interposition of the great, has always a bad effect upon the morals of the common people. The peasants too are often rendered desperate and savage, by the misery they suffer from the oppression and tyranny of their landlords. In this neighbourhood the labouring people are ill lodged and wretchedly fed; and they have no idea of cleanliness. There is a substantial burgher[12] in the High Town, who was some years ago convicted of a most barbarous murder. He received sentence to be broke alive upon the wheel; but was pardoned by the interposition of the governor of the county, and carries on his business as usual in the face of the whole community. A furious *abbé*, being refused orders by the bishop, on account of his irregular life, took an opportunity to stab the prelate with a knife, one Sunday, as he walked out of the cathedral. The good bishop desired he might be permitted to escape; but it was thought proper to punish, with the utmost severity, such an atrocious attempt. He was accordingly apprehended, and, though the wound was not mortal, condemned to be broke.[13] When this dreadful sentence was executed, he cried out, that it was hard he should undergo such torments, for having wounded a worthless priest, by whom he had been injured, while such-a-one (naming the burgher mentioned above) lived in ease and security, after having brutally murdered a poor man, and a helpless woman big with child, who had not given him the least provocation.

The inhabitants of Boulogne may be divided into three classes; the noblesse or gentry, the burghers, and the canaille. I don't mention the clergy, and the people belonging to the law, because I shall occasionally trouble you with my thoughts upon the religion and ecclesiastics of this country; and as for the lawyers, exclusive of their profession, they may be considered as belonging to one or other of these divisions. The noblesse are vain, proud, poor, and slothful. Very few of them have above six thousand livres a year, which may amount to about two hundred and fifty pounds sterling; and many of them have not half this revenue. I think there is one heiress, said to be worth one hundred thousand livres, about four thousand two hundred pounds; but then her jewels, her cloaths, and even her linen, are reckoned part of this fortune. The noblesse have not the common sense to reside at their houses in the country, where, by farming their own grounds, they might live at a small expence, and improve their estates at the same time. They allow their country-houses to go to decay, and their gardens and fields to waste; and reside in dark holes in the Upper Town of Boulogne, without light, air, or convenience. There they starve within doors, that they may have wherewithal to purchase fine cloaths, and appear dressed once a day in the church, or on the rampart. They have no education, no taste for reading, no housewifery, nor indeed any earthly occupation, but that of dressing their hair, and adorning their bodies. They hate walking, and would never go abroad, if they were not stimulated by the vanity of being seen. I ought to except indeed those who turn devotees, and spend the greatest part of their time with the priest, either at church, or in their own houses. Other amusements they have none in this place, except private parties of card-playing, which are far from being expensive. Nothing can be more parsimonious than the œconomy of these people: they live upon soupe and bouillê, fish and sallad: they never think of giving dinners, or entertaining their friends; they even save the expence of coffee and tea, though both are very cheap at Boulogne. They presume that every person drinks coffee at home, immediately after dinner, which is always over by one o'clock; and, in lieu of tea in the afternoon, they treat with a glass of sherbet, or capillaire.[14] In a word, I know not a more insignificant set of mortals than the noblesse of Boulogne; helpless in themselves, and useless to the community; without dignity, sense, or sentiment; contemptible from pride, and ridiculous from vanity. They pretend to be jealous of their rank, and will entertain no correspondence with the merchants, whom they term plebeians. They likewise keep at a great distance from strangers, on pretence of a delicacy in the article of punctilio: but, as I am informed, this statelieness is in a great measure affected, in order to conceal their poverty, which would appear to greater disadvantage, if they admitted of a more familiar communication. Considering the vivacity of the French people, one would imagine they could not possibly lead such an insipid life, altogether unanimated by society, or diversion. True it is, the only profane diversions of this place are a puppet-show and a mountebank; but then their religion affords a perpetual comedy. Their high masses, their feasts, their processions, their pilgrimages, confessions, images, tapers, robes, incense, benedictions, spectacles, representations, and innumerable ceremonies, which revolve almost incessantly, furnish a variety of entertainment from one end of the year to the other. If superstition implies *fear*, never was a word more misapplied than it is to the mummery of the religion of Rome. The people are so far from being impressed with awe and religious terror by this sort of machinery, that it amuses their imaginations in the most agreeable manner, and keeps them always in good humour. A Roman catholic longs as impatiently for the festival of *St. Suaire*, or *St. Croix*, or *St. Veronique*, as a school-boy in England for the representation of punch and the devil; and there is generally as much laughing at one farce as at the other. Even when the descent from the cross is acted, in the holy week, with all the circumstances that ought naturally to inspire the gravest sentiments, if you cast your eyes among the multitude that croud the place, you will not discover one melancholy face: all is prattling, tittering, or laughing; and ten to one but you perceive a number of them employed in hissing the female who personates the Virgin Mary. And here it may not be amiss to observe, that the Roman catholics, not content with the infinite number of saints who really existed, have not only personified *the cross*, but made two female saints out of a piece of linen. *Veronique*, or *Veronica*, is no other than a corruption of *vera icon*, or *vera effigies*, said to be the exact representation of our Saviour's face, impressed upon a piece of linen, with which he wiped the sweat from his forehead in his way to the place of crucifixion. The same is worshipped under the name of *St. Suaire*, from the Latin word *sudarium*. This same handkerchief is said to have had three folds, on every one of which was the impression: one of these remains at Jerusalem, a second was brought to Rome, and a third was conveyed to Spain. Baronius says, there is a very antient history of the *sancta facies* in the Vatican.[15] Tillemont, however, looks upon the whole as a fable.[16] Some suppose *Veronica* to be the same with St. Hæmorrhoissa, the patroness of those who are afflicted with the piles,[17] who make their joint invocations to her and St. Fiacre,[18] the son of a Scotch king, who lived and died a hermit in France. The troops of Henry V. of England are said to have pillaged the chapel of this Highland saint; who, in revenge, assisted his countrymen, in the French service, to defeat the English at Baugé,[19] and afterwards afflicted Henry with the piles, of which he died. This prince complained, that he was not only plagued by the living Scots, but even persecuted by those who were dead.

I know not whether I may be allowed to compare the Romish religion to comedy, and Calvinism to tragedy. The first amuses the senses, and excites ideas of mirth and good-humour; the other, like tragedy, deals in the passions of terror and pity. Step into a conventicle of dissenters, you will, ten to one, hear the minister holding forth upon the sufferings of Christ, or the torments of hell, and see many marks of religious horror in the faces of the hearers. This is perhaps one reason why the reformation did not succeed in France, among a volatile, giddy, unthinking people, shocked at the mortified appearances of the Calvinists; and accounts for its rapid progress among nations of a more melancholy turn of character and complexion: for, in the conversion of the multitude, reason is generally out of the question. Even the penance imposed upon the catholics is little more than mock mortification: a murderer is often quit with his confessor for saying three prayers extraordinary; and these easy terms, on which absolution is obtained, certainly encourage the repetition of the most enormous crimes. The pomp and ceremonies of this religion, together with the great number of holidays they observe, howsoever they may keep up the spirits of the commonalty, and help to diminish the sense of their own misery, must certainly, at the same time, produce a frivolous taste for frippery and shew, and encourage a habit of idleness, to which I, in a great measure, ascribe the extreme poverty of the lower people. Very near half of their time, which might be profitably employed in the exercise of industry, is lost to themselves and the community, in attendance upon the different exhibitions of religious mummery.

But as this letter has already run to an unconscionable length, I shall defer, till another occasion, what I have further to say on the people of this place, and in the mean time assure you, that I am always

Yours affectionately.

# LETTER V.

*Boulogne, September* 12, 1763.

DEAR SIR,

My stay in this place now draws towards a period. 'Till within these few days I have continued bathing, with some advantage to my health, though the season has been cold and wet, and disagreeable. There was a fine prospect of a plentiful harvest in this neighbourhood. I used to have great pleasure in driving between the fields of wheat, oats, and barley; but the crop has been entirely ruined by the rain, and nothing is now to be seen on the ground but the tarnished straw, and the rotten spoils of the husbandman's labour. The ground scarce affords subsistence to a few flocks of meagre sheep, that crop the stubble, and the intervening grass; each flock under the protection of its shepherd, with his crook and dogs, who lies every night in the midst of the fold, in a little thatched travelling lodge, mounted on a wheel-carriage. Here he passes the night, in order to defend his flock from the wolves, which are sometimes, especially in winter, very bold and desperate.

Two days ago we made an excursion with Mrs. B——[1] and Capt. L——[2] to the village of Samers, on the Paris road, about three leagues from Boulogne. Here is a venerable abbey of Benedictines, well endowed, with large agreeable gardens prettily laid out. The monks are well lodged, and well entertained. Though restricted from flesh meals by the rules of their order, they are allowed to eat wild duck and teal, as a species of fish; and when they long for a good *bouillon*, or a partridge, or a pullet, they have nothing to do but to say they are out of order. In that case the appetite of the patient is indulged in his own apartment. Their church is elegantly contrived, but kept in a very dirty condition. The greatest curiosity I saw in this place was an English boy, about eight or nine years old, from Dover, whom his father had sent hither to learn the French language. In less than eight weeks, he was become captain of the boys of the place, spoke French perfectly well, and had almost forgot his mother tongue. But to return to the people of Boulogne.

The burghers here, as in other places, consist of merchants,

30

shop-keepers, and artisans. Some of the merchants have got fortunes, by fitting out privateers during the war. A great many single ships were taken from the English, notwithstanding the good look-out of our cruisers, who were so alert, that the privateers from this coast were often taken in four hours after they sailed from the French harbour; and there is hardly a captain of an *armateur* in Boulogne, who has not been prisoner in England five or six times in the course of the war. They were fitted out at a very small expence, and used to run over in the night to the coast of England, where they hovered as English fishing smacks, until they kidnapped some coaster, with which they made the best of their way across the Channel. If they fell in with a British cruizer, they surrendered without resistance: the captain was soon exchanged, and the loss of the proprietor was not great: if they brought their prize safe into harbour, the advantage was considerable. In time of peace the merchants of Boulogne deal in wine, brandies, and oil, imported from the South, and export fish, with the manufactures of France, to Portugal, and other countries; but the trade is not great. Here are two or three considerable houses of wine-merchants from Britain, who deal in Bourdeaux wine, with which they supply London and other parts of England, Scotland, and Ireland. The fishery of mackarel and herring is so considerable on this coast, that it is said to yield annually eight or nine hundred thousand livres, about thirty-five thousand pounds sterling.

The shop-keepers here drive a considerable traffic with the English smugglers, whose cutters are almost the only vessels one sees in the harbour of Boulogne, if we except about a dozen of those flat-bottomed boats, which raised such alarms in England, in the course of the war.[3] Indeed they seem to be good for nothing else, and perhaps they were built for this purpose only. The smugglers from the coast of Kent and Sussex pay English gold for great quantities of French brandy, tea, coffee, and small wine, which they run from this country. They likewise buy glass trinkets, toys, and coloured prints, which sell in England, for no other reason, but that they come from France, as they may be had as cheap, and much better finished, of our own manufacture. They likewise take off ribbons, laces, linen, and cambrics; though this branch of trade is chiefly in the hands of traders that come from London, and make their purchases at Dunkirk, where they pay no duties. It is certainly worth while for any traveller to lay in a stock of linen either at Dunkirk or Boulogne; the difference of the price at these two places is not great. Even here I have made a provision of shirts for one half of the money they would have cost in London. Undoubtedly the practice of smuggling is very detrimental to the fair trader, and carries considerable sums of money out of the kingdom, to enrich our rivals and enemies. The custom-house officers are very watchful, and make a great number of seizures: nevertheless, the smugglers find their account in continuing this contraband commerce; and are said to indemnify themselves, if they save one cargo out of three. After all, the best way to prevent smuggling, is to lower the duties upon the commodities which are thus introduced. I have been told, that the revenue upon tea has encreased ever since the duty upon it was diminished.[4] By the bye, the tea smuggled on the coast of Sussex is most execrable stuff. While I stayed at Hastings,[5] for the conveniency of bathing, I must have changed my breakfast, if I had not luckily brought tea with me from London: yet we have as good tea at Boulogne for nine livres a pound, as that which sells at fourteen shillings at London.

The bourgeois of this place seem to live at their ease, probably in consequence of their trade with the English. Their houses consist of the ground-floor, one story above, and garrets. In those which are well furnished, you see pier-glasses[6] and marble slabs; but the chairs are either paultry things, made with straw bottoms, which cost about a shilling a-piece, or old-fashioned, high-backed seats of needle-work, stuffed, very clumsy and incommodious. The tables are square fir boards, that stand on edge in a corner, except when they are used, and then they are set upon cross legs that open and shut occasionally. The king of France dines off a board of this kind. Here is plenty of table-linen however. The poorest tradesman in Boulogne has a napkin on every cover, and silver forks with four prongs, which are used with the right hand, there being very little occasion for knives; for the meat is boiled or roasted to rags. The French beds are so high, that sometimes one is obliged to mount them by the help of steps; and this is also the case in Flanders. They very seldom use feather-beds; but they lie upon a *paillasse*, or bag of straw, over which are laid two, and sometimes three mattrasses. Their testers[7] are high and old-fashioned, and their curtains generally of thin bays, red, or green, laced with taudry yellow, in imitation of gold. In some houses, however, one meets with furniture of stamped linen; but there is no such thing as a carpet to be seen, and the floors are in a very dirty condition. They have not even the implements of cleanliness in this country. Every chamber is furnished with an *armoire*, or clothes-press, and a chest of drawers, of very clumsy workmanship. Every thing shews a deficiency in the mechanic arts. There is not a door, nor a window, that shuts close. The hinges, locks, and latches, are of iron, coarsely made, and ill contrived. The very chimnies are built so open, that they admit both rain and sun, and all of them smoke intolerably. If there is no cleanliness among these people, much less shall we find delicacy, which is the cleanliness of the mind. Indeed they are utter strangers to what we call common decency; and I could give you some high-flavoured instances, at which even a native of Edin-burgh would stop his nose.[8] There are certain mortifying views of human nature, which undoubtedly ought to be concealed as much as possible, in order to prevent giving offence: and nothing can be more absurd, than to plead the difference of custom in different countries, in defence of those usages which cannot fail giving disgust to the organs and senses of all mankind. Will custom exempt from the imputation of gross indecency a French lady, who shifts her frowsy smock in presence of a male visitant, and talks to him of her *lavement*, her *medicine*, and her *bidet*! An Italian *signora* makes no scruple of telling you, she is such a day to begin a course of physic for the *pox*. The celebrated reformer of the Italian comedy introduces a child befouling itself on the stage, OE, NO TI SENTI? BISOGNA DESFASSARLO, ( *fa cenno che sentesi mal odore*).[9] I have known a lady handed to the house of office by her admirer, who stood at the door, and entertained her with *bons mots* all the time she was within. But I should be glad to know, whether it is possible for a fine lady to speak and act in this manner, without exciting ideas to her own disadvantage in the mind of every man who has any imagination left, and enjoys the intire use of his senses, howsoever she may be authorised by the customs of her country? There is nothing so vile or repugnant to nature, but you may plead prescription for it, in the customs of some nation or other. A Parisian likes mortified flesh: a native of Legiboli[10] will not taste his fish till it is quite putrefied: the civilized inhabitants of Kamschatka[11] get drunk with the urine of their guests, whom they have already intoxicated: the Nova Zemblans make merry on train-oil: the Groen-landers eat in the same dish with their dogs: the Caffres, at the Cape of Good Hope, piss upon those whom they delight to honour, and feast upon a sheep's intestines with their contents, as the greatest dainty that can be presented. A true-bred Frenchman dips his fingers, imbrowned with snuff, into his plate filled with ragout: between every three mouth-fuls, he produces his snuff-box, and takes a fresh pinch, with the most graceful gesticulations; then he displays his hand-kerchief, which may be termed the *flag of abomination*, and, in the use of both, scatters his favours among those who have the happiness to sit near him. It must be owned, however, that a Frenchman will not drink out of a tankard, in which, perhaps, a dozen of filthy mouths have slabbered, as is the custom in England. Here every individual has his own gobelet, which stands before him, and he helps himself occasionally with wine, or water, or both, which likewise stand upon the table. But I know no custom more beastly than that of using water-glasses, in which polite company spirt, and squirt, and spue the filthy scourings of their gums, under the eyes of each other. I knew a lover cured of his passion, by seeing this nasty cascade discharged from the mouth of his mistress. I don't doubt but I shall live to see the day, when the hospitable custom of the antient Ægyptians will be revived; then a conveniency will be placed behind every chair in company, with a proper provision of waste paper, that individuals may make themselves easy without parting company. I insist upon it, that this practice would not be more indelicate than that which is now in use. What then, you will say, must a man sit with his chops and fingers up to the ears and knuckles in grease? No; let those who cannot eat without defiling themselves, step into another room, provided with basons and towels: but I think it would be better to institute schools, where youth may learn to eat their victuals, without daubing themselves, or giving offence to the eyes of one another.

The bourgeois of Boulogne have commonly soup and bouillé at noon, and a roast, with a sallad, for supper; and at all their meals there is a desert of fruit. This indeed is the practice all over France. On meagre days they eat fish, omelettes, fried beans, fricassees of eggs and onions, and burnt cream. The tea which they drink in the afternoon is rather boiled than infused; it is sweetened all together with coarse sugar, and drank with an equal quantity of boiled milk.

We had the honour to be entertained the other day by our landlord, Mr. B——,[12] who spared no cost on this banquet, exhibited for the glory of France. He had invited a new-married couple, together with the husband's mother, and the lady's father, who was one of the noblesse of Montreuil, his name Mons. L——y.[13] There were likewise some merchants of the town, and Mons. B——'s uncle, a facetious little man, who had served in the English navy, and was as big and as round as a hogshead; we were likewise favoured with the company of father K——, a native of Ireland, who is *vicaire*, or curate of the parish;[14] and among the guests was Mons. L——y's son, a pretty boy, about thirteen or fourteen years of age. The *repas* served up in three services, or courses, with *entrées* and *hors d'œuvres*, exclusive of the fruit, consisted of above twenty dishes, extremely well dressed by the *rotisseur*, who is the best cook I ever knew, in France, or elsewhere; but the *plats* were not presented with much order. Our young ladies did not seem to be much used to do the honours of the table. The most extraordinary circumstance that I observed on this occasion was, that all the French who were present ate of every dish that appeared; and I am told, that if there had been an hundred articles more, they would have had a trial of each. This is what they call doing justice to the founder. Mons. L——y was placed at the head of the table; and indeed he was the oracle and orator of the company; tall, thin, and weather-beaten, not unlike the picture of Don Quixote after he had lost his teeth.[15] He had been *garde du corps*, or life-guardsman at Versailles; and by virtue of this office he was perfectly well acquainted with the persons of the king and the dauphin, with the characters of the ministers and grandees, and, in a word, with all the secrets of state, on which he held forth with equal solemnity and elocution. He exclaimed against the jesuits, and the farmers of the revenue, who, he said, had ruined France. Then, addressing himself to me, asked, if the English did not every day drink to the health of *madame la marquise*?[16] I did not at first comprehend his meaning; but answered in general, that the English were not deficient in complaisance for the ladies. "Ah! (cried he) she is the best friend they have in the world. If it had not been for her, they would not have such reason to boast of the advantages of the war." I told him the only conquest which the French had made in the war, was atchieved by one of her generals: I meant the taking of Mahon.[17] But I did not choose to prosecute the discourse, remembering that in the year 1749, I had like to have had an affair with a Frenchman at Ghent, who affirmed, that all the battles gained by the great duke of Marlborough were purposely lost by the French generals, in order to bring the schemes of madame de Maintenon into disgrace.[18] This is no bad resource for the national vanity of these people: though, in general, they are really persuaded, that theirs is the richest, the bravest, the happiest, and the most powerful nation under the sun; and therefore, without some such cause, they must be invincible. By the bye, the common people here still frighten their wayward children with the name of *Marlborough*. Mr. B——'s son, who was nursed at a peasant's house, happening one day, after he was brought home, to be in disgrace with his father, who threatened to correct him, the child ran for protection to his mother, crying, *"faites sortir ce vilain Malbroug,"* "turn out that rogue Malbrough."[19] It is amazing to hear a sensible Frenchman assert, that the revenues of France amount to four hundred millions of livres, about twenty millions sterling, clear of all incumbrances, when in fact their clear revenue is not much above ten. Without all doubt they have reason to inveigh against the *fermiers généraux*,[20] who oppress the people in raising the taxes, not above two thirds of which are brought into the king's coffers: the rest enriches themselves, and enables them to bribe high for the protection of the great, which is the only support they have against the remonstrances of the states and parliaments, and the suggestions of common sense; which will ever demonstrate this to be, of all others, the most pernicious method of supplying the necessities of government.

Mons. L——y seasoned the severity of his political apothegms with intermediate sallies of mirth and gallantry. He ogled the venerable gentlewoman his *commère*, who sat by him. He looked, sighed, and languished, sung tender songs, and kissed the old lady's hand with all the ardour of a youthful admirer. I unfortunately congratulated him on having such a pretty young gentleman to his son. He answered, sighing, that the boy had talents, but did not put them to a proper use —"long before I attained his age (said he) I had finished my rhetoric." Captain B——, who had eaten himself black in the face, and, with the napkin under his chin, was no bad representation of Sancho Panza in the suds, with the dishclout about his neck, when the duke's scullions insisted upon shaving him,[21] this sea-wit, turning to the boy, with a waggish leer, "I suppose (said he) you don't understand the figure of *amplification* so well as Monsieur your father." At that instant, one of the nieces, who knew her uncle to be very ticklish, touched him under the short ribs, on which the little man attempted to spring up, but lost the centre of gravity. He overturned his own plate in the lap of the person that sat next to him, and falling obliquely upon his own chair, both tumbled down upon the floor together, to the great discomposure of the whole company; for the poor man would have been actually strangled, had not his nephew loosed his stock with great expedition. Matters being once more adjusted, and the captain condoled on his disaster, Mons. L——y took it in his head to read his son a lecture upon filial obedience. This was mingled with some sharp reproof, which the boy took so ill that he retired. The old lady observed that he had been too severe: her daughter-in-law, who was very pretty, said her brother had given him too much reason; hinting, at the same time, that he was addicted to some terrible vices; upon which several individuals repeated the interjection, ah! ah! "Yes (said Mons. L——y, with a rueful aspect) the boy has a pernicious turn for gaming: in one afternoon he lost, at billiards, such a sum as gives me horror to think of it." "Fifty sols in one afternoon," (cried the sister). "Fifty sols! (exclaimed the mother-in-law, with marks of astonishment) that's too much —that's too much!—he's to blame—he's to blame! but youth, you know Mons. L——y— ah! vive la jeunesse!" "et l'amour!" cried the father, wiping his eyes, squeezing her hand, and looking tenderly upon her. Mr. B— took this opportunity to bring in the young gentleman, who was admitted into favour, and received a second exhortation. Thus harmony was restored, and the entertainment concluded with fruit, coffee, and *liqueurs*.

When a bourgeois of Boulogne takes the air, he goes in a one-horse chaise, which is here called *cabriolet*, and hires it for half-a-crown a day. There are also travelling chaises, which hold four persons, two seated with their faces to the horses, and two behind their backs; but those vehicles are all very ill made, and extremely inconvenient. The way of riding most used in this place is on assback. You will see every day, in the skirts of the town, a great number of females thus mounted, with the feet on either side occasionally, according as the wind blows, so that sometimes the right and sometimes the left hand guides the beast: but in other parts of France, as well as in Italy, the ladies sit on horseback with their legs astride, and are provided with drawers for that purpose.

When I said the French people were kept in good humour by the fopperies of their religion, I did not mean that there were no gloomy spirits among them. There will be fanatics in religion, while there are people of a saturnine disposition, and melancholy turn of mind. The character of a *devotee*, which is hardly known in England, is very common here. You see them walking to and from church at all hours, in their hoods and long camblet cloaks, with a slow pace, demure aspect, and downcast eye. Those who are poor become very troublesome to the monks, with their scruples and cases of conscience: you may see them on their knees, at the confessional, every hour in the day. The rich *devotee* has her favourite confessor, whom she consults and regales in private, at her own house; and this spiritual director generally governs the whole family. For my part, I never knew a fanatic that was not an hypocrite at bottom. Their pretensions to superior sanctity, and an absolute conquest over all the passions, which human reason was never yet able to subdue, introduce a habit of dissimulation, which, like all other habits, is confirmed by use, till at length they become adepts in the art and science of hypocrisy. Enthusiasm and hypocrisy are by no means incompatible. The wildest fanatics I ever knew, were real sensualists in their way of living, and cunning cheats in their dealings with mankind.

Among the lower class of people at Boulogne, those who take the lead, are the seafaring men, who live in one quarter, divided into classes, and registered for the service of the king. They are hardy and raw-boned, exercise the trade of fishermen and boatmen, and propagate like rabbits. They have put themselves under the protection of a miraculous image of the Virgin Mary, which is kept in one of their churches, and every year carried in procession. According to the legend, this image was carried off, with other pillage, by the English, when they took Boulogne, in the reign of Henry VIII. The lady, rather than reside in England, where she found a great many heretics, trusted herself alone in an open boat, and crossed the sea to the road of Boulogne, where she was seen waiting for a pilot. Accordingly a boat put off to her assistance, and brought her safe into the harbour: since which time she has continued to patronize the watermen of Boulogne. At present she is very black and very ugly, besides being cruelly mutilated in different parts of her body, which I suppose have been amputated, and converted into tobacco-stoppers; but once a year she is dressed in very rich attire, and carried in procession, with a silver boat, provided at the expence of the sailors.[22] That vanity which characterises the French extends even to the canaille. The lowest creature among them is sure to have her ear-rings and golden cross hanging about her neck. Indeed this last is an implement of superstition as well as of dress, without which no female appears. The common people here, as in all countries where they live poorly and dirtily, are hard-featured, and of very brown, or rather tawny complexions. As they seldom eat meat, their juices are destitute of that animal oil which gives a plumpness and smoothness to the skin, and defends those fine capillaries from the injuries of the weather, which would otherwise coalesce, or be shrunk up, so as to impede the circulation on the external surface of the body. As for the dirt, it undoubtedly blocks up the pores of the skin, and disorders the perspiration; consequently must contribute to the scurvy, itch, and other cutaneous distempers.

In the quarter of the *matelots* at Boulogne, there is a number of poor Canadians, who were removed from the island of St. John, in the gulph of St. Laurence, when it was reduced by the English.[23] These people are maintained at the expence of the king, who allows them soldier's pay, that is five sols, or two-pence halfpenny a day; or rather three sols and ammunition bread. How the soldiers contrive to subsist upon this wretched allowance, I cannot comprehend: but, it must be owned, that those invalids who do duty at Boulogne betray no marks of want. They are hale and stout, neatly and decently cloathed, and on the whole look better than the pensioners of Chelsea.

About three weeks ago I was favoured with a visit by one Mr. M——,[24] an English gentleman, who seems far gone in a consumption. He passed the last winter at Nismes in Languedoc, and found himself much better in the beginning of summer, when he embarked at Cette, and returned by sea to England. He soon relapsed, however, and (as he imagines) in consequence of a cold caught at sea. He told me, his intention was to try the South again, and even to go as far as Italy. I advised him to make trial of the air of Nice, where I myself proposed to reside. He seemed to relish my advice, and proceeded towards Paris in his own carriage.

I shall to-morrow ship my great chests on board of a ship bound to Bourdeaux; they are directed, and recommended to the care of a merchant of that place, who will forward them by Thoulouse, and the canal of Languedoc, to his correspondent at Cette, which is the sea-port of Montpellier. The charge of their conveyance to Bourdeaux does not exceed one guinea. They consist of two very large chests and a trunk, about a thousand pounds weight; and the expence of transporting them from Bourdeaux to Cette, will not exceed thirty livres. They are already sealed with lead at the custom-house, that they may be exempted from further visitation. This is a precaution which every traveller takes, both by sea and land: he must likewise provide himself with a *passe-avant* at the bureau, otherwise he may be stopped, and rummaged at every town through which he passes.[25] I have hired a berline and four horses to Paris, for fourteen loui'dores; two of which the *voiturier* is obliged to pay for a permission from the farmers of the poste; for every thing is farmed in this country; and if you hire a carriage, as I have done, you must pay twelve livres, or half a guinea, for every person that travels in it. The common coach between Calais and Paris, is such a vehicle as no man would use, who has any regard to his own ease and convenience; and it travels at the pace of an English waggon.

In ten days I shall set out on my journey; and I shall leave Boulogne with regret. I have been happy in the acquaintance of Mrs. B——, and a few British families in the place; and it was my good fortune to meet here with two honest gentlemen, whom I had formerly known in Paris, as well as with some of my countrymen, officers in the service of France. My next will be from Paris. Remember me to our friends at A——'s.[26] I am a little heavy-hearted at the prospect of removing to such a distance from you. It is a moot point whether I shall ever return. My health is very precarious.

Adieu.

# LETTER VI.

*Paris, October 12, 1763.*

DEAR SIR,

Of our journey from Boulogne I have little to say. The weather was favourable, and the roads were in tolerable order. We found good accommodation at Montreuil and Amiens; but in every other place where we stopped, we met with abundance of dirt, and the most flagrant imposition. I shall not pretend to describe the cities of Abbeville and Amiens, which we saw only *en passant*; nor take up your time with an account of the stables and palace of Chantilly, belonging to the prince of Condé,[1] which we visited the last day of our journey; nor shall I detain you with a detail of the *Tresors de St. Denis*,[2] which, together with the tombs in the abbey church, afforded us some amusement while our dinner was getting ready. All these particulars are mentioned in twenty different books of tours, travels, and directions, which you have often perused. I shall only observe, that the abbey church is the lightest piece of Gothic architecture I have seen, and the air within seems perfectly free from that damp and moisture, so perceivable in all our old cathedrals. This must be owing to the nature of its situation. There are some fine marble statues that adorn the tombs of certain individuals here interred; but they are mostly in the French taste, which is quite contrary to the simplicity of the antients. Their attitudes are affected, unnatural, and desultory; and their draperies fantastic; or, as one of our English artists expressed himself, *they are all of a flutter*. As for the treasures, which are shewn on certain days to the populace gratis, they are contained in a number of presses, or armoires, and, if the stones are genuine, they must be inestimable: but this I cannot believe. Indeed I have been told, that what they shew as diamonds are no more than composition: nevertheless, exclusive of these, there are some rough stones of great value, and many curiosities worth seeing. The monk that shewed them was the very image of our friend Hamilton,[3] both in his looks and manner.

I have one thing very extraordinary to observe of the French auberges, which seems to be a remarkable deviation from the general character of the nation. The landlords, hostesses, and servants of the inns upon the road, have not the least dash of complaisance in their behaviour to strangers. Instead of coming to the door, to receive you as in England, they take no manner of notice of you; but leave you to find or enquire your way into the kitchen, and there you must ask several times for a chamber, before they seem willing to conduct you up stairs. In general, you are served with the appearance of the most mortifying indifference, at the very time they are laying schemes for fleecing you of your money. It is a very odd contrast between France and England; in the former all the people are complaisant but the publicans; in the latter there is hardly any complaisance but among the publicans. When I said all the people in France, I ought also to except those vermin who examine the baggage of travellers in different parts of the kingdom. Although our portmanteaus were sealed with lead, and we were provided with a passe-avant from the douane, our coach was searched at the gate of Paris by which we entered; and the women were obliged to get out, and stand in the open street, till this operation was performed.

I had desired a friend to provide lodgings for me at Paris, in the Fauxbourg St. Germain; and accordingly we found ourselves accommodated at the Hotel de Montmorency,[4] with a first floor, which costs me ten livres a day. I should have put up with it had it been less polite; but as I have only a few days to stay in this place, and some visits to receive, I am not sorry that my friend has exceeded his commission. I have been guilty of another piece of extravagance in hiring a *carosse de remise*, for which I pay twelve livres a day. Besides the article of visiting, I could not leave Paris, without carrying my wife and the girls to see the most remarkable places in and about this capital, such as the Luxemburg, the Palais-Royal, the Thuilleries, the Louvre, the Invalids, the Gobelins, &c. together with Versailles, Trianon, Marli, Meudon, and Choissi; and therefore, I thought the difference in point of expence would not be great, between a *carosse de remise* and a hackney coach. The first are extremely elegant, if not too much ornamented, the last are very shabby and disagreeable. Nothing gives me such chagrin, as the necessity I am under to hire a *valet de place*, as my own servant does not speak the language. You cannot conceive with what eagerness and dexterity those rascally valets exert themselves in pillaging strangers. There is always one ready in waiting on your arrival, who begins by assisting your own servant to unload your baggage, and interests himself in your affairs with such artful officiousness, that you will find it difficult to shake him off, even though you are determined beforehand against hiring any such domestic. He produces recommendations from his former masters, and the people of the house vouch for his honesty. The truth is, those fellows are very handy, useful, and obliging; and so far honest, that they will not steal in the usual way. You may safely trust one of them to bring you a hundred loui'dores from your banker; but they fleece you without mercy in every other article of expence. They lay all your tradesmen under contribution; your taylor, barber, mantua-maker,[5] milliner, perfumer, shoemaker, mercer, jeweller, hatter, traiteur, and wine-merchant: even the bourgeois who owns your coach pays him twenty sols per day. His wages amount to twice as much, so that I imagine the fellow that serves me, makes above ten shillings a day, besides his victuals, which, by the bye, he has no right to demand. Living at Paris, to the best of my recollection, is very near twice as dear as it was fifteen years ago; and, indeed, this is the case in London; a circumstance that must be undoubtedly owing to an increase of taxes; for I don't find that in the articles of eating and drinking, the French people are more luxurious than they were heretofore. I am told the *entrées*, or duties, payed upon provision imported into Paris, are very heavy. All manner of butcher's meat and poultry are extremely good in this place. The beef is excellent. The wine, which is generally drank, is a very thin kind of Burgundy. I can by no means relish their cookery; but one breakfasts deliciously upon their *petit pains* and their *patés* of butter, which last is exquisite.

The common people, and even the bourgeois of Paris live, at this season, chiefly on bread and grapes, which is undoubtedly very wholsome fare. If the same simplicity of diet prevailed in England, we should certainly undersel the French at all foreign markets: for they are very slothful with all their vivacity; and the great number of their holidays not only encourages this lazy disposition, but actually robs them of one half of what their labour would otherwise produce; so that, if our common people were not so expensive in their living, that is, in their eating and drinking, labour might be afforded cheaper in England than in France. There are three young lusty hussies, nieces or daughters of a blacksmith, that lives just opposite to my windows, who do nothing from morning till night. They eat grapes and bread from seven till nine, from nine till twelve they dress their hair, and are all the afternoon gaping at the window to view passengers. I don't perceive that they give themselves the trouble either to make their beds, or clean their apartment. The same spirit of idleness and dissipation I have observed in every part of France, and among every class of people.

Every object seems to have shrunk in its dimensions since I was last in Paris. The Louvre, the Palais-Royal, the bridges, and the river Seine, by no means answer the ideas I had formed of them from my former observation. When the memory is not very correct, the imagination always betrays her into such extravagances. When I first revisited my own country, after an absence of fourteen years, I found every thing diminished in the same manner, and I could scarce believe my own eyes.

Notwithstanding the gay disposition of the French, their houses are all gloomy. In spite of all the ornaments that have been lavished on Versailles, it is a dismal habitation. The apartments are dark, ill-furnished, dirty, and unprincely. Take the castle, chapel, and garden all together, they make a most fantastic composition of magnificence and littleness, taste and foppery. After all, it is in England only, where we must look for cheerful apartments, gay furniture, neatness, and convenience. There is a strange incongruity in the French genius. With all their volatility, prattle, and fondness for *bons mots*, they delight in a species of drawling, melancholy, church music. Their most favourite dramatic pieces are almost without incident; and the dialogue of their comedies consists of moral, insipid apophthegms, intirely destitute of wit, or repartee. I know what I hazard by this opinion among the implicit admirers of Lully,[6] Racine, and Moliere.

I don't talk of the busts, the statues, and pictures which abound at Versailles, and other places, in and about Paris, particularly the great collection of capital pieces in the Palais-Royal, belonging to the duke of Orleans. I have neither capacity, nor inclination, to give a critique on these *chef d'œuvres*, which indeed would take up a whole volume. I have seen this great magazine of painting three times, with astonishment; but I should have been better pleased, if there had not been half the number: one is bewildered in such a profusion, as not to know where to begin, and hurried away before there is time to consider one piece with any sort of deliberation. Besides, the rooms are all dark, and a great many of the pictures hang in a bad light. As for Trianon, Marli, and Choissi, they are no more than pigeon-houses, in respect to palaces; and, notwithstanding the extravagant eulogiums which you have heard of the French king's houses, I will venture to affirm, that the king of England is better, I mean more comfortably, lodged. I ought, however, to except Fontainbleau, which I have not seen.

The city of Paris is said to be five leagues, or fifteen miles, in circumference; and if it is really so, it must be much more populous than London; for the streets are very narrow, and the houses very high, with a different family on every floor. But I have measured the best plans of these two royal cities, and am certain that Paris does not take up near so much ground as London and Westminster occupy; and I suspect the number of its inhabitants is also exaggerated by those who say it amounts to eight hundred thousand, that is two hundred thousand more than are contained in the bills of mortality.[7] The hotels of the French noblesse, at Paris, take up a great deal of room, with their court-yards and gardens; and so do their convents and churches. It must be owned, indeed, that their streets are wonderfully crouded with people and carriages.

The French begin to imitate the English, but only in such particulars as render them worthy of imitation. When I was last at Paris, no person of any condition, male or female, appeared, but in full dress, even when obliged to come out early in the morning, and there was not such a thing to be seen as a *peruque ronde*; but at present I see a number of frocks and scratches in a morning, in the streets of this metropolis. They have set up a *petite poste*, on the plan of our penny-post, with some improvements;[8] and I am told there is a scheme on foot for supplying every house with water, by leaden pipes, from the river Seine. They have even adopted our practice of the cold bath, which is taken very conveniently, in wooden houses, erected on the side of the river, the water of which is let in and out occasionally, by cocks fixed in the sides of the bath. There are different rooms for the different sexes: the accommodations are good, and the expence is a trifle. The tapestry of the Gobelins is brought to an amazing degree of perfection; and I am surprised that this furniture is not more in fashion among the great, who alone are able to purchase it. It would be a most elegant and magnificent ornament, which would always nobly distinguish their apartments from those of an inferior rank; and in this they would run no risque of being rivalled by the bourgeois. At the village of Chaillot, in the neighbourhood of Paris, they make beautiful carpets and screen-work; and this is the more extraordinary, as there are hardly any carpets used in this kingdom. In almost all the lodging-houses, the floors are of brick, and have no other kind of cleaning, than that of being sprinkled with water, and swept once a day. These brick floors, the stone stairs, the want of wainscotting in the rooms, and the thick party-walls of stone, are, however, good preservatives against fire, which seldom does any damage in this city. Instead of wainscotting, the walls are covered with tapestry or damask. The beds in general are very good, and well ornamented, with testers and curtains.

Twenty years ago the river Seine, within a mile of Paris, was as solitary as if it had run through a desert. At present the banks of it are adorned with a number of elegant houses and plantations, as far as Marli. I need not mention the machine at this place for raising water,[9] because I know you are well acquainted with its construction; nor shall I say any thing more of the city of Paris, but that there is a new square, built upon an elegant plan, at the end of the garden of the Thuilleries: it is called Place de Louis XV. and, in the middle of it, there is a good equestrian statue of the reigning king.

You have often heard that Louis XIV. frequently regretted,

that his country did not afford gravel for the walks of his gardens, which are covered with a white, loose sand, very disagreeable both to the eyes and feet of those who walk upon it; but this is a vulgar mistake. There is plenty of gravel on the road between Paris and Versailles, as well as in many other parts of this kingdom; but the French, who are all for glare and glitter, think the other is more gay and agreeable: one would imagine they did not feel the burning reflexion from the white sand, which in summer is almost intolerable.

In the character of the French, considered as a people, there are undoubtedly many circumstances truly ridiculous. You know the fashionable people, who go a hunting, are equipped with their jack boots, bag wigs, swords and pistols: but I saw the other day a scene still more grotesque. On the road to Choissi, a *fiacre*, or hackney-coach, stopped, and out came five or six men, armed with musquets, who took post, each behind a separate tree. I asked our servant who they were, imagining they might be *archers*, or footpads of justice, in pursuit of some malefactor. But guess my surprise, when the fellow told me, they were gentlemen *à la chasse*. They were in fact come out from Paris, in this equipage, to take the diversion of hare-hunting; that is, of shooting from behind a tree at the hares that chanced to pass. Indeed, if they had nothing more in view, but to destroy the game, this was a very effectual method; for the hares are in such plenty in this neighbourhood, that I have seen a dozen together, in the same field. I think this way of hunting, in a coach or chariot, might be properly adopted at London, in favour of those aldermen of the city, who are too unwieldy to follow the hounds a horseback.

The French, however, with all their absurdities, preserve a certain ascendancy over us, which is very disgraceful to our nation; and this appears in nothing more than in the article of dress. We are contented to be thought their apes in fashion; but, in fact, we are slaves to their taylors, mantua-makers, barbers, and other tradesmen. One would be apt to imagine that our own tradesmen had joined them in a combination against us. When the natives of France come to London, they appear in all public places, with cloaths made according to the fashion of their own country, and this fashion is generally admired by the English. Why, therefore, don't we follow it implicitly? No, we pique ourselves upon a most ridiculous deviation from the very modes we admire, and please ourselves with thinking this deviation is a mark of our spirit and liberty. But, we have not spirit enough to persist in this deviation, when we visit their country: otherwise, perhaps, they would come to admire and follow our example: for, certainly, in point of true taste, the fashions of both countries are equally absurd. At present, the skirts of the English descend from the fifth rib to the calf of the leg, and give the coat the form of a Jewish gaberdine;[10] and our hats seem to be modelled after that which Pistol wears upon the stage.[11] In France, the haunch buttons and pocket-holes are within half a foot of the coat's extremity: their hats look as if they had been pared round the brims, and the crown is covered with a kind of cordage, which, in my opinion produces a very beggarly effect. In every other circumstance of dress, male and female, the contrast between the two nations, appears equally glaring. What is the consequence? when an Englishman comes to Paris, he cannot appear until he has undergone a total metamorphosis. At his first arrival he finds it necessary to send for the taylor, peruquier, hatter, shoemaker, and every other tradesman concerned in the equipment of the human body. He must even change his buckles, and the form of his ruffles; and, though at the risque of his life, suit his cloaths to the mode of the season. For example, though the weather should be never so cold, he must wear his *habit d'été*, or *de mi-saison*, without presuming to put on a warm dress before the day which fashion has fixed for that purpose; and neither old age nor infirmity will excuse a man for wearing his hat upon his head, either at home or abroad. Females are (if possible) still more subject to the caprices of fashion; and as the articles of their dress are more manifold, it is enough to make a man's heart ake to see his wife surrounded by a multitude of *cotturieres*, milliners, and tire-women. All her sacks and negligees must be altered and new trimmed. She must have new caps, new laces, new shoes, and her hair new cut. She must have her taffaties for the summer, her flowered silks for the spring and autumn, her sattins and damasks for winter. The good man, who used to wear the *beau drap d'Angleterre*, quite plain all the year round, with a long bob, or tye perriwig, must here provide himself with a camblet suit trimmed with silver for spring and autumn, with silk cloaths for summer, and cloth laced with gold, or velvet for winter; and he must wear his bag-wig *à la pigeon*.[12] This variety of dress is absolutely indispensible for all those who pretend to any rank above the meer bourgeois. On his return to his own country, all this frippery is useless. He cannot appear in London until he has undergone another thorough metamorphosis; so that he will have some reason to think, that the tradesmen of Paris and London have combined to lay him under contribution: and they, no doubt, are the directors who regulate the fashions in both capitals; the English, however, in a subordinate capacity: for the puppets of their making will not pass at Paris, nor indeed in any other part of Europe; whereas a French *petit maitre* is reckoned a complete figure every where, London not excepted. Since it is so much the humour of the English at present to run abroad, I wish they had antigallican spirit enough to produce themselves in their own genuine English dress, and treat the French modes with the same philosophical contempt, which was shewn by an honest gentleman, distinguished by the name of Wig-Middleton.[13] That unshaken patriot still appears in the same kind of scratch perriwig, skimming-dish hat, and slit sleeve, which were worn five-and-twenty years ago, and has invariably persisted in this garb, in defiance of all the revolutions of the mode. I remember a student in the temple, who, after a long and learned investigation of the το χαλον, or *beautiful*, had resolution enough to let his beard grow, and wore it in all public places, until his heir at law applied for a commission of lunacy against him; then he submitted to the razor, rather than run any risque of being found *non compos*.

Before I conclude, I must tell you, that the most reputable shop-keepers and tradesmen of Paris think it no disgrace to practise the most shameful imposition. I myself know an instance of one of the most creditable table *marchands* in this capital, who demanded six francs an ell for some lutestring, laying his hand upon his breast at the same time, and declaring *en conscience*, that it had cost him within three sols of the money. Yet, in less than three minutes, he sold it for four and a half, and when the buyer upbraided him with his former declaration, he shrugged up his shoulders, saying, *il faut marchander*. I don't mention this as a particular instance. The same mean disingenuity is universal all over France, as I have been informed by several persons of veracity.

The next letter you have from me will probably be dated at Nismes, or Montpellier. Mean-while, I am ever

Yours.

To Mrs. M——.[1]

*Paris, October* 12, 1763.

MADAM,

I shall be much pleased if the remarks I have made on the characters of the French people, can afford you the satisfaction you require. With respect to the ladies, I can only judge from their exteriors: but, indeed, these are so characteristic, that one can hardly judge amiss; unless we suppose that a woman of taste and sentiment may be so overruled by the absurdity of what is called fashion, as to reject reason, and disguise nature, in order to become ridiculous or frightful. That this may be the case with some individuals, is very possible. I have known it happen in our own country, where the follies of the French are adopted, and exhibited in the most aukward imitation: but the general prevalence of those preposterous modes, is a plain proof that there is a general want of taste, and a general depravity of nature. I shall not pretend to describe the particulars of a French lady's dress. These you are much better acquainted with than I can pretend to be: but this I will be bold to affirm, that France is the general reservoir from which all the absurdities of false taste, luxury, and extravagance have overflowed the different kingdoms and states of Europe. The springs that fill this reservoir, are no other than vanity and ignorance. It would be superfluous to attempt proving from the nature of things, from the first principles and use of dress, as well as from the consideration of natural beauty, and the practice of the ancients, who certainly understood it as well as the connoisseurs of these days, that nothing can be more monstrous, inconvenient, and contemptible, than the fashion of modern drapery. You yourself are well aware of all its defects, and have often ridiculed them in my hearing. I shall only mention one particular of dress essential to the fashion in this country, which seems to me to carry human affectation to the very farthest verge of folly and extravagance; that is, the manner in which the faces of the ladies are primed and painted. When the Indian chiefs were in England every body ridiculed their preposterous method of painting their cheeks and eye-lids;[2] but this ridicule was wrong placed. Those critics ought to have considered, that the Indians do not use paint to make themselves agreeable; but in order to be the more terrible to their enemies. It is generally supposed, I think, that your sex make use of *fard*[3] and vermillion for very different purposes; namely, to help a bad or faded complexion, to heighten the graces, or conceal the defects of nature, as well as the ravages of time. I shall not enquire at present, whether it is just and honest to impose in this manner on mankind: if it is not honest, it may be allowed to be artful and politic, and shews, at least, a desire of being agreeable. But to lay it on as the fashion in France prescribes to all the ladies of condition, who indeed cannot appear without this badge of distinction, is to disguise themselves in such a manner, as to render them odious and detestable to every spectator, who has the least relish left for nature and propriety. As for the *fard*, or *white*, with which their necks and shoulders are plaistered, it may be in some measure excusable, as their skins are naturally brown, or sallow; but the *rouge*, which is daubed on their faces, from the chin up to the eyes, without the least art or dexterity, not only destroys all distinction of features, but renders the aspect really frightful, or at best conveys nothing but ideas of disgust and aversion. You know, that without this horrible masque no married lady is admitted at court, or in any polite assembly; and that it is a mark of distinction which no bourgeoise dare assume. Ladies of fashion only have the privilege of exposing themselves in these ungracious colours. As their faces are concealed under a false complexion, so their heads are covered with a vast load of false hair, which is frizzled on the forehead, so as exactly to resemble the wooly heads of the Guinea negroes. As to the natural hue of it, this is a matter of no consequence, for powder makes every head of hair of the same colour; and no woman appears in this country, from the moment she rises till night, without being compleatly whitened. Powder or meal was first used in Europe by the Poles, to conceal their scald heads;[4] but the present fashion of using it, as well as the modish method of dressing the hair, must have been borrowed from the Hottentots, who grease their wooly heads with mutton suet, and then paste it over with the powder called *buchu*.[5] In like manner, the hair of our fine ladies is frizzled into the appearance of negroes wool, and stiffened with an abominable paste of hog's grease, tallow, and white powder. The present fashion, therefore, of painting the face, and adorning the head, adopted by the beau monde in France, is taken from those two polite nations the Chickesaws of America and the Hottentots of Afric. On the whole, when I see one of those fine creatures sailing along, in her taudry robes of silk and gauze, frilled, and flounced, and furbelowed, with her false locks, her false jewels, her paint, her patches, and perfumes, I cannot help looking upon her as the vilest piece of sophistication that art ever produced.

This hideous masque of painting, though destructive of all beauty, is, however, favourable to natural homeliness and deformity. It accustoms the eyes of the other sex, and in time reconciles them to frightful objects; it disables them from perceiving any distinction of features between woman and woman; and, by reducing all faces to a level, gives every female an equal chance for an admirer; being in this particular analagous to the practice of the antient Lacedemonians, who were obliged to chuse their help-mates in the dark. In what manner the insides of their heads are furnished, I would not presume to judge from the conversation of a very few to whom I have had access: but from the nature of their education, which I have heard described, and the natural vivacity of their tempers, I should expect neither sense, sentiment, nor discretion. From the nursery they are allowed, and even encouraged, to say every thing that comes uppermost; by which means they acquire a volubility of tongue, and a set of phrases, which constitutes what is called polite conversation. At the same time they obtain an absolute conquest over all sense of shame, or rather, they avoid acquiring this troublesome sensation; for it is certainly no innate idea. Those who have not governesses at home, are sent, for a few years, to a convent, where they lay in a fund of superstition that serves them for life: but I never heard they had the least opportunity of cultivating the mind, of exercising the powers of reason, or of imbibing a taste for letters, or any rational or useful accomplishment. After being taught to

prattle, to dance and play at cards, they are deemed sufficiently qualified to appear in the *grand monde*, and to perform
all the duties of that high rank and station in life. In
mentioning cards, I ought to observe, that they learn to play
not barely for amusement, but also with a view to advantage;
and, indeed, you seldom meet with a native of France,
whether male or female, who is not a compleat gamester,
well versed in all the subtleties and finesses of the art. This is
likewise the case all over Italy. A lady of a great house in
Piedmont, having four sons, makes no scruple to declare, that
the first shall represent the family, the second enter into the
army, the third into the church, and that she will breed the
fourth a gamester. These noble adventurers devote themselves in a particular manner to the entertainment of travellers from our country, because the English are supposed to be
full of money, rash, incautious, and utterly ignorant of play.
But such a sharper is most dangerous, when he hunts in
couple with a female. I have known a French count and his
wife, who found means to lay the most wary under contribution. He was smooth, supple, officious, and attentive: she was
young, handsome, unprincipled, and artful. If the Englishman marked for prey was found upon his guard against the
designs of the husband, then madam plied him on the side of
gallantry. She displayed all the attractions of her person. She
sung, danced, ogled, sighed, complimented, and complained.
If he was insensible to all her charms, she flattered his vanity,
and piqued his pride, by extolling the wealth and generosity
of the English; and if he proved deaf to all these insinuations,
she, as her last stake, endeavoured to interest his humanity
and compassion. She expatiated, with tears in her eyes, on the
cruelty and indifference of her great relations; represented
that her husband was no more than the cadet of a noble
family; that his provision was by no means suitable, either to
the dignity of his rank, or the generosity of his disposition:
that he had a law-suit of great consequence depending, which
had drained all his finances; and, finally, that they should be
both ruined, if they could not find some generous friend,
who would accommodate them with a sum of money to
bring the cause to a determination.[6] Those who are not
actuated by such scandalous motives, become gamesters

from meer habit, and, having nothing more solid to engage their thoughts, or employ their time, consume the best part of their lives, in this worst of all dissipation. I am not ignorant that there are exceptions from this general rule: I know that France has produced a Maintenon, a Sevigné, a Scuderi, a Dacier, and a Chatelet;[7] but I would no more deduce the general character of the French ladies from these examples, than I would call a field of hemp a flower-garden, because there might be in it a few *lillies* or *renunculas* planted by the hand of accident.

Woman has been defined a weaker man; but in this country the men are, in my opinion, more ridiculous and insignificant than the women. They certainly are more disagreeable to a rational enquirer, because they are more troublesome. Of all the coxcombs on the face of the earth, a French *petit maitre* is the most impertinent: and they are all *petit maitres*, from the marquis who glitters in lace and embroidery, to the *garçon barbier* covered with meal, who struts with his hair in a long queue, and his hat under his arm. I have already observed, that vanity is the great and universal mover among all ranks and degrees of people in this nation; and as they take no pains to conceal or controul it, they are hurried by it into the most ridiculous and indeed intolerable extravagance.

When I talk of the French nation, I must again except a great number of individuals, from the general censure. Though I have a hearty contempt for the ignorance, folly, and presumption which characterise the generality, I cannot but respect the talents of many great men, who have eminently distinguished themselves in every art and science: these I shall always revere and esteem as creatures of a superior species, produced, for the wise purposes of providence, among the refuse of mankind. It would be absurd to conclude that the Welch or Highlanders are a gigantic people, because those mountains may have produced a few individuals near seven feet high. It would be equally absurd to suppose the French are a nation of philosophers, because France has given birth to a Des Cartes, a Maupertuis, a Reaumur, and a Buffon.[8]

I shall not even deny, that the French are by no means deficient in natural capacity; but they are at the same time remarkable for a natural levity, which hinders their youth from cultivating that capacity. This is reinforced by the most preposterous education, and the example of a giddy people, engaged in the most frivolous pursuits. A Frenchman is by some Jesuit, or other monk, taught to read his mother tongue, and to say his prayers in a language he does not understand. He learns to dance and to fence, by the masters of those noble sciences. He becomes a compleat connoisseur in dressing hair, and in adorning his own person, under the hands and instructions of his barber and valet de chambre. If he learns to play upon the flute or the fiddle, he is altogether irresistible. But he piques himself upon being polished above the natives of any other country by his conversation with the fair sex. In the course of this communication, with which he is indulged from his tender years, he learns like a parrot, by rote, the whole circle of French compliments, which you know are a set of phrases, ridiculous even to a proverb; and these he throws out indiscriminately to all women, without distinction, in the exercise of that kind of address, which is here distinguished by the name of gallantry: it is no more than his making love to every woman who will give him the hearing. It is an exercise, by the repetition of which he becomes very pert, very familiar, and very impertinent. Modesty, or diffidence, I have already said, is utterly unknown among them, and therefore I wonder there should be a term to express it in their language.

If I was obliged to define politeness, I should call it, the art of making one's self agreeable. I think it an art that necessarily implies a sense of decorum, and a delicacy of sentiment. These are qualities, of which (as far as I have been able to observe) a Frenchman has no idea; therefore he never can be deemed polite, except by those persons among whom they are as little understood. His first aim is to adorn his own person with what he calls fine cloaths, that is the frippery of the fashion. It is no wonder that the heart of a female, unimproved by reason, and untinctured with natural good sense, should flutter at the sight of such a gaudy thing, among the number of her admirers: this impression is enforced by fustian compliments, which her own vanity interprets in a literal sense, and still more confirmed by the assiduous attention of the gallant, who, indeed, has nothing else to mind. A Frenchman in consequence of his mingling with the females from his infancy, not only becomes acquainted with all their customs and humours; but grows wonderfully alert in performing a thousand little offices, which are overlooked by other men, whose time hath been spent in making more valuable acquisitions. He enters, without ceremony, a lady's bed-chamber, while she is in bed, reaches her whatever she wants, airs her shift, and helps to put it on. He attends at her toilette, regulates the distribution of her patches, and advises where to lay on the paint. If he visits her when she is dressed, and perceives the least impropriety in her *coeffure*, he insists upon adjusting it with his own hands: if he sees a curl, or even a single hair amiss, he produces his comb, his scissars, and pomatum,[9] and sets it to rights with the dexterity of a professed *friseur*. He 'squires her to every place she visits, either on business, or pleasure; and, by dedicating his whole time to her, renders himself necessary to her occasions. This I take to be the most agreeable side of his character: let us view him on the quarter of impertinence. A Frenchman pries into all your secrets with the most impudent and importunate curiosity, and then discloses them without remorse. If you are indisposed, he questions you about the symptoms of your disorder, with more freedom than your physician would presume to use; very often in the grossest terms. He then proposes his remedy (for they are all quacks), he prepares it without your knowledge, and worries you with solicitation to take it, without paying the least regard to the opinion of those whom you have chosen to take care of your health. Let you be ever so ill, or averse to company, he forces himself at all times into your bed-chamber, and if it is necessary to give him a peremptory refusal, he is affronted. I have known one of those *petit maitres* insist upon paying regular visits twice a day to a poor gentleman who was delirious; and he conversed with him on different subjects, till he was in his last agonies. This attendance is not the effect of attachment, or regard, but of sheer vanity, that he may afterwards boast of his charity and humane disposition: though, of all the people I have ever known, I think the French are the least capable of feeling for the distresses of their fellow creatures. Their hearts are not susceptible of deep impressions; and, such is their levity, that the imagination has not time to brood long over any disagreeable idea, or sensation. As a Frenchman piques himself on his gallantry, he no sooner makes a conquest of a female's heart, than he exposes her character, for the gratification of his vanity. Nay, if he should miscarry in his schemes, he will forge letters and stories, to the ruin of the lady's reputation. This is a species of perfidy which one would think should render them odious and detestable to the whole sex; but the case is otherwise. I beg your pardon, Madam; but women are never better pleased, than when they see one another exposed; and every individual has such confidence in her own superior charms and discretion, that she thinks she can fix the most volatile, and reform the most treacherous lover.

If a Frenchman is admitted into your family, and distinguished by repeated marks of your friendship and regard, the first return he makes for your civilities is to make love to your wife, if she is handsome; if not, to your sister, or daughter, or niece. If he suffers a repulse from your wife, or attempts in vain to debauch your sister, or your daughter, or your niece, he will, rather than not play the traitor with his gallantry, make his addresses to your grandmother; and ten to one, but in one shape or another, he will find means to ruin the peace of a family, in which he has been so kindly entertained. What he cannot accomplish by dint of compliment, and personal attendance, he will endeavour to effect, by reinforcing these with billets-doux, songs, and verses, of which he always makes a provision for such purposes. If he is detected in these efforts of treachery, and reproached with his ingratitude, he impudently declares, that what he had done was no more than simple gallantry, considered in France as an indispensible duty on every man who pretended to good breeding. Nay, he will even affirm, that his endeavours to corrupt your wife, or deflower your daughter, were the most genuine proofs he could give of his particular regard for your family.

If a Frenchman is capable of real friendship, it must certainly be the most disagreeable present he can possibly make to a man of a true English character. You know, Madam, we are naturally taciturn, soon tired of impertinence, and much subject to fits of disgust. Your French friend intrudes upon you at all hours: he stuns you with his loquacity: he teases you with impertinent questions about your domestic and private affairs: he attempts to meddle in all your concerns; and forces his advice upon you with the most unwearied importunity: he asks the price of every thing you wear, and, so sure as you tell him, undervalues it, without hesitation: he affirms it is in a bad taste, ill-contrived, ill-made; that you have been imposed upon both with respect to the fashion and the price; that the marquise of this, or the countess of that, has one that is perfectly elegant, quite in the *bon ton*, and yet it cost her little more than you gave for a thing that nobody would wear.

If there were five hundred dishes at table, a Frenchman will eat of all of them, and then complain he has no appetite. This I have several times remarked. A friend of mine gained a considerable wager upon an experiment of this kind: the *petit maitre* ate of fourteen different *plats*, besides the desert; then disparaged the cook, declaring he was no better than a *marmiton*, or turnspit.

The French have a most ridiculous fondness for their hair, and this I believe they inherit from their remote ancestors. The first race of French kings were distinguished by their long hair, and certainly the people of this country consider it as an indispensible ornament. A Frenchman will sooner part with his religion than with his hair, which, indeed, no consideration will induce him to forego. I know a gentleman afflicted with a continual head-ach, and a defluxion on his eyes, who was told by his physician that the best chance he had for being cured, would be to have his head close shaved, and bathed every day in cold water. "How (cried he) cut my hair? Mr. Doctor, your most humble servant!" He dismissed his physician, lost his eye-sight, and almost his senses, and is now led about with his hair in a bag, and a piece of green silk hanging like a screen before his face. Count Saxe, and other military writers, have demonstrated the absurdity of a soldier's wearing a long head of hair;[10] nevertheless, every soldier in this country wears a long queue, which makes a delicate mark on his white cloathing; and this ridiculous foppery has descended even to the lowest class of people. The *decrotteur*, [11] who cleans your shoes at the corner of the Pont Neuf, has a tail of this kind hanging down to his rump, and even the peasant who drives an ass loaded with dung, wears his hair *en queue*, though, perhaps, he has neither shirt nor breeches. This is the ornament upon which he bestows much time and pains, and in the exhibition of which he finds full gratification for his vanity. Considering the harsh features of the common people in this country, their diminutive stature, their grimaces, and that long appendage, they have no small resemblance to large baboons walking upright; and perhaps this similitude has helped to entail upon them the ridicule of their neighbours. [12]

A French friend tires out your patience with long visits; and, far from taking the most palpable hints to withdraw, when he perceives you uneasy, he observes you are low-spirited, and therefore declares he will keep you company. This perseverance shews that he must either be void of all penetration, or that his disposition must be truly diabolical. Rather than be tormented with such a fiend, a man had better turn him out of doors, even though at the hazard of being run through the body.

The French are generally counted insincere, and taxed with want of generosity. But I think these reproaches are not well founded. High-flown professions of friendship and attachment constitute the language of common compliment in this country, and are never supposed to be understood in the literal acceptation of the words; and, if their acts of generosity are but very rare, we ought to ascribe that rarity, not so much to a deficiency of generous sentiments, as to their vanity and ostentation, which engrossing all their funds, utterly disable them from exerting the virtues of beneficence. Vanity, indeed, predominates among all ranks, to such a degree, that they are the greatest *egotists* in the world; and the most insignificant individual talks in company with the same conceit and arrogance, as a person of the greatest importance. Neither conscious poverty nor disgrace will restrain him in the least either from assuming his full share of the conversation, or making his addresses to the finest lady, whom he has the smallest opportunity to approach: nor is he restrained by any other consideration whatsoever. It is all one to him whether he himself has a wife of his own, or the lady a husband; whether she is designed for the cloister, or pre-ingaged to his best friend and benefactor. He takes it for granted that his addresses cannot but be acceptable; and, if he meets with a repulse, he condemns her taste; but never doubts his own qualifications.

I have a great many things to say of their military character, and their punctilios of honour, which last are equally absurd and pernicious; but as this letter has run to an unconscionable length, I shall defer them till another opportunity. Mean-while, I have the honour to be, with very particular esteem,

Madam,

Your most obedient servant.

# LETTER VIII.

## To Mr. M——.[1]

*Lyons, October 19, 1763.*

DEAR SIR,

I was favoured with yours at Paris, and look upon your reproaches as the proof of your friendship. The truth is, I considered all the letters I have hitherto written on the subject of my travels, as written to your society in general, though they have been addressed to one individual of it; and if they contain any thing that can either amuse or inform, I desire that henceforth all I send may be freely perused by all the members.

With respect to my health, about which you so kindly enquire, I have nothing new to communicate. I had reason to think that my bathing in the sea at Boulogne produced a good effect, in strengthening my relaxed fibres. You know how subject I was to colds in England; that I could not stir abroad after sun-set, nor expose myself to the smallest damp, nor walk till the least moisture appeared on my skin, without being laid up for ten days or a fortnight. At Paris, however, I went out every day, with my hat under my arm, though the weather was wet and cold: I walked in the garden at Versailles even after it was dark, with my head uncovered, on a cold evening, when the ground was far from being dry: nay, at Marli, I sauntered above a mile through damp alleys, and wet grass: and from none of these risques did I feel the least inconvenience.

In one of our excursions we visited the manufacture for porcelain, which the king of France has established at the village of St. Cloud,[2] on the road to Versailles, and which is, indeed, a noble monument of his munificence. It is a very large building, both commodious and magnificent, where a great number of artists are employed, and where this elegant superfluity is carried to as great perfection as it ever was at Dresden. Yet, after all, I know not whether the porcelain made at Chelsea[3] may not vie with the productions either of Dresden, or St. Cloud. If it falls short of either, it is not in the design, painting, enamel, or other ornaments, but only in the

63

composition of the metal, and the method of managing it in the furnace. Our porcelain seems to be a partial vitrification of levigated flint and fine pipe clay, mixed together in a certain proportion; and if the pieces are not removed from the fire in the very critical moment, they will be either too little, or too much vitrified. In the first case, I apprehend they will not acquire a proper degree of cohesion; they will be apt to be corroded, discoloured, and to crumble, like the first essays that were made at Chelsea; in the second case, they will be little better than imperfect glass.

There are three methods of travelling from Paris to Lyons, which, by the shortest road is a journey of about three hundred and sixty miles. One is by the *diligence*, or stage-coach, which performs it in five days; and every passenger pays one hundred livres, in consideration of which, he not only has a seat in the carriage, but is maintained on the road. The inconveniences attending this way of travelling are these. You are crouded into the carriage, to the number of eight persons, so as to sit very uneasy, and sometimes run the risque of being stifled among very indifferent company. You are hurried out of bed, at four, three, nay often at two o'clock in the morning. You are obliged to eat in the French way, which is very disagreeable to an English palate; and, at Chalons, you must embark upon the Soane in a boat, which conveys you to Lyons, so that the two last days of your journey are by water. All these were insurmountable objections to me, who am in such a bad state of health, troubled with an asthmatic cough, spitting, slow fever, and restlessness, which demands a continual change of place, as well as free air, and room for motion. I was this day visited by two young gentlemen, sons of Mr. Guastaldi, late minister from Genoa at London.[4] I had seen them at Paris, at the house of the dutchess of Douglas.[5] They came hither, with their conductor, in the *diligence*, and assured me, that nothing could be more disagreeable than their situation in that carriage.

Another way of travelling in this country is to hire a coach and four horses; and this method I was inclined to take: but when I went to the bureau, where alone these voitures are to be had, I was given to understand, that it would cost me six-and-twenty guineas, and travel so slow that I should be ten days upon the road. These carriages are let by the same persons who farm the diligence; and for this they have an exclusive privilege, which makes them very saucy and insolent. When I mentioned my servant, they gave me to understand, that I must pay two loui'dores more for his seat upon the coach box. As I could not relish these terms, nor brook the thoughts of being so long upon the road, I had recourse to the third method, which is going post.

In England you know I should have had nothing to do, but to hire a couple of post-chaises from stage to stage, with two horses in each; but here the case is quite otherwise. The post is farmed from the king, who lays travellers under contribution for his own benefit, and has published a set of oppressive ordonnances, which no stranger nor native dares transgress. The postmaster finds nothing but horses and guides: the carriage you yourself must provide. If there are four persons within the carriage, you are obliged to have six horses, and two postilions; and if your servant sits on the outside, either before or behind, you must pay for a seventh. You pay double for the first stage from Paris, and twice double for passing through Fontainbleau when the court is there, as well as at coming to Lyons, and at leaving this city. These are called royal posts, and are undoubtedly a scandalous imposition.

There are two post roads from Paris to Lyons, one of sixty-five posts, by the way of Moulins; the other of fifty-nine, by the way of Dijon in Burgundy. This last I chose, partly to save sixty livres, and partly to see the wine harvest of Burgundy, which, I was told, was a season of mirth and jollity among all ranks of people. I hired a very good coach for ten loui'dores to Lyons, and set out from Paris on the thirteenth instant, with six horses, two postilions, and my own servant on horseback. We made no stop at Fontainbleau, though the court was there; but lay at Moret, which is one stage further, a very paltry little town; where, however, we found good accommodation.

I shall not pretend to describe the castle or palace of Fontainbleau, of which I had only a glimpse in passing; but the forest, in the middle of which it stands, is a noble chace of great extent, beautifully wild and romantic, well stored with game of all sorts, and abounding with excellent timber. It put me in mind of the New Forest in Hampshire; but the hills, rocks, and mountains, with which it is diversified, render it more agreeable.

The people of this country dine at noon, and travellers always find an ordinary[6] prepared at every *auberge*, or public-house, on the road. Here they sit down promiscuously, and dine at so much a head. The usual price is thirty sols for dinner, and forty for supper, including lodging; for this moderate expence they have two courses and a desert. If you eat in your own apartment, you pay, instead of forty sols, three, and in some places, four livres a head. I and my family could not well dispense with our tea and toast in the morning, and had no stomach to eat at noon. For my own part, I hate the French cookery, and abominate garlick, with which all their ragouts, in this part of the country, are highly seasoned: we therefore formed a different plan of living upon the road. Before we left Paris, we laid in a stock of tea, chocolate, cured neats tongues,[7] and *saucissons*, or Bologna sausages, both of which we found in great perfection in that capital, where, indeed, there are excellent provisions of all sorts. About ten in the morning we stopped to breakfast at some auberge, where we always found bread, butter, and milk. In the mean time, we ordered a *poulard* or two to be roasted, and these, wrapped in a napkin, were put into the boot of the coach, together with bread, wine, and water. About two or three in the afternoon, while the horses were changing, we laid a cloth upon our knees, and producing our store, with a few earthen plates, discussed our short meal without further ceremony. This was followed by a desert of grapes and other fruit, which we had also provided. I must own I found these transient refreshments much more agreeable than any regular meal I ate upon the road. The wine commonly used in Burgundy is so weak and thin, that you would not drink it in England. The very best which they sell at Dijon, the capital of the province, for three livres a bottle, is in strength, and even in flavour, greatly inferior to what I have drank in London. I believe all the first growth is either consumed in the houses of the noblesse, or sent abroad to foreign markets. I have drank excellent Burgundy at Brussels for a florin a bottle; that is, little more than twenty pence sterling.

The country from the forest of Fontainbleau to the Lyonnois, through which we passed, is rather agreeable than fertile, being part of Champagne and the dutchy of Burgundy, watered by three pleasant pastoral rivers, the Seine, the Yonne, and the Soane. The flat country is laid out chiefly for corn; but produces more rye than wheat. Almost all the ground seems to be ploughed up, so that there is little or nothing lying fallow. There are very few inclosures, scarce any meadow ground, and, so far as I could observe, a great scarcity of cattle. We sometimes found it very difficult to procure half a pint of milk for our tea. In Burgundy I saw a peasant ploughing the ground with a jack-ass, a lean cow, and a he-goat, yoked together. It is generally observed, that a great number of black cattle are bred and fed on the mountains of Burgundy, which are the highest lands in France; but I saw very few. The peasants in France are so wretchedly poor, and so much oppressed by their landlords, that they cannot afford to inclose their grounds, or give a proper respite to their lands; or to stock their farms with a sufficient number of black cattle to produce the necessary manure, without which agriculture can never be carried to any degree of perfection. Indeed, whatever efforts a few individuals may make for the benefit of their own estates, husbandry in France will never be generally improved, until the farmer is free and independent.

From the frequency of towns and villages, I should imagine this country is very populous; yet it must be owned, that the towns are in general thinly inhabited. I saw a good number of country seats and plantations near the banks of the rivers, on each side; and a great many convents, sweetly situated, on rising grounds, where the air is most pure, and the prospect most agreeable. It is surprising to see how happy the founders of those religious houses have been in their choice of situations, all the world over.

In passing through this country, I was very much struck with the sight of large ripe clusters of grapes, entwined with the briars and thorns of common hedges on the wayside. The mountains of Burgundy are covered with vines from the bottom to the top, and seem to be raised by nature on purpose to extend the surface, and to expose it the more advantageously to the rays of the sun. The *vandange* was just begun, and the people were employed in gathering the grapes; but I saw no signs of festivity among them. Perhaps their joy was a little damped by the bad prospect of their harvest; for they complained that the weather had been so unfavourable as to hinder the grapes from ripening. I thought, indeed, there was something uncomfortable in seeing the vintage thus retarded till the beginning of winter: for, in some parts, I found the weather extremely cold; particularly at a place called Maison-neuve, where we lay, there was a hard frost, and in the morning the pools were covered with a thick crust of ice. My personal adventures on the road were such as will not bear a recital. They consisted of petty disputes with landladies, post-masters, and posti-lions. The highways seem to be perfectly safe. We did not find that any robberies were ever committed, although we did not see one of the *maréchaussée* from Paris to Lyons. You know the *maréchaussée* are a body of troopers well mounted, maintained in France as safe-guards to the public roads. It is a reproach upon England that some such patrol is not appointed for the protection of travellers.

At Sens in Champagne, my servant, who had rode on before to bespeak fresh horses, told me, that the domestic of another company had been provided before him, although it was not his turn, as he had arrived later at the post. Provoked at this partiality, I resolved to chide the post-master, and accordingly addressed myself to a person who stood at the door of the auberge. He was a jolly figure, fat and fair, dressed in an odd kind of garb, with a gold laced cap on his head, and a cambric handkerchief pinned to his middle. The sight of such a fantastic *petit maitre*, in the character of a post-master, increased my spleen. I called to him with an air of authority, mixed with indignation, and when he came up to the coach, asked in a peremptory tone, if he did not understand the king's ordonnance concerning the regulation of the posts? He laid his hand upon his breast; but before he could make any answer, I pulled out the post-book,[8] and began to read, with great vociferation, the article which orders, that the traveller who comes first shall be first served. By this time the fresh horses being put to the carriage, and the postilions mounted, the coach set off all of a sudden, with uncommon speed. I imagined the post-master had given the fellows a signal to be gone, and, in this persuasion, thrusting my head out at the window, I bestowed some epithets upon him, which must have sounded very harsh in the ears of a Frenchman. We stopped for a refreshment at a little town called Joigne-ville,[9] where (by the bye) I was scandalously imposed upon, and even abused by a virago of a landlady; then proceeding to the next stage, I was given to understand we could not be supplied with fresh horses. Here I perceived at the door of the inn, the same person whom I had reproached at Sens. He came up to the coach, and told me, that notwithstanding what the guides had said, I should have fresh horses in a few minutes. I imagined he was master both of this house and the auberge at Sens, between which he passed and repassed occasionally; and that he was now desirous of making me amends for the affront he had put upon me at the other place. Observing that one of the trunks behind was a little displaced, he assisted my servant in adjusting it: then he entered into conversation with me, and gave me to understand, that in a post-chaise, which we had passed, was an English gentleman on his return from Italy. I wanted to know who he was, and when he said he could not tell, I asked him, in a very abrupt manner, why he had not enquired of his servant. He shrugged up his shoulders, and retired to the inn door. Having waited about half an hour, I beckoned to him, and when he approached, upbraided him with having told me that I should be supplied with fresh horses in a few minutes: he seemed shocked, and answered, that he thought he had reason for what he said, observing, that it was as disagreeable to him as to me to wait for a relay. As it began to rain, I pulled up the glass in his face, and he withdrew again to the door, seemingly ruffled at my deportment. In a little time the horses arrived, and three of them were immediately put to a very handsome post-chaise, into which he stepped, and set out, accompanied by a man in a rich livery on horseback. Astonished at this circumstance, I asked the hostler who he was, and he replied, that he was a man of fashion (un seigneur) who lived in the neighbourhood of Auxerre. I was much mortified to find that I had treated a nobleman so scurvily, and scolded my own people for not having more penetration than myself. I dare say he did not fail to descant upon the brutal behaviour of the Englishman; and that my mistake served with him to confirm the national reproach of bluntness, and ill breeding, under which we lie in this country. The truth is, I was that day more than usually peevish, from the bad weather, as well as from the dread of a fit of the asthma, with which I was threatened: and I dare say my appearance seemed as uncouth to him, as his travelling dress appeared to me. I had a grey mourning frock under a wide great coat, a bob wig without powder, a very large laced hat, and a meagre, wrinkled, discontented countenance.

The fourth night of our journey we lay at Macon, and the next day passed through the Lyonnois, which is a fine country, full of towns, villages, and gentlemen's houses. In passing through the Maconnois, we saw a great many fields of Indian corn, which grows to the height of six or seven feet: it is made into flour for the use of the common people, and goes by the name of *Turkey wheat*. Here likewise, as well as in Dauphiné, they raise a vast quantity of very large pompions,[10] with the contents of which they thicken their soup and ragouts.

As we travelled only while the sun was up, on account of my ill health, and the post horses in France are in bad order, we seldom exceeded twenty leagues a day.

I was directed to a lodging-house at Lyons, which being full they shewed us to a tavern, where I was led up three pair of stairs, to an apartment consisting of three paltry chambers, for which the people demanded twelve livres a day: for dinner and supper they asked thirty-two, besides three livres for my servant; so that my daily expence would have amounted to about forty-seven livres, exclusive of breakfast and coffee in the afternoon. I was so provoked at this extortion, that, without answering one word, I drove to another auberge, where I now am, and pay at the rate of two-and-thirty livres a day, for which I am very badly lodged, and but very indifferently entertained. I mention these circumstances to give you an idea of the imposition to which strangers are subject in this country. It must be owned, however, that in the article of eating, I might save half the money by going to the public ordinary; but this is a scheme of œconomy, which (exclusive of other disagreeable circumstances) neither my own health, nor that of my wife permits me to embrace. My journey from Paris to Lyons, including the hire of the coach, and all expences on the road, has cost me, within a few shillings, forty loui'dores. From Paris our baggage (though not plombé) was not once examined till we arrived in this city, at the gate of which we were questioned by one of the searchers, who, being tipt with half a crown, allowed us to proceed without further enquiry.

I purposed to stay in Lyons until I should receive some letters I expected from London, to be forwarded by my banker at Paris: but the enormous expence of living in this manner has determined me to set out in a day or two for Montpellier, although that place is a good way out of the road to Nice. My reasons for taking that route I shall communicate in my next. Mean-while, I am ever,

> Dear Sir,
>
> Your affectionate and obliged humble servant.

# LETTER IX.

DEAR SIR,

The city of Lyons has been so often and so circumstantially described, that I cannot pretend to say any thing new on the subject. Indeed, I know very little of it, but what I have read in books; as I had but one day to make a tour of the streets, squares, and other remarkable places. The bridge over the Rhone seems to be so slightly built, that I should imagine it would be one day carried away by that rapid river; especially as the arches are so small, that, after great rains they are sometimes *bouchées*, or stopped up; that is, they do not admit a sufficient passage for the encreased body of the water. In order to remedy this dangerous defect, in some measure, they found an artist some years ago, who has removed a middle pier, and thrown two arches into one. This alteration they looked upon as a master-piece in architecture, though there is many a common mason in England, who would have undertaken and performed the work, without valuing himself much upon the enterprize. This bridge, as well as that of St. Esprit, is built, not in a strait line across the river, but with a curve, which forms a convexity to oppose the current. Such a bend is certainly calculated for the better resisting the general impetuosity of the stream, and has no bad effect to the eye.

Lyons is a great, populous, and flourishing city; but I am surprised to find it is counted a healthy place, and that the air of it is esteemed favourable to pulmonic disorders. It is situated on the confluence of two large rivers,[1] from which there must be a great evaporation, as well as from the low marshy grounds, which these rivers often overflow. This must render the air moist, frouzy, and even putrid, if it was not well ventilated by winds from the mountains of Swisserland; and in the latter end of autumn, it must be subject to fogs. The morning we set out from thence, the whole city and adjacent plains were covered with so thick a fog, that we could not distinguish from the coach the head of the foremost mule that drew it. Lyons is said to be very hot in summer, and very cold in winter; therefore I imagine must abound

72

with inflammatory and intermittent disorders in the spring and fall of the year.

My reasons for going to Montpellier, which is out of the strait road to Nice, were these. Having no acquaintance nor correspondents in the South of France, I had desired my credit might be sent to the same house to which my heavy baggage was consigned. I expected to find my baggage at Cette, which is the sea-port of Montpellier; and there I also hoped to find a vessel, in which I might be transported by sea to Nice, without further trouble. I longed to try what effect the boasted air of Montpellier would have upon my constitution; and I had a great desire to see the famous monuments of antiquity in and about the ancient city of Nismes, which is about eight leagues short of Montpellier.

At the inn where we lodged, I found a return berline, belonging to Avignon, with three mules, which are the animals commonly used for carriages in this country. This I hired for five loui'dores. The coach was large, commodious, and well-fitted; the mules were strong and in good order; and the driver, whose name was Joseph, appeared to be a sober, sagacious, intelligent fellow, perfectly well acquainted with every place in the South of France. He told me he was owner of the coach: but I afterwards learned, he was no other than a hired servant. I likewise detected him in some knavery, in the course of our journey; and plainly perceived he had a fellow-feeling with the innkeepers on the road; but, in other respects, he was very obliging, serviceable, and even entertaining. There are some knavish practices of this kind, at which a traveller will do well to shut his eyes, for his own ease and convenience. He will be lucky if he has to do with a sensible knave, like Joseph, who understood his interest too well to be guilty of very flagrant pieces of imposition.

A man impatient to be at his journey's end, will find this a most disagreeable way of travelling. In summer it must be quite intolerable. The mules are very sure, but very slow. The journey seldom exceeds eight leagues, about four and twenty miles a day: and as those people have certain fixed stages, you are sometimes obliged to rise in a morning before day; a circumstance very grievous to persons in ill health. These inconveniences, however, were over-balanced by other *agreemens*. We no sooner quitted Lyons, than we got into summer weather, and travelling through a most romantic country, along the banks of the Rhone, had opportunities (from the slowness of our pace) to contemplate its beauties at leisure.

The rapidity of the Rhone is, in a great measure, owing to its being confined within steep banks on each side. These are formed almost through its whole course, by a double chain of mountains, which rise with an abrupt ascent from both banks of the river. The mountains are covered with vineyards, interspersed with small summer-houses, and in many places they are crowned with churches, chapels, and convents, which add greatly to the romantic beauty of the prospect. The highroad, as far as Avignon, lies along the side of the river, which runs almost in a straight line, and affords great convenience for inland commerce. Travellers, bound to the southern parts of France, generally embark in the *diligence* at Lyons, and glide down this river with great velocity, passing a great number of towns and villages on each side, where they find ordinaries every day at dinner and supper. In good weather, there is no danger in this method of travelling, 'till you come to the Pont St. Esprit, where the stream runs through the arches with such rapidity, that the boat is sometimes overset. But those passengers who are under any apprehension are landed above-bridge, and taken in again, after the boat has passed, just in the same manner as at London Bridge. The boats that go up the river are drawn against the stream by oxen, which swim through one of the arches of this bridge, the driver sitting between the horns of the foremost beast. We set out from Lyons early on Monday morning, and as a robbery had been a few days before committed in that neighbourhood, I ordered my servant to load my musquetoon with a charge of eight balls. By the bye, this piece did not fail to attract the curiosity and admiration of the people in every place through which we passed. The carriage no sooner halted, than a crowd immediately surrounded the man to view the blunderbuss, which they dignified with the title of *petit canon*. At Nuys in Burgundy, he fired it in the air, and the whole mob dispersed, and scampered off like a flock of sheep. In our journey hither, we generally set out in a morning at eight o'clock, and travelled 'till noon, when the mules were put up and rested a couple of hours. During this halt, Joseph went to dinner, and we went to breakfast, after which we ordered provision for our refreshment in the coach, which we took about three or four in the afternoon, halting for that purpose, by the side of some transparent brook, which afforded excellent water to mix with our wine. In this country I was almost poisoned with garlic, which they mix in their ragouts, and all their sauces; nay, the smell of it perfumes the very chambers, as well as every person you approach. I was also very sick of *beca ficas*,[2] *grieves*,[3] or *thrushes*, and other little birds, which are served up twice a day at all ordinaries on the road. They make their appearance in vine-leaves, and are always half raw, in which condition the French choose to eat them, rather than run the risque of losing the juice by over-roasting.

The peasants on the South of France are poorly clad, and look as if they were half starved, diminutive, swarthy, and meagre; and yet the common people who travel, live luxuriously on the road. Every carrier and mule-driver has two meals a day, consisting each of a couple of courses and a desert, with tolerable small wine.—That which is called *hermitage*, and grows in this province of Dauphiné, is sold on the spot for three livres a bottle. The common draught, which you have at meals in this country, is remarkably strong, though in flavour much inferior to that of Burgundy. The accommodation is tolerable, though they demand (even in this cheap country) the exorbitant price of four livres a head for every meal, of those who choose to eat in their own apartments. I insisted, however, upon paying them with three, which they received, though not without murmuring and seeming discontented. In this journey, we found plenty of good mutton, pork, poultry, and game, including the red partridge, which is near twice as big as the partridge of England. Their hares are likewise surprisingly large and juicy. We saw great flocks of black turkeys feeding in the fields, but no black cattle; and milk was so scarce, that sometimes we were obliged to drink our tea without it.

One day perceiving a meadow on the side of the road, full of a flower which I took to be the crocus, I desired my servant to alight and pull some of them. He delivered the musquetoon to Joseph, who began to tamper with it, and off it went with a prodigious report, augmented by an eccho from the mountains that skirted the road. The mules were so frightened, that they went off at the gallop; and Joseph, for some minutes, could neither manage the reins, nor open his mouth. At length he recollected himself, and the cattle were stopt, by the assistance of the servant, to whom he delivered the musquetoon, with a significant shake of the head. Then alighting from the box, he examined the heads of his three mules, and kissed each of them in his turn. Finding they had received no damage, he came up to the coach, with a pale visage and staring eyes, and said it was God's mercy he had not killed his beasts. I answered, that it was a greater mercy he had not killed his passengers; for the muzzle of the piece might have been directed our way as well as any other, and in that case Joseph might have been hanged for murder. "I had as good be hanged (said he) for murder, as be ruined by the loss of my cattle." This adventure made such an impression upon him, that he recounted it to every person we met; nor would he ever touch the blunderbuss from that day. I was often diverted with the conversation of this fellow, who was very arch and very communicative. Every afternoon, he used to stand upon the foot-board, at the side of the coach, and discourse with us an hour together. Passing by the gibbet of Valencia, which stands very near the high-road, we saw one body hanging quite naked, and another lying broken on the wheel. I recollected, that Mandrin[4] had suffered in this place, and calling to Joseph to mount the foot-board, asked if he had ever seen that famous adventurer. At mention of the name of Mandrin, the tear started in Joseph's eye, he discharged a deep sigh, or rather groan, and told me he was his dear friend. I was a little startled at this declaration; however, I concealed my thoughts, and began to ask questions about the character and exploits of a man who had made such noise in the world.

He told me, Mandrin was a native of Valencia, of mean extraction: that he had served as a soldier in the army, and afterwards acted as *maltotier*, or tax-gatherer: that at length he turned *contrebandier*, or smuggler, and by his superior qualities, raised himself to the command of a formidable gang, consisting of five hundred persons well armed with carbines and pistols. He had fifty horse for his troopers, and three hundred mules for the carriage of his merchandize. His head-quarters were in Savoy: but he made incursions into Dauphiné, and set the *maréchaussée* at defiance. He maintained several bloody skirmishes with these troopers, as well as with other regular detachments, and in all those actions signalized himself by his courage and conduct. Coming up at one time with fifty of the *maréchaussée*, who were in quest of him, he told them very calmly, he had occasion for their horses and acoutrements, and desired them to dismount. At that instant his gang appeared, and the troopers complied with his request, without making the least opposition. Joseph said he was as generous as he was brave, and never molested travellers, nor did the least injury to the poor; but, on the contrary, relieved them very often. He used to oblige the gentlemen in the country to take his merchandize, his tobacco, brandy, and muslins, at his own price; and, in the same manner, he laid the open towns under contribution. When he had no merchandize, he borrowed money of them upon the credit of what he should bring when he was better provided. He was at last betrayed, by his wench, to the colonel of a French regiment, who went with a detachment in the night to the place where he lay in Savoy, and surprized him in a wood-house, while his people were absent in different parts of the country. For this intrusion, the court of France made an apology to the king of Sardinia, in whose territories he was taken. Mandrin being conveyed to Valencia, his native place, was for some time permitted to go abroad, under a strong guard, with chains upon his legs; and here he conversed freely with all sorts of people, flattering himself with the hopes of a pardon, in which, however, he was disappointed. An order came from court to bring him to his trial, when he was found guilty, and condemned to be broke on the wheel. Joseph said he drank a bottle of wine with him the night before his execution. He bore his fate with great resolution, observing that if the letter which he had written to the King, had been delivered, he certainly should have obtained his Majesty's pardon. His executioner was one of his own gang, who was pardoned on condition of performing this office. You know, that criminals broke upon the wheel are first strangled, unless the sentence imports, that they shall be broke alive. As Mandrin had not been guilty of cruelty in the course of his delinquency, he was indulged with this favour. Speaking to the executioner, whom he had formerly commanded, "Joseph (dit il) je ne veux pas que tu me touche, jusqu'à ce que je sois roid mort." "Joseph, said he, thou shalt not touch me till I am quite dead." — Our driver had no sooner pronounced these words, than I was struck with a suspicion, that he himself was the executioner of his friend Mandrin. On that suspicion, I exclaimed, "ah! ah! Joseph!" The fellow blushed up to the eyes, and said, *oui, son nom étoit Joseph aussi bien que le mien*, "yes, he was called *Joseph*, as I am." I did not think proper to prosecute the inquiry; but did not much relish the nature of Joseph's connexions. The truth is, he had very much the looks of a ruffian; though, I must own, his behaviour was very obliging and submissive.

On the fifth day of our journey, in the morning, we passed the famous bridge at St. Esprit, which to be sure is a great curiosity, from its length, and the number of its arches: but these arches are too small; the passage above is too narrow; and the whole appears to be too slight, considering the force and impetuosity of the river.[5] It is not comparable to the bridge at Westminster, either for beauty or solidity.[6] Here we entered Languedoc, and were stopped to have our baggage examined: but the searcher being tipped with a three-livre piece, allowed it to pass. — Before we leave Dauphiné, I must observe, that I was not a little surprized to see figs and chesnuts growing in the open fields, at the discretion of every passenger. It was this day I saw the famous Pont du Garde; but as I cannot possibly include, in this letter, a description of that beautiful bridge, and of the other anti-quities belonging to Nismes, I will defer it till the next opportunity, being, in the mean time, with equal truth and affection,

Dear Sir,
Your obliged humble Servant.

# LETTER X.

*Montpellier, November 10, 1763.*

DEAR SIR,

By the Pont St. Esprit we entered the province of Languedoc, and breakfasted at Bagnole, which is a little paltry town; from whence, however, there is an excellent road through a mountain, made at a great expence, and extending about four leagues. About five in the afternoon, I had the first glimpse of the famous Pont du Garde, which stands on the right hand, about the distance of a league from the post-road to Nismes, and about three leagues from that city. I would not willingly pass for a false enthusiast in taste; but I cannot help observing, that from the first distant view of this noble monument, till we came near enough to see it perfectly, I felt the strongest emotions of impatience that I had ever known; and obliged our driver to put his mules to the full gallop, in the apprehension that it would be dark before we reached the place. I expected to find the building, in some measure, ruinous; but was agreeably disappointed, to see it look as fresh as the bridge at Westminster. The climate is either so pure and dry, or the free-stone, with which it is built, so hard, that the very angles of them remain as acute as if they had been cut last year. Indeed, some large stones have dropped out of the arches; but the whole is admirably preserved, and presents the eye with a piece of architecture, so unaffectedly elegant, so simple, and majestic, that I will defy the most phlegmatic and stupid spectator to behold it without admiration. It was raised in the Augustan age, by the Roman colony of Nismes, to convey a stream of water between two mountains, for the use of that city. It stands over the river Gardon, which is a beautiful pastoral stream, brawling among rocks, which form a number of pretty natural cascades, and overshadowed on each side with trees and shrubs, which greatly add to the rural beauties of the scene. It rises in the Cevennes, and the sand of it produces gold, as we learn from Mr. Reaumur, in his essay on this subject, inserted in the French Memoirs, for the year 1718.[1]—If I lived at Nismes, or Avignon (which last city is within four short leagues of it) I should take pleasure in forming parties to

79

come hither, in summer, to dine under one of the arches of the Pont du Garde, on a cold collation.

This work consists of three bridges, or tire of arches, one above another; the first of six, the second of eleven, and the third of thirty-six. The height, comprehending the aqueduct on the top, amounts to 174 feet three inches: the length between the two mountains, which it unites, extends to 723. The order of architecture is the Tuscan: but the symmetry of it is inconceivable. By scooping the bases of the pilasters of the second tire of arches, they had made a passage for foot-travellers: but though the antients far excelled us in beauty, they certainly fell short of the moderns in point of conveniency. The citizens of Avignon have, in this particular, improved the Roman work with a new bridge by apposition, constructed on the same plan with that of the lower tire of arches, of which indeed it seems to be a part, affording a broad and commodious passage over the river, to horses and carriages of all kinds. The aqueduct, for the continuance of which this superb work was raised, conveyed a stream of sweet water from the fountain of Eure, near the city of Uzés, and extended near six leagues in length.

In approaching Nismes, you see the ruins of a Roman tower, built on the summit of a hill, which over-looks the city. It seems to have been intended, at first, as a watch, or signal-tower, though, in the sequel, it was used as a fortress: what remains of it, is about ninety feet high; the architecture of the Doric order. I no sooner alighted at the inn, than I was presented with a pamphlet, containing an account of Nismes and its antiquities,[2] which every stranger buys. There are persons too who attend in order to shew the town, and you will always be accosted by some shabby antiquarian, who presents you with medals for sale, assuring you they are genuine antiques, and were dug out of the ruins of the Roman temple and baths. All those fellows are cheats; and they have often laid under contribution raw English travellers, who had more money than discretion. To such they sell the vilest and most common trash: but when they meet with a connoisseur, they produce some medals which are really valuable and curious.

Nismes, antiently called Nemausis, was originally a colony

of Romans, settled by Augustus Cæsar, after the battle of
Actium. It is still of considerable extent, and said to contain
twelve thousand families; but the number seems, by this
account, to be greatly exaggerated. Certain it is, the city must
have been formerly very extensive, as appears from the
circuit of the antient walls, the remains of which are still to be
seen. Its present size is not one third of its former extent. Its
temples, baths, statues, towers, basilica, and amphitheatre,
prove it to have been a city of great opulence and magnificence. At present, the remains of these antiquities are all that
make it respectable or remarkable; though here are manufactures of silk and wool, carried on with good success. The
water necessary for these works is supplied by a source at the
foot of the rock, upon which the tower is placed; and here
were discovered the ruins of Roman baths, which had been
formed and adorned with equal taste and magnificence.
Among the rubbish they found a vast profusion of columns,
vases, capitals, cornices, inscriptions, medals, statues, and
among other things, the finger of a colossal statue in bronze,
which, according to the rules of proportion, must have been
fifteen feet high. From these particulars, it appears that the
edifices must have been spacious and magnificent. Part of a
tesselated pavement still remains. The antient pavement of
the bath is still intire; all the rubbish has been cleared away;
and the baths, in a great measure, restored on the old plan,
though they are not at present used for any thing but
ornament. The water is collected into two vast reservoirs,
and a canal built and lined with hewn stone. There are three
handsome bridges thrown over this vast canal. It contains a
great body of excellent water, which by pipes and other small
branching canals, traverses the town, and is converted to
many different purposes of œconomy and manufacture.
Between the Roman bath and these great canals, the ground
is agreeably laid out in pleasure-walks, for the recreation of
the inhabitants. Here are likewise ornaments of architecture,
which savour much more of French foppery, than of the
simplicity and greatness of the antients. It is very surprizing,
that this fountain should produce such a great body of water,
as fills the basin of the source, the Roman basin, two large
deep canals three hundred feet in length, two vast basins that

make part of the great canal, which is eighteen hundred feet long, eighteen feet deep, and forty-eight feet broad. When I saw it, there was in it about eight or nine feet of water, transparent as crystal. It must be observed, however, for the honour of French cleanliness, that in the Roman basin, through which this noble stream of water passes, I perceived two washerwomen at work upon children's clouts and dirty linnen. Surprized, and much disgusted at this filthy phænomenon, I asked by what means, and by whose permission, those dirty hags had got down into the basin, in order to contaminate the water at its fountain-head; and understood they belonged to the commandant of the place, who had the keys of the subterranean passage.

Fronting the Roman baths are the ruins of an antient temple, which, according to tradition, was dedicated to Diana: but it has been observed by connoisseurs, that all the antient temples of this goddess were of the Ionic order; whereas, this is partly Corinthian, and partly composite. It is about seventy foot long, and six and thirty in breadth, arched above, and built of large blocks of stone, exactly joined together without any cement. The walls are still standing, with three great tabernacles at the further end, fronting the entrance. On each side, there are niches in the intercolumniation of the walls, together with pedestals, and shafts of pillars, cornices, and an entablature, which indicate the former magnificence of the building. It was destroyed during the civil war that raged in the reign of Henry III. of France.[3]

It is amazing, that the successive irruptions of barbarous nations, of Goths, Vandals, and Moors; of fanatic croisards,[4] still more sanguinary and illiberal than those Barbarians, should have spared this temple, as well as two other still more noble monuments of architecture, that to this day adorn the city of Nismes: I mean the amphitheatre and the edifice, called *Maison Carrée*. — The former of these is counted the finest monument of the kind, now extant; and was built in the reign of Antoninus Pius,[5] who contributed a large sum of money towards its erection. It is of an oval figure, one thousand and eighty feet in circumference, capacious enough to hold twenty thousand spectators. The architecture is of the Tuscan order, sixty feet high, composed of two open galleries, built one over another, consisting each of threescore arcades. The entrance into the arena was by four great gates, with porticos; and the seats, of which there were thirty, rising one above another, consisted of great blocks of stone, many of which still remain. Over the north gate, appear two bulls, in *alto relievo*, extremely well executed, emblems which, according to the custom of the Romans, signified that the amphitheatre was erected at the expence of the people. There are in other parts of it some work in *bas relief*, and heads or busts but indifferently carved. It stands in the lower part of the town, and strikes the spectator with awe and veneration. The external architecture is almost intire in its whole circuit; but the arena is filled up with houses. — This amphitheatre was fortified as a citadel by the Visigoths, in the beginning of the sixth century. They raised within it a castle, two towers of which are still extant; and they surrounded it with a broad and deep fossée, which was filled up in the thirteenth century. In all the subsequent wars to which this city was exposed, it served as the last resort of the citizens, and sustained a great number of successive attacks; so that its preservation is almost miraculous. It is likely, however, to suffer much more from the Gothic avarice of its own citizens, some of whom are mutilating it every day, for the sake of the stones, which they employ in their own private buildings. It is surprizing, that the King's authority has not been exerted to put an end to such sacrilegious violation.

If the amphitheatre strikes you with an idea of greatness, the *Maison Carrée* enchants you with the most exquisite beauties of architecture and sculpture. This is an edifice, supposed formerly to have been erected by Adrian, who actually built a basilica in this city, though no vestiges of it remain: but the following inscription, which was discovered on the front of it, plainly proves, that it was built by the inhabitants of Nismes, in honour of Caius and Lucius Cæsar, the grand-children of Augustus, by his daughter Julia, the wife of Agrippa.[6]

C. CAESARI. AVGVSTI. F. COS.
L. CAESARI. AVGVSTI. F. COS
DESIGNATO.

## PRINCIPIBVS IVVENTVTIS.

To *Caius*, and *Lucius Cæsar*, Sons of *Augustus*,
Consuls elect, Princes of the Roman youth.

This beautiful edifice, which stands upon a pediment six feet high, is eighty-two feet long, thirty-five broad, and thirty-seven high, without reckoning the pediment. The body of it is adorned with twenty columns engaged in the wall, and the peristyle, which is open, with ten detached pillars that support the entablature. They are all of the Corinthian order, fluted and embellished with capitals of the most exquisite sculpture: the frize and cornice are much admired, and the foliage is esteemed inimitable. The proportions of the building are so happily united, as to give it an air of majesty and grandeur, which the most indifferent spectator cannot behold without emotion. A man needs not be a connoisseur in architecture, to enjoy these beauties. They are indeed so exquisite that you may return to them every day with a fresh appetite for seven years together. What renders them the more curious, they are still entire, and very little affected, either by the ravages of time, or the havoc of war. Cardinal Alberoni[7] declared, that it was a jewel that deserved a cover of gold to preserve it from external injuries. An Italian painter, perceiving a small part of the roof repaired by modern French masonry, tore his hair, and exclaimed in a rage, "Zounds! what do I see? harlequin's hat on the head of Augustus!"

Without all doubt it is ravishingly beautiful. The whole world cannot parallel it; and I am astonished to see it standing entire, like the effects of inchantment, after such a succession of ages, every one more barbarous than another. The history of the antiquities of Nismes takes notice of a grotesque statue, representing two female bodies and legs, united under the head of an old man; but, as it does not inform us where it is kept, I did not see it.

The whole country of Languedoc is shaded with olive trees, the fruit of which begins to ripen, and appears as black as sloes; those they pickle are pulled green, and steeped for some time in a lye made of quick lime or wood ashes, which extracts the bitter taste, and makes the fruit tender. Without this preparation it is not eatable. Under the olive and fig trees, they plant corn and vines, so that there is not an inch of ground unlaboured: but here are no open fields, meadows, or cattle to be seen. The ground is overloaded; and the produce of it crowded to such a degree, as to have a bad effect upon the eye, impressing the traveller with the ideas of indigence and rapacity. The heat in summer is so excessive, that cattle would find no green forage, every blade of grass being parched up and destroyed. The weather was extremely hot when we entered Montpellier, and put up at the *Cheval Blanc*,[8] counted the best *auberge* in the place, tho' in fact it is a most wretched hovel, the habitation of darkness, dirt, and imposition. Here I was obliged to pay four livres a meal for every person in my family, and two livres at night for every bed, though all in the same room: one would imagine that the further we advance to the southward the living is the dearer, though in fact every article of housekeeping is cheaper in Languedoc than many other provinces of France. This imposition is owing to the concourse of English who come hither, and, like simple birds of passage, allow themselves to be plucked by the people of the country, who know their weak side, and make their attacks accordingly. They affect to believe, that all the travellers of our country are grand seigneurs, immensely rich and incredibly generous; and we are silly enough to encourage this opinion, by submitting quietly to the most ridiculous extortion, as well as by committing acts of the most absurd extravagance. This folly of the English, together with a concourse of people from different quarters, who come hither for the re-establishment of their health, has rendered Montpellier one of the dearest places in the South of France. The city, which is but small, stands upon a rising ground fronting the Mediterranean, which is about three leagues to the southward: on the other side is an agreeable plain, extending about the same distance towards the mountains of the Cevennes. The town is reckoned well built, and what the French call *bien percée*; yet the streets are in general narrow, and the houses dark. The air is counted salutary in catarrhous consumptions, from its dryness and elasticity: but too sharp in cases of pulmonary imposthumes.

It was at Montpellier that we saw for the first time any signs of that gaiety and mirth for which the people of this country are celebrated. In all other places through which we passed since our departure from Lyons, we saw nothing but marks of poverty and chagrin. We entered Montpellier on a Sunday, when the people were all dressed in their best apparel. The streets were crowded; and a great number of the better sort of both sexes sat upon stone seats at their doors, conversing with great mirth and familiarity. These conversations lasted the greatest part of the night; and many of them were improved with musick both vocal and instrumental: next day we were visited by the English residing in the place, who always pay this mark of respect to new comers. They consist of four or five families, among whom I could pass the winter very agreeably, if the state of my health and other reasons did not call me away.

Mr. L——[9] had arrived two days before me, troubled with the same asthmatic disorder, under which I have laboured so long. He told me he had been in quest of me ever since he left England. Upon comparing notes, I found he had stopped at the door of a country inn in Picardy, and drank a glass of wine and water, while I was at dinner up stairs; nay, he had even spoke to my servant, and asked who was his master, and the man, not knowing him, replied, he was a gentleman from Chelsea.[10] He had walked by the door of the house where I lodged at Paris, twenty times, while I was in that city; and the very day before he arrived at Montpellier, he had passed our coach on the road.

The garrison of this city consists of two battalions, one of which is the Irish regiment of Berwick,[11] commanded by lieutenant colonel Teuts,[12] a gentleman with whom we contracted an acquaintance at Boulogne. He treats us with great politeness, and indeed does every thing in his power to make the place agreeable to us. The duke of Fitz-James,[13] the governor, is expected here in a little time. We have already a tolerable concert twice a week; there will be a comedy in the winter; and the states of Provence[14] assemble in January, so that Montpellier will be extremely gay and brilliant. These very circumstances would determine me to leave it. I have not health to enjoy these pleasures: I cannot bear a croud of company, such as pours in upon us unexpectedly at all hours; and I foresee, that in staying at Montpellier, I should be led into an expence, which I can ill afford. I have therefore forwarded the letter I received from general P——n,[15] to Mr. B——d,[16] our consul at Nice, signifying my intention of going thither, and explaining the kind of accommodation I would chuse to have at that place.

The day after our arrival, I procured tolerable lodgings in the High Street, for which I pay fifty sols, something more than two shillings per day; and I am furnished with two meals a day by a *traiteur* for ten livres: but he finds neither the wine nor the desert; and indeed we are but indifferently served. Those families who reside here find their account in keeping house. Every traveller who comes to this, or any other, town in France with a design to stay longer than a day or two, ought to write beforehand to his correspondent to procure furnished lodgings, to which he may be driven immediately, without being under the necessity of lying in an execrable inn; for all the inns of this country are execrable.

My baggage is not yet arrived by the canal of Languedoc;[17] but that gives me no disturbance, as it is consigned to the care of Mr. Ray,[18] an English merchant and banker of this place; a gentleman of great probity and worth, from whom I have received repeated marks of uncommon friendship and hospitality.

The next time you hear of me will be from Nice: meanwhile, I remain always,

      Dear Sir,

          Your affectionate humble servant.

# LETTER XI.

*Montpellier, November* 12.

DEAR DOCTOR,

I flattered myself with the hope of much amusement during my short stay at Montpellier. — The University, the Botanical Garden,[1] the State of Physic in this part of the world, and the information I received of a curious collection of manuscripts, among which I hoped to find something for our friend Dr. H——r;[2] all these particulars promised a rich fund of entertainment, which, however, I cannot enjoy.

A few days after my arrival, it began to rain with a southerly wind, and continued without ceasing the best part of a week, leaving the air so loaded with vapours, that there was no walking after sun-set, without being wetted by the dew almost to the skin. I have always found a cold and damp atmosphere the most unfavourable of any to my constitution. My asthmatical disorder, which had not given me much disturbance since I left Boulogne, became now very troublesome, attended with fever, cough, spitting, and lowness of spirits; and I wasted visibly every day. I was favoured with the advice of Dr. Fitz-maurice,[3] a very worthy sensible physician settled in this place: but I had the curiosity to know the opinion of the celebrated professor F——,[4] who is the Boerhaave[5] of Montpellier. The account I had of his private character, and personal deportment, from some English people to whom he was well known, left me no desire to converse with him: but I resolved to consult with him on paper. This great lanthorn of medicine is become very rich and very insolent; and in proportion as his wealth increases, he is said to grow the more rapacious. He piques himself upon being very slovenly, very blunt, and very unmannerly; and perhaps to these qualifications he owes his reputation rather than to any superior skill in medicine. I have known them succeed in our own country; and seen a doctor's parts estimated by his brutality and presumption.

F—— is in his person and address not unlike our old acquaintance Dr. Sm——ie;[6] he stoops much, dodges along, and affects to speak the *Patois*, which is a corruption of the old *Provencial* tongue, spoken by the vulgar in Languedoc and

Provence. Notwithstanding his great age and great wealth, he will scramble up two pair of stairs for a fee of six livres; and without a fee he will give his advice to no person whatsoever. He is said to have great practice in the venereal branch, and to be frequented by persons of both sexes infected with this distemper, not only from every part of France, but also from Spain, Italy, Germany, and England. I need say nothing of the Montpellier method of cure, which is well known at London; but I have some reason to think the great professor F——, has, like the famous Mrs. Mapp, the bone-setter,[7] cured many patients that were never diseased.

Be that as it may, I sent my *valet de place*, who was his townsman and acquaintance, to his house, with the following case, and a loui'dore.

*Annum ætatis post quadragesimum tertium. Temperamentum humidum, crassum, pituitâ repletum, catarrhis sæpissimè profligatum. Catarrhus, febre, anxietate et dyspnœa, nunquam non comitatus. Irritatio membranæ pituitariæ trachæalis, tussim initio aridam, siliquosam, deinde vero excreationem copiosam excitat: sputum albumini ovi simillimum.*

*Accedente febre, urina pallida, limpida: ad ἀχμὴy flagrante, colorem rubrum, subflavum induit: coctione peractâ, sedimentum lateritium deponit.*

*Appetitus rarò deest: digestio segnior sed secura, non autem sine ructu perfecta. Alvus plerumque stipata: excretio intestinalis minima, ratione ingestorum habitâ. Pulsus frequens, vacillans, exilis, quandoquidem etiam intermittens.*

*Febre una extinctâ, non deficit altera. Aliaque et eadem statim nascitur. Aer paulo frigidior, vel humidior, vestimentum inusitatum indutum; exercitatio paululum nimia; ambulatio, equitatio, in quovis vehiculo jactatio; hæc omnia novos motus suscitant. Systema nervosum maxime irritabile, orgasmos patitur. Ostiola in cute hiantia, materiei perspirabili exitum præbentia, clauduntur. Materies obstructa cumulatur; sanguine aliisque humoribus circumagitur: fit plethora. Natura opprimi nolens, excessus hujus expulsionem conatur. Febris nova accenditur. Pars oneris, in membranam trachæalem laxatam ac debilitatam transfertur. Glandulæ pituitariæ turgentes bronchia comprimunt. Liber aeri transitus negatur: hinc respiratio difficilis. Hac vero translatione febris minuitur: interdiu remittitur. Dyspnœa autem aliaque symptomata verè hypochondriaca, recedere nolunt. Vespere febris exacerbatur. Calor, inquietudo, anxietas et asthma, per noctem grassantur. Ita quotidie res agitur, donec vis vitœ paulatim crisim efficit. Seminis jactura, sive in somniis effusi, seu in gremio veneris ejaculati, inter causas horum malorum nec-non numeretur.*

*Quibusdam abhinc annis, exercitationibus juvenilibus subito remissis, in vitam sedentariam lapsum. Animo in studia severiora converso, fibrœ gradatim laxabantur. Inter legendum et scribendum inclinato corpore in pectus malum ruebat. Morbo ingruenti affectio scorbutica auxilium tulit. Invasio prima nimium aspernata. Venientibus hostibus non occursum. Cunctando res non restituta. Remedia convenientia stomachus perhorrescebat. Gravescente dyspnœa phlebotomia frustra tentata. Sanguinis missione vis vitœ diminuta: fiebat pulsus debilior, respiratio difficilior. In pejus ruunt omnia. Febris anomala in febriculam continuam mutata. Dyspnœa confirmata. Fibrarum compages soluta. Valetudo penitus eversa.*

*His agitatus furiis, æger ad mare provolat: in fluctus se precipitem dat: periculum factum spem non fefellit: decies iteratum, felix faustumque evasit. Elater novus fibris conciliatur. Febricula fugatur. Acris dyspnœa solvitur. Beneficium dextrâ ripâ partum, sinistrâ perditum. Superficie corporis, aquæ marinæ frigore et pondere, compressâ et contractâ, interstitia fibrarum occluduntur: particulis incrementi novis partes abrasas reficientibus, locus non datur. Nutritio corporis, viâ pristinâ clausâ, qua data porta ruit: in membranam pulmonum minus firmatam facile fertur, et glandulis per sputum rejicitur.*

*Hieme pluviosâ regnante dolores renovantur; tametsi tempore sereno equitatio profuit. Æstate morbus vix ullum progrediebatur. Autumno, valetudine plus declinatâ, thermis Bathoniensibus solatium haud frustra quæsitum. Aqua ista miré medicata, externe æque ac interne adhibita, malis levamen attulit. Hiems altera, frigida, horrida, diuturna, innocua tamen successit. Vere novo casus atrox diras procellas animo immisit: toto corpore, totâ mente tumultuatur. Patriâ relictâ, tristitia, sollicitudo, indignatio, et sævissima recordatio sequuntur. Inimici priores furore inveterato revertuntur. Rediit febris hectica: rediit asthma cum anxietate, tusse et dolore lateris lancinante.*

*Desperatis denique rebus, iterum ad mare, veluti ad anceps remedium recurritur. Balneum hoc semper benignum. Dolor statim avolat. Tertio die febris retrocessit. Immersio quotidiana antemeridiana, ad vices quinquaginta repetita, symptomata graviora subjugavit.—Manet vero tabes pituitaria: manet temperamentum in catarrhos proclive. Corpus macrescit. Vires delabuntur.*

"The patient's age is forty three; his constitution moist, gross, abounding with phlegm, and very subject to rheums, accompanied with fever, dejection and difficulty of breathing. An irritation of the pituitous membrane that lines the *trachæa arteria*,[8] produces a cough which is at first hard and husky, but afterwards it is attended with a copious expectoration of phlegm or *pituita* that resembles the whites of eggs: at the accession of the fever, the urine is pale and limpid; but in the progress of it, becomes red and yellowish; and at the crisis deposits a brick dust sediment.

"The appetite seldom fails: the digestion, tho' slow is sure; but not performed without flatulency or eructation.—He is generally costive; and the discharge of the intestinal canal is very inconsiderable in proportion to the quantity of the *ingesta*. The pulse is quick, low, wavering, and sometimes intermitting.

"One fever being expelled, another of the same nature immediately succeeds. The least alteration in the weather, towards cold or moisture, change of dress, the smallest excess in point of exercise, whether afoot, on horseback, or in a carriage, occasion fresh commotions in the animal œconomy. The nervous system, being extremely irritable, undergoes a variety of spasms. The pores of the skin, that transmit the insensible perspiration, are obstructed; this obstructed matter being accumulated in the habit, circulates with the blood and humours, untill a plethora ensues; then Nature finding herself in danger of being oppressed, endeavours to expell the excess, by means of a new fever. Part of the incumbrance is thrown upon the weakened and relaxed membrane of the *trachæa*, the glands of which being thus distended, press upon the *bronchia*, so as to impede the free passage of the air, and hence arises the difficulty in the spiration. By this translation, however, the fever abates, and in the day time there is a total remission, tho' the shortness of breath and other symptoms which are really hypochondriac, never totally intermit. In the evening there is always an *exacerbation* or increase of the fever; and all night long, the heat, restlessness, anxiety and asthma prevail. Such is the constant progress of the disorder, 'till the strength of nature insensibly concocts and expels the offending matter. Nocturnal emissions, whether voluntary or involuntary, never fail to produce the same disorders.

"Some years ago, the patient underwent a sudden transition from an active to a sedentary life of hard study and application, by which the fibres were gradually relaxed; and in consequence of reading and writing in a stooping posture, his breast became affected. A scorbutical taint in the constitution favoured the disorder which was too much neglected in the beginning—no steps were taken to repel it in the first attack; and delay bred danger. The patient had the utmost aversion to those medicines which his case required. The asthma growing very troublesome, bleeding was tried in vain. The *vis vitæ* being weakened by venesection,[9] the pulse sunk; the difficulty of breathing increased; every symptom was aggravated; the *anomalous* fever[10] degenerated into a *febricula*[11] without remission; the asthma seemed confirmed; the whole fibrile system untwined; and the constitution quite broke.

"Stimulated by this complication of distress, the patient hied him to the sea and bathed without hesitation: nor was he disappointed in the trial; the bath ten times repeated, had the most happy effects.[12] His nerves were new braced; the fever was dispelled; and the asthma in a great measure removed. But, what he gained on one side, he lost on the other. By the cold and pressure of the sea water on the surface of the body, the interstices of the fibres were so closed or contracted, that no room seemed to be left for the nutritive particles appropriated to repair the necessary waste of the solids, so that being denied their former passage, they rushed where they found the least resistance, upon the debilitated membrane of the lungs; and thus the whole nourishment of the body was hawked up from the *trachæa arteria*.

"The succeeding winter proving raw and rainy, the symptoms recurred, but were mitigated by riding on horseback when the weather was fair. In the summer, the disorder could not be said to gain ground: but growing more serious in the autumn, the Bath in Somersetshire was tried with good effect. All his complaints were relieved by the external and internal use of that excellent water, so that he happily passed the ensuing winter, though it proved remarkably cold, dreary and tedious. In the spring however, he was visited by a domestic calamity which grievously affected him both in mind and body. He fled from the scene of this misfortune, to foreign climes, but found himself pursued by unutterable grief, anxiety, indignation, and the cruel remembrance of his irretrievable loss. The hectic fever, asthma, and dejection returned, attended with an almost incessant cough, and an acute pain in the side.

"In this emergency, recourse was had again to sea bathing as a doubtfull and desperate remedy; and this as usual, proved propitious. The stitch was immediately removed, and in three days the fever disappeared. By bathing in the forenoon for fifty days successively, all the severer symptoms were subdued: but the cough and consumptive spitting still remain, together with the susceptibility of cold: the patient's flesh wastes apace, and his strength continues to decay."

The professor's eyes sparkled at sight of the fee; and he desired the servant to call next morning for his opinion of the case, which accordingly I received in these words:

"On voit par cette relation que monsieur le consultant dont on n'a pas jugé à propos de dire l'age, mais qui nous paroit etre adulte et d'un age passablement avancé, a été sujet cy devant à des rhumes frequens accompagnés de fievre; on ne detaille point (aucune epoque), on parle dans la relation d'asthme auquel il a été sujet, de scorbut ou affection scorbutique dont on ne dit pas les symptomes. On nous fair sçavoir qu'il s'est bien trouvé de l'immersion dans l'eau de la mer, et des eaux de Bath.

"On dit à present qu'il a une *fievre pituitaire* sans dire depuis combien de temps. Qu'il lui reste toujours son temperament enclin aux catharres. Que le corps maigrit, et que les forces se perdent. On ne dit point s'il y a des exacerbations dans cette fievre ou non, si le malade a appetit ou non, si'il tousse ou non, s'il crache ou non, en un mot on n'entre dans aucun detail sur ces objets, sur quoi le conseil soussigné estime que monsieur le consultant est en fievre lente, et que vraisemblable le poumon souffre de quelque tubercules qui peut-etre sont en fonte, ce que nous aurions determiné si dans la relation on avoit marqué les qualités de crachats.

"La cause fonchere de cette maladie doit etre imputée à une lymphe epaisse et acrimonieuse, qui donne occasion à des tubercules au poumon, qui étant mis en fonte fournissent au sang des particules acres et le rendent tout acrimonieux.

"Les vües que l'on doit avoir dans ce cas sont de procurer des bonnes digestions (quoique dans la relation on ne dit pas un mot sur les digestions) de jetter un douce detrempe dans la masse du sang, d'en chasser l'acrimonie et de l'adoucir, de diviser fort doucement la lymphe, et de deterger le poumon, lui procurant meme du calme supposé que la toux l'inquiete, quoique cependant on ne dit pas un mot sur la toux dans la relation. C'est pourquoi on le purgera avec 3 onces de manne, dissoutes dans un verre de decoction de 3 dragmes de polypode de chesne, on passera ensuite à des bouillons qui seront faits avec un petit poulet, la chair, le sang, le cœur et le foye d'une tortue de grandeur mediocre, c'est à dire du poid de 8 à 12 onces avec sa coquille, une poignée de chicorée amere de jardin, et une pincée de feuilles de lierre terrestre vertes ou seches. Ayant pris ces bouillons 15 matins on se purgera comme auparavant, pour en venir à des bouillons qui seront faits avec la moitié d'un moü de veau, une poignée de pimprenelle de jardin, et une dragme de racine d'angelique concassée.

"Ayant pris ces bouillons 15 matins, on se purgera comme auparavant pour en venir au lait d'anesse que l'on prendra le matin à jeun, à la dose de 12 à 16 onces y ajoutant un cuillerée de sucre rapé, on prendra ce lait le matin à jeun observant de prendre pendant son usage de deux jours l'un un moment avant le lait un bolus fait avec 15 grains de craye de Briançon en poudre fine, 20 grains de corail preparé, 8 grains d'antihectique de poterius, et ce qu'il faut de syrop de lierre terrestre, mais les jours ou on ne prendra pas le bolus on prendra un moment avant le lait 3 ou 4 gouttes de bon baume de Canada detrempées dans un demi cuillerée de syrop de lierre terrestre. Si le corps maigrit de plus en plus, je suis d'avis que pendant l'usage du lait d'anesse on soupe tous les soirs avec une soupe au lait de vache.

"On continuera l'usage du lait d'anesse tant, que le malade pourra le supporter, ne le purgeant que par necessité et toujours avec la medicine ordonnée.

"Au reste, si monsieur le consultant ne passe pas les nuits bien calmes, il prendra chaque soir à l'heure de sommeil six grains des pilules de cynoglosse, dont il augmentera la dose d'un grain de plus toutes les fois que la dose du jour precedent, n'aura pas été suffisante pour lui faire passer la nuit bien calme.

"Si le malade tousse il usera soit de jour soit de nuit par petites cuillerées à caffé d'un looch, qui sera fait avec un once de syrop de violat et une dragme de blanc de baleine.

"Si les crachats sont epais et qu'il crache difficilement, en ce cas il prendra une ou deux fois le jour, demi dragme de blanc de baleine reduit en poudre avec un peu de sucre candit qu'il avalera avec une cuillerée d'eau.

"Enfin il doit observer un bon regime de vivre, c'est pourquoi il fera toujours gras et seulement en soupes, bouilli et roti, il ne mangera pas les herbes des soupes, et on salera peu son pot, il se privera du beuf, cochon, chair noir, oiseaux d'eau, ragouts, fritures, patisseries, alimens sales, epicês, vinagrés, salades, fruits, cruds, et autres crudités, alimens grossiers, ou de difficille digestion, la boisson sera de l'eau tant soit peu rougée de bon vin au diner seulement, et il ne prendra à souper qu'une soupe.[13]

Délibéré à Montpellier

  le 11 Novembre.

F—,

Professeur en l'université

honoraire.

Reçeu vint et quatre livres."

"It appears by this case that the *consultor*, who has not thought proper to mention his age, but who seems to be adult and even pretty well advanced in years, has been heretofore subject to frequent rheums; tho' there is no detail of circumstances, (no epocha). In his account of the asthma to which he has been subject, he talks of the scurvy, or scorbutic affection, but says not a word of the symptoms. We are given to understand that he found benefit from bathing in the sea, and in the waters at Bath.—At present he says he has a *pituitous fever*, without saying how long it has been upon him; that his constitution is still subject to catarrhs; that his flesh wastes, and his strength decays. No mention is made whether the fever has any *exacerbations*; whether the patient has a good appetite; whether he coughs or spits; in a word, he says nothing of these particulars. The under subscribing physician, therefore, is of opinion that the *consultor* has got a slow fever, and probably there are tubercules now in suppuration on the lungs, a circumstance which we should have ascertained, had the nature of the spitting been described in the case.

"The fundamental cause of this disorder must be imputed to a thick, acrimonious lymph which produces tubercules on the lungs, which tubercules suppurating, supply the blood with acrid particles, and render it wholly acrimonious.

"The views to be pursued in this case are to procure a good digestion, (tho' in the case, not a word is said of digestion) to throw a soft dilution into the mass of blood, to expell the acrimony, to sweeten it, to attenuate the lymph very gently, and heal the ulcerated lungs, procuring ease and rest to the patient, provided he is disturbed by the cough, tho' there is not a word said of the cough in the relation of the case. Therefore, he must be purged with three ounces of manna dissolved in a glass of decoction made with three drachms of *polypodium* of the oak;[14] then he must go upon a course of *bouillons* (broths) made of a young chicken, with the flesh, blood, heart and liver of a land tortoise of a middling size, weighing from eight to twelve ounces, including the shell, a handfull of bitter garden *succory*, and a pinch of ground-ivy, either green or dried. Having taken these *bouillons*, fifteen mornings successively, he shall purge as before, in order to begin another course of *bouillons* made with the lights of veal, a handfull of garden *pimpernel* and a drachm of bruised *angelica* root.

"Having taken these *bouillons*, fifteen days, he shall purge as before, in order to begin a course of asses milk which he shall take in the morning fasting, to the quantity of twelve or sixteen ounces, with a spoonfull of powdered sugar. This milk must be taken in the morning fasting, and during the use of it, the patient must take every second day immediately before this milk, a bolus composed of 15 grains of *chalk of Briançon*[15] in fine powder, 20 grains of prepared *coral*, and 8 grains of the *antihecticum* of *poterius*,[16] with a sufficient quantity of syrup of ground-ivy; but the days on which this bolus is not taken, he shall take immediately before the milk, three of four drops of *balm of Canada*[17] in half a spoonfull of syrup of ground-ivy. If his flesh continues to waste I am of opinion that during the use of the asses milk, he should sup every night on cow's milk.

"The asses milk shall be continued as long as the patient can bear it; and he shall never purge but when there is a necessity for it, and then only with the medicine prescribed above.

"If, nevertheless, the *consultor* should have bad nights, he shall take every evening when going to bed, six grains of the *pilulæ cynoglossæ*,[18] to which he may add one grain as often, as the dose of the preceding night shall have failed in procuring him repose.

"If he is troubled with a cough he may take either by day or by night, a teaspoonfull of a linctus made with one drachm of *sperma cete* mixed with an ounce of *syrup* of *violets*. —If what he spits up be thick and it comes off with difficulty, in that case he shall take, once, or twice a day, half a drachm of *sperma cete* rubbed with sugar candy, to be swallowed in a spoonfull of water.

"In fine he must observe a good regimen in his diet, and eat flesh meat every day, in soup, boiled or roasted, but without tasting the greens that are in the soup, or putting a great deal of salt in his pottage. He must abstain from beef, pork, game, water-fowl, ragouts, fried meats, pastry, high seasoned food of all kinds, pickles, sallads, raw fruit and other crudities, gross feeding and victuals hard of digestion. His drink at dinner must be water just tinctured with good wine, and at supper, nothing but soup.

prescribed at *Montpellier*
Nov.! 11th.

*Fizes*
*Honorary Professor in the univer-*
*sity.*
*Received twenty four livres.*"

97

I thought it was a little extraordinary that a learned professor should reply in his mother tongue to a case put in Latin: but I was much more surprised, as you will also be, at reading his answer, from which I was obliged to conclude, either that he did not understand Latin, or that he had not taken the trouble to read my *memoire*. I shall not make any remarks upon the stile of his prescription, replete as it is with a disgusting repetition of low expressions: but I could not but, in justice to myself, point out to him the passages in my case which he had overlooked. Accordingly, having marked them with letters, I sent it back, with the following billet.

"Apparement Mons. F—— n'a pas donné beaucoup d'attention au memoire de ma santé que j'ai eu l'honneur de lui presenter—'Monsieur le consultant (dit il) dont on n'a pas jugé à propos de dire l'age.'—Mais on voit dans le memoire à No. 1. '*Annum ætatis post quadragesimum tertium.*'

"Mons. F—— dit que 'je n'ai pas marqué aucune epoque.' Mais à No. 2. du memoire il trouvera ces mots. '*Quibusdam abhinc annis.*' J'ai meme detaillé le progrès de la maladie pour trois ans consecutifs.

"Mons. F—— observe, 'On ne dit point si'l y a des exacerbations dans cette fievre ou non.' Qu'il regarde la lettre B, il verra, '*Vespere febris exacerbatur. Calor, inquietudo, anxietas et asthma per noctem grassantur.*'

"Mons. F—— remarque, 'On ne dit point si le malade a appetit ou non, s'il tousse ou non, s'il crache ou non, en un mot on n'entre dans aucun detail sur ces objets.' Mais on voit toutes ces circonstances detaillées dans le memoire à lettre A, '*Irritatio membranæ trachæalis tussim, initio aridam, siliquosam, deinde vero excreationem copiosam excitat. Sputum albumini ovi simillimum. Appetitus raro deest. Digestio segnior sed secura.*'

"Mons. F—— observe encore, 'qu'on ne dit pas un mot sur la toux dans la relation.' Mais j'ai dit encore à No. 3. de memoire, '*Rediit febris hectica; rediit asthma cum anxietate, tusse et dolore lateris lancinante.*'

"Au reste, je ne puis pas me persuader qu'il y ait des tubercules au poumon, parce que j'ai ne jamais craché de pus, ni autre chose que de la pituite qui a beaucoup de resemblance au blanc des oeufs. *Sputum albumini ovi simillimum.* Il me paroit donc que ma maladie doit son origine à la suspension de l'exercise du corps, au grand attachement d'esprit, et à une vie sedentaire qui a relaché le sisteme fibreux; et qu'à present on peut l'appeler *tabes pituitaria*, non *tabes purulenta*. J'espere que Mons. F—— aura la bonté de faire revision du memoire, et de m'en dire encore son sentiment."

"Monsieur *Fizes* seems to have given very little attention to the case I had the honour to send him.

" 'The *consultor* (says he) who has not thought proper to mention his age,' —But he may see in the case at No. 1. *Annum ætatis post quadragesimum tertium*.' 'The patient's age is forty three.'

"Mr. *Fizes* says I have not mentioned any *epocha* or date,—But at No. 2, he will find these words. '*Quibusdam abhinc annis*.' 'Some years ago.' I have even given a detail of the progress of the distemper, for three years successively. Mr. *Fizes* observes, that I take no notice of any *exacerbations* in the fever. — Let him look at the letter B, where he will see, '*Vespere febris exacerbatur. Calor, inquietudo, anxietas* et *asthma per noctem grassantur*.' 'In the evening there is always an *exacerbation* of the fever and all night long the heat, restlessness, anxiety and asthma prevail.'—Mons. *Fizes* remarks, 'No mention is made whether the patient has a good appetite, whether he coughs, or spits; in a word, he says nothing of these particulars.' But all these particulars are mentioned in the case, at the letter A. '*Irritatio membranæ trachæalis tussim, initio aridam, siliquosam, deinde vero excreationem copiosam excitat. Sputum albumini ovi simillimum. Appetitus rare deest. Digestio segnior sed secura*.' 'An irritation of the pituitous membrane that lines the *trachæa arteria*, produces a *cough* which is at first, hard and husky; but, afterwards it is attended with a copious *expectoration* of *phlegm that resembles the whites of eggs*. — The *appetite* seldom fails; the *digestion*, tho' slow, is sure.'

"Finally Mons? *Fizes* observes that 'not a word is said of the *cough* in the relation of the case.' But I have mentioned it once more at No. 3 of the relation. '*Rediit febris hectica; rediit asthma cum anxietate, tusse et dolore lateris lancinante*.' 'The hectic fever, asthma, and dejection returned, attended with an almost incessant *cough*, and an acute pain in the side.'

"Besides, I cannot think there are any tubercules on my lungs, as I never spit up purulent matter, nor any thing but phlegm or *pituita* in colour and consistence like the whites of eggs. *Sputum albumini ovi simillimum.* I imagine, therefore, that my disorder was originally owing to a sudden intermission of bodily exercise, intense application of the mind, and a sedentary life which hath relaxed the whole fibrile system, and that now it may be called a *pituitary*, not a *purulent*, consumption. *Tabes pituitaria*, non *tabes purulenta*.

"I hope Mons.! *Fizes* will be so good as to reexamine the relation, and once more favour me with his opinion of my case."

Considering the nature of the case, you see I could not treat him more civilly. I desired the servant to ask when he should return for an answer, and whether he expected another fee. He desired him to come next morning, and, as the fellow assured me, gave him to understand, that whatever monsieùr might send, should be for his (the servant's) advantage. In all probability he did not expect another gratification, to which, indeed, he had no title. Mons. F—— was undoubtedly much mortified to find himself detected in such flagrant instances of unjustifiable negligence, and like all other persons in the same ungracious dilemma, instead of justifying himself by reason or argument, had recourse to recrimination. In the paper which he sent me next day, he insisted in general that he had carefully perused the case (which you will perceive was a self-evident untruth) he said the theory it contained was idle; that he was sure it could not be written by a physician; that, with respect to the disorder, he was still of the same opinion; and adhered to his former prescription; but if I had any doubts I might come to his house, and he would resolve them.

I wrapt up twelve livres in the following note, and sent it to his house.

"C'est ne pas sans raison que monsieur F—— jouit d'une si grande reputation. Je n'ai plus de doutes, graces à Dieu et à monsieur F——e."

"It is not without reason that *Mons.! Fizes* enjoys such a

large share of reputation. I have no doubts remaining; thank Heaven and *monsieur Fizes*."

To this I received for answer. "Monsieur n'a plus de doutes: j'en suis charmé. Reçeu douze livres. F——, &c."

"Sir, you have no doubts remaining: I am very glad of it—received twelve livres. *Fizes* &c."

Instead of keeping his promise to the valet, he put the money in his pocket; and the fellow returned in a rage, exclaiming that he was *un gros cheval de carosse*, a great coach-horse.

I shall make no other comment upon the medicines, and the regimen which this great Doctor prescribed; but that he certainly mistook the case: that upon the supposition I actually laboured under a purulent discharge from the lungs, his remedies savour strongly of the old woman; and that there is a total blank with respect to the article of exercise, which you know is so essential in all pulmonary disorders. But after having perused my remarks upon his first prescription, he could not possibly suppose that I had tubercules, and was spitting up pus; therefore his persisting in recommending the same medicines he had prescribed on that supposition, was a flagrant absurdity. —If, for example, there was no *vomica*[19] in the lungs; and the business was to attenuate the lymph, what could be more preposterous than to advise the chalk of Briançon, coral, antihecticum poterii, and the balm of Canada? As for the turtle-soupe, it is a good restorative and balsamic; but, I apprehend, will tend to thicken rather than attenuate the phlegm. He mentions not a syllable of the air, though it is universally allowed, that the climate of Montpellier is pernicious to ulcerated lungs; and here I cannot help recounting a small adventure which our doctor had with a son of Mr. O——d,[20] merchant in the city of London. I had it from Mrs. St——e[21] who was on the spot. The young gentleman, being consumptive, consulted Mr. F——, who continued visiting and prescribing for him a whole month. At length, perceiving that he grew daily worse, "Doctor (said he) I take your prescriptions punctually; but, instead of being the better for them, I have now not an hour's remission from the fever in the four-and-twenty.—I cannot conceive the meaning of it." F——, who perceived he had not long to live, told him the reason was very plain: the air of Montpellier was too sharp for his lungs, which required a softer climate. "Then you're a sordid villain (cried the young man) for allowing me to stay here till my constitution is irretrievable." He set out immediately for Thoulouse, and in a few weeks died in the neighbourhood of that city.

I observe that the physicians in this country pay no regard to the state of the solids in chronical disorders: that exercise and the cold bath are never prescribed: that they seem to think the scurvy is entirely an English disease;[22] and that, in all appearance, they often confound the symptoms of it, with those of the venereal distemper. Perhaps I may be more particular on this subject in a subsequent letter. In the mean time, I am ever,

Dear Sir,
Yours sincerely.

# LETTER XII.

DEAR SIR,

The inhabitants of Montpellier are sociable, gay, and good tempered. They have a spirit of commerce, and have erected several considerable manufactures in the neighbourhood of the city. People assemble every day to take the air on the esplanade, where there is a very good walk, just without the gate of the citadel: but, on the other side of the town, there is another still more agreeable, called the *peirou*, from whence there is a prospect of the Mediterranean on one side, and of the Cevennes on the other. Here is a good equestrian statue of Louis XIV. fronting one gate of the city, which is built in form of a triumphal arch, in honour of the same monarch. Immediately under the *peirou* is the physic garden, and near it an arcade just finished for an aqueduct, to convey a stream of water to the upper parts of the city. Perhaps I should have thought this a neat piece of work, if I had not seen the *Pont du Garde*: but, after having viewed the Roman arches, I could not look upon this but with pity and contempt. It is a wonder how the architect could be so fantastically modern, having such a noble model, as it were, before his eyes.

There are many protestants at this place, as well as at Nismes, and they are no longer molested on the score of religion. They have their conventicles in the country, where they assemble privately for worship. These are well known; and detachments are sent out every Sunday to intercept them; but the officer has always private directions to take another route. Whether this indulgence comes from the wisdom and lenity of the government, or is purchased with money of the commanding officer, I cannot determine: but certain it is, the laws of France punish capitally every protestant minister convicted of having performed the functions of his ministry in this kingdom; and one was hanged about two years ago, in the neighbourhood of Montauban.[1]

The markets in Montpellier are well supplied with fish, poultry, butcher's meat, and game, at reasonable rates. The wine of the country is strong and harsh, and never drank, but when mixed with water. Burgundy is dear, and so is the sweet wine of Frontignan,[2] though made in the neighbourhood of Cette. You know it is famous all over Europe, and so are the *liqueurs*, or drams of various sorts, compounded and distilled at Montpellier. Cette is the sea-port, about four leagues from that city: but the canal of Languedoc comes up within a mile of it; and is indeed a great curiosity: a work in all respects worthy of a Colbert, under whose auspices it was finished. When I find such a general tribute of respect and veneration paid to the memory of that great man, I am astonished to see so few monuments of public utility left by other ministers. One would imagine, that even the desire of praise would prompt a much greater number to exert themselves for the glory and advantage of their country; yet, in my opinion, the French have been ungrateful to Colbert, in the same proportion as they have over-rated the character of his master.[3] Through all France one meets with statues and triumphal arches erected to Louis XIV. in consequence of his victories; by which, likewise, he acquired the title of Louis le Grand. But how were those victories obtained? Not by any personal merit of Louis. It was Colbert who improved his finances, and enabled him to pay his army. It was Louvois that provided all the necessaries of war. It was a Condé, a Turenne, a Luxemburg, a Vendome,[4] who fought his battles; and his first conquests, for which he was deified by the pen of adulation, were obtained almost without bloodshed, over weak, dispirited, divided, and defenceless nations. It was Colbert that improved the marine, instituted manufactures, encouraged commerce, undertook works of public utility, and patronized the arts and sciences. But Louis (you will say) had the merit of choosing and supporting those ministers, and those generals. I answer, no. He found Colbert and Louvois already chosen: he found Condé and Turenne in the very zenith of military reputation. Luxemburg was Condé's pupil; and Vendome, a prince of the blood, who at first obtained the command of armies in consequence of his high birth, and happened to turn out a man of genius. The same Louis had the sagacity to revoke the edict of Nantz;[5] to entrust his armies to a Tallard, a Villeroy, and a Marsin.[6] He had the humanity to ravage the country, burn the towns, and massacre the people of the Palatinate.[7] He had the patriotism to impoverish and depopulate his own kingdom, in order to prosecute schemes of the most lawless ambition. He had the consolation to beg a peace from those he had provoked to war by the most outrageous insolence; and he had the glory to espouse Mrs. Maintenon in her old age, the widow of the buffoon Scarron.[8] Without all doubt, it was from irony he acquired the title *le Grand*.[9]

Having received a favourable answer from Mr. B——,[10] the English consul at Nice, and recommended the care of my heavy baggage to Mr. Ray, who undertook to send it by sea from Cette to Villefranche, I hired a coach and mules for seven loui'dores, and set out from Montpellier on the 13th of November, the weather being agreeable, though the air was cold and frosty. In other respects there were no signs of winter: the olives were now ripe, and appeared on each side of the road as black as sloes; and the corn was already half a foot high. On the second day of our journey, we passed the Rhone on a bridge of boats at Buccaire,[11] and lay on the other side at Tarrascone. Next day we put up at a wretched place called Orgon, where, however, we were regaled with an excellent supper; and among other delicacies, with a dish of green pease. Provence is a pleasant country, well cultivated; but the inns are not so good here as in Languedoc, and few of them are provided with a certain convenience which an English traveller can very ill dispense with. Those you find are generally on the tops of houses, exceedingly nasty; and so much exposed to the weather, that a valetudinarian cannot use them without hazard of his life. At Nismes in Languedoc, where we found the temple of Cloacina[12] in a most shocking condition, the servant-maid told me her mistress had caused it to be made on purpose for the English travellers; but now she was very sorry for what she had done, as all the French who frequented her house, instead of using the seat, left their offerings on the floor, which she was obliged to have cleaned three or four times a day. This is a degree of beastliness, which would appear detestable even in the capital of North-Britain.[13] On the fourth day of our pilgrimage, we lay in the suburbs of Aix, but did not enter the city, which I had a great curiosity to see. The villainous asthma baulked me of that satisfaction. I was pinched with the cold, and impatient to reach a warmer climate. Our next stage was at a paltry village, where we were poorly entertained. I looked so ill in the morning, that the good woman of the house, who was big with child, took me by the hand at parting, and even shed tears, praying fervently that God would restore me to my health. This was the only instance of sympathy, compassion, or goodness of heart, that I had met with among the publicans of France. Indeed, at Valencia, our landlady understanding I was travelling to Montpellier for my health, would have dissuaded me from going thither; and exhorted me, in particular, to beware of the physicians, who were all a pack of assassins. She advised me to eat fricassees of chickens, and white meat, and to take a good *bouillon* every morning.

A *bouillon* is an universal remedy among the good people of France; insomuch, that they have no idea of any person's dying, after having swallowed *un bon bouillon*. One of the English gentlemen, who were robbed and murdered about thirty years ago between Calais and Boulogne, being brought to the post-house of Boulogne with some signs of life, this remedy was immediately administered. "What surprises me greatly, (said the post-master, speaking of this melancholy story to a friend of mine, two years after it happened) I made an excellent *bouillon*, and poured it down his throat with my own hands, and yet he did not recover." Now, in all probability, this *bouillon* it was that stopped his breath.[14] When I was a very young man, I remember to have seen a person suffocated by such impertinent officiousness. A young man of uncommon parts and erudition, very well esteemed at the university of G——ow,[15] was found early one morning in a subterranean vault among the ruins of an old archiepiscopal palace, with his throat cut from ear to ear. Being conveyed to a public-house in the neighbourhood, he made signs for pen, ink, and paper, and in all probability would have explained the cause of this terrible catastrophe, when an old woman, seeing the windpipe which was cut, sticking out of the wound, and mistaking it for the gullet, by way of giving him a cordial to support his spirits, poured into it, through a small funnel, a glass of burnt brandy, which strangled him in the tenth part of a minute. The gash was so hideous, and formed by so many repeated strokes of a razor, that the surgeons believed he could not possibly be the perpetrator himself; nevertheless, this was certainly the case.

At Brignolles, where we dined, I was obliged to quarrel with the landlady, and threaten to leave her house, before she would indulge us with any sort of flesh-meat. It was meagre day, and she had made her provision accordingly. She even hinted some dissatisfaction at having heretics in her house: but, as I was not disposed to eat stinking fish, with ragouts of eggs and onions, I insisted upon a leg of mutton, and a brace of fine partridges, which I found in the larder. Next day, when we set out in the morning from Luc, it blew a north-westerly wind so extremely cold and biting, that even a flannel wrapper could not keep me tolerably warm in the coach. Whether the cold had put our coachman in a bad humour, or he had some other cause of resentment against himself, I know not; but we had not gone above a quarter of a mile, when he drove the carriage full against the corner of a garden wall, and broke the axle-tree, so that we were obliged to return to the inn on foot, and wait a whole day, until a new piece could be made and adjusted. The wind that blew, is called *Maestral*, in the Provencial dialect, and indeed is the severest that ever I felt. At this inn, we met with a young French officer who had been a prisoner in England, and spoke our language pretty well. He told me, that such a wind did not blow above twice or three times in a winter, and was never of long continuance: that in general, the weather was very mild and agreeable during the winter months; that living was very cheap in this part of Provence, which afforded greaty plenty of game. Here, too, I found a young Irish recolet,[16] in his way from Rome to his own country. He complained, that he was almost starved by the inhospitable disposition of the French people; and that the regular clergy, in particular, had treated him with the most cruel disdain. I relieved his necessities, and gave him a letter to a gentleman of his own country at Montpellier.

When I rose in the morning, and opened a window that looked into the garden, I thought myself either in a dream, or bewitched. All the trees were cloathed with snow, and all the country covered at least a foot thick. "This cannot be the south of France, (said I to myself) it must be the Highlands of

Scotland!" At a wretched town called Muy, where we dined,
I had a warm dispute with our landlord, which, however, did
not terminate to my satisfaction. I sent on the mules before,
to the next stage, resolving to take post-horses, and bespoke
them accordingly of the aubergiste, who was, at the same
time, inn-keeper and post-master. We were ushered into the
common eating-room, and had a very indifferent dinner;
after which, I sent a loui'dore to be changed, in order to pay
the reckoning. The landlord, instead of giving the full
change, deducted three livres a head for dinner, and sent in
the rest of the money by my servant. Provoked more at his ill
manners, than at his extortion, I ferretted him out of a
bed-chamber, where he had concealed himself, and obliged
him to restore the full change, from which I paid him at the
rate of two livres a head. He refused to take the money,
which I threw down on the table; and the horses being ready,
stepped into the coach, ordering the postilions to drive on.
Here I had certainly reckoned without my host. The fellows
declared they would not budge, until I should pay their
master; and as I threatened them with manual chastisement,
they alighted, and disappeared in a twinkling. I was now so
incensed, that though I could hardly breathe; though the
afternoon was far advanced, and the street covered with wet
snow, I walked to the consul of the town, and made my
complaint in form. This magistrate, who seemed to be a
taylor, accompanied me to the inn, where by this time the
whole town was assembled, and endeavoured to persuade me
to compromise the affair. I said, as he was the magistrate, I
would stand to his award. He answered, "that he would not
presume to determine what I was to pay." I have already paid
him a reasonable price for his dinner, (said I) and now I
demand post-horses according to the king's ordonnance. The
aubergiste said the horses were ready, but the guides were
run away; and he could not find others to go in their place. I
argued with great vehemence, offering to leave a loui'dore
for the poor of the parish, provided the consul would oblige
the rascal to do his duty. The consul shrugged up his
shoulders, and declared it was not in his power. This was a
lie, but I perceived he had no mind to disoblige the publican.
If the mules had not been sent away, I should certainly have

not only payed what I thought proper, but corrected the landlord into the bargain, for his insolence and extortion; but now I was entirely at his mercy, and as the consul continued to exhort me in very humble terms, to comply with his demands, I thought proper to acquiesce. Then the postilions immediately appeared: the crowd seemed to exult in the triumph of the aubergiste; and I was obliged to travel in the night, in very severe weather, after all the fatigue and mortification I had undergone.

We lay at Frejus, which was the *Forum Julianum* of the antients, and still boasts of some remains of antiquity; particularly the ruins of an amphitheatre, and an aqueduct. The first we passed in the dark, and next morning the weather was so cold that I could not walk abroad to see it. The town is at present very inconsiderable, and indeed in a ruinous condition. Nevertheless, we were very well lodged at the post-house, and treated with more politeness than we had met with in any other part of France.

As we had a very high mountain to ascend in the morning, I ordered the mules on before to the next post, and hired six horses for the coach. At the east end of Frejus, we saw close to the road on our left-hand, the arcades of the antient aqueduct, and the ruins of some Roman edifices, which seemed to have been temples. There was nothing striking in the architecture of the aqueduct. The arches are small and low, without either grace or ornament, and seem to have been calculated for mere utility.

The mountain of Esterelles, which is eight miles over, was formerly frequented by a gang of desperate banditti, who are now happily exterminated: the road is very good, but in some places very steep and bordered by precipices. The mountain is covered with pines, and the *laurus cerasus*, the fruit of which being now ripe, made a most romantic appearance through the snow that lay upon the branches. The cherries were so large that I at first mistook them for dwarf oranges. I think they are counted poisonous in England, but here the people eat them without hesitation. In the middle of the mountain is the post-house, where we dined in a room so cold, that the bare remembrance of it makes my teeth chatter. After dinner I chanced to look into another chamber that fronted the south, where the sun shone; and opening a window perceived, within a yard of my hand, a large tree loaded with oranges, many of which were ripe. You may judge what my astonishment was to find Winter in all his rigour reigning on one side of the house, and Summer in all her glory on the other. Certain it is, the middle of this mountain seemed to be the boundary of the cold weather. As we proceeded slowly in the afternoon we were quite enchanted. This side of the hill is a natural plantation of the most agreeable ever-greens, pines, firs, laurel, cypress, sweet myrtle, tamarisc, box, and juniper, interspersed with sweet marjoram, lavender, thyme, wild thyme, and sage. On the right-hand the ground shoots up into agreeable cones, between which you have delightful vistas of the Mediterranean, which washes the foot of the rock; and between two divisions of the mountains, there is a bottom watered by a charming stream, which greatly adds to the rural beauties of the scene.

This night we passed at Cannes, a little fishing town, agreeably situated on the beach of the sea, and in the same place lodged Monsieur Nadeau d'Etrueil,[17] the unfortunate French governor of Guadeloupe, condemned to be imprisoned for life in one of the isles of Marguerite, which lie within a mile of this coast.

Next day we journeyed by the way of Antibes, a small maritime town, tolerably well fortified; and passing the little river Loup, over a stone-bridge, arrived about noon at the village of St. Laurent, the extremity of France, where we passed the Var, after our baggage had undergone examination. From Cannes to this village the road lies along the sea-side; and sure nothing can be more delightful. Though in the morning there was a frost upon the ground, the sun was as warm as it is in May in England. The sea was quite smooth, and the beach formed of white polished pebbles; on the left-hand the country was covered with green olives, and the side of the road planted with large trees of sweet myrtle growing wild like the hawthorns in England. From Antibes we had the first view of Nice, lying on the opposite side of the bay, and making a very agreeable appearance. The author of the Grand Tour says, that from Antibes to Nice the roads are very bad, through rugged mountains bordered with precipices on the left, and by the sea to the right;[18] whereas, in fact, there is neither precipice nor mountain near it.

The Var, which divides the county of Nice from Provence, is no other than a torrent fed chiefly by the snow that melts on the Maritime Alps, from which it takes its origin. In the summer it is swelled to a dangerous height, and this is also the case after heavy rains: but at present the middle of it is quite dry, and the water divided into two or three narrow streams, which, however, are both deep and rapid. This river has been absurdly enough by some supposed the Rubicon, in all probability from the description of that river in the Pharsalia of Lucan, who makes it the boundary betwixt Gaul and Italy—

> —et Gallica certus
> Limes ab Ausoniis disterminat arva colonis;

> A sure frontier that parts the Gallic plains,
> From the rich meadows of th'Ausonian swains;[19]

whereas, in fact, the Rubicon, now called Pisatello, runs between Ravenna and Rimini.—But to return to the Var. At the village of St. Laurent, famous for its Muscadine wines, there is a set of guides always in attendance to conduct you in your passage over the river. Six of those fellows, tucked up above the middle, with long poles in their hands, took charge of our coach, and by many windings guided it safe to the opposite shore. Indeed there was no occasion for any; but it is a sort of a perquisite, and I did not choose to run any risque, how small soever it might be, for the sake of saving half a crown, with which they were satisfied. If you do not gratify the searchers at St. Laurent with the same sum, they will rummage your trunks, and turn all your cloaths topsy turvy. And here, once for all, I would advise every traveller who consults his own ease and convenience, to be liberal of his money to all that sort of people; and even to wink at the imposition of aubergistes on the road, unless it be very flagrant. So sure as you enter into disputes with them, you will be put to a great deal of trouble, and fret yourself to no manner of purpose. I have travelled with œconomists in

England, who declared they would rather give away a crown than allow themselves to be cheated of a farthing. This is a good maxim, but requires a great share of resolution and self-denial to put it in practice. In one excursion of about two hundred miles, my fellow-traveller was in a passion, and of consequence very bad company from one end of the journey to the other. He was incessantly scolding either at landlords, landladies, waiters, hostlers, or postilions. We had bad horses, and bad chaises; set out from every stage with the curses of the people; and at this expence I saved about ten shillings in the whole journey. For such a paltry considera-tion, he was contented to be miserable himself, and to make every other person unhappy with whom he had any concern. When I came last from Bath it rained so hard, that the postilion who drove the chaise was wet to the skin before we had gone a couple of miles. When we arrived at the Devizes, I gave him two shillings instead of one, out of pure compas-sion. The consequence of this liberality was, that in the next stage we seemed rather to fly than to travel upon solid ground. I continued my bounty to the second driver, and indeed through the whole journey, and found myself accommodated in a very different manner from what I had experienced before. I had elegant chaises, with excellent horses; and the postilions of their own accord used such diligence, that although the roads were broken by the rain, I travelled at the rate of twelve miles an hour; and my extraordinary expence from Bath to London, amounted precisely to six shillings.

The river Var falls into the Mediterranean a little below St. Laurent, about four miles to the westward of Nice. Within the memory of persons now living, there have been three wooden bridges thrown over it, and as often destroyed in consequence of the jealousy subsisting between the kings of France and Sardinia; this river being the boundary of their dominions on the side of Provence.[20] However, this is a consideration that ought not to interfere with the other advantages that would accrue to both kingdoms from such a convenience. If there was a bridge over the Var, and a post-road made from Nice to Genoa, I am very confident that all those strangers who now pass the Alps in their way to and from Italy, would choose this road as infinitely more safe, commodious, and agreeable. This would also be the case with all those who hire felucas from Marseilles or Antibes, and expose themselves to the dangers and inconveniences of travelling by sea in an open boat.

In the afternoon we arrived at Nice, where we found Mr. M——e,[21] the English gentleman whom I had seen at Boulogne, and advised to come hither. He had followed my advice, and reached Nice about a month before my arrival, with his lady, child, and an old gouvernante. He had travelled with his own post-chaise and horses, and is now lodged just without one of the gates of the city, in the house of the count de V——n,[22] for which he pays five loui'dores a month. I could hire one much better in the neighbourhood of London, for the same money. Unless you will submit to this extortion, and hire a whole house for a length of time, you will find no ready-furnished lodgings at Nice. After having stewed a week in a paltry inn, I have taken a ground floor for ten months at the rate of four hundred livres a year, that is twenty pounds sterling, for the Piedmontese livre is about an English shilling.[23] The apartments are large, lofty, and commodious enough, with two small gardens, in which there is plenty of sallad, and a great number of oranges and lemons: but as it required some time to provide furniture, our consul Mr. B——d,[24] one of the best natured and most friendly men in the world, has lent me his lodgings, which are charmingly situated by the sea-side, and open upon a terrace, that runs parallel to the beach, forming part of the town wall. Mr. B——d himself lives at Villa Franca, which is divided from Nice by a single mountain, on the top of which there is a small fort, called the castle of Montalban. Immediately after our arrival we were visited by one Mr. de Martines,[25] a most agreeable young fellow, a lieutenant in the Swiss regiment,[26] which is here in garrison. He is a Protestant, extremely fond of our nation, and understands our language tolerably well. He was particularly recommended to our acquaintance by general P——[27] and his lady; we are happy in his conversation; find him wonderfully obliging, and extremely serviceable on many occasions. We have likewise made acquaintance with some other individuals, particularly with Mr. St. Pierre, junior,[28] who is a considerable merchant, and consul for Naples. He is a well-bred, sensible young man, speaks English, is an excellent performer on the lute and mandolin, and has a pretty collection of books. In a word, I hope we shall pass the winter agreeably enough, especially if Mr. M——e should hold out; but I am afraid he is too far gone in a consumption to recover. He spent the last winter at Nismes, and consulted F——[29] at Montpellier. I was impatient to see the prescription, and found it almost verbatim the same he had sent to me; although I am persuaded there is a very essential difference between our disorders. Mr. M——e has been long afflicted with violent spasms, colliquative sweats, prostration of appetite, and a disorder in his bowels. He is likewise jaundiced all over, and I am confident his liver is unsound. He tried the tortoise soup, which he said in a fortnight stuffed him up with phlegm. This gentleman has got a smattering of physic, and I am afraid tampers with his own constitution, by means of Brookes's Practice of Physic,[30] and some dispensatories, which he is continually poring over. I beg pardon for this tedious epistle, and am,

Very sincerely, dear Sir,

Your affectionate,

Humble servant.

# LETTER XIII.

DEAR SIR,

I am at last settled at Nice, and have leisure to give you some account of this very remarkable place. The county of Nice extends about fourscore miles in length, and in some places it is thirty miles broad. It contains several small towns, and a great number of villages; all of which, this capital excepted, are situated among mountains, the most extensive plain of the whole country being this where I now am, in the neighbourhood of Nice. The length of it does not exceed two miles, nor is the breadth of it, in any part, above one. It is bounded by the Mediterranean on the south. From the sea-shore, the Maritime Alps begin with hills of a gentle ascent, rising into mountains that form a sweep or amphitheatre ending at Montalban, which over-hangs the town of Villa Franca. On the west side of this mountain, and in the eastern extremity of the amphitheatre, stands the city of Nice, wedged in between a steep rock and the little river Paglion, which descends from the mountains, and washing the town-walls on the west side, falls into the sea, after having filled some canals for the use of the inhabitants. There is a stone-bridge of three arches over it, by which those who come from Provence enter the city. The channel of it is very broad, but generally dry in many places; the water (as in the Var) dividing itself into several small streams. The Paglion being fed by melted snow and rain in the mountains, is quite dry in summer; but it is sometimes swelled by sudden rains to a very formidable torrent. This was the case in the year 1744,[1] when the French and Spanish armies attacked eighteen Piedmontese battalions, which were posted on the side of Montalban. The assailants were repulsed with the loss of four thousand men, some hundreds of whom perished in repassing the Paglion, which had swelled to a surprising degree during the battle, in consequence of a heavy continued rain. This rain was of great service to the Piedmontese, as it prevented one half of the enemy from passing the river to sustain the other. Five hundred were taken prisoners: but the Piedmontese, foreseeing they should be surrounded next day by the French, who had penetrated behind them, by a pass in the mountains, retired in the night. Being received on board the English fleet, which lay at Villa Franca, they were conveyed to Oneglia. In examining the bodies of those that were killed in the battle, the inhabitants of Nice perceived, that a great number of the Spanish soldiers were circumcised; a circumstance, from which they concluded, that a great many Jews engage in the service of his Catholic majesty. I am of a different opinion. The Jews are the least of any people that I know, addicted to a military life. I rather imagine they were of the Moorish race, who have subsisted in Spain, since the expulsion of their brethren; and though they conform externally to the rites of the Catholic religion, still retain in private their attachment to the law of Mahomet.

The city of Nice is built in form of an irregular isosceles triangle, the base of which fronts the sea. On the west side it is surrounded by a wall and rampart; on the east, it is over-hung by a rock, on which we see the ruins of an old castle, which, before the invention of artillery, was counted impregnable. It was taken and dismantled by marechal Catinat,[2] in the time of Victor Amadæus, the father of his Sardinian majesty.[3] It was afterwards finally demolished by the duke of Berwick towards the latter end of queen Anne's war.[4] To repair it would be a very unnecessary expence, as it is commanded by Montalban, and several other eminences.

The town of Nice is altogether indefensible, and therefore without fortifications. There are only two iron guns upon a bastion that fronts the beach; and here the French had formed a considerable battery against the English cruisers, in the war of 1744, when the mareschal duke de Belleisle[5] had his head quarters at Nice. This little town, situated in the bay of Antibes, is almost equidistant from Marseilles, Turin, and Genoa, the first and last being about thirty leagues from hence by sea; and the capital of Piedmont at the same distance to the northward, over the mountains. It lies exactly opposite to Capo di Ferro, on the coast of Barbary; and the islands of Sardinia and Corsica are laid down about two degrees to the eastward, almost exactly in a line with Genoa. This little town, hardly a mile in circumference, is said to contain twelve thousand inhabitants. The streets are narrow; the houses are built of stone, and the windows in general are fitted with paper instead of glass. This expedient would not answer in a country subject to rain and storms; but here, where there is very little of either, the paper lozenges answer tolerably well. The bourgeois, however, begin to have their houses sashed with glass. Between the town-wall and the sea, the fishermen haul up their boats upon the open beach; but on the other side of the rock, where the castle stood, is the port or harbour of Nice, upon which some money has been expended. It is a small basin, defended to seaward by a mole of free-stone, which is much better contrived than executed: for the sea has already made three breaches in it; and in all probability, in another winter, the extremity of it will be carried quite away. It would require the talents of a very skilful architect to lay the foundation of a good mole, on an open beach like this, exposed to the swell of the whole Mediterranean, without any island or rock in the offing, to break the force of the waves. Besides, the shore is bold, and the bottom foul. There are seventeen feet of water in the basin, sufficient to float vessels of one hundred and fifty ton; and this is chiefly supplied by a small stream of very fine water; another great convenience for shipping. On the side of the mole, there is a constant guard of soldiers, and a battery of seven cannon, pointing to the sea. On the other side, there is a curious manufacture for twisting or reeling silk; a tavern, a coffee-house, and several other buildings, for the convenience of the sea-faring people. Without the harbour is a lazarette, where persons coming from infected places, are obliged to perform quarantine. The harbour has been declared a free-port, and it is generally full of tartanes, polacres,[6] and other small vessels, that come from Sardinia, Ivica, Italy, and Spain, loaded with salt, wine, and other commodities; but here is no trade of any great consequence.

The city of Nice is provided with a senate, which administers justice under the auspices of an avocat-general, sent hither by the king. The internal œconomy of the town is managed by four consuls; one for the noblesse, another for the merchants, a third for the bourgeois, and a fourth for the peasants. These are chosen annually from the town-council. They keep the streets and markets in order, and superintend the public works. There is also an intendant, who takes care of his majesty's revenue: but there is a discretionary power lodged in the person of the commandant, who is always an officer of rank in the service, and has under his immediate command the regiment which is here in garrison. That which is here now is a Swiss battalion, of which the king has five or six in his service.[7] There is likewise a regiment of militia, which is exercised once a year. But of all these particulars, I shall speak more fully on another occasion.

When I stand upon the rampart, and look round me, I can scarce help thinking myself inchanted. The small extent of country which I see, is all cultivated like a garden. Indeed, the plain presents nothing but gardens, full of green trees, loaded with oranges, lemons, citrons, and bergamots, which make a delightful appearance. If you examine them more nearly, you will find plantations of green pease ready to gather; all sorts of sallading, and pot-herbs, in perfection; and plats of roses, carnations, ranunculas, anemonies, and daffodils, blowing in full glory, with such beauty, vigour, and perfume, as no flower in England ever exhibited.

I must tell you, that presents of carnations are sent from hence, in the winter, to Turin and Paris; nay, sometimes as far as London, by the post. They are packed up in a wooden box, without any sort of preparation, one pressed upon another: the person who receives them, cuts off a little bit of the stalk, and steeps them for two hours in vinegar and water, when they recover their full bloom and beauty. Then he places them in water-bottles, in an apartment where they are screened from the severities of the weather; and they will continue fresh and unfaded, the best part of a month.

Amidst the plantations in the neighbourhood of Nice, appear a vast number of white *bastides*, or country-houses, which make a dazzling shew. Some few of these are good villas, belonging to the noblesse of this county; and even some of the bourgeois are provided with pretty lodgeable *cassines*; but in general, they are the habitations of the peasants, and contain nothing but misery and vermin. They are all built square; and, being whitened with lime or plaister, contribute greatly to the richness of the view. The hills are shaded to the tops with olive-trees, which are always green; and those hills are over-topped by more distant mountains, covered with snow. When I turn myself towards the sea, the view is bounded by the horizon; yet, in a clear morning, one can perceive the high lands of Corsica. On the right hand, it is terminated by Antibes, and the mountain of Esterelles, which I described in my last. As for the weather, you will conclude, from what I have said of the oranges, flowers, &c. that it must be wonderfully mild and serene: but of the climate, I shall speak hereafter. Let me only observe, *en passant*, that the houses in general have no chimnies, but in their kitchens; and that many people, even of condition, at Nice, have no fire in their chambers, during the whole winter. When the weather happens to be a little more sharp than usual, they warm their apartments with a *brasiere* or pan of charcoal.

Though Nice itself retains few marks of antient splendor, there are considerable monuments of antiquity in its neighbourhood. About two short miles from the town, upon the summit of a pretty high hill, we find the ruins of the antient city Cemenelion, now called Cimia,[8] which was once the metropolis of the Maritime Alps, and the seat of a Roman president. With respect to situation, nothing could be more agreeable or salubrious. It stood upon the gentle ascent and summit of a hill, fronting the Mediterranean; from the shore of which, it is distant about half a league; and, on the other side, it overlooked a bottom, or narrow vale, through which the Paglion (antiently called Paulo) runs towards the walls of Nice. It was inhabited by a people, whom Ptolomy and Pliny[9] call the *Vedantij*: but these were undoubtedly mixed with a Roman colony, as appears by the monuments which still remain; I mean the ruins of an amphitheatre, a temple of Apollo, baths, aqueducts, sepulchral, and other stones, with inscriptions, and a great number of medals, which the peasants have found by accident, in digging and labouring the vineyards and cornfields, which now cover the ground where the city stood. Touching this city, very little is to be learned from the antient historians: but that it was the seat of a Roman præses,[10] is proved by the two following inscriptions, which are still extant.

## LETTER XIII.

P. AELIO. SEVERINO.
V. E. P.
PRAESIDI. OPTIMO.
ORDO. CEMEN.
PATRONO.

By the Senate of *Cemenelion* Dedicated to his Excellency P. Ælius Severinus, the best of Governors and Patrons.

This is now in the possession of the count de Gubernatis,[11] who has a country-house upon the spot. The other, found near the same place, is in praise of the præses Marcus Aurelius Masculus.

M. AVRELIO. MASCVLO.
V. E.
OB. EXIMIAM. PRAESIDATVS
EIVS. INTEGRITATEM. ET
EGREGIAM. AD OMNES HOMINES
MANSVETVDINEM. ET. VRGENTIS
ANNONAE. SINCERAM. PRAEBITIONEM.
AC. MVNIFICENTIAM. ET. QVOD. AQVAE
VSVM. VETVSTATE. LAPSVM. REQVI-
SITVM. AC. REPERTVM. SAECVLI
FELICITATE. CVRSVI. PRISTINO
REDDIDERIT.
COLLEG. III.
QVIB. EX. SCC. P. EST
PATRONO. DIGNISS.

Inscribed by the three Corporations under the authority of the Senate, to their most worthy Patron, his Excellency *M. Aurelius Masculus*, in testimony of their gratitude for the blessings of his incorruptible administration, his wonderfull affability to all without distinction, his generous distribution of corn in time of dearth, his munificence in repairing the ruinous aqueduct, in searching for, discovering and restoring the water to its former course for the benefit of the community.

This president well deserved such a mark of respect from a people whom he had assisted in two such essential articles, as their corn and their water. You know, the præses of a Roman province had the *jus figendi clavi*, the right to drive a nail in the Kalendar, the privilege of wearing the *latus clavus*, or broad studs on his garment, the *gladius, infula, prætexta purpura, & annulus aureus*, the sword, diadem, purple robe, and gold ring: he had his *vasa, vehicula, apparitores, Scipio eburneus, & sella curulis*, his kettle drums, chariots, pursuivants, ivory staff and chair of state. I know the kettle drum is a modern invention, but the *vasa militari modo conclamata*, was something analogous.

I shall give you one more sepulchral inscription on a marble, which is now placed over the gate of the church belonging to the convent of St. Pont, a venerable building, which stands at the bottom of the hill, fronting the north side of the town of Nice. This St. Pont, or Pontius, was a Roman convert to Christianity, who suffered martyrdom at Cemene-lion in the year 261, during the reigns of the emperors Valerian and Gallienus.[12] The legends recount some ridiculous miracles wrought in favour of this saint, both before and after his death.[13] Charles V. emperor of Germany and king of Spain,[14] caused this monastery to be built on the spot where Pontius suffered decapitation. But to return to the inscription: it appears in these words.

M. M. A.
FLAVIAE. BASILLAE. CONIVG. CARISSIM.
DOM. ROMA. MIRAE. ERGA. MARITVM. AMORIS.
ADQ. CASTITAT. FAEMINAE. QVAE VIXIT
ANN. XXXV. M. III. DIEB. XII. AVRELIVS
RHODISMANVS. AVG. LIB. COMMEM. ALP.
MART. ET. AVRELIA. ROMVLA. FILII.
IMPATIENTISSIM. DOLOR. EIVS. ADFLICTI
ADQ. DESOLATI. CARISSIM. AC MERENT. FERET.
FEC. ET. DED.

Freely consecrated by *Aurelius Rhodismanus* the Emperor's Freedman, to the much honoured memory of his dear Consort *Flavia Aurelia* of *Rome*, a woman equally distinguished by her unblemished vertue and conjugal affection. His children *Martial*, and *Aurelia Romula* deeply affected and distressed by the violence of his grief, erected and dedicated a monument to their dear, deserving parent.*

The amphitheatre of Cemenelion is but very small, compared to that of Nismes. The arena is ploughed up, and bears corn: some of the seats remain, and part of two opposite porticos; but all the columns, and the external façade of the building, are taken away; so that it is impossible to judge of the architecture: all we can perceive is, that it was built in an oval form. About one hundred paces from the amphitheatre stood an antient temple, supposed to have been dedicated to Apollo. The original roof is demolished, as well as the portico; the vestiges of which may still be traced. The part called the Basilica, and about one half of the Cella Sanctior, remain, and are converted into the dwelling-house and stable of the peasant who takes care of the count de Gubernatis's garden, in which this monument stands. In the Cella Sanctior, I found a lean cow, a he-goat, and a jack-ass; the very same conjunction of animals which I had seen drawing a plough in Burgundy. Several mutilated statues have been dug up from the ruins of this temple; and a great number of medals have been found in the different vineyards which now occupy the space upon which stood the antient city of Cemenelion. These were of gold, silver, and brass. Many of them were presented to Charles Emanuel I. duke of Savoy.[15] The prince of Monaco has a good number of them in his collection; and the rest are in private hands. The peasants, in digging, have likewise found many urns, lachrymatories,[16] and sepulchral stones, with epitaphs, which are now dispersed among different convents and private houses. All this ground is a rich mine of antiquities, which, if properly worked, would produce a great number of valuable curiosities. Just by the temple of Apollo were the ruins of a bath, composed of great blocks of marble, which have been taken away for the purposes of modern building. In all probability, many other noble monuments of this city have been dilapidated by the same barbarous œconomy. There are some subterranean vaults, through which the water was conducted to this bath, still extant in the garden of the count

---

*N.B. I don't pretend to translate these inscriptions literally, because I am doubtfull about the meaning of some abbreviations.

de Gubernatis. Of the aqueduct that conveyed water to the town, I can say very little, but that it was scooped through a mountain: that this subterranean passage was discovered some years ago, by removing the rubbish which choaked it up: that the people penetrating a considerable way, by the help of lighted torches, found a very plentiful stream of water flowing in an aqueduct, as high as an ordinary man, arched over head, and lined with a sort of cement. They could not, however, trace this stream to its source; and it is again stopped up with earth and rubbish. There is not a soul in this country, who has either spirit or understanding to conduct an inquiry of this kind. Hard by the amphitheatre is a convent of Recolets, built in a very romantic situation, on the brink of a precipice. On one side of their garden, they ascend to a kind of esplanade, which they say was part of the citadel of Cemenelion. They have planted it with cypress-trees, and flowering-shrubs. One of the monks told me, that it is vaulted below, as they can plainly perceive by the sound of their instruments used in houghing the ground. A very small expence would bring the secrets of this cavern to light. They have nothing to do, but to make a breach in the wall, which appears uncovered towards the garden.

The city of Cemenelion was first sacked by the Longobards,[17] who made an irruption into Provence, under their king Alboinus,[18] about the middle of the sixth century. It was afterwards totally destroyed by the Saracens, who, at different times, ravaged this whole coast. The remains of the people are supposed to have changed their habitation, and formed a coalition with the inhabitants of Nice.

What further I have to say of Nice, you shall know in good time; at present, I have nothing to add, but what you very well know, that I am always your affectionate humble servant.

*Nice, January 20,* 1764.

DEAR SIR,

Last Sunday I crossed Montalban on horseback, with some Swiss officers, on a visit to our consul, Mr. B——d,[1] who lives at Ville Franche, about half a league from Nice. It is a small town, built upon the side of a rock, at the bottom of the harbour, which is a fine basin, surrounded with hills on every side, except to the south, where it lies open to the sea. If there was a small island in the mouth of it, to break off the force of the waves, when the wind is southerly, it would be one of the finest harbours in the world; for the ground is exceeding good for anchorage: there is a sufficient depth of water, and room enough for the whole navy of England. On the right hand, as you enter the port, there is an elegant fanal, or light-house, kept in good repair: but in all the charts of this coast which I have seen, this lanthorn is laid down to the westward of the harbour; an error equally absurd and dangerous, as it may mislead the navigator, and induce him to run his ship among the rocks, to the eastward of the light-house, where it would undoubtedly perish. Opposite to the mouth of the harbour is the fort, which can be of no service, but in defending the shipping and the town by sea; for, by land, it is commanded by Montalban, and all the hills in the neighbourhood. In the war of 1744,[2] it was taken and re-taken. At present, it is in tolerable good repair. On the left of the fort, is the basin for the gallies, with a kind of dock, in which they are built, and occasionally laid up to be refitted. This basin is formed by a pretty stone mole; and here his Sardinian majesty's two gallies lie perfectly secure, moored with their sterns close up to the jetté. I went on board one of these vessels, and saw about two hundred miserable wretches, chained to the banks on which they sit and row, when the galley is at sea. This is a sight which a British subject, sensible of the blessing he enjoys, cannot behold without horror and compassion. Not but that if we consider the nature of the case, with coolness and deliberation, we must acknowledge the justice, and even sagacity, of employing for the service of the public, those malefactors who have forfeited their title to the privileges of the community. Among the slaves at Ville Franche is a Piedmontese count, condemned to the gallies for life, in consequence of having been convicted of forgery. He is permitted to live on shore; and gets money by employing the other slaves to knit stockings for sale. He appears always in the Turkish habit, and is in a fair way of raising a better fortune than that which he has forfeited.

It is a great pity, however, and a manifest outrage against the law of nations, as well as of humanity, to mix with those banditti, the Moorish and Turkish prisoners who are taken in the prosecution of open war. It is certainly no justification of this barbarous practice, that the Christian prisoners are treated as cruelly at Tunis and Algiers. It would be for the honour of Christendom, to set an example of generosity to the Turks; and, if they would not follow it, to join their naval forces, and extirpate at once those nests of pirates, who have so long infested the Mediterranean. Certainly, nothing can be more shameful, than the treaties which France and the Maritime Powers have concluded with those barbarians. They supply them with artillery, arms, and ammunition, to disturb their neighbours. They even pay them a sort of tribute, under the denomination of presents; and often put up with insults tamely, for the sordid consideration of a little gain in the way of commerce. They know that Spain, Sardinia, and almost all the Catholic powers in the Mediterranean, Adriatic, and Levant, are at perpetual war with those Mahometans; that while Algiers, Tunis, and Sallee,[3] maintain armed cruisers at sea, those Christian powers will not run the risque of trading in their own bottoms,[4] but rather employ as carriers the maritime nations, who are at peace with the infidels. It is for our share of this advantage, that we cultivate the piratical States of Barbary, and meanly purchase passports of them, thus acknowledging them masters of the Mediterranean.

The Sardinian gallies are mounted each with five-and-twenty oars, and six guns, six-pounders, of a side, and a large piece of artillery a midships, pointing a-head, which (so far as I am able to judge) can never be used point-blank, without demolishing the head or prow of the galley. The accommodation on board for the officers is wretched. There is a paltry cabin in the poop for the commander; but all the other officers lie below the slaves, in a dungeon, where they have neither light, air, nor any degree of quiet; half suffocated by the heat of the place; tormented by fleas, bugs, and lice; and disturbed by the incessant noise over head. The slaves lie upon the naked banks, without any other covering than a tilt.[5] This, however, is no great hardship, in a climate where there is scarce any winter. They are fed with a very scanty allowance of bread, and about fourteen beans a day; and twice a week they have a little rice, or cheese: but most of them, while they are in harbour, knit stockings, or do some other kind of work, which enables them to make some addition to this wretched allowance. When they happen to be at sea in bad weather, their situation is truly deplorable. Every wave breaks over the vessel, and not only keeps them continually wet, but comes with such force, that they are dashed against the banks with surprising violence: sometimes their limbs are broke, and sometimes their brains dashed out. It is impossible (they say) to keep such a number of desperate people under any regular command, without exercising such severities as must shock humanity. It is almost equally impossible to maintain any tolerable degree of cleanliness, where such a number of wretches are crouded together without conveniences, or even the necessaries of life. They are ordered twice a week to strip, clean, and bathe themselves in the sea; but, notwithstanding all the precautions of discipline, they swarm with vermin, and the vessel smells like an hospital, or crouded jail. They seem, nevertheless, quite insensible of their misery, like so many convicts in Newgate: they laugh and sing, and swear, and get drunk when they can. When you enter by the stern, you are welcomed by a band of musick selected from the slaves; and these expect a gratification. If you walk forwards, you must take care of your pockets. You will be accosted by one or other of the slaves, with a brush and blacking-ball for cleaning your shoes; and if you undergo this operation, it is ten to one but your pocket is picked. If you decline his service, and keep aloof, you will find it almost impossible to avoid a colony of vermin, which these fellows have a very dexterous method of conveying to strangers. Some of the Turkish prisoners, whose ransom or exchange is expected, are allowed to go ashore, under proper inspection; and those *forçats*,[6] who have served the best part of the time for which they were condemned, are employed in public works, under a guard of soldiers. At the harbour of Nice, they are hired by ship-masters to bring ballast, and have a small proportion of what they earn, for their own use: the rest belongs to the king. They are distinguished by an iron shackle about one of their legs. The road from Nice to Ville Franche is scarce passable on horseback: a circumstance the more extraordinary, as those slaves, in the space of two or three months, might even make it fit for a carriage, and the king would not be one farthing out of pocket, for they are quite idle the greatest part of the year.

The gallies go to sea only in the summer. In tempestuous weather, they could not live out of port. Indeed, they are good for nothing but in smooth water, during a calm, when, by dint of rowing, they make good way. The king of Sardinia is so sensible of their inutility, that he intends to let his gallies rot; and, in lieu of them, has purchased two large frigates in England, one of fifty, and another of thirty guns, which are now in the harbour of Ville Franche.[7] He has also procured an English officer, one Mr. A——,[8] who is second in command on board of one of them, and has the title of captain *consulteur*, that is, instructor to the first captain, the marquis de M——i,[9] who knows as little of seamanship as I do of Arabic.

The king, it is said, intends to have two or three more frigates, and then he will be more than a match for the Barbary corsairs, provided care be taken to man his fleet in a proper manner: but this will never be done, unless he invites foreigners into his service, officers as well as seamen; for his own dominions produce neither at present. If he is really determined to make the most of the maritime situation of his dominions, as well as of his alliance with Great-Britain, he ought to supply his ships with English mariners, and put a British commander at the head of his fleet. He ought to erect magazines and docks at Villa Franca; or if there is not conveniency for building, he may at least have pits and wharfs for heaving down and careening;[10] and these ought to be under the direction of Englishmen, who best understand all the particulars of marine œconomy. Without all doubt, he will not be able to engage foreigners, without giving them liberal appointments; and their being engaged in his service will give umbrage to his own subjects: but, when the business is to establish a maritime power, these considerations ought to be sacrificed to reasons of public utility. Nothing can be more absurd and unreasonable, than the murmurs of the Piedmontese officers at the preferment of foreigners, who execute those things for the advantage of their country, of which they know themselves incapable. When Mr. P——n[11] was first promoted in the service of his Sardinian majesty, he met with great opposition, and numberless mortifications, from the jealousy of the Piedmontese officers, and was obliged to hazard his life in many rencounters with them, before they would be quiet. Being a man of uncommon spirit, he never suffered the least insult or affront to pass unchastised. He had repeated opportunities of signalizing his valour against the Turks; and by dint of extraordinary merit, and long services, not only attained the chief command of the gallies, with the rank of lieutenant-general, but also acquired a very considerable share of the king's favour, and was appointed commandant of Nice. His Sardinian majesty found his account more ways then one, in thus promoting Mr. P——n. He made the acquisition of an excellent officer, of tried courage and fidelity, by whose advice he conducted his marine affairs. This gentleman was perfectly well esteemed at the court of London. In the war of 1744, he lived in the utmost harmony with the British admirals who commanded our fleet in the Mediterranean. In consequence of this good understanding, a thousand occasional services were performed by the English ships, for the benefit of his master, which otherwise could not have been done, without a formal application to our ministry; in which case, the opportunities would have been lost. I know our admirals had general orders and instructions, to co-operate in all things with his Sardinian majesty; but I know, also, by experience, how little these general instructions avail, when the admiral is not cordially interested in the service. Were the king of Sardinia at present engaged with England in a new war against France, and a British squadron stationed upon this coast, as formerly, he would find a great difference in this particular. He should therefore carefully avoid having at Nice a Savoyard commandant, utterly ignorant of sea affairs; unacquainted with the true interest of his master; proud, and arbitrary; reserved to strangers, from a prejudice of national jealousy; and particularly averse to the English.[12]

With respect to the antient name of Villa Franca, there is a dispute among antiquarians. It is not at all mentioned in the *Itinerarium* of Antoninus, unless it is meant as the port. of Nice.[13] But it is more surprising, that the accurate Strabo, in describing this coast, mentions no such harbour. Some people imagine it is the Portus Herculis Monæci.[14] But this is undoubtedly what is now called Monaco; the harbour of which exactly tallies with what Strabo says of the Portus Monæci—*neque magnas, neque multas capit naves,*[15] it holds but a few vessels and those of small burthen. Ptolomy, indeed, seems to mention it under the name of Herculis Portus, different from the Portus Monæci. His words are these: *post vari ostium ad Ligustrium mare, massiliensium sunt* Nicæa, Herculis Portus, Trophæa Augusti, Monæci Portus.[16] Beyond the mouth of the *Var* upon the *Ligurian* coast, the Marsilian colonies are *Nice*, Port *Hercules*, *Trophæa* and *Monaco*. In that case, Hercules was worshipped both here and at Monaco, and gave his name to both places. But on this subject, I shall perhaps speak more fully in another letter, after I have seen the *Trophæa Augusti*, now called Tourbia, and the town of Monaco, which last is about three leagues from Nice. Here I cannot help taking notice of the following elegant description from the Pharsalia, which seems to have been intended for this very harbour.

> *Finis et Hesperiæ promoto milite varus,*
> *Quaque sub Herculeo sacratus numine Portus*
> *Urget rupe cava pelagus, non* Corus *in illum*
> *Jus habet, aut* Zephirus, *solus sua littora turbat*
> Circius, *et tuta prohibet statione Monæci.*[17]

> —The troops advanc'd as far,
> As flows th'Hesperian[18] boundary, the *Var*;

> And where the mountain scoop'd by nature's
> hands,
> The spacious Port of *Hercules* expands;
> Here the tall ships at anchor, safe remain
> Tho' *Zephyr*[19] blows, or *Caurus* sweeps the plain;
> The southern blast alone disturbs the bay;
> And to *Monaco's* safer port obstructs the way.

The present town of Villa Franca was built and settled in the thirteenth century by order of Charles II. king of the Sicilies, and count of Provence,[20] in order to defend the harbour from the descents of the Saracens, who at that time infested the coast. The inhabitants were removed hither from another town, situated on the top of a mountain in the neighbourhood, which those pirates had destroyed. Some ruins of the old town are still extant. In order to secure the harbour still more effectually, Emanual Philibert,[21] duke of Savoy, built the fort in the beginning of the last century, together with the mole where the gallies are moored. As I said before, Ville Franche is built on the face of a barren rock, washed by the sea; and there is not an acre of plain ground within a mile of it. In summer, the reflexion of the sun from the rocks must make it intolerably hot; for even at this time of the year, I walked myself into a profuse sweat, by going about a quarter of a mile to see the gallies.

Pray remember me to our friends at A——'s,[22] and believe me to be ever yours.

# LETTER XV.

MADAM,

In your favour which I received by Mr. M——l,[1] you remind me of my promise, to communicate the remarks I have still to make on the French nation; and at the same time you signify your opinion, that I am too severe in my former observations. You even hint a suspicion, that this severity is owing to some personal cause of resentment; but, I protest, I have no particular cause of animosity against any individual of that country. I have neither obligation to, nor quarrel with, any subject of France; and when I meet with a Frenchman worthy of my esteem, I can receive him into my friendship with as much cordiality, as I could feel for any fellow citizen of the same merit. I even respect the nation, for the number of great men it has produced in all arts and sciences. I respect the French officers, in particular, for their gallantry and valour; and especially for that generous humanity which they exercise towards their enemies, even amidst the horrors of war. This liberal spirit is the only circumstance of antient chivalry, which I think was worth preserving. It had formerly flourished in England, but was almost extinguished in a succession of civil wars, which are always productive of cruelty and rancour. It was Henry IV. of France,[2] (a real knight errant) who revived it in Europe. He possessed that greatness of mind, which can forgive injuries of the deepest dye: and as he had also the faculty of distinguishing characters, he found his account, in favouring with his friendship and confidence, some of those who had opposed him in the field with the most inveterate perseverance. I know not whether he did more service to mankind in general, by reviving the practice of treating his prisoners with generosity, than he prejudiced his own country by patronizing the absurd and pernicious custom of duelling, and establishing a *punto*,[3] founded in diametrical opposition to common sense and humanity.

I have often heard it observed, that a French officer is generally an agreeable companion when he is turned of fifty. Without all doubt, by that time, the fire of his vivacity, which makes him so troublesome in his youth, will be considerably abated, and in other respects, he must be improved by his experience. But there is a fundamental error in the first principles of his education, which time rather confirms than removes. Early prejudices are for the most part converted into habits of thinking; and accordingly you will find the old officers in the French service more bigotted than their juniors, to the punctilios of false honour.

A lad of a good family no sooner enters into the service, than he thinks it incumbent upon him to shew his courage in a rencontre.[4] His natural vivacity prompts him to hazard in company every thing that comes uppermost, without any respect to his seniors or betters; and ten to one but he says something, which he finds it necessary to maintain with his sword. The old officer, instead of checking his petulance, either by rebuke or silent disapprobation, seems to be pleased with his impertinence, and encourages every sally of his presumption. Should a quarrel ensue, and the parties go out, he makes no efforts to compromise the dispute; but sits with a pleasing expectation to learn the issue of the rencontre. If the young man is wounded, he kisses him with transport, extols his bravery, puts him into the hands of the surgeon, and visits him with great tenderness every day, until he is cured. If he is killed on the spot, he shrugs up his shoulders—says, *quelle dommage! c'étoit un aimable enfant! ah, patience!* what pity! he was a fine boy! it can't be helpt! and in three hours the defunct is forgotten. You know, in France, duels are forbid, on pain of death:[5] but this law is easily evaded. The person insulted walks out; the antagonist understands the hint, and follows him into the street, where they justle as if by accident, draw their swords, and one of them is either killed or disabled, before any effectual means can be used to part them. Whatever may be the issue of the combat, the magistrate takes no cognizance of it; at least, it is interpreted into an accidental rencounter, and no penalty is incurred on either side. Thus the purpose of the law is entirely defeated, by a most ridiculous and cruel connivance. The meerest trifles in conversation, a rash word, a distant hint, even a look or smile of contempt, is sufficient to produce one of these combats; but injuries of a deeper dye, such as terms of reproach, the lie direct, a blow, or even the menace of a blow, must be discussed with more formality. In any of these cases, the parties agree to meet in the dominions of another prince, where they can murder each other, without fear of punishment. An officer who is struck, or even threatened with a blow, must not be quiet, until he either kills his antagonist, or loses his own life. A friend of mine, (a Nissard) who was in the service of France, told me, that some years ago, one of their captains, in the heat of passion, struck his lieutenant. They fought immediately: the lieutenant was wounded and disarmed. As it was an affront that could not be made up, he no sooner recovered of his wounds, than he called out the captain a second time. In a word, they fought five times before the combat proved decisive; at last, the lieutenant was left dead on the spot. This was an event which sufficiently proved the absurdity of the punctilio that gave rise to it. The poor gentleman who was insulted, and outraged by the brutality of the aggressor, found himself under the necessity of giving him a further occasion to take away his life. Another adventure of the same kind happened a few years ago in this place. A French officer having threatened to strike another, a formal challenge ensued; and it being agreed that they should fight until one of them dropped, each provided himself with a couple of pioneers[6] to dig his grave on the spot. They engaged just without one of the gates of Nice, in presence of a great number of spectators, and fought with surprising fury, until the ground was drenched with their blood. At length one of them stumbled, and fell; upon which the other, who found himself mortally wounded, advancing, and dropping his point, said, "*Je te donne ce que tu m'as ôté.*" "I give thee that which thou has taken from me." So saying, he dropped dead upon the field. The other, who had been the person insulted, was so dangerously wounded, that he could not rise. Some of the spectators carried him forthwith to the beach, and putting him into a boat, conveyed him by sea to Antibes. The body of his antagonist was denied Christian burial, as he died without absolution, and every body allowed that his soul went to hell: but the gentlemen of the army declared, that he died like a man of honour. Should a man be never so well inclined to make atonement in a peaceable manner, for an insult given in the heat of passion, or in the fury of intoxication, it cannot be received. Even an involuntary trespass from ignorance, or absence of mind, must be cleansed with blood. A certain noble lord, of our country, when he was yet a commoner, on his travels, involved himself in a dilemma of this sort, at the court of Lorrain.[7] He had been riding out, and strolling along a public walk, in a brown study, with his horse-whip in his hand, perceived a caterpillar crawling on the back of a marquis, who chanced to be before him. He never thought of the *petit maitre*; but lifting up his whip, in order to kill the insect, laid it across his shoulders with a crack, that alarmed all the company in the walk. The marquis's sword was produced in a moment, and the aggressor in great hazard of his life, as he had no weapon of defence. He was no sooner waked from his reverie, than he begged pardon, and offered to make all proper concessions for what he had done through mere inadvertency. The marquis would have admitted his excuses, had there been any precedent of such an affront washed away without blood. A conclave of honour was immediately assembled; and after long disputes, they agreed that an involuntary offence, especially from *such a kind of man, d'un tel homme*, might be attoned by concessions. That you may have some idea of the small beginning, from which many gigantic quarrels arise, I shall recount one that lately happened at Lyons, as I had it from the mouth of a person who was an ear and eye-witness of the transaction. Two Frenchmen, at a public ordinary, stunned the rest of the company with their loquacity. At length one of them, with a supercilious air, asked the other's name. "I never tell my name, (said he) but in a whisper." "You may have very good reasons for keeping it secret," replied the first. "I will tell you," (resumed the other): with these words, he rose; and going round to him, pronounced, loud enough to be heard by the whole company, "*Je m'appelle Pierre Paysan; et vous êtes un impertinent*." "My name is *Peter Peasant*, and you are an impertinent fellow." So saying, he walked out: the interrogator followed him into the street, where they justled, drew their swords, and engaged. He who asked the question was run through the body; but his relations were so powerful, that the victor was obliged to fly his country. He was tried and condemned in his absence; his goods were confiscated; his wife broke her heart; his children were reduced to beggary; and he himself is now starving in exile. In England, we have not yet adopted all the implacability of the punctilio. A gentleman may be insulted even with a blow, and survive, after having once hazarded his life against the aggressor. The laws of honour in our country do not oblige him either to slay the person from whom he received the injury, or even to fight to the last drop of his own blood. One finds no examples of duels among the Romans, who were certainly as brave and as delicate in their notions of honour, as the French. Cornelius Nepos tells us, that a famous Athenian general, having a dispute with his colleague, who was of Sparta, a man of a fiery disposition, this last lifted up his cane to strike him. Had this happened to a French *petit maitre*, death must have ensued: but mark what followed. — The Athenian, far from resenting the outrage, in what is now called a gentleman-like manner, said, "Do, strike if you please; but hear me." He never dreamed of cutting the Lacedemonian's throat; but bore with his passionate temper, as the infirmity of a friend who had a thousand good qualities to overbalance that defect.[8]

I need not expatiate upon the folly and the mischief which are countenanced and promoted by the modern practice of duelling. I need not give examples of friends who have murdered each other, in obedience to this savage custom, even while their hearts were melting with mutual tenderness; nor will I particularize the instances which I myself know, of whole families ruined, of women and children made widows and orphans, of parents deprived of only sons, and of valuable lives lost to the community, by duels, which had been produced by one unguarded expression, uttered without intention of offence, in the heat of dispute and altercation. I shall not insist upon the hardship of a worthy man's being obliged to devote himself to death, because it is his misfortune to be insulted by a brute, a bully, a drunkard, or a madman: neither will I enlarge upon this side of the absurdity, which indeed amounts to a contradiction in terms; I mean the dilemma to which a gentleman in the army is reduced, when he receives an affront: if he does not challenge and fight his antagonist, he is broke with infamy by a court-martial; if he fights and kills him, he is tried by the civil power, convicted of murder, and, if the royal mercy does not interpose, he is infallibly hanged: all this, exclusive of the risque of his own life in the duel, and his conscience being burthened with the blood of a man, whom perhaps he has sacrificed to a false punctilio, even contrary to his own judgment. These are reflections which I know your own good sense will suggest, but I will make bold to propose a remedy for this gigantic evil, which seems to gain ground every day: let a court be instituted for taking cognizance of all breaches of honour, with power to punish by fine, pillory, sentence of infamy, outlawry, and exile, by virtue of an act of parliament made for this purpose; and all persons insulted, shall have recourse to this tribunal: let every man who seeks personal reparation with sword, pistol, or other instrument of death, be declared infamous, and banished the kingdom: let every man, convicted of having used a sword or pistol, or other mortal weapon, against another, either in duel or rencontre, occasioned by any previous quarrel, be subject to the same penalties: if any man is killed in a duel, let his body be hanged upon a public gibbet, for a certain time, and then given to the surgeons:[9] let his antagonist be hanged as a murderer, and dissected also; and some mark of infamy be set on the memory of both. I apprehend such regulations would put an effectual stop to the practice of duelling, which nothing but the fear of infamy can support; for I am persuaded, that no being, capable of reflection, would prosecute the trade of assassination at the risque of his own life, if this hazard was at the same time reinforced by the certain prospect of infamy and ruin. Every person of sentiment would in that case allow, that an officer, who in a duel robs a deserving woman of her husband, a number of children of their father, a family of its support, and the community of a fellow citizen, has as little merit to plead from exposing his own person, as a highwayman, or housebreaker, who every day risques his life to rob or plunder that which is not of half the importance to society. I think it was from the Buccaneers of America, that the English have learned to abolish one solecism in the practice of duelling: those adventurers decided their personal quarrels with pistols; and this improvement has been adopted in Great Britain with good success; though in France, and other parts of the continent, it is looked upon as a proof of their barbarity. It is, however, the only circumstance of duelling, which savours of common sense, as it puts all mankind upon a level, the old with the young, the weak with the strong, the unwieldy with the nimble, and the man who knows not how to hold a sword with the *spadassin*,[10] who has practised fencing from the cradle. What glory is there in a man's vanquishing an adversary over whom he has a manifest advantage? To abide the issue of a combat in this case, does not even require that moderate share of resolution which nature has indulged to her common children. Accordingly, we have seen many instances of a coward's provoking a man of honour to battle. In the reign of our second Charles, when duels flourished in all their absurdity, and the seconds fought while their principals were engaged, Villiers, duke of Buckingham, not content with having debauched the countess of Shrewsbury, and publishing her shame, took all opportunities of provoking the earl to single combat, hoping he should have an easy conquest, his lordship being a puny little creature, quiet, inoffensive, and every way unfit for such personal contests. He ridiculed him on all occasions; and at last declared in public company, that there was no glory in cuckolding Shrewsbury, who had not spirit to resent the injury. This was an insult which could not be overlooked. The earl sent him a challenge; and they agreed to fight, at Barns-Elms, in presence of two gentlemen, whom they chose for their seconds. All the four engaged at the same time: the first thrust was fatal to the earl of Shrewsbury; and his friend killed the duke's second at the same instant. Buckingham, elated with his exploit, set out immediately for the earl's seat at Cliefden, where he lay with his wife, after having boasted of the murder of her husband, whose blood he shewed her upon his sword, as a trophy of his prowess.[11] But this very duke of Buckingham was little better than a poltroon at bottom. When the gallant earl of Ossory challenged him to fight in Chelsea fields, he crossed the water to Battersea, where he pretended to wait for his lordship; and then complained to the house of lords, that Ossory had given him the rendez-vous, and did not keep his appointment. He knew the house would interpose in the quarrel, and he was not disappointed. Their lordships obliged them both to give their word of honour, that their quarrel should have no other conse-quences.[12]

I ought to make an apology for having troubled a lady with so many observations on a subject so unsuitable to the softness of the fair sex; but I know you cannot be indifferent to any thing that so nearly affects the interests of humanity, which I can safely aver have alone suggested every thing which has been said, by

Madam,

Your very humble servant.

*Nice, May 2, 1764.*

DEAR DOCTOR,

A few days ago, I rode out with two gentlemen of this country, to see a stream of water which was formerly conveyed in an aqueduct to the antient city of Cemenelion, from whence this place is distant about a mile, though separated by abrupt rocks and deep hollows, which last are here honoured with the name of vallies. The water, which is exquisitely cool, and light and pure, gushes from the middle of a rock by a hole which leads to a subterranean aqueduct carried through the middle of the mountain. This is a Roman work, and the more I considered it, appeared the more stupendous. A peasant who lives upon the spot told us, he had entered by this hole at eight in the morning, and advanced so far, that it was four in the afternoon before he came out. He said he walked in the water, through a regular canal formed of a hard stone, lined with a kind of cement, and vaulted over-head; but so high in most parts he could stand upright, yet in others, the bed of the canal was so filled with earth and stones, that he was obliged to stoop in passing. He said that there were air-holes at certain distances (and indeed I saw one of these not far from the present issue) that there were some openings and stone seats on the sides, and here and there figures of men formed of stone, with hammers and working tools in their hands. I am apt to believe the fellow romanced a little, in order to render his adventure the more marvellous: but I am certainly informed, that several persons have entered this passage, and proceeded a considerable way by the light of torches, without arriving at the source, which (if we may believe the tradition of the country) is at the distance of eight leagues from this opening; but this is altogether incredible. The stream is now called *la fontaine de muraille*, and is carefully conducted by different branches into the adjacent vineyards and gardens, for watering the ground. On the side of the same mountain, more southerly, at the distance of half a mile, there is another still more copious discharge of the same kind of water, called *la source du temple*. It was conveyed through the same kind of passage, and put to the same use as the other; and I should imagine they are both from the same source, which, though hitherto undiscovered, must be at a considerable distance, as the mountain is continued for several leagues to the westward, without exhibiting the least signs of water in any other part. But, exclusive of the subterranean conduits, both these streams must have been conveyed through aqueducts extending from hence to Cemenelion over steep rocks and deep ravines, at a prodigious expence. The water from this *source du temple*, issues from a stone building which covers the passage in the rock. It serves to turn several olive, corn, and paper mills, being conveyed through a modern aqueduct raised upon paultry arcades at the expence of the public, and afterwards is branched off in very small streams, for the benefit of this parched and barren country. The Romans were so used to bathing, that they could not exist without a great quantity of water; and this, I imagine, is one reason that induced them to spare no labour and expence in bringing it from a distance, when they had not plenty of it at home. But, besides this motive, they had another: they were so nice and delicate in their taste of water, that they took great pains to supply themselves with the purest and lightest from afar, for drinking and culinary uses, even while they had plenty of an inferior sort for their baths, and other domestic purposes. There are springs of good water on the spot where Cemenelion stood: but there is a hardness in all well-water, which quality is deposited in running a long course, especially if exposed to the influence of the sun and air. The Romans, therefore, had good reason to soften and meliorate this element, by conveying it a good length of way in open aqueducts. What was used in the baths of Cemenelion, they probably brought in leaden pipes, some of which have been dug up very lately by accident. You must know, I made a second excursion to these antient ruins, and measured the arena of the amphitheatre with packthread. It is an oval figure; the longest diameter extending to about one hundred and thirteen feet, and the shortest to eighty-eight; but I will not answer for the exactness of the measurement. In the center of it, there was a square stone, with an iron ring, to which I suppose the wild beasts were tied, to prevent their springing upon the spectators. Some of the seats remain, with two opposite entrances, consisting each of one large gate, and two lateral smaller doors, arched: there is also a considerable portion of the external wall; but no columns, or other ornaments of architecture. Hard by, in the garden of the count de Gubernatis, I saw the remains of a bath, fronting the portal of the temple, which I have described in a former letter; and here were some shafts of marble pillars, particularly a capital of the Corinthian order, beautifully cut, of white alabaster. Here the count found a large quantity of fine marble, which he has converted to various uses; and some mutilated statues, bronze as well as marble. The peasant shewed me some brass and silver medals, which he has picked up at different times in labouring the ground; together with several oblong beads of coloured glass, which were used as ear-rings by the Roman ladies; and a small seal of agate, very much defaced. Two of the medals were of Maximian[1] and Gallienus; the rest were so consumed, that I could not read the legend. You know, that on public occasions, such as games, and certain sacrifices, handfuls of medals were thrown among the people; a practice, which accounts for the great number which have been already found in this district. I saw some subterranean passages, which seemed to have been common-sewers; and a great number of old walls still standing along the brink of a precipice, which overhangs the Paglion. The peasants tell me, that they never dig above a yard in depth, without finding vaults or cavities. All the vineyards and garden-grounds, for a considerable extent, are vaulted underneath; and all the ground that produces their grapes, fruit, and garden-stuff, is no more than the crumbled lime and rubbish of old Roman buildings, mixed with manure brought from Nice. This antient town commanded a most noble prospect of the sea; but is altogether inaccessible by any kind of wheel carriage. If you make shift to climb to it on horseback, you cannot descend to the plain again, without running the risque of breaking your neck.

About seven or eight miles on the other side of Nice, are the remains of another Roman monument, which has greatly suffered from the barbarity of successive ages. It was a trophy erected by the senate of Rome, in honour of Augustus Cæsar,

when he had totally subdued all the ferocious nations of these
Maritime Alps; such as the Trumpilini, Camuni, Vennonetes,
Isnarci, Breuni,[2] &c. It stands upon the top of a mountain
which overlooks the town of Monaco, and now exhibits the
appearance of an old ruined tower. There is a description of
what it was, in an Italian manuscript,[3] by which it appears to
have been a beautiful edifice of two stories, adorned with
columns and trophies in alto relievo, with a statue of
Augustus Cæsar on the top. On one of the sides was an
inscription, some words of which are still legible, upon the
fragment of a marble found close to the old building: but the
whole is preserved in Pliny, who gives it in these words. lib.
iii. cap. 20.[4]

IMPERATORI CAESARI DIVI. F. AVG. PONT.
MAX. IMP. XIV. TRIBVNIC. POTEST. XVIII.
S. P. Q. R.
QVOD EIVS DVCTV, AVSPICIISQ. GENTES ALPINÆ
OMNES, QVÆ A MARI SVPERO AD INFERVM PERTI-
NEBANT, SVB IMPERIVM PO. RO. SVNT REDAC.
GENTES ALPINÆ DEVICTÆ. TRVMPILINI CAMV-
-NI, VENNONETES, ISNARCI, BREVNI, NAVNES,
FOCVNATES, VINDELICORVM GENTES QVATVOR,
CONSVANETES, VIRVCINATES, LICATES, CATE-
-NATES, ABISONTES, RVGVSCI, SVANETES, CA-
-LVCONES, BRIXENTES, LEPONTII, VIBERI, NAN-
TVATES, SEDVNI, VERAGRI, SALASSI, ACITAVONES
MEDVLLI, VCINI, CATVRIGES, BRIGIANI, SOGI-
-VNTII, EBRODVNTII, NEMALONES, EDENETES,
ESVBIANI, VEAMINI, GALLITÆ, TRIVLLATI,
ECTINI, VERGVNNI, EGVITVRI, NEMENTVRI,
ORATELLI, NERVSCI, VELAVNI, SVETRI.

This trophy is erected by the Senate and people of *Rome*, to
the Emperor *Cæsar Augustus*, son of the divine *Julius*, in the
fourteenth year of his imperial dignity, and in the eighteenth
of his tribunician power, because under his command and
auspices all the nations of the Alps from the Adriatic to the
Tuscan Sea, were reduced under the dominion of Rome. The
Alpine nations subdued, were the *Trumpelini* &c.

Pliny, however, is mistaken in placing this inscription on a trophy near the *Augusta prætoria*, now called *Aosta*, in Piedmont: where, indeed, there is a triumphal arch, but no inscription. This noble monument of antiquity was first of all destroyed by fire; and afterwards, in Gothic times, converted into a kind of fortification. The marbles belonging to it were either employed in adorning the church of the adjoining village,* which is still called Turbia, a corruption of Trophæa; or converted into tomb-stones, or carried off to be preserved in one or two churches of Nice. At present, the work has the appearance of a ruinous watch-tower, with Gothic battlements; and as such stands undistinguished by those who travel by sea from hence to Genoa, and other ports of Italy. I think I have now described all the antiquities in the neighbourhood of Nice, except some catacombs or caverns, dug in a rock at St. Hospice, which Busching, in his Geography,[5] has described as a strong town and sea-port, though in fact, there is not the least vestige either of town or village. It is a point of land almost opposite to the tower of Turbia, with the mountains of which it forms a bay, where there is a great and curious fishery of the tunny fish, farmed of the king of Sardinia. Upon this point there is a watch-tower still kept in repair, to give notice to the people in the neighbourhood, in case any Barbary corsairs should appear on the coast. The catacombs were in all probability dug, in former times, as places of retreat for the inhabitants upon sudden descents of the Saracens, who greatly infested these seas for several successive centuries. Many curious persons

---

* This was formerly a considerable town called Villa Martis, and pretends to the honour of having given birth to Aulus Helvius,[6] who succeeded Commodus[7] as emperor of Rome, by the name of Pertinax, which he acquired from his obstinate refusal of that dignity, when it was forced upon him by the senate. You know this man, though of very low birth, possessed many excellent qualities, and was basely murdered by the prætorian guards, at the instigation of Didius Julianus.[8] For my part, I could never read without emotion, that celebrated elogium of the senate who exclaimed after his death, *Pertinace imperante, securi viximus, neminem timuimus, patre pio, patre senatus, patre omnium bonorum*.[9] "We lived secure and were afraid of nothing under the government of *Pertinax* our affectionate father, father of the senate, father to all the children of virtue!"

have entered them and proceeded a considerable way by torch-light, without arriving at the further extremity; and the tradition of the country is, that they reach as far as the ancient city of Cemenelion; but this is an idle supposition, almost as ridiculous as that which ascribes them to the labour and ingenuity of the fairies: they consist of narrow subterranean passages, vaulted with stone and lined with cement. Here and there one finds detached apartments like small chambers, where I suppose the people remained concealed till the danger was over. Diodorus Siculus tells us, that the antient inhabitants of this country usually lived under ground. "*Ligures in terrâ cubant ut plurimum: plures ad cava saxa speluncasque ab natura factas, ubi tegantur corpora, divertunt.*"[10] "The *Ligurians* mostly lie on the bare ground; many of them lodge in natural caves and caverns where they are sheltered from the inclemency of the weather." This was likewise the custom of the Troglodytæ,[11] a people bordering upon Æthiopia, who, according to Ælian,[12] lived in subterranean caverns; from whence, indeed, they took their name τρωγλη, signifying a cavern; and Virgil, in his Georgics, thus describes the *Sarmatæ*,[13]

> "*Ipsi in defossis specubus, secura sub alta*
> *Ocia agunt terra.*"——[14]

In subterranean caves secure they lie.
Nor heed the transient seasons as they fly.

These are dry subjects; but such as the country affords. If we have not white paper, we must snow with brown. Even that which I am now scrawling may be useful, if not entertaining: it is therefore the more confidently offered by,

Dear Sir,

Yours affectionately.

*Nice, July 2, 1764.*

DEAR SIR,

Nice was originally a colony from Marseilles. You know the Phocians[1] (if we may believe Justin[2] and Polybius[3]) settled in Gaul, and built Marseilles, during the reign of Tarquinius Priscus[4] at Rome. This city flourished to such a degree, that long before the Romans were in a condition to extend their dominion, it sent forth colonies, and established them along the coast of Liguria. Of these, Nice, or Nicæa, was one of the most remarkable; so called, in all probability, from the Greek word Νιχή, signifying *Victoria*, in consequence of some important victory obtained over the Salij[5] and Ligures, who were the antient inhabitants of this country. Nice, with its mother city, being in the sequel subdued by the Romans, fell afterwards successively under the dominion of the Goths, Burgundians, and Franks, the kings of Arles, and the kings of Naples, as counts of Provence. In the year one thousand three hundred and eighty-eight, the city and county of Nice being but ill protected by the family of Durazzo, voluntarily surrendered themselves to Amadæus, surnamed the Red, duke of Savoy;[6] and since that period, they have continued as part of that potentate's dominions, except at such times as they have been over-run and possessed by the power of France, which hath always been a troublesome neighbour to this country. The castle was begun by the Arragonian counts of Provence, and afterwards enlarged by several successive dukes of Savoy, so as to be deemed impregnable, until the modern method of besieging began to take place. A fruitless attempt was made upon it in the year one thousand five hundred and forty-three, by the French and Turks in conjunction: but it was reduced several times after that period, and is now in ruins. The celebrated engineer Vauban,[7] being commanded by Louis XIV. to give in a plan for fortifying Nice, proposed, that the river Paglion should be turned into a new channel, so as to surround the town to the north, and fall into the harbour; that where the Paglion now runs to the westward of the city walls, there should be a deep ditch to be filled with sea-water; and that a fortress should be built to the westward of this fosse. These particulars might be executed at no very great expence; but, I apprehend, they would be ineffectual, as the town is commanded by every hill in the neighbourhood; and the exhalations from stagnating sea-water would infallibly render the air unwholesome. Notwithstanding the undoubted antiquity of Nice, very few monuments of that antiquity now remain. The inhabitants say, they were either destroyed by the Saracens in their successive descents upon the coast, by the barbarous nations in their repeated incursions, or used in fortifying the castle, as well as in building other edifices. The city of Cemenelion, however, was subject to the same disasters, and even entirely ruined; nevertheless, we still find remains of its antient splendor. There have been likewise a few stones found at Nice, with antient inscriptions; but there is nothing of this kind standing, unless we give the name of antiquity to a marble cross on the road to Provence, about half a mile from the city. It stands upon a pretty high pedestal with steps, under a pretty stone cupola or dome, supported by four Ionic pillars, on the spot where Charles V. emperor of Germany, Francis I. of France,[8] and pope Paul II.[9] agreed to have a conference, in order to determine all their disputes. The emperor came hither by sea, with a powerful fleet, and the French king by land, at the head of a numerous army. All the endeavours of his holiness, however, could not effect a peace; but they agreed to a truce of ten years. Mezerai affirms, that these two great princes never saw one another on this occasion; and that this shyness was owing to the management of the pope, whose private designs might have been frustrated, had they come to a personal interview.[10] In the front of the colonnade, there is a small stone, with an inscription in Latin, which is so high, and so much defaced, that I cannot read it.

In the sixteenth century there was a college erected at Nice, by Emanuel Philibert, duke of Savoy, for granting degrees to students of law; and in the year one thousand six hundred and fourteen, Charles Emanuel I. instituted the senate of Nice; consisting of a president, and a certain number of senators, who are distinguished by their purple robes, and other ensigns of authority. They administer justice, having the power of life and death, not only through the whole county of Nice, but causes are evoked from Oneglia, and some other places, to their tribunal, which is the *dernier resort*, from whence there is no appeal. The commandant, however, by virtue of his military power and unrestricted authority, takes upon him to punish individuals by imprisonment, corporal pains, and banishment, without consulting the senate, or indeed, observing any form of trial. The only redress against any unjust exercise of this absolute power, is by complaint to the king; and you know what chance a poor man has for being redressed in this manner.

With respect to religion, I may safely say, that here superstition reigns under the darkest shades of ignorance and prejudice. I think there are ten convents and three nunneries within and without the walls of Nice; and among them all, I never could hear of one man who had made any tolerable advances in any kind of human learning. All ecclesiastics are exempted from any exertion of civil power, being under the immediate protection and authority of the bishop, or his vicar. The bishop of Nice is suffragan of the archbishop of Ambrun[11] in France; and the revenues of the see amount to between five and six hundred pounds sterling. We have likewise an office of the inquisition, though I do not hear that it presumes to execute any acts of jurisdiction, without the king's special permission. All the churches are sanctuaries for all kinds of criminals, except those guilty of high treason; and the priests are extremely jealous of their privileges in this particular. They receive, with open arms, murderers, robbers, smugglers, fraudulent bankrupts, and felons of every denomination; and never give them up, until after having stipulated for their lives and liberty. I need not enlarge upon the pernicious consequences of this infamous prerogative, calculated to raise and extend the power and influence of the Roman church, on the ruins of morality and good order. I saw a fellow, who had three days before murdered his wife in the last month of pregnancy, taking the air with great composure and serenity, on the steps of a church in Florence; and nothing is more common, than to see the most execrable villains diverting themselves in the cloysters of some convents at Rome.

Nice abounds with noblesse, marquisses, counts, and barons. Of these, three or four families are really respectable: the rest are *novi homines*, sprung from Bourgeois, who have saved a little money by their different occupations, and raised themselves to the rank of noblesse by purchase. One is descended from an avocat; another from an apothecary; a third from a retailer of wine, a fourth from a dealer in anchovies; and I am told, there is actually a count at Villefranche, whose father sold macaroni in the streets. A man in this country may buy a marquisate, or a county, for the value of three or four hundred pounds sterling, and the title follows the fief: but he may purchase *lettres de noblesse* for about thirty or forty guineas. In Savoy, there are six hundred families of noblesse; the greater part of which have not above one hundred crowns a year to maintain their dignity. In the mountains of Piedmont, and even in this county of Nice, there are some representatives of very antient and noble families, reduced to the condition of common peasants; but they still retain the antient pride of their houses, and boast of the noble blood that runs in their veins. A gentleman told me, that in travelling through the mountains, he was obliged to pass a night in the cottage of one of these rusticated nobles, who called to his son in the evening, "*Chevalier, as tu donné à manger aux cochons?*" "Have you fed the hogs, Sir Knight?" This, however, is not the case with the noblesse of Nice. Two or three of them have about four or five hundred a year: the rest, in general, may have about one hundred pistoles, arising from the silk, oil, wine, and oranges, produced in their small plantations, where they have also country houses. Some few of these are well built, commodious, and agreeably situated; but, for the most part, they are miserable enough. Our noblesse, notwithstanding their origin, and the cheap rate at which their titles have been obtained, are nevertheless extremely tenacious of their privileges, very delicate in maintaining the *etiquette*, and keep at a very stately distance from the Bourgeoisie. How they live in their families, I do not choose to enquire; but, in public, Madame appears in her robe of gold, or silver stuff, with her powder and frisure, her perfumes, her paint and her patches; while Monsieur Le Comte struts about in his lace and embroidery. Rouge and fard are more peculiarly necessary in this country, where the complexion and skin are naturally swarthy and yellow. I have likewise observed, that most of the females are pot-bellied; a circumstance owing, I believe, to the great quantity of vegetable trash which they eat. All the horses, mules, asses, and cattle, which feed upon grass, have the same distension. This kind of food produces such acid juices in the stomach, as excite a perpetual sense of hunger. I have been often amazed at the voracious appetites of these people. You must not expect that I should describe the tables and the hospitality of our Nissard gentry. Our consul, who is a very honest man, told me, he had lived four and thirty years in the country, without having once eat or drank in any of their houses.

The noblesse of Nice cannot leave the country without express leave from the king; and this leave, when obtained, is for a limited time, which they dare not exceed, on pain of incurring his majesty's displeasure. They must, therefore, endeavour to find amusements at home; and this, I apprehend, would be no easy task for people of an active spirit or restless disposition. True it is, the religion of the country supplies a never-failing fund of pastime to those who have any relish for devotion; and this is here a prevailing taste. We have had transient visits of a puppet-shew, strolling musicians, and rope-dancers; but they did not like their quarters, and decamped without beat of drum. In the summer, about eight or nine at night, part of the noblesse may be seen assembled in a place called the Parc; which is, indeed, a sort of a street formed by a row of very paltry houses on one side, and on the other, by part of the town-wall, which screens it from a prospect of the sea, the only object that could render it agreeable. Here you may perceive the noblesse stretched in pairs upon logs of wood, like so many seals upon the rocks by moon-light, each dame with her *cicisbeo*: for, you must understand, this Italian fashion prevails at Nice among all ranks of people; and there is not such a passion as jealousy known. The husband and the *cicisbeo* live together as sworn brothers; and the wife and the mistress embrace each other with marks of the warmest affection.[12] I do not choose to enter into particulars. I cannot open the scandalous chronicle of Nice, without hazard of contamination. With respect to delicacy and decorum, you must peruse dean Swift's description of the Yahoos,[13] and then you will have some idea of the *porcheria*,[14] that distinguishes the gallantry of Nice. But the Parc is not the only place of public resort for our noblesse in a summer's evening. Just without one of our gates, you will find them seated in ditches on the highway side, serenaded with the croaking of frogs, and the bells and braying of mules and asses continually passing in a perpetual cloud of dust. Besides these amusements, there is a public *conversazione* every evening at the commandant's house called the Government, where those noble personages play at cards for farthings. In carnival time, there is also, at this same government, a ball twice or thrice a week, carried on by subscription. At this assembly every person, without distinction, is permitted to dance in masquerade: but, after dancing, they are obliged to unmask, and if Bourgeois, to retire. No individual can give a ball, without obtaining a permission and guard of the commandant; and then his house is open to all masques, without distinction, who are provided with tickets, which tickets are sold by the commandant's secretary, at five sols a-piece, and delivered to the guard at the door. If I have a mind to entertain my particular friends, I cannot have more than a couple of violins; and, in that case, it is called a *conversazione*.

Though the king of Sardinia takes all opportunities to distinguish the subjects of Great-Britain with particular marks of respect, I have seen enough to be convinced, that our nation is looked upon with an evil eye by the people of Nice; and this arises partly from religious prejudices, and partly from envy, occasioned by a ridiculous notion of our superior wealth. For my own part, I owe them nothing on the score of civilities; and therefore, I shall say nothing more on the subject, lest I should be tempted to deviate from that temperance and impartiality which I would fain hope have hitherto characterised the remarks of,

Dear Sir,
Your faithful humble servant.

# LETTER XVIII.

*Nice, September 2, 1764.*

DEAR DOCTOR,

I wrote in May to Mr. B——[1] at Geneva, and gave him what information he desired to have, touching the conveniences of Nice. I shall now enter into the same detail, for the benefit of such of your friends or patients, as may have occasion to try this climate.

The journey from Calais to Nice, of four persons in a coach, or two post-chaises, with a servant on horseback, travelling post, may be performed with ease, for about one hundred and twenty pounds, including every expence. Either at Calais or at Paris, you will always find a travelling coach or berline, which you may buy for thirty or forty guineas, and this will serve very well to reconvey you to your own country.

In the town of Nice, you will find no ready-furnished lodgings for a whole family. Just without one of the gates, there are two houses to be let, ready-furnished, for about five loui'dores per month. As for the country houses in this neighbourhood, they are damp in winter, and generally without chimneys; and in summer they are rendered uninhabitable by the heat and the vermin. If you hire a tenement in Nice, you must take it for a year certain; and this will cost you about twenty pounds sterling. For this price, I have a ground floor paved with brick, consisting of a kitchen, two large halls, a couple of good rooms with chimneys, three large closets that serve for bed-chambers, and dressing-rooms, a butler's room, and three apartments for servants, lumber or stores, to which we ascend by narrow wooden stairs. I have likewise two small gardens, well stocked with oranges, lemons, peaches, figs, grapes, corinths, sallad, and pot-herbs. It is supplied with a draw-well of good water, and there is another in the vestibule of the house, which is cool, large, and magnificent. You may hire furniture for such a tenement, for about two guineas a month: but I chose rather to buy what was necessary; and this cost me about sixty pounds. I suppose it will fetch me about half the money when I leave the place. It is very difficult to find a tolerable cook at

151

Nice. A common maid, who serves the people of the country, for three or four livres a month, will not live with an English family under eight or ten. They are all slovenly, slothful, and unconscionable cheats. The markets at Nice are tolerably well supplied. Their beef, which comes from Piedmont, is pretty good, and we have it all the year. In the winter, we have likewise excellent pork, and delicate lamb; but the mutton is indifferent. Piedmont, also, affords us delicious capons, fed with maiz; and this country produces excellent turkeys, but very few geese. Chickens and pullets are extremely meagre. I have tried to fatten them, without success. In summer they are subject to the pip, and die in great numbers. Autumn and winter are the seasons for game; hares, partridges, quails, wild-pigeons, woodcocks, snipes, thrushes, beccaficas, and ortolans.[2] Wild-boar is sometimes found in the mountains: it has a delicious taste, not unlike that of the wild hog in Jamaica;[3] and would make an excellent barbecue, about the beginning of winter, when it is in good case: but, when meagre, the head only is presented at tables. Pheasants are very scarce. As for the heath-game, I never saw but one cock, which my servant bought in the market, and brought home; but the commandant's cook came into my kitchen, and carried it off, after it was half plucked, saying, his master had company to dinner. The hares are large, plump, and juicy. The partridges are generally of the red sort; large as pullets, and of a good flavour: there are also some grey partridges in the mountains; and another sort of a white colour, that weigh four or five pounds each. Beccaficas are smaller than sparrows, but very fat, and they are generally eaten half raw. The best way of dressing them, is to stuff them into a roll, scooped of its crum; to baste them well with butter, and roast them, until they are brown and crisp. The ortolans are kept in cages, and crammed, until they die of fat, then eaten as dainties. The thrush is presented with the trail,[4] because the bird feeds on olives. They may as well eat the trail of a sheep, because it feeds on the aromatic herbs of the mountain. In the summer, we have beef, veal, and mutton, chicken, and ducks; which last are very fat, and very flabby. All the meat is tough in this season, because the excessive heat, and great number of flies, will not admit of its being kept any time after it is killed. Butter and milk, though not very delicate, we have all the year. Our tea and fine sugar come from Marseilles, at a very reasonable price.

Nice is not without variety of fish; though they are not counted so good in their kinds as those of the ocean. Soals, and flat-fish in general, are scarce. Here are some mullets, both grey and red. We sometimes see the dory, which is called *St. Pierre*; with rock-fish, bonita,[5] and mackarel. The gurnard[6] appears pretty often; and there is plenty of a kind of large whiting, which eats pretty well, but has not the delicacy of that which is caught on our coast. One of the best fish of this country, is called *le loup*,[7] about two or three pounds in weight; white, firm, and well-flavoured. Another, no-way inferior to it, is the *moustel*,[8] about the same size, of a dark-grey colour, and short, blunt snout, growing thinner and flatter from the shoulders downwards, so as to resemble a soal at the tail. This cannot be the *mustela* of the antients,[9] which is supposed to be the sea lamprey. Here too are found the *vyvre*, or, as we call it, weaver;[10] remarkable for its long, sharp spines, so dangerous to the fingers of the fishermen. We have abundance of the *sæpie*, or cuttle-fish, of which the people in this country make a delicate ragout; as also of the *polype de mer*,[11] which is an ugly animal, with long feelers, like tails, which they often wind about the legs of the fishermen. They are stewed with onions, and eat something like cow-heel. The market sometimes affords the *ecrivisse de mer*,[12] which is a lobster without claws, of a sweetish taste; and there are a few rock oysters, very small and very rank. Sometimes the fishermen find under water, pieces of a very hard cement, like plaister of Paris, which contain a kind of muscle, called *la datte*, from its resemblance to a date. These petrefactions are commonly of a triangular form, and may weigh about twelve or fifteen pounds each; and one of them may contain a dozen of these muscles, which have nothing extraordinary in the taste or flavour, though extremely curious, as found alive and juicy, in the heart of a rock, almost as hard as marble, without any visible communication with the air or water. I take it for granted, however, that the inclosing cement is porous, and admits the finer parts of the surrounding fluid. In order to reach the muscles, this cement must be broke with large hammers; and it may be truly said, the kernel is not worth the trouble of cracking the shell.* Among the fish of this country, there is a very ugly animal of the eel species, which might pass for a serpent: it is of a dusky, black colour, marked with spots of yellow, about eighteen inches, or two feet long. The Italians call it *murena*;[14] but whether it is the fish which had the same name among the antient Romans, I cannot pretend to determine. The antient murena was counted a great delicacy, and was kept in ponds for extraordinary occasions. Julius Cæsar borrowed six thousand for one entertainment: but I imagined this was the river lamprey.[15] The murena of this country is in no esteem, and only eaten by the poor people. Craw-fish and trout are rarely found in the rivers among the mountains. The sword-fish is much esteemed in Nice, and called *l'empereur*, about six or seven feet long: but I have never seen it.† They are very scarce; and when taken, are generally concealed, because the head belongs to the commandant, who has likewise the privilege of buying the best fish at a very low price. For which reason, the choice pieces are concealed by the fishermen, and sent privately to Piedmont or Genoa. But, the chief fisheries on this coast, are of the sardines, anchovies, and tunny. These are taken in small quantities all the year: but spring and summer is the season when they mostly abound. In June and July, a fleet of about fifty fishing-boats, puts to sea every evening about eight o'clock, and catch anchovies in immense quantities. One small boat sometimes takes in one night twenty-five rup,[16] amounting to six hundred weight; but it must be observed, that the pound here, as well as in other parts of Italy, consists but of twelve ounces. Anchovies, besides their making a considerable article in the commerce of Nice, are a great resource in all families. The noblesse and bourgeois sup on sallad and anchovies, which are eaten on all their meagre

---

* These are found in great plenty at *Ancona* and other parts of the *Adriatic*, where they go by the name of *Bollani*, as we are informed by *Keysler*.[13]

† Since I wrote the above letter, I have eaten several times of this fish, which is as white as the finest veal, and extremely delicate. The emperor associates with the tunny fish, and is always taken in their company.

days. The fishermen and mariners all along this coast have scarce any other food but dry bread, with a few pickled anchovies; and when the fish is eaten, they rub their crusts with the brine. Nothing can be more delicious than fresh anchovies fried in oil: I prefer them to the smelts of the Thames. I need not mention, that the sardines and anchovies are caught in nets; salted, barrelled, and exported into all the different kingdoms and states of Europe. The sardines, however, are largest and fattest in the month of September. A company of adventurers have farmed the tunny-fishery of the king, for six years; a monopoly, for which they pay about three thousand pounds sterling. They are at a very considerable expence for nets, boats, and attendance. Their nets are disposed in a very curious manner across the small bay of St. Hospice, in this neighbourhood, where the fish chiefly resort. They are never removed, except in the winter, and when they want repair: but there are avenues for the fish to enter, and pass, from one inclosure to another. There is a man in a boat, who constantly keeps watch. When he perceives they are fairly entered, he has a method for shutting all the passes, and confining the fish to one apartment of the net, which is lifted up into the boat, until the prisoners are taken and secured. The tunny-fish generally runs from fifty to one hundred weight; but some of them are much larger. They are immediately gutted, boiled, and cut in slices. The guts and head afford oil: the slices are partly dried, to be eaten occasionally with oil and vinegar, or barrelled up in oil, to be exported. It is counted a delicacy in Italy and Piedmont, and tastes not unlike sturgeon. The famous pickle of the ancients, called *garum*,[17] was made of the gills and blood of the tunny, or thynnus. There is a much more considerable fishery of it in Sardinia, where it is said to employ four hundred persons; but this belongs to the duc de St. Pierre.[18] In the neighbourhood of Villa Franca, there are people always employed in fishing for coral and sponge, which grow adhering to the rocks under water. Their methods do not savour much of ingenuity. For the coral, they lower down a swab, composed of what is called spunyarn on board our ships of war, hanging in distinct threads, and sunk by means of a great weight, which striking against the coral in its descent, disengages it from the rocks; and some of the pieces being intangled among the threads of the swab, are brought up with it above water. The sponge is got by means of a cross-stick, fitted with hooks, which being lowered down, fastens upon it, and tears it from the rocks. In some parts of the Adriatic and Archipelago, these substances are gathered by divers, who can remain five minutes below water. But I will not detain you one minute longer; though I must observe, that there is plenty of fine samphire growing along all these rocks, neglected and unknown. Adieu.

# LETTER XIX.

*Nice, October* 10, 1764.

DEAR SIR,

Before I tell you the price of provisions at Nice, it will be necessary to say something of the money. The gold coin of Sardinia consists of the doppia di Savoia, value twenty-four livres Piedmontese, about the size of a loui'dore; and the mezzo doppia, or piece of twelve livres. In silver, there is the scudo of six livres, the mezzo scudo of three; and the quarto, or pezza di trenta soldi: but all these are very scarce. We seldom see any gold and silver coin, but the loui'dore, and the six, and three-livre pieces of France; a sure sign that the French suffer by their contraband commerce with the Nissards. The coin chiefly used at market is a piece of copper silvered, that passes for seven sols and a half; and another of the same sort, value two sols and a half. They have on one side the impression of the king's head; and on the other, the arms of Savoy, with a ducal crown, inscribed with his name and titles. There are of genuine copper, pieces of one sol, stamped on one side with a cross fleuree; and on the reverse, with the king's cypher and crown, inscribed as the others: finally, there is another small copper piece, called piccalon, the sixth part of a sol, with a plain cross, and on the reverse, a slip-knot surmounted with a crown; the legend as above. The impression and legend on the gold and silver coins, are the same as those on the pieces of seven sols and a half. The livre of Piedmont consists of twenty sols, and is very near of the same value as an English shilling: ten sols, therefore, are equal to six-pence sterling.[1] Butcher's meat in general sells at Nice for three sols a pound; and veal is something dearer: but then there are but twelve ounces in the pound, which being allowed for, sixteen ounces come for something less than twopence halfpenny English. Fish commonly sells for four sols the twelve ounces, or five for the English pound; and these five are equivalent to three-pence of our money: but sometimes we are obliged to pay five, and even six sols for the Piedmontese pound of fish. A turkey that would sell for five or six shillings at the London market, costs me but three at Nice. I can buy a good capon for thirty sols, or eighteen-

157

pence; and the same price I pay for a brace of partridges, or a good hare. I can have a woodcock for twenty-four sols; but the pigeons are dearer than in London. Rabbits are very rare; and there is scarce a goose to be seen in the whole county of Nice. Wild-ducks and teal are sometimes to be had in the winter; and now I am speaking of sea-fowl, it may not be amiss to tell you what I know of the halcyon, or king's-fisher. It is a bird, though very rare in this country, about the size of a pigeon; the body brown, and the belly white: by a wonderful instinct, it makes its nest upon the surface of the sea, and lays its eggs in the month of November, when the Mediterranean is always calm and smooth as a mill-pond. The people here call them martinets, because they begin to hatch about Martinmass.[2] Their nests are sometimes seen floating near the shore, and generally become the prize of the boys, who are very alert in catching them.

You know all sea-birds are allowed by the church of Rome to be eaten on meagre days, as a kind of fish; and the monks especially do not fail to make use of this permission. Sea turtle, or tortoises, are often found at sea by the mariners, in these latitudes: but they are not the green sort, so much in request among the aldermen of London. All the Mediterranean turtle are of the kind called loggerhead, which in the West-Indies are eaten by none but hungry seamen, negroes, and the lowest class of people. One of these, weighing about two hundred pounds, was lately brought on shore by the fishermen of Nice, who found it floating asleep on the surface of the sea. The whole town was alarmed at sight of such a monster, the nature of which they could not comprehend. However, the monks, called *minims*, of St. Francisco di Paolo,[3] guided by a sure instinct, marked it as their prey, and surrounded it accordingly. The friars of other convents, not quite so hungry, crowding down to the beach, declared it should not be eaten; dropped some hints about the possibility of its being something præternatural and diabolical, and even proposed exorcisms and aspersions with holy water. The populace were divided according to their attachment to this, or that convent: a mighty clamour arose; and the police, in order to remove the cause of their contention, ordered the tortoise to be re-committed to the waves; a sentence which the Franciscans saw executed, not without sighs and lamentation. The land-turtle, or terrapin, is much better known at Nice, as being a native of this county; yet the best are brought from the island of Sardinia. The soup or *bouillon* of this animal is always prescribed here as a great restorative to consumptive patients. The bread of Nice is very indifferent, and I am persuaded very unwholsome. The flour is generally musty, and not quite free of sand. This is either owing to the particles of the mill-stone rubbed off in grinding, or to what adheres to the corn itself, in being threshed upon the common ground; for there are no threshing-floors in this country. I shall now take notice of the vegetables of Nice. In the winter, we have green pease, asparagus, artichoaks, cauliflower, beans, French beans, celery, and endive; cabbage, coleworts, radishes, turnips, carrots, betteraves, sorrel, lettuce, onions, garlic, and chalot.[4] We have potatoes from the mountains, mushrooms, champignons, and truffles. Piedmont affords white truffles, counted the most delicious in the world: they sell for about three livres the pound. The fruits of this season are pickled olives, oranges, lemons, citrons, citronelles, dried figs, grapes, apples, pears, almonds, chesnuts, walnuts, filberts, medlars, pomegranates, and a fruit called azerolles,*[5] about the size of a nutmeg, of an oblong shape, red colour, and agreeable acid taste. I might likewise add the cherry of the *laurus cerasus*, which is sold in the market; very beautiful to the eye, but insipid to the palate. In summer we have all those vegetables in perfection. There is also a kind of small courge, or gourd,[6] of which the people of the country made a very savoury ragout, with the help of eggs, cheese, and fresh anchovies. Another is made of the badenjean, which the Spaniards call berengena:[7] it is much eaten in Spain and the Levant, as well as by the Moors in Barbary.† It is about the size and shape of a hen's egg, inclosed in a cup like an acorn; when ripe, of a faint purple colour. It grows on a stalk about a foot high, with long spines

* The Italians call them *Lazerruole*.

†This fruit is called *Melanzana* in *Italy* and as much esteemed by the *Jews* in Leghorn; perhaps *Melanzana* is a corruption of *mala insana*.[8]

or prickles. The people here have different ways of slicing and dressing it, by broiling, boiling, and stewing, with other ingredients: but it is at best an insipid dish. There are some caper-bushes in this neighbourhood, which grow wild in holes of garden walls, and require no sort of cultivation: in one or two gardens, there are palm-trees; but the dates never ripen. In my register of the weather, I have marked the seasons of the principal fruits in this country. In May we have strawberries, which continue in season two or three months. These are of the wood kind; very grateful, and of a good flavour; but the scarlets and hautboys[9] are not known at Nice. In the beginning of June, and even sooner, the cherries begin to be ripe. They are a kind of bleeding hearts;[10] large, fleshy, and high flavoured, though rather too luscious. I have likewise seen a few of those we call Kentish cherries, which are much more cool, acid, and agreeable, especially in this hot climate. The cherries are succeeded by the apricots and peaches, which are all standards, and of consequence better flavoured than what we call wall-fruit. The trees, as well as almonds, grow and bear without care and cultivation, and may be seen in the open fields about Nice: but without proper culture, the fruit degenerates. The best peaches I have seen at Nice are the amberges, of a yellow hue, and oblong shape, about the size of a small lemon. Their consistence is much more solid than that of our English peaches, and their taste more delicious. Several trees of this kind I have in my own garden. Here is likewise plenty of other sorts; but no nectarines. We have little choice of plumbs. Neither do I admire the pears or apples of this country: but the most agreeable apples I ever tasted, come from Final, and are called *pomi carli*. The greatest fault I find with most fruits in this climate, is, that they are too sweet and luscious, and want that agreeable acid which is so cooling and so grateful in a hot country. This, too, is the case with our grapes, of which there is great plenty and variety, plump and juicy, and large as plumbs. Nature, however, has not neglected to provide other agreeable vegetable juices to cool the human body. During the whole summer, we have plenty of musk melons. I can buy one as large as my head for the value of an English penny: but one of the best and largest, weighing ten or twelve pounds, I can have for twelve sols, or about eight-pence sterling. From Antibes and Sardinia, we have another fruit called a water-melon, which is well known in Jamaica, and some of our other colonies. Those from Antibes are about the size of an ordinary bomb-shell: but the Sardinian and Jamaica water-melons are four times as large. The skin is green, smooth, and thin. The inside is a purple pulp, studded with broad, flat, black seeds, and impregnated with a juice the most cool, delicate, and refreshing, that can well be conceived. One would imagine the pulp itself dissolved in the stomach; for you may eat of it until you are filled up to the tongue, without feeling the least inconvenience. It is so friendly to the constitution, that in ardent inflammatory fevers, it is drank as the best emulsion. At Genoa, Florence, and Rome, it is sold in the streets, ready cut in slices; and the porters, sweating under their burthens, buy and eat them as they pass. A porter of London quenches his thirst with a draught of strong beer: a porter of Rome, or Naples, refreshes himself with a slice of water-melon, or a glass of iced-water. The one costs three half-pence; the last, half a farthing—which of them is most effectual? I am sure the men are equally pleased. It is commonly remarked, that beer strengthens as well as refreshes. But the porters of Constan-tinople, who never drink any thing stronger than water, and eat very little animal food, will lift and carry heavier burthens than any other porters in the known world. If we may believe the most respectable travellers, a Turk will carry a load of seven hundred weight, which is more (I believe) than any English porter ever attempted to carry any length of way.

Among the refreshments of these warm countries, I ought not to forget mentioning the sorbettes, which are sold in coffee-houses, and places of public resort. They are iced froth, made with juice of oranges, apricots, or peaches; very agreeable to the palate, and so extremely cold, that I was afraid to swallow them in this hot country, until I found from information and experience, that they may be taken in moderation, without any bad consequence.

Another considerable article in house-keeping is wine, which we have here good and reasonable. The wine of Tavelle in Languedoc is very near as good as Burgundy, and may be had at Nice, at the rate of six-pence a bottle. The sweet wine of St. Laurent, counted equal to that of Frontignan,[11] costs about eight or nine-pence a quart: pretty good Malaga may be had for half the money. Those who make their own wine choose the grapes from different vineyards, and have them picked, pressed, and fermented at home. That which is made by the peasants, both red and white, is generally genuine: but the wine-merchants of Nice brew and balderdash,[12] and even mix it with pigeons' dung and quick-lime. It cannot be supposed, that a stranger and sojourner should buy his own grapes, and make his own provision of wine: but he may buy it by recommendation from the peasants, for about eighteen or twenty livres the charge, consisting of eleven rup five pounds; in other words, of two hundred and eighty pounds of this country, so as to bring it for something less than three-pence a quart. The Nice wine, when mixed with water, makes an agreeable beverage. There is an inferior sort for servants, drank by the common people, which in the cabaret[13] does not cost above a penny a bottle. The people here are not so nice as the English, in the management of their wine. It is kept in flacons, or large flasks, without corks, having a little oil at top. It is not deemed the worse for having been opened a day or two before; and they expose it to the hot sun, and all kinds of weather, without hesitation. Certain it is, this treatment has little or no effect upon its taste, flavour, and transparency.

The brandy of Nice is very indifferent; and the *liqueurs* are so sweetened with coarse sugar, that they scarce retain the taste or flavour of any other ingredient.

The last article of domestic œconomy which I shall mention is fuel, or wood for firing, which I buy for eleven sols (a little more than six-pence halfpenny) a quintal,[14] consisting of one hundred and fifty pound Nice weight. The best, which is of oak, comes from Sardinia. The common sort is olive, which being cut with the sap in it, ought to be laid in during the summer; otherwise, it will make a very uncomfortable fire. In my kitchen and two chambers, I burned fifteen thousand weight of wood in four weeks, exclusive of charcoal for the kitchen stoves, and of pine-tops for lighting the fires. These last are as large as pine-apples, which they greatly resemble in shape, and to which, indeed, they give their name; and being full of turpentine, make a wonderful blaze. For the same purpose, the people of these countries use the sarments,[15] or cuttings of the vines, which they sell made up in small fascines.[16] This great consumption of wood is owing to the large fires used in roasting pieces of beef, and joints, in the English manner. The roasts of this country seldom exceed two or three pounds of meat; and their other plats are made over stove-holes. But it is now high time to conduct you from the kitchen, where you have been too long detained by

Your humble servant.

*P.S.* I have mentioned the prices of almost all the articles in house-keeping, as they are paid by the English: but exclusive of butcher's meat, I am certain the natives do not pay so much by thirty per cent. Their imposition on us, is not only a proof of their own villany and hatred, but a scandal on their government; which ought to interfere in favour of the subjects of a nation, to which they are so much bound in point of policy, as well as gratitude.

*Nice, October 22, 1764.*

SIR,

As I have nothing else to do, but to satisfy my own curiosity, and that of my friends, I obey your injunctions with pleasure; though not without some apprehension that my inquiries will afford you very little entertainment. The place where I am is of very little importance or consequence as a state or community; neither is there any thing curious or interesting in the character or œconomy of its inhabitants.

There are some few merchants in Nice, said to be in good circumstances. I know one of them, who deals to a considerable extent, and goes twice a year to London to attend the sales of the East-India company.[1] He buys up a very large quantity of muslins, and other India goods, and freights a ship in the river to transport them to Villa Franca. Some of these are sent to Swisserland; but, I believe, the greater part is smuggled into France, by virtue of counterfeit stamps, which are here used without any ceremony. Indeed, the chief commerce of this place is a contraband traffick carried on to the disadvantage of France; and I am told, that the farmers of the Levant company[2] in that kingdom find their account in conniving at it. Certain it is, a great quantity of merchandize is brought hither every week by mules from Turin and other parts in Piedmont, and afterwards conveyed to the other side of the Var, either by land or water. The mules of Piedmont are exceeding strong and hardy. One of them will carry a burthen of six hundred weight. They are easily nourished, and require no other respite from their labour, but the night's repose. They are the only carriage that can be used in crossing the mountains, being very sure-footed: and it is observed, that in choosing their steps, they always march upon the brink of the precipice. You must let them take their own way; otherwise you will be in danger of losing your life; for they are obstinate, even to desperation. It is very dangerous for a person on horseback to meet those animals: they have such an aversion to horses, that they will attack them with incredible fury, so as even to tear them and their riders in pieces; and the best method for avoiding this fate, is to clap spurs to your beast, and seek your safety in flight. I have been more than once obliged to fly before them. They always give you warning, by raising a hideous braying as soon as they perceive the horse at a distance. The mules of Provence are not so mischievous, because they are more used to the sight and society of horses: but those of Piedmont are by far the largest and the strongest I have seen.

Some very feasible schemes for improving the commerce of Nice have been presented to the ministry of Turin; but hitherto without success. The English import annually between two and three thousand bales of raw silk, the growth of Piedmont; and this is embarked either at Genoa or Leghorn. We likewise take a considerable quantity of fruit and oil at Oneglia, St. Remo, and other places in this neighbourhood. All these commodities might be embarked at a smaller expence at Nice, which is a free port, where no duties are paid by the exporter. Besides, the county of Nice itself produces a considerable quantity of hemp, oranges, lemons, and very good oil and anchovies, with some silk and wine, which last is better than that of Languedoc, and far excels the port drank in England. This wine is of a strong body, a good flavour, keeps very well, and improves by sea-carriage. I am told, that some of the wine-merchants here transport French wine from Languedoc and Provence, and enter it in England as the produce of Nice or Italy. If the merchants of Nice would establish magazines of raw silk, oil, wine, &c. at Nice; and their correspondents at London send hither ships at stated periods, laden with India goods, hard-ware, and other manufactures of England, which would find a vent in this country, in Piedmont, Savoy, Swisserland, and Provence, then the commerce of this town would flourish, more especially if the king would lay out the necessary expence for rendering the harbour more commodious and secure. But this is not a matter of very great consequence, as there is an excellent harbour at Ville Franche, which is not more than a mile and a half from that of Nice. But the great objection to the improvement of commerce at Nice, is the want of money, industry, and character. The natives themselves are in general such dirty knaves, that no foreigners will trust them in the way of trade. They have been known to fill their oil-casks half full of water, and their anchovy-barrels with stinking heads of that fish, in order to cheat their correspondents.

The shopkeepers of this place are generally poor, greedy, and over-reaching. Many of them are bankrupts of Marseilles, Genoa, and other countries, who have fled from their creditors to Nice; which, being a free-port, affords an asylum to foreign cheats and sharpers of every denomination. Here is likewise a pretty considerable number of Jews, who live together in a street appropriated for their use, which is shut up every night.[3] They act as brokers; but are generally poor, and deal in frippery, remnants, old cloaths, and old household furniture. There is another branch of traffick engrossed by the monks. Some convents have such a number of masses bequeathed to them, that they find it impossible to execute the will of the donors. In this case, they agree by the lump with the friars of poorer convents, who say the masses for less money than has been allowed by the defunct, and their employers pocket the difference: for example; my grandfather bequeaths a sum of money to a certain convent, to have such a number of masses said for the repose of his soul, at the price of ten sols each; and this convent, not having time to perform them, bargains with the friars of another to say them for six sols a-piece, so that they gain four sols upon every mass; for it matters not to the soul of the deceased where they are said, so they be properly authenticated. A poor gentleman of Nice, who piques himself much on the noble blood that runs in his veins, though he has not a pair of whole breeches to wear, complained to me, that his great grandmother had founded a perpetual mass for the repose of her own soul, at the rate of fifteen sols (nine-pence English) a day; which indeed was all that now remained of the family estate. He said, what made the hardship the greater on him, she had been dead above fifty years, and in all probability her soul had got out of purgatory long ago; therefore the continuance of the mass was an unnecessary expence. I told him, I thought in such a case, the defunct should appear before the civil magistrate, and make affidavit of her being at peace, for the advantage of the family. He mused a little, and shrugging up his shoulders, replied, that where the interest of the church was at stake, he did not believe a spirit's declaration would be held legal evidence. In some parts of France, the curé of the parish, on All Soul's day,[4] which is called *le jour des morts*, says a *libera domine* for two sols, at every grave in the burying-ground, for the release of the soul whose body is there interred.

The artisans of Nice are very lazy, very needy, very aukward, and void of all ingenuity. The price of their labour is very near as high as at London or Paris. Rather than work for moderate profit, arising from constant employment, which would comfortably maintain them and their families, they choose to starve at home, to lounge about the ramparts, bask themselves in the sun, or play at bowls in the streets from morning 'till night.

The lowest class of people consists of fishermen, day labourers, porters, and peasants: these last are distributed chiefly in the small cassines in the neighbourhood of the city, and are said to amount to twelve thousand. They are employed in labouring the ground, and have all the outward signs of extreme misery. They are all diminutive, meagre, withered, dirty, and half naked; in their complexions, not barely swarthy, but as black as Moors; and I believe many of them are descendants of that people. They are very hard favoured; and their women in general have the coarsest features I have ever seen: it must be owned, however, they have the finest teeth in the world. The nourishment of those poor creatures consists of the refuse of the garden, very coarse bread, a kind of meal called *polenta*, made of Indian corn, which is very nourishing and agreeable, and a little oil: but even in these particulars, they seem to be stinted to very scanty meals. I have known a peasant feed his family with the skins of boiled beans. Their hogs are much better fed than their children. 'Tis pity they have no cows, which would yield milk, butter, and cheese, for the sustenance of their families. With all this wretchedness, one of these peasants will not work in your garden for less than eighteen sols, about eleven-pence sterling, *per diem*; and then he does not half the work of an English labourer. If there is fruit in it, or any thing he can convey, he will infallibly steal it, if you do not keep a very watchful eye over him. All the common people are thieves and beggars; and I believe this is always the case with people who are extremely indigent and miserable. In other respects, they are seldom guilty of excesses. They are remarkably respectful and submissive to their superiors. The populace of Nice are very quiet and orderly. They are little addicted to drunkenness. I have never heard of one riot since I lived among them; and murder and robbery are altogether unknown. A man may walk alone over the county of Nice, at midnight, without danger of insult. The police is very well regulated. No man is permitted to wear a pistol or dagger, on pain of being sent to the gallies. I am informed, that both murder and robbery are very frequent in some parts of Piedmont. Even here, when the peasants quarrel in their cups, (which very seldom happens) they draw their knives, and the one infallibly stabs the other. To such extremities, however, they never proceed, except when there is a woman in the case; and mutual jealousy co-operates with the liquor they have drank, to inflame their passions. In Nice, the common people retire to their lodgings at eight o'clock in winter, and nine in summer. Every person found in the streets after these hours, is apprehended by the patrole; and, if he cannot give a good account of himself, sent to prison. At nine in winter, and ten in summer, there is a curfew-bell rung, warning the people to put out their lights, and go to bed. This is a very necessary precaution in towns subject to conflagrations; but of small use in Nice, where there is very little combustible in the houses.

The punishments inflicted upon malefactors and delinquents at Nice are hanging for capital crimes; slavery on board the gallies for a limited term, or for life, according to the nature of the transgression; flagellation, and the corda or strappado.[5] This last is performed, by hoisting up the criminal by his hands tied behind his back, on a pulley about two stories high; from whence, the rope being suddenly slackened, he falls to within a yard or two of the ground, where he is stopped with a violent shock, arising from the weight of his body, and the velocity of his descent, which generally dislocates his shoulders, with incredible pain. This dreadful execution is sometimes repeated in a few minutes on the same delinquent; so that the very ligaments are tore from his joints, and his arms are rendered useless for life.

The poverty of the people in this country, as well as in the South of France, may be conjectured from the appearance of their domestic animals. The draught-horses, mules, and asses, of the peasants, are so meagre, as to excite compassion. There is not a dog to be seen in tolerable case; and the cats are so many emblems of famine, frightfully thin, and dangerously rapacious. I wonder the dogs and they do not devour young children. Another proof of that indigence which reigns among the common people, is this: you may pass through the whole South of France, as well as the county of Nice, where there is no want of groves, woods, and plantations, without hearing the song of black-bird, thrush, linnet, gold-finch, or any other bird whatsoever. All is silent and solitary. The poor birds are destroyed, or driven for refuge, into other countries, by the savage persecution of the people, who spare no pains to kill, and catch them for their own subsistence. Scarce a sparrow, red-breast, tom-tit, or wren, can 'scape the guns and snares of those indefatigable fowlers. Even the noblesse make parties to go *à la chasse*, a-hunting; that is, to kill those little birds, which they eat as *gibier* or game.

The great poverty of the people here, is owing to their religion. Half of their time is lost in observing the great number of festivals; and half of their substance is given to mendicant friars and parish priests. But if the church occasions their indigence, it likewise, in some measure, alleviates the horrors of it, by amusing them with shows, processions, and even those very feasts, which afford a recess from labour, in a country where the climate disposes them to idleness. If the peasants in the neighbourhood of any chapel dedicated to a saint, whose day is to be celebrated, have a mind to make a *festin*, in other words, a fair, they apply to the commandant of Nice for a licence, which costs them about a French crown. This being obtained, they assemble after service, men and women, in their best apparel, and dance to the musick of fiddles, and pipe and tabor, or rather pipe and drum. There are hucksters' stands, with pedlary ware and knick-knacks for presents; cakes and bread, *liqueurs* and wine; and thither generally resort all the company of Nice. I have seen our whole noblesse at one of these *festins*, kept on the highway in summer, mingled with an immense crowd of peasants, mules, and asses, covered with dust, and sweating at every pore with the excessive heat of the weather. I should be much puzzled to tell whence their enjoyment arises on such occasions; or to explain their motives for going thither, unless they are prescribed it for penance, as a fore-taste of purgatory.

Now I am speaking of religious institutions, I cannot help observing, that the antient Romans were still more superstitious than the modern Italians; and that the number of their religious feasts, sacrifices, fasts, and holidays, was even greater than those of the Christian church of Rome. They had their *festi* and *profesti*;[6] their *feriæ stativæ*, and *conceptivæ*, their fixed and moveable feasts; their *esuriales*, or fasting days, and their *precidaneæ*, or vigils. The *agonales* were celebrated in January; the *carmentales*, in January and February; the *lupercales* and *matronales*, in March; the *megalesia* in April; the *floralia*, in May; and the *matralia* in June. They had their *saturnalia*, *robigalia*, *venalia*, *vertumnalia*, *fornacalia*, *palilia*, *laralia*; their *latinæ*, their *paganales*, their *sementinæ*, their *compitales*, and their *imperativæ*; such as the *novemdalia*,[7] instituted by the senate, on account of a supposed shower of stones. Besides, every private family had a number of *feriæ*, kept either by way of rejoicing for some benefit, or mourning for some calamity. Every time it thundered, the day was kept holy. Every ninth day was a holiday, thence called *nundinæ quasi novendinæ*. There was the *dies denominalis*, which was the fourth of the kalends, nones and ides[8] of every month, over and above the anniversary of every great defeat which the republic had sustained, particularly the *dies alliensis*,[9] or fifteenth of the kalends of December, on which the Romans were totally defeated by the Gauls and Veientes; as Lucan says—*et damnata diu Romanis allia fastis*,[10] and *Allia in Rome's* calendar condemn'd.[11] The vast variety of their deities, said to amount to thirty thousand, with their respective rites of adoration, could not fail to introduce such a number of ceremonies, shews, sacrifices, lustrations, and public processions, as must have employed the people almost constantly from one end of the year to the other. This continual dissipation must have been a great enemy to industry; and the people must have been idle and effeminate. I think it would be no difficult matter to prove, that there is very little difference, in point of character, between the antient and modern inhabitants of Rome; and that the great figure which this empire made of old, was not so much owing to the intrinsic virtue of its citizens, as to the barbarism, ignorance, and imbecility of the nations they subdued. Instances of public and private virtue I find as frequent and as striking in the history of other nations, as in the annals of antient Rome; and now that the kingdoms and states of Europe are pretty equally enlightened, and ballanced in the scale of political power, I am of opinion, that if the most fortunate generals of the Roman commonwealth were again placed at the head of the very armies they once commanded, instead of extending their conquests over all Europe and Asia, they would hardly be able to subdue, and retain under their dominion, all the petty republics that subsist in Italy.

But I am tired with writing; and I believe you will be tired with reading this long letter, notwithstanding all your prepossession in favour of

Your very humble servant.

# LETTER XXI.

DEAR DOCTOR,

In my enquiries about the revenues of Nice, I am obliged to trust to the information of the inhabitants, who are much given to exaggerate. They tell me, the revenues of this town amount to one hundred thousand livres, or five thousand pounds sterling; of which I would strike off at least one fourth, as an addition of their own vanity: perhaps, if we deduct a third, it will be nearer the truth. For, I cannot find out any other funds they have, but the butchery and the bakery, which they farm at so much a year to the best bidder; and the *droits d'entrée*, or duties upon provision brought into the city; but these are very small. The king is said to draw from Nice one hundred thousand livres annually, arising from a free-gift, amounting to seven hundred pounds sterling, in lieu of the taille, from which this town and county are exempted; an inconsiderable duty upon wine sold in public-houses; and the *droits du port*. These last consist of anchorage, paid by all vessels in proportion to their tonnage, when they enter the harbours of Nice and Villa Franca. Besides, all foreign vessels, under a certain stipulated burthen, that pass between the island of Sardinia and this coast, are obliged, in going to the eastward, to enter and pay a certain regulated imposition, on pain of being taken and made prize. The prince of Monaco exacts a talliage of the same kind; and both he and the king of Sardinia maintain armed cruisers to assert this prerogative; from which, however, the English and French are exempted by treaty, in consequence of having paid a sum of money at once. In all probability, it was originally given as a consideration for maintaining lights on the shore, for the benefit of navigators, like the toll paid for passing the Sound in the Baltic.* The fanal, or lanthorn,[1] to the eastward of Villa Franca, is kept in good repair, and still lighted in the winter. The toll, however, is a very trouble-

---

* Upon further inquiry I find it was given in consideration of being protected from the Corsairs by the naval force of the Duke of Savoy, and, Prince of *Monaco*.

some tax upon feluccas,[2] and other small craft, which are greatly retarded in their voyages, and often lose the benefit of a fair wind, by being obliged to run in shore, and enter those harbours. The tobacco, the king manufactures at his own expence, and sells for his own profit, at a very high price; and every person convicted of selling this commodity in secret, is sent to the gallies for life. The salt comes chiefly from Sardinia, and is stored up in the king's magazine; from whence it is exported to Piedmont, and other parts of his inland dominions. And here it may not be amiss to observe, that Sardinia produces very good horses, well-shaped, though small; strong, hardy, full of mettle, and easily fed. The whole county of Nice is said to yield the king half a million of livres, about twenty-five thousand pounds sterling, arising from a small donative made by every town and village: for the lands pay no tax, or imposition, but the tithes to the church. His revenue then flows from the *gabelle* on salt and wine, and these free-gifts; so that we may strike off one fifth of the sum at which the whole is estimated; and conclude, that the king draws from the county of Nice, about four hundred thousand livres, or twenty thousand pounds sterling. That his revenues from Nice are not great, appears from the smallness of the appointments allowed to his officers. The president has about three hundred pounds per annum; and the intendant about two. The pay of the commandant does not exceed three hundred and fifty pounds: but he has certain privileges called the *tour du baton*,[3] some of which a man of spirit would not insist upon. He who commands at present, having no estate of his own, enjoys a small commandery, which being added to his appointments at Nice, make the whole amount to about five hundred pounds sterling.

If we may believe the politicians of Nice, the king of Sardinia's whole revenue does not fall short of twenty millions of Piedmontese livres, being above one million of our money. It must be owned, that there is no country in Christendom less taxed than that of Nice; and as the soil produces the necessaries of life, the inhabitants, with a little industry, might renew the golden age in this happy climate, among their groves, woods, and mountains, beautified with fountains, brooks, rivers, torrents, and cascades. In the midst of these pastoral advantages, the peasants are poor and miserable. They have no stock to begin the world with. They have no leases of the lands they cultivate; but entirely depend, from year to year, on the pleasure of the arbitrary landholder, who may turn them out at a minute's warning; and they are oppressed by the mendicant friars and parish priests, who rob them of the best fruits of their labour. After all, the ground is too scanty for the number of families which are crouded on it.

You desire to know the state of the arts and sciences at Nice; which, indeed, is almost a total blank. I know not what men of talents this place may have formerly produced; but at present, it seems to be consecrated to the reign of dulness and superstition. It is very surprising, to see a people established between two enlightened nations, so devoid of taste and literature. Here are no tolerable pictures, busts, statues, nor edifices: the very ornaments of the churches are wretchedly conceived, and worse executed. They have no public, nor private libraries, that afford any thing worth perusing. There is not even a bookseller in Nice. Though they value themselves upon their being natives of Italy, they are unacquainted with music. The few that play upon instruments, attend only to the execution. They have no genius nor taste, nor any knowledge of harmony and composition. Among the French, a Nissard piques himself on being Provençal; but in Florence, Milan, or Rome, he claims the honour of being born a native of Italy. The people of condition here speak both languages equally well; or, rather, equally ill; for they use a low, uncouth phraseology; and their pronunciation is extremely vitious. Their vernacular tongue is what they call *Patois*; though in so calling it, they do it injustice. —*Patois*, from the Latin word *patavinitas*, means no more than a provincial accent, or dialect. It takes its name from *Patavium*, or Padua, which was the birthplace of Livy, who, with all his merit as a writer, has admitted into his history, some provincial expressions of his own country.[4] The *Patois*, or native tongue of Nice, is no other than the ancient Provençal, from which the Italian, Spanish, and French languages, have been formed. This is the language that rose upon the ruins of the Latin tongue, after the irruptions of the Goths,

Vandals, Huns, and Burgundians, by whom the Roman empire was destroyed. It was spoke all over Italy, Spain, and the southern parts of France, until the thirteenth century, when the Italians began to polish it into the language which they now call their own. The Spaniards and French, likewise, improved it into their respective tongues. From its great affinity to the Latin, it was called *Romance*, a name which the Spaniards still give to their own language. As the first legends of knight-errantry were written in Provençal, all subsequent performances of the same kind, have derived from it the name of romance; and as those annals of chivalry contained extravagant adventures of knights, giants, and necromancers, every improbable story or fiction is to this day called a romance. Mr. Walpole, in his Catalogue of royal and noble Authors, has produced two sonnets in the antient Provençal, written by our king Richard I. surnamed *Cœur de Lion*;[5] and Voltaire, in his Historical Tracts, has favoured the world with some specimens of the same language.[6] The *Patois* of Nice, must, without doubt, have undergone changes and corruptions in the course of so many ages, especially as no pains have been taken to preserve its original purity, either in orthography or pronunciation. It is neglected, as the language of the vulgar; and scarce any-body here knows either its origin or constitution. I have in vain endeavoured to procure some pieces in the antient Provençal, that I might compare them with the modern *Patois*: but I can find no person to give me the least information on the subject. The shades of ignorance, sloth, and stupidity, are impenetrable. Almost every word of the *Patois* may still be found in the Italian, Spanish, and French languages, with a small change in the pronunciation. *Cavallo*, signifying a *horse* in Italian and Spanish, is called *cavao*; *maison*, the French word for a *house*, is changed into *maion*; *agua*, which means *water* in Spanish, the Nissards call *daigua*. To express, *what a slop is here!* they say *acco fa lac aqui*, which is a sentence composed of two Italian words, one French, and one Spanish. This is nearly the proportion in which these three languages will be found mingled in the *Patois* of Nice; which, with some variation, extends over all Provence, Languedoc, and Gascony. I will now treat you with two or three stanzas of a *canzon*, or hymn, in this language, to the Virgin Mary, which was lately printed at Nice.[7]

| 1. | 1. |
|---|---|
| Vierge, mairé de Dieu, | Virgin, mother of God, |
| Nuostro buono avocado, | Our good advocate, |
| Embél car uvostre sieu, | With your dear son, |
| En Fenestro* adourado, | In Fenestro adored, |
| Jeu vous saludi, | I salute you, |
| E demandi en socours; | And ask his assistance; |
| E senso autre preludi, | And without further prelude, |
| Canti lous uvostre honours. | I sing your honours. |

| 2. | 2. |
|---|---|
| Qu' ario de Paradis! | What air of Paradise! |
| Que maestà divino! | What majesty divine! |
| Salamon es d'advis, | Solomon is of opinion, |
| Giugiar de uvostro mino; | To judge of your appearance; |
| Vous dis plus bello: | Says you are the fairest: |
| E lou dis ben sovèn | And it is often said |
| De toutoi lei femello, | Of all females, |
| E non s'engano ren. | And we are not at all deceived. |

| 3. | 3. |
|---|---|
| Qu' ario de Paradis! | What air of Paradise! |
| Que maestà divino! | What majesty divine! |
| La bellezzo eblovis; | The beauty dazzles; |
| La bontà l'ueigl raffino. | The goodness purifies the eye: |
| Sias couronado: | You are crowned: |
| Tenes lou monde en man: | You hold the world in your hand: |
| Sus del trono assettado, | Seated on the throne, |
| Riges lou uvostre enfan. | You support your child. |

You see I have not chosen this *canzon* for the beauty and elegance of thought and expression; but give it you as the only printed specimen I could find of the modern Provençal. If you have any curiosity to be further acquainted with the *Patois*. I will endeavour to procure you satisfaction. Mean while, I am, in plain English,

Dear Sir,

Ever yours.

* Fenestro is the name of a place in this neighbourhood, where there is a supposed miraculous sanctuary, or chapel, of the Virgin Mary.

# LETTER XXII.

*Nice, November* 10, 1764.

DEAR SIR,

I had once thoughts of writing a complete natural history of this town and county: but I found myself altogether unequal to the task. I have neither health, strength, nor opportunity, to make proper collections of the mineral, vegetable, and animal productions. I am not much conversant with these branches of natural philosophy. I have no books to direct my inquiries. I can find no person capable of giving me the least information or assistance; and I am strangely puzzled by the barbarous names they give to many different species, the descriptions of which I have read under other appellations; and which, as I have never seen them before, I cannot pretend to distinguish by the eye. You must therefore be contented with such imperfect intelligence as my opportunities can afford.

The useful arts practised at Nice, are these, gardening and agriculture, with their consequences, the making of wine, oil, and cordage; the rearing of silk-worms, with the subsequent management and manufacture of that production; and the fishing, which I have already described.

Nothing can be more unpromising than the natural soil of this territory, except in a very few narrow bottoms, where there is a stiff clay, which when carefully watered, yields tolerable pasturage. In every other part, the soil consists of a light sand mingled with pebbles, which serves well enough for the culture of vines and olives: but the ground laid out for kitchen herbs, as well as for other fruit, must be manured with great care and attention. They have no black cattle to afford such compost as our farmers use in England. The dung of mules and asses, which are their only beasts of burthen, is of very little value for this purpose; and the natural sterility of their ground requires something highly impregnated with nitre and volatile salts. They have recourse therefore to pigeon's dung and ordure, which fully answer their expectations. Every peasant opens, at one corner of his wall, a public house of office for the reception of passengers; and in the town of Nice, every tenement is provided with one of these receptacles, the contents of which are carefully preserved for sale. The peasant comes with his asses and casks to carry it off before day, and pays for it according to its quality, which he examines and investigates, by the taste and flavour. The jakes of a protestant family, who eat *gras* every day, bears a much higher price than the privy of a good catholic who lives *maigre* one half of the year. The vaults belonging to the convent of Minims are not worth emptying.

The ground here is not delved with spades as in England, but laboured with a broad sharp hough,[1] having a short horizontal handle; and the climate is so hot and dry in the summer, that the plants must be watered every morning and evening, especially where it is not shaded by trees. It is surprising to see how the productions of the earth are crouded together. One would imagine they would rob one another of nourishment; and moreover be stifled for want of air; and doubtless this is in some measure the case. Olive and other fruit-trees are planted in rows very close to each other. These are connected by vines, and the interstices, between the rows, are filled with corn. The gardens that supply the town with sallad and pot-herbs, lye all on the side of Provence, by the highway. They are surrounded with high stone-walls, or ditches, planted with a kind of cane or large reed, which answers many purposes in this country. The leaves of it afford sustenance to the asses, and the canes not only serve as fences to the inclosures, but are used to prop the vines and pease, and to build habitations for the silkworms: they are formed into arbours, and wore as walking-staves. All these gardens are watered by little rills that come from the mountains, particularly, by the small branches of the two sources which I have described in a former letter, as issuing from the two sides of a mountain, under the names of *Fontaine de Muraille*, and *Fontaine du Temple*.

In the neighbourhood of Nice, they raise a considerable quantity of hemp, the largest and strongest I ever saw. Part of this, when dressed, is exported to other countries; and part is manufactured into cordage. However profitable it may be to the grower, it is certainly a great nusance in the summer. When taken out of the pits, where it has been put to rot, the stench it raises is quite insupportable; and must undoubtedly be unwholesome.

There is such a want of land in this neighbourhood, that terraces are built over one another with loose stones, on the faces of bare rocks, and these being covered with earth and manured, are planted with olives, vines, and corn. The same shift was practised all over Palestine, which was rocky and barren, and much more populous than the county of Nice.

Notwithstanding the small extent of this territory, there are some pleasant meadows in the skirts of Nice, that produce excellent clover; and the corn which is sown in open fields, where it has the full benefit of the soil, sun, and air, grows to a surprizing height. I have seen rye seven or eight feet high. All vegetables have a wonderful growth in this climate. Besides wheat, rye, barley, and oats, this country produces a good deal of Meliga, or Turkish wheat, which is what we call Indian corn.[2] I have, in a former letter, observed that the meal of this grain goes by the name *polenta*, and makes excellent hasty-pudding,[3] being very nourishing, and counted an admirable pectoral.[4] The pods and stalks are used for fuel; and the leaves are much preferable to common straw, for making *paillasses*.[5]

The pease and beans in the garden appear in the winter like beautiful plantations of young trees in blossom; and perfume the air. Myrtle, sweet-briar, sweet-marjoram, sage, thyme, lavender, rosemary, with many other aromatic herbs and flowers, which with us require the most careful cultivation, are here found wild in the mountains.

It is not many years since the Nissards learned the culture of silk-worms, of their neighbours the Piedmontese; and hitherto the progress they have made is not very considerable: the whole county of Nice produces about one hundred and thirty-three bales of three hundred pounds each, amounting in value to four hundred thousand livres.

In the beginning of April, when the mulberry-leaves begin to put forth, the eggs or grains that produce the silk-worm, are hatched. The grains are washed in wine, and those that swim on the top, are thrown away as good for nothing. The rest being deposited in small bags of linen, are worn by women in their bosoms, until the worms begin to appear: then they are placed in shallow wooden boxes, covered with a piece of white paper, cut into little holes, through which the worms ascend as they are hatched, to feed on the young mulberry-leaves, of which there is a layer above the paper. These boxes are kept for warmth between two mattrasses, and visited every day. Fresh leaves are laid in, and the worms that feed are removed successively to the other place prepared for their reception. This is an habitation, consisting of two or three stories, about twenty inches from each other, raised upon four wooden posts. The floors are made of canes, and strewed with fresh mulberry-leaves: the corner posts, and other occasional props, for sustaining the different floors, are covered with a coat of loose heath, which is twisted round the wood. The worms when hatched are laid upon the floors; and here you may see them in all the different stages of moulting or casting the slough, a change which they undergo three times successively before they begin to work. The silk-worm is an animal of such acute and delicate sensations, that too much care cannot be taken to keep its habitation clean, and to refresh it from time to time with pure air. I have seen them languish and die in scores, in consequence of an accidental bad smell. The soiled leaves, and the filth which they necessarily produce, should be carefully shifted every day; and it would not be amiss to purify the air sometimes with fumes of vinegar, rose, or orange-flower water. These niceties, however, are but little observed. They commonly lie in heaps as thick as shrimps in a plate, some feeding on the leaves, some new hatched, some intranced in the agonies of casting their skin, some languishing, and some actually dead, with a litter of half eaten faded leaves about them, in a close room, crouded with women and children, not at all remarkable for their cleanliness. I am assured by some persons of credit, that if they are touched, or even approached, by a woman in her catamenia,[6] they infallibly expire. This, however, must be understood of those females whose skins have naturally a very rank flavour, which is generally heightened at such periods. The mulberry-leaves used in this country are of the tree which bears a small white fruit not larger than a damascene.[7] They are planted on purpose, and the leaves are sold at so much a pound. By the middle of June all the mulberry-trees are stripped; but new leaves succeed, and in a few weeks, they are cloathed again with fresh verdure. In about ten days after the last moulting, the silk-worm climbs upon the props of his house, and choosing a situation among the heath, begins to spin in a most curious manner, until he is quite inclosed, and the cocon or pod of silk, about the size of a pigeon's egg, which he has produced, remains suspended by several filaments. It is not unusual to see double cocons, spun by two worms included under a common cover. There must be an infinite number of worms to yield any considerable quantity of silk. One ounce of eggs or grains produces four rup, or one hundred Nice pounds of cocons; and one rup, or twenty-five pounds of cocons, if they are rich, gives three pounds of raw silk; that is, twelve pounds of silk are got from one ounce of grains, which ounce of grains is produced by as many worms as are inclosed in one pound, or twelve ounces of cocons. In preserving the cocons for breed, you must choose an equal number of males and females; and these are very easily distinguished by the shape of the cocons; that which contains the male is sharp, and the other obtuse, at the two ends. In ten or twelve days after the cocon is finished, the worm makes its way through it, in the form of a very ugly, unwieldy, aukward butterfly, and as the different sexes are placed by one another on paper or linen, they immediately engender. The female lays her eggs, which are carefully preserved; but neither she nor her mate takes any nourishment, and in eight or ten days after they quit the cocons, they generally die. The silk of these cocons cannot be wound, because the animals in piercing through them, have destroyed the continuity of the filaments. It is therefore, first boiled, and then picked and carded like wool, and being afterwards spun, is used in the coarser stuffs of the silk manufacture. The other cocons, which yield the best silk, are managed in a different manner. Before the inclosed worm has time to penetrate, the silk is reeled off with equal care and ingenuity. A handful of the cocons are thrown into a kettle of boiling water, which not only kills the animal, but dissolves the glutinous substance by which the fine filaments of the silk cohere or stick together, so that they are easily wound off, without breaking. Six or seven of these small filaments being joined together are passed over a kind of twisting iron, and fixed to the wheel, which one girl turns, while another, with her hands in the boiling water, disentangles the threads, joins them when they chance to break, and supplies fresh cocons with admirable dexterity and dispatch. There is a manufacture of this kind just without one of the gates of Nice, where forty or fifty of these wheels are worked together, and give employment for some weeks to double the number of young women. Those who manage the pods that float in the boiling water must be very alert, otherwise they will scald their fingers. The smell that comes from the boiling cocons is extremely offensive. Hard by the harbour, there is a very curious mill for twisting the silk, which goes by water. There is in the town of Nice, a well regulated hospital for poor orphans of both sexes, where above one hundred of them are employed in dressing, dying, spinning and weaving the silk. In the villages of Provence, you see the poor women in the streets spinning raw silk upon distaves: but here the same instrument is only used for spinning hemp and flax; which last, however, is not of the growth of Nice.—But lest I should spin this letter to a tedious length, I will now wind up my bottom,[8] and bid you heartily farewell.

# LETTER XXIII.

*Nice, November* 19, 1764.

Sir,

In my last, I gave you a succinct account of the silk-worm, and the management of that curious insect in this country. I shall now proceed to describe the methods of making wine and oil.

The vintage begins in September. The grapes being chosen and carefully picked, are put into a large vat, where they are pressed by a man's naked feet, and the juices drawn off by a cock below. When no more is procured by this operation, the bruised grapes are put into the press, and yield still more liquor. The juice obtained by this double pressure, being put in casks, with their bungs open, begins to ferment and discharge its impurities at the openings. The waste occasioned by this discharge, is constantly supplied with fresh wine; so that the casks are always full. The fermentation continues for twelve, fifteen, or twenty days, according to the strength and vigour of the grape. In about a month, the wine is fit for drinking. When the grapes are of a bad, meagre kind, the wine dealers mix the juice with pigeons-dung or quick-lime, in order to give it a spirit which nature has denied: but this is a very mischievous adulteration.

The process for oil-making is equally simple. The best olives are those that grow wild; but the quantity of them is very inconsiderable. Olives begin to ripen and drop in the beginning of November: but some remain on the trees till February, and even till April, and these are counted the most valuable. When the olives are gathered, they must be man-ufactured immediately, before they fade and grow wrinkled, otherwise they will produce bad oil. They are first of all ground into a paste by a mill-stone set edge-ways in a circular stone-trough, the wheel being turned by water. This paste is put into frails[1] or circular cases made of grass woven, having a round hole at top and bottom; when filled they resemble in shape our Cheshire cheeses. A number of these placed one upon another, are put in a press, and being squeezed, the oil with all its impurities, runs into a receptacle below fixed in the ground. From hence it is laded into a wooden vat, half filled with water. The sordes or dirt falls to the bottom; the oil swims a-top; and being skimmed off, is barrelled up in small oblong casks. What remains in the vat, is thrown into a large stone cistern with water, and after being often stirred, and standing twelve or fourteen days, yields a coarser oil used for lamps and manufactures. After these processes, they extract an oil still more coarse and fetid from the refuse of the whole. Sometimes, in order to make the olives grind the more easily into a paste, and part with more oil, they are mixed with a little hot water: but the oil thus procured is apt to grow rancid. The very finest, called virgin oil, is made chiefly of green olives, and sold at a very high price, because a great quantity is required to produce a very little oil. Even the stuff that is left after all these operations, consisting of the dried pulp, is sold for fuel, and used in *brasieres* for warming apartments which have no chimney.

I have now specified all the manufactures of Nice which are worth mentioning. True it is, there is some coarse paper made in this neighbourhood; there are also people here who dress skins and make leather for the use of the inhabitants: but this business is very ill performed: the gloves and shoes are generally rotten as they come from the hands of the maker. Carpenter's, joiner's, and blacksmith's work is very coarsely and clumsily done. There are no chairs to be had at Nice, but crazy things made of a few sticks, with rush bottoms, which are sold for twelve livres a dozen. Nothing can be more contemptible than the hard-ware made in this place, such as knives, scissars, and candle-snuffers. All utensils in brass and copper are very ill made and finished. The silver-smiths make nothing but spoons, forks, paultry rings, and crosses for the necks of the women.

The houses are built of a ragged stone dug from the mountains, and the interstices are filled with rubble; so that the walls would appear very ugly, if they were not covered with plaister, which has a good effect. They generally consist of three stories, and are covered with tiles. The apartments of the better sort are large and lofty, the floors paved with brick, the roofs covered with a thick coat of stucco, and the walls white-washed. People of distinction hang their chambers with damask, striped silk, painted cloths, tapestry, or printed linnen. All the doors, as well as the windows, consist of folding leaves. As there is no wainscot in the rooms, which are divided by stone partitions, and the floors and cieling are covered with brick and stucco, fires are of much less dreadful consequence here than in our country. Wainscot would afford harbour for bugs: besides, white walls have a better effect in this hot climate. The beds commonly used in this place, and all over Italy, consist of a *paillasse*, with one or two mattrasses, laid upon planks, supported by two wooden benches. Instead of curtains there is a *couziniere* or mosquito net, made of a kind of gauze, that opens and contracts occasionally, and incloses the place where you lie: persons of condition, however, have also bedsteads and curtains; but these last are never used in the summer.

In these countries, people of all ranks dine exactly at noon; and this is the time I seize in winter, for making my daily tour of the streets and ramparts, which at all other hours of the day are crowded with men, women, children and beasts of burthen. The rampart is the common road for carriages of all kinds. I think there are two private coaches in Nice, besides that of the commandant: but there are sedan chairs, which may be had at a reasonable rate. When I bathed in the summer, I paid thirty sols, equal to eighteen-pence, for being carried to and from the bathing place, which was a mile from my own house. Now I am speaking of bathing, it may not be amiss to inform you that though there is a fine open beach, extending several miles to the westward of Nice, those who cannot swim ought to bathe with great precaution, as the sea is very deep, and the descent very abrupt from within a yard or two of the water's edge. The people here were much surprised when I began to bathe in the beginning of May. They thought it very strange, that a man seemingly con-sumptive should plunge into the sea, especially when the weather was so cold; and some of the doctors prognosticated immediate death. But, when it was perceived that I grew better in consequence of the bath, some of the Swiss officers tried the same experiment, and in a few days, our example was followed by several inhabitants of Nice. There is, however, no convenience for this operation, from the benefit of which the fair sex must be intirely excluded, unless they lay aside all regard to decorum; for the shore is always lined with fishing-boats, and crouded with people. If a lady should be at the expence of having a tent pitched on the beach where she might put on and off her bathing-dress, she could not pretend to go into the sea without proper attendants; nor could she possibly plunge headlong into the water, which is the most effectual, and least dangerous way of bathing. All that she can do is to have the sea-water brought into her house, and make use of a bathing-tub, which may be made according to her own, or physician's direction.

What further I have to say of this climate and country, you shall have in my next; and then you will be released from a subject, which I am afraid has been but too circumstantially handled by,

Sir,

Your very humble servant.

# LETTER XXIV.

*Nice, January 4, 1765.*

DEAR SIR,

The constitution of this climate may be pretty well ascertained, from the inclosed register of the weather, which I kept with all possible care and attention. From a perusal of it, you will see that there is less rain and wind at Nice, than in any other part of the world that I know; and such is the serenity of the air, that you see nothing above your head for several months together, but a charming blue expanse, without cloud or speck. Whatever clouds may be formed by evaporation from the sea, they seldom or never hover over this small territory; but, in all probability, are attracted by the mountains that surround it, and there fall in rain or snow: as for those that gather from other quarters, I suppose their progress hitherward is obstructed by those very Alps which rise one over another, to an extent of many leagues. This air being dry, pure, heavy, and elastic, must be agreeable to the constitution of those who labour under disorders arising from weak nerves, obstructed perspiration, relaxed fibres, a viscidity of lymph, and a languid circulation. In other respects, it encourages the scurvy, the atmosphere being undoubtedly impregnated with sea-salt. Ever since my arrival at Nice, I have had a scorbutical eruption on my right hand, which diminishes and increases according to the state of my health.[1] One day last summer, when there was a strong breeze from the sea, the surface of our bodies was covered with a salt brine, very perceptible to the taste; my gums, as well as those of another person in my family, began to swell, and grow painful, though this had never happened before; and I was seized with violent pains in the joints of my knees. I was then at a country-house fronting the sea, and particularly exposed to the marine air. The swelling of our gums subsided as the wind fell: but what was very remarkable, the scurvy-spot on my hand disappeared, and did not return for a whole month. It is affirmed, that sea-salt will dissolve, and render the blood so fluid, that it will exude through the coats of the vessels. Perhaps the sea-scurvy is a partial dissolution of it, by that mineral absorbed from the air

187

by the lymphatics on the surface of the body, and by those of the lungs in respiration. Certain it is, in the last stages of the sea-scurvy, the blood often bursts from the pores; and this phænomenon is imputed to a high degree of putrefaction: sure enough it is attended with putrefaction. We know that a certain quantity of salt is required to preserve the animal juices from growing putrid: but, how a greater quantity should produce putrefaction, I leave to wiser heads to explain. Many people here have scorbutical complaints, though their teeth are not affected. They are subject to eruptions on the skin, putrid gums, pains in the bones, lassitude, indigestion, and low spirits; but the reigning distemper is a *marasmus*, or consumption, which proceeds gradually, without any pulmonary complaint, the complexion growing more and more florid, 'till the very last scene of the tragedy. This I would impute to the effects of a very dry, saline atmosphere, upon a thin habit, in which there is an extraordinary waste by perspiration. The air is remarkably salt in this district, because the mountains that hem it in, prevent its communication with the circumambient atmosphere, in which the saline particles would otherwise be diffused; and there is no rain, nor dew, to precipitate or dissolve them. Such an air as I have described, should have no bad effect upon a moist, phlegmatic constitution, such as mine; and yet it must be owned, I have been visibly wasting since I came hither, though this decay I considered as the progress of the *tabes*[2] which began in England. But the air of Nice has had a still more sensible effect upon Mr. Sch——z,[3] who laboured under nervous complaints to such a degree, that life was a burthen to him. He had also a fixed pain in his breast, for which complaint he had formerly tried the air of Naples, where he resided some considerable time, and in a great measure recovered: but, this returning with weakness, faintness, low spirits, and entire loss of appetite, he was advised to come hither; and the success of his journey has greatly exceeded his expectation. Though the weather has been remarkably bad for this climate, he has enjoyed perfect health. Since he arrived at Nice, the pain in his breast has vanished; he eats heartily, sleeps well, is in high spirits, and so strong, that he is never off his legs in the day-time. He can walk to the Var, and back again, before dinner; and he has climbed to the tops of all the mountains in this neighbourhood. I never saw before such sudden and happy effects from the change of air. I must also acknowledge, that ever since my arrival at Nice, I have breathed more freely than I had done for some years, and my spirits have been more alert. The father of my housekeeper, who was a dancing-master, had been so afflicted with an asthmatic disorder, that he could not live in France, Spain, or Italy; but found the air of Nice so agreeable to his lungs, that he was enabled to exercise his profession for above twenty years, and died last spring turned of seventy. Another advantage I have reaped from this climate is my being, in a great measure, delivered from a slow fever which used to hang about me, and render life a burthen. Neither am I so apt to catch cold as I used to be in England and France; and the colds I do catch are not of the same continuance and consequence, as those to which I was formerly subject. The air of Nice is so dry, that in summer, and even in winter, (except in wet weather) you may pass the evening, and indeed the whole night, *sub Dio*,[4] without feeling the least dew or moisture; and as for fogs, they are never seen in this district. In summer, the air is cooled by a regular sea-breeze blowing from the east, like that of the West-Indies. It begins in the forenoon, and increases with the heat of the day. It dies away about six or seven; and immediately after sun-set, is succeeded by an agreeable land-breeze from the mountains. The sea-breeze from the eastward, however, is not so constant here, as in the West-Indies between the tropicks, because the sun, which produces it, is not so powerful. This country lies nearer the region of variable winds, and is surrounded by mountains, capes, and straights, which often influence the constitution and current of the air. About the winter solstice, the people of Nice expect wind and rain, which generally lasts, with intervals, 'till the beginning of February: but even during this, their worst weather, the sun breaks out occasionally, and you may take the air either a-foot or on horseback every day; for the moisture is immediately absorbed by the earth, which is naturally dry. They likewise lay their account with being visited by showers of rain and gusts of wind in April. A

week's rain in the middle of August makes them happy. It
not only refreshes the parched ground, and plumps up the
grapes and other fruit, but it cools the air and assuages the
heats, which then begin to grow very troublesome; but the
rainy season is about the autumnal equinox, or rather something later. It continues about twelve days or a fortnight, and
is extremely welcome to the natives of this country. This
rainy season is often delayed 'till the latter end of November,
and sometimes 'till the month of December; in which case,
the rest of the winter is generally dry. The heavy rains in this
country generally come with a south-west wind, which was
the *creberque procellis Africus*, the stormy southwest, of the
antients. It is here called *Lebeche*, a corruption of *Lybicus*:[5] it
generally blows high for a day or two, and rolls the Mediterranean before it in huge waves, that often enter the town of
Nice. It likewise drives before it all the clouds which had
been formed above the surface of the Mediterranean. These
being expended in rain, fair weather naturally ensues. For this
reason, the Nissards observe *le lebeche raccommode le tems*, the
*Lebeche* settles the weather. During the rains of this season,
however, the winds have been variable. From the sixteenth of
November, 'till the fourth of January, we have had two and
twenty days of heavy rain: a very extraordinary visitation in
this country: but the seasons seem to be more irregular than
formerly, all over Europe. In the month of July, the mercury
in Fahrenheit's thermometer,[6] rose to eighty-four at Rome,
the highest degree at which it was ever known in that
country; and the very next day, the Sabine mountains[7] were
covered with snow. The same phænomenon happened on the
eleventh of August, and the thirtieth of September. The
consequence of these sudden variations of weather, was this:
putrid fevers were less frequent than usual; but the sudden
check of perspiration from the cold, produced colds, inflammatory sore throats, and the rheumatism. I know instances of
some English valetudinarians, who have passed the winter at
Aix, on the supposition that there was little or no difference
between that air and the climate of Nice: but this is a very
great mistake, which may be attended with fatal consequences. Aix is altogether exposed to the north and north-west
winds, which blow as cold in Provence as ever I felt them on

the mountains of Scotland: whereas Nice is entirely screened from these winds by the Maritime Alps, which form an amphitheatre, to the land-side, around this little territory: but another incontestible proof of the mildness of this climate, is deduced from the oranges, lemons, citrons, roses, narcissus's, july-flowers,[8] and jonquils, which ripen and blow in the middle of winter. I have described the agreeable side of this climate; and now I will point out its inconveniences. In the winter, but especially in the spring, the sun is so hot, that one can hardly take exercise of any sort abroad, without being thrown into a breathing sweat; and the wind at this season is so cold and piercing, that it often produces a mischievous effect on the pores thus opened. If the heat rarifies the blood and juices, while the cold air constringes the fibres, and obstructs the perspiration, inflammatory disorders must ensue. Accordingly, the people are then subject to colds, pleurisies, peripneumonies, and ardent fevers.[9] An old count advised me to stay within doors in March, *car alors les humeurs commencent à se remuer*, for then the humours begin to be in motion. During the heats of summer, some few persons of gross habits have, in consequence of violent exercise and excess, been seized with putrid fevers, attended with exanthemata, erisipelatous, and miliary eruptions,[10] which commonly prove fatal: but the people in general are healthy, even those that take very little exercise: a strong presumption in favour of the climate! As to medicine, I know nothing of the practice of the Nice physicians. Here are eleven in all; but four or five make shift to live by the profession. They receive, by way of fee, ten sols (an English six-pence) a visit, and this but ill paid; so you may guess whether they are in a condition to support the dignity of physic; and whether any man, of a liberal education, would bury himself at Nice on such terms. I am acquainted with an Italian physician settled at Villa Franca, a very good sort of a man, who practises for a certain salary, raised by annual contribution among the better sort of people; and an allowance from the king, for visiting the sick belonging to the garrison and the gallies. The whole may amount to near thirty pounds.

Among the inconveniences of this climate, the vermin form no inconsiderable article. Vipers and snakes are found in the mountains. Our gardens swarm with lizzards; and there are some few scorpions; but as yet I have seen but one of this species. In summer, notwithstanding all the care and precautions we can take, we are pestered with incredible swarms of flies, fleas, and bugs; but the gnats, or *couzins*, are more intolerable than all the rest. In the day-time, it is impossible to keep the flies out of your mouth, nostrils, eyes, and ears. They croud into your milk, tea, chocolate, soup, wine, and water: they soil your sugar, contaminate your victuals, and devour your fruit; they cover and defile your furniture, floors, cielings, and indeed your whole body. As soon as candles are lighted, the *couzins* begin to buz about your ears in myriads, and torment you with their stings, so that you have no rest nor respite 'till you get into bed, where you are secured by your musquito-net. This inclosure is very disagreeable in hot weather; and very inconvenient to those, who, like me, are subject to a cough and spitting. It is moreover ineffectual; for some of those cursed insects insinuate themselves within it, almost every night; and half a dozen of them are sufficient to disturb you 'till morning. This is a plague that continues all the year; but in summer it is intolerable. During this season, likewise, the moths are so mischievous, that it requires the utmost care to preserve woollen cloths from being destroyed. From the month of May, 'till the beginning of October, the heat is so violent, that you cannot stir abroad after six in the morning 'till eight at night, so that you are entirely deprived of the benefit of exercise. There is no shaded walk in, or near the town; and there is neither coach nor chaise to hire, unless you travel post. Indeed, there is no road fit for any wheel carriage, but the common highway to the Var, in which you are scorched by the reflexion of the sun from the sand and stones, and at the same time half stifled with dust. If you ride out in the cool of the evening, you will have the disadvantage of returning in the dark.

Among the demerits of Nice, I must also mention the water which is used in the city. It is drawn from wells; and for the most part so hard, that it curdles with soap. There are many fountains and streams in the neighbourhood, that afford excellent water, which, at no great charge, might be conveyed into the town, so as to form conduits in all the public streets: but the inhabitants are either destitute of public spirit, or cannot afford the expence.* I have a draw-well in my porch, and another in my garden, which supply tolerable water for culinary uses; but what we drink, is fetched from a well belonging to a convent of Dominicans in this neighbourhood. Our linnen is washed in the river Paglion; and when that is dry, in the brook called Limpia, which runs into the harbour.

In mentioning the water of this neighbourhood, I ought not to omit the baths of Rocabiliare,[11] a small town among the mountains, above five and twenty miles from Nice. There are three sources, each warmer than the other; the warmest being nearly equal to the heat of the king's bath at Bath in Somersetshire, as far as I can judge from information. I have perused a Latin manuscript, which treats of these baths at Rocabiliare, written by the duke of Savoy's first physician about sixty years ago. He talks much of the sulphur and the nitre which they contain: but I apprehend their efficacy is owing to the same volatile vitriolic principle, which characterises the waters at Bath. They are attenuating and deobstruent, consequently of service in disorders arising from a languid circulation, a viscidity of the juices, a lax fibre, and obstructed viscera. The road from hence to Rocabiliare is in some parts very dangerous, lying along the brink of precipices, impassable to any other carriage but a mule. The town itself affords bad lodging and accommodation, and little or no society. The waters are at the distance of a mile and a half from the town: there are no baths nor shelter, nor any sort of convenience for those that drink them; and the best part of their efficacy is lost, unless they are drank at the fountain-head. If these objections were in some measure removed, I would advise valetudinarians, who come hither for the benefit of this climate, to pass the heats of summer at Rocabiliare, which being situated among mountains, enjoys a

---

* General Paterson delivered a plan to the king of *Sardinia* for supplying Nice with excellent water for so small an expence as one livre a house per annum; but the inhabitants remonstrated against it as an intolerable imposition.

cool temperate air all the summer. This would be a salutary respite from the salt air of Nice, to those who labour under scorbutical complaints; and they would return with fresh vigour and spirits, to pass the winter in this place, where no severity of weather is known. Last June, when I found myself so ill at my *cassine*, I had determined to go to Rocabiliare, and even to erect a hut at the spring, for my own convenience. A gentleman of Nice undertook to procure me a tolerable lodging in the house of the curé,[12] who was his relation. He assured me, there was no want of fresh butter, good poultry, excellent veal, and delicate trout; and that the articles of living might be had at Rocabiliare for half the price we paid at Nice: but finding myself grow better immediately on my return from the *cassine* to my town house, I would not put myself to the trouble and expence of a further removal.

I think I have now communicated all the particulars relating to Nice, that are worth knowing; and perhaps many more than you desired to know: but, in such cases, I would rather be thought prolix and unentertaining, than deficient in that regard and attention with which I am very sincerely,

Your friend and servant.

## END OF VOLUME I.

*Nice, January* 1, 1765.

DEAR SIR,

It was in deference to your opinion, reinforced by my own inclination, and the repeated advice of other friends, that I resolved upon my late excursion to Italy. I could plainly perceive from the anxious sollicitude, and pressing exhortations contained in all the letters I had lately received from my correspondents in Britain, that you had all despaired of my recovery. You advised me to make a pilgrimage among the Alps, and the advice was good. In scrambling among those mountains, I should have benefited by the exercise, and at the same time have breathed a cool, pure, salubrious air, which, in all probability, would have expelled the slow fever arising in a great measure from the heat of this climate. But, I wanted a companion and fellow-traveller, whose conversation and society could alleviate the horrors of solitude. Besides, I was not strong enough to encounter the want of conveniencies, and even of necessaries, to which I must have been exposed in the course of such an expedition. My worthy friend Dr. A——[1] earnestly intreated me to try the effect of a sea-voyage, which you know has been found of wonderful efficacy in consumptive cases. After some deliberation, I resolved upon the scheme, which I have now happily executed. I had a most eager curiosity to see the antiquities of Florence and Rome: I longed impatiently to view those wonderful edifices, statues, and pictures, which I had so often admired in prints and descriptions. I felt an enthusiastic ardor to tread that very classical ground which had been the scene of so many great atchievements; and I could not bear the thought of returning to England from the very skirts of Italy, without having penetrated to the capital of that renowned country. With regard to my health, I knew I could manage matters so as to enjoy all the benefits that could be expected from the united energy of a voyage by sea, a journey by land, and a change of climate.

Rome is betwixt four and five hundred miles distant from Nice, and one half of the way I was resolved to travel by water. Indeed there is no other way of going from hence to

Genoa, unless you take a mule, and clamber along the mountains at the rate of two miles an hour, and at the risque of breaking your neck every minute. The Appenine mountains, which are no other than a continuation of the Maritime Alps, form an almost continued precipice from Villefranche to Lerici, which is almost forty-five miles on the other side of Genoa; and as they are generally washed by the sea, there is no beach or shore, consequently the road is carried along the face of the rocks, except at certain small intervals, which are occupied by towns and villages. But, as there is a road for mules and foot passengers, it might certainly be enlarged and improved so as to render it practicable by chaises and other wheel-carriages, and a toll might be exacted, which in a little time would defray the expence: for certainly no person who travels to Italy, from England, Holland, France, or Spain, would make a troublesome circuit to pass the Alps by the way of Savoy and Piedmont, if he could have the convenience of going post by the way of Aix, Antibes, and Nice, along the side of the Mediterranean, and through the Riviera of Genoa,[2] which from the sea affords the most agreeable and amazing prospect I ever beheld. What pity it is, they cannot restore the celebrated *Via Aurelia*, mentioned in the Itinerarium of Antoninus,[3] which extended from Rome by the way of Genoa, and through this country as far as Arles upon the Rhone. It was said to have been made by the emperor Marcus Aurelius;[4] and some of the vestiges of it are still to be seen in Provence. The truth is, the nobility of Genoa, who are all merchants, from a low, selfish, and absurd policy, take all methods to keep their subjects of the Riviera in poverty and dependence. With this view, they carefully avoid all steps towards rendering that country accessible by land; and at the same time discourage their trade by sea, lest it should interfere with the commerce of their capital, in which they themselves are personally concerned.

Those who either will not or cannot bear the sea, and are equally averse to riding, may be carried in a common chair, provided with a foot-board, on men's shoulders: this is the way of travelling practised by the ladies of Nice, in crossing the mountains to Turin; but it is very tedious and expensive, as the men must be often relieved.

The most agreeable carriage from hence to Genoa, is a feluca, or open boat, rowed by ten or twelve stout mariners. Though none of these boats belong to Nice, they are to be found every day in our harbour, waiting for a fare to Genoa; and they are seen passing and repassing continually, with merchandize or passengers, between Marseilles, Antibes, and the Genoese territories. A feluca is large enough to take in a post-chaise; and there is a tilt over the stern-sheets, where the passengers sit, to protect them from the rain: between the seats one person may lie commodiously upon a mattrass, which is commonly supplied by the patron. A man in good health may put up with any thing; but I would advise every valetudinarian who travels this way, to provide his own chaise, mattrass, and bed-linnen, otherwise he will pass his time very uncomfortably. If you go as a simple passenger in a feluca, you pay about a loui'dore for your place, and you must be intirely under the direction of the patron, who, while he can bear the sea, will prosecute his voyage by night as well as by day, and expose you to many other inconveniencies: but for eight zequines, or four loui'dores, you can have a whole feluca to yourself, from Nice to Genoa, and the master shall be obliged to put a-shore every evening. If you would have it still more at your command, you may hire it at so much per day, and in that case, go on shore as often, and stay as long as you please. This is the method I should take, were I to make the voyage again; for I am persuaded I should find it very near as cheap, and much more agreeable than any other.

The distance between this place and Genoa, when measured on the carte, does not exceed ninety miles: but the people of the felucas insist upon its being one hundred and twenty. If they creep along shore round the bottoms of all the bays, this computation may be true: but, except when the sea is rough, they stretch directly from one head-land to another, and even when the wind is contrary, provided the gale is not fresh, they perform the voyage in two days and a half, by dint of rowing: when the wind is favourable, they will sail it easily in fourteen hours.

A man, who has nothing but expedition in view, may go with the courier, who has always a light boat well manned, and will be glad to accommodate a traveller for a reasonable gratification. I know an English gentleman who always travels with the courier in Italy, both by sea and land. In posting by land, he is always sure of having part of a good calash,[5] and the best horses that can be found; and as the expence of both is defrayed by the public, it costs him nothing but a present to his companion, which does not amount to one fourth part of the expence he would incur by travelling alone. These opportunities may be had every week in all the towns of Italy.

For my own part, I hired a gondola from hence to Genoa. This is a boat smaller than a feluca, rowed by four men, and steered by the patron; but the price was nine zequines, rather more than I should have payed for a feluca of ten oars. I was assured that being very light, it would make great way; and the master was particularly recommended to me, as an honest man and an able mariner. I was accompanied in this voyage by my wife and Miss C——,[6] together with one Mr. R——,[7] a native of Nice, whom I treated with the jaunt, in hopes that as he was acquainted with the customs of the country, and the different ways of travelling in it, he would save us much trouble, and some expence: but I was much disappointed. Some persons at Nice offered to lay wagers that he would return by himself from Italy; but they were also disappointed.

We embarked in the beginning of September, attended by one servant. The heats, which render travelling dangerous in Italy, begin to abate at this season. The weather was extremely agreeable; and if I had postponed my voyage a little longer, I foresaw that I should not be able to return before winter; in which case I might have found the sea too rough, and the weather too cold for a voyage of one hundred and thirty-five miles in an open boat.

Having therefore provided myself with a proper pass, signed and sealed by our consul, as well as with letters of recommendation from him to the English consuls at Genoa and Leghorn, a precaution which I would advise all travellers to take, in case of meeting with accidents on the road, we went on board about ten in the morning, stopped about half an hour at a friend's country-house in the bay of St. Hospice, and about noon entered the harbour of Monaco, where the patron was obliged to pay toll, according to the regulation which I have explained in a former letter. This small town, containing about eight or nine hundred souls, besides the garrison, is built on a rock which projects into the sea, and makes a very romantic appearance. The prince's palace stands in the most conspicuous part, with a walk of trees before it. The apartments are elegantly furnished, and adorned with some good pictures. The fortifications are in good repair, and the place is garrisoned by two French battalions. The present prince of Monaco is a Frenchman, son of the duke de Matignon, who married the heiress of Monaco, whose name was Grimaldi.[8] The harbour is well sheltered from the wind; but has not water sufficient to admit vessels of any great burthen. Towards the north, the king of Sardinia's territories extend to within a mile of the gate; but the prince of Monaco can go upon his own ground along shore about five or six miles to the eastward, as far as Menton, another small town, which also belongs to him, and is situated on the sea-side. His revenues are computed at a million of French livres, amounting to something more than forty thousand pounds sterling: but, the principality of Monaco, consisting of three small towns,[9] and an inconsiderable tract of barren rock, is not worth above seven thousand a year; the rest arises from his French estate. This consists partly of the dutchy of Matignon, and partly of the dutchy of Valentinois, which last was given to the ancestors of this prince of Monaco, in the year 1640, by the French king, to make up the loss of some lands in the kingdom of Naples, which were confiscated when he expelled the Spanish garrison from Monaco, and threw himself into the arms of France: so that he is duke of Valentinois as well as of Matignon, in that kingdom.[10] He lives almost constantly in France; and has taken the name and arms of Grimaldi.

The Genoese territories begin at Ventimiglia, another town lying on the coast, at the distance of twenty miles from Nice, a circumstance from which it borrows the name. Having passed the towns of Monaco, Menton, Ventimiglia, and several other places of less consequence that lie along this coast, we turned the point of St. Martin with a favourable breeze, and might have proceeded twenty miles further before night: but the women began to be sick, as well as afraid at the roughness of the water; Mr. R—— was so discomposed, that he privately desired the patron to put ashore at St. Remo, on pretence that we should not find a tolerable auberge in any other place between this and Noli, which was at the distance of forty miles. We accordingly landed, and were conducted to the poste, which our gondeliere assured us was the best auberge in the whole Riviera of Genoa. We ascended by a dark, narrow, steep stair, into a kind of public room, with a long table and benches, so dirty and miserable, that it would disgrace the worst hedge ale-house[11] in England. Not a soul appeared to receive us. This is a ceremony one must not expect to meet with in France; far less in Italy. Our patron going into the kitchen, asked a servant if the company could have lodging in the house; and was answered, "he could not tell: the patron was not at home." When he desired to know where the patron was, the other answered, "he was gone to take the air." *E andato a passeggiare.* In the mean time, we were obliged to sit in the common room among watermen and muleteers. At length the landlord arrived, and gave us to understand, that he could accommodate us with chambers. In that where I lay, there was just room for two beds, without curtains or bedstead, an old rotten table covered with dried figs, and a couple of crazy chairs. The walls had been once whitewashed: but were now hung with cobwebs, and speckled with dirt of all sorts; and I believe the brick-floor had not been swept for half a century. We supped in an outward room suitable in all respects to the chamber, and fared villainously. The provision was very ill-dressed, and served up in the most slovenly manner. You must not expect cleanliness or conveniency of any kind in this country. For this accommodation I payed as much as if I had been elegantly entertained in the best auberge of France or Italy.

Next day, the wind was so high that we could not prosecute our voyage, so that we were obliged to pass other four and twenty hours in this comfortable situation. Luckily Mr. R—— found two acquaintances in the place; one a Franciscan monk, a jolly fellow; and the other a *maestro di capella*,[12] who sent a spinnet to the inn, and entertained us agreeably with his voice and performance, in both of which accomplishments he excelled. The padre was very good humoured, and favoured us with a letter of recommendation to a friend of his, a professor in the university of Pisa. You would laugh to see the hyperbolical terms in which he mentioned your humble servant: but Italy is the native country of hyperbole.

St. Remo is a pretty considerable town, well-built upon the declivity of a gently rising hill, and has a harbour capable of receiving small vessels, a good number of which are built upon the beach: but ships of any burden are obliged to anchor in the bay, which is far from being secure. The people of St. Remo form a small republic, which is subject to Genoa. They enjoyed particular privileges, till the year 1753, when in consequence of a new gabelle upon salt, they revolted: but this effort in behalf of liberty did not succeed. They were soon reduced by the Genoese, who deprived them of all their privileges, and built a fort by the sea-side, which serves the double purpose of defending the harbour and over-awing the town. The garrison at present does not exceed two hundred men. The inhabitants are said to have lately sent a deputation to Ratisbon, to crave the protection of the diet of the empire.[13] There is very little plain ground in this neighbourhood; but the hills are covered with oranges, lemons, pomegranates, and olives, which produce a considerable traffic in fine fruit and excellent oil. The women of St. Remo are much more handsome and better tempered than those of Provence. They have in general good eyes, with open ingenuous countenances. Their dress, though remarkable, I cannot describe; but upon the whole, they put me in mind of some portraits I have seen, representing the females of Georgia and Mingrelia.[14]

On the third day, the wind being abated, though still unfavourable, we reimbarked and rowed along shore, passing by Porto-mauricio, and Oneglia; then turning the promontory called Capo di Melle, we proceeded by Albenga, Finale, and many other places of inferior note. Porto-mauricio is seated on a rock washed by the sea, but indifferently fortified, with an inconsiderable harbour, which none but very small vessels can enter. About two miles to the eastward is Oneglia, a small town with some fortifications, lying along the open beach, and belonging to the king of Sardinia. This small territory abounds with olive-trees, which produce a considerable quantity of oil, counted the best of the whole Riviera. Albenga is a small town, the see of a bishop, suffragan to the archbishop of Genoa. It lies upon the sea, and the country produces a great quantity of hemp. Finale is the capital of a marquisate belonging to the Genoese, which has been the source of much trouble to the republic; and indeed was the sole cause of their rupture with the king of Sardinia and the house of Austria in the year 1745.[15] The town is pretty well built; but the harbour is shallow, open, and unsafe: nevertheless, they build a good number of tartans and other vessels on the beach; and the neighbouring country abounds with oil and fruit, particularly with those excellent apples called *pomi carli*, which I have mentioned in a former letter.

In the evening we reached the Capo di Noli, counted very dangerous in blowing weather. It is a very high perpendicular rock or mountain washed by the sea, which has eaten into it in divers places, so as to form a great number of caverns. It extends about a couple of miles, and in some parts is indented into little creeks or bays, where there is a narrow margin of sandy beach between it and the water. When the wind is high, no feluca will attempt to pass it; even in a moderate breeze, the waves dashing against the rocks and caverns, which echo with the sound, make such an awful noise, and at the same time occasion such a rough sea, as one cannot hear, and see, and feel, without a secret horror.

On this side of the Cape, there is a beautiful strand cultivated like a garden; the plantations extend to the very tops of the hills, interspersed with villages, castles, churches, and villas. Indeed the whole Riviera is ornamented in the same manner, except in such places as admit of no building nor cultivation.

Having passed the Cape, we followed the winding of the coast, into a small bay, and arrived at the town of Noli, where we proposed to pass the night. You will be surprized that we did not go ashore sooner, in order to take some refreshment; but the truth is, we had a provision of ham, tongues, roasted pullets, cheese, bread, wine, and fruit, in the feluca, where we every day enjoyed a slight repast about one or two o'clock in the afternoon. This I mention as a necessary piece of information to those who may be inclined to follow the same route. We likewise found it convenient to lay in store of *l'eau de vie*, or brandy, for the use of the rowers, who always expect to share your comforts. On a meagre day, however, those ragamuffins will rather die of hunger than suffer the least morsel of flesh-meat to enter their mouths. I have frequently tried the experiment, by pressing them to eat something *gras*, on a Friday or Saturday: but they always declined it with marks of abhorrence, crying, *Dio me ne libere*! God deliver me from it! or some other words to that effect. I moreover observed, that not one of those fellows ever swore an oath, or spoke an indecent word. They would by no means put to sea, of a morning, before they had heard mass; and when the wind was unfavourable, they always set out with a hymn to the Blessed Virgin, or St. Elmo,[16] keeping time with their oars as they sung. I have indeed remarked all over this country, that a man who transgresses the institutions of the church in these small matters, is much more infamous than one who has committed the most flagrant crimes against nature and morality. A murderer, adulterer, or s—m—te,[17] will obtain easy absolution from the church, and even find favour with society; but a man who eats a pidgeon on a Saturday, without express licence, is avoided and abhorred, as a monster of reprobation. I have conversed with several intelligent persons on the subject; and have reason to believe, that a delinquent of this sort is considered as a luke-warm catholic, little better than a heretic; and of all crimes they look upon heresy as the most damnable.

Noli is a small republic of fishermen subject to Genoa; but very tenacious of their privileges. The town stands on the beach, tolerably well built, defended by a castle situated on a rock above it; and the harbour is of little consequence. The auberge was such as made us regret even the inn we had left at St. Remo. After a very odd kind of supper, which I cannot pretend to describe, we retired to our repose: but I had not been in bed five minutes, when I felt something crawling on different parts of my body, and taking a light to examine, perceived above a dozen large bugs. You must know I have the same kind of antipathy to these vermin, that some persons have to a cat or breast of veal. I started up immediately, and wrapping myself in a great coat, sick as I was, laid down in the outer room upon a chest, where I continued till morning.

One would imagine that in a mountainous country like this, there should be plenty of goats; and indeed, we saw many flocks of them feeding among the rocks, yet we could not procure half a pint of milk for our tea, if we had given the weight of it in gold. The people here have no idea of using milk, and when you ask them for it, they stand gaping with a foolish face of surprize, which is exceedingly provoking. It is amazing that instinct does not teach the peasants to feed their children with goat's milk, so much more nourishing and agreeable than the wretched sustenance on which they live. Next day we rowed by Vado and Savona, which last is a large town, with a strong citadel, and a harbour, which was formerly capable of receiving large ships: but it fell a sacrifice to the jealousy of the Genoese, who have partly choaked it up, on pretence that it should not afford shelter to the ships of war belonging to those states which might be at enmity with the republic.

Then we passed Albisola, Sestri di Ponente, Novi, Voltri, and a great number of villages, villas, and magnificent palaces belonging to the Genoese nobility, which form almost a continued chain of buildings along the strand for thirty miles.

About five in the afternoon, we skirted the fine suburbs of St. Pietro D'arena, and arrived at Genoa, which makes a dazzling appearance when viewed from the sea, rising like an amphitheatre in a circular form, from the water's edge, a considerable way up the mountains, and surrounded on the land side by a double wall, the most exterior of which is said to extend fifteen miles in circuit. The first object that strikes your eye at a distance, is a very elegant pharos, or lighthouse, built on the projection of a rock on the west side of the harbour, so very high, that, in a clear day, you may see it at the distance of thirty miles. Turning the light-house point, you find yourself close to the mole, which forms the harbour of Genoa. It is built at a great expence from each side of the bay, so as to form in the sea two long magnificent jettés. At the extremity of each is another smaller lanthorn. These moles are both provided with brass-cannon, and between them is the entrance into the harbour. But this is still so wide as to admit a great sea, which, when the wind blows hard from south and south-west, is very troublesome to the shipping. Within the mole there is a smaller harbour or wet dock, called *Darsena*, for the gallies of the republic. We passed through a considerable number of ships and vessels lying at anchor, and landing at the water-gate, repaired to an inn called *La Croix de Malthe*,[18] in the neighbourhood of the harbour. Here we met with such good entertainment as prepossessed us in favour of the interior parts of Italy, and contributed with other motives to detain us some days in this city. But, I have detained you so long, that I believe you wish I may proceed no farther; and therefore I take my leave for the present, being very sincerely,

Yours.

# LETTER XXVI.

Dear Sir,

It is not without reason that Genoa is called *La superba*. The city itself is very stately; and the nobles are very proud. Some few of them may be proud of their wealth: but, in general, their fortunes are very small. My friend Mr. R——[1] assured me that many Genoese noblemen had fortunes of half a million of livres *per annum*: but the truth is, the whole revenue of the state does not exceed this sum; and the livre of Genoa is but about nine pence sterling. There are about half a dozen of their nobles who have ten thousand a year: but the majority have not above a twentieth part of that sum. They live with great parsimony in their families; and wear nothing but black in public; so that their expences are but small. If a Genoese nobleman gives an entertainment once a quarter, he is said to live upon the fragments all the rest of the year. I was told that one of them lately treated his friends, and left the entertainment to the care of his son, who ordered a dish of fish that cost a zechine, which is equal to about ten shillings sterling. The old gentleman no sooner saw it appear on the table, than unable to suppress his concern, he burst into tears, and exclaimed, *Ah Figliuolo indegno! Siamo in Rovina! Siamo in precipizio!* Ah Prodigal! ruined! undone!

I think the pride or ostentation of the Italians in general takes a more laudable turn than that of other nations. A Frenchman lays out his whole revenue upon tawdry suits of cloaths, or in furnishing a magnificent *repas* of fifty or a hundred dishes, one half of which are not eatable, nor intended to be eaten. His wardrobe goes to the *fripier*;[2] his dishes to the dogs, and himself to the devil, and after his decease no vestige of him remains. A Genoese, on the other hand, keeps himself and his family at short allowance, that he may save money to build palaces and churches, which remain to after-ages so many monuments of his taste, piety, and munificence; and in the mean time give employment and bread to the poor and industrious. There are some Genoese nobles who have each five or six elegant palaces magnificently furnished, either in the city, or in different parts of the

Riviera. The two streets called *Strada Balbi* and *Strada Nuova*, are continued double ranges of palaces adorned with gardens and fountains: but their being painted on the outside has, in my opinion, a poor effect.

The commerce of this city is, at present, not very considerable; yet it has the face of business. The streets are crouded with people; the shops are well furnished; and the markets abound with all sorts of excellent provision. The wine made in this neighbourhood is, however, very indifferent; and all that is consumed must be bought at the public cantine, where it is sold for the benefit of the state. Their bread is the whitest and the best I have tasted any where; and the beef, which they have from Piedmont, is juicy and delicious. The expence of eating in Italy is nearly the same as in France, about three shillings a head for every meal. The state of Genoa is very poor, and their bank of St. George[3] has received such rude shocks, first from the revolt of the Corsicans, and afterwards from the misfortunes of the city, when it was taken by the Austrians in the war of 1745,[4] that it still continues to languish without any near prospect of its credit being restored. Nothing shews the weakness of their state more than their having recourse to the assistance of France to put a stop to the progress of Paoli in Corsica; for after all that has been said of the gallantry and courage of Paoli and his islanders, I am very credibly informed that they might be very easily suppressed, if the Genoese had either vigour in the council or resolution in the field.[5]

True it is, they made a noble effort in expelling the Austrians who had taken possession of their city; but this effort was the effect of oppression and despair, and if I may believe the insinuations of some politicians in this part of the world, the Genoese would not have succeeded in that attempt, if they had not previously purchased with a large sum of money the connivance of the only person who could defeat the enterprize. For my own part, I can scarce entertain thoughts so prejudicial to the character of human nature, as to suppose a man capable of sacrificing to such a consideration, the duty he owed his prince, as well as all regard to the lives of his soldiers, even those who lay sick in hospitals, and who being dragged forth, were miserably butchered by the furious populace. There is one more presumption of his innocence; he still retains the favour of his sovereign, who could not well be supposed to share in the booty.[6] "There are mysteries in politics which were never dreamed of in our philosophy, Horatio!"[7] The possession of Genoa might have proved a troublesome bone of contention, which it might be convenient to lose by accident. Certain it is, when the Austrians returned after their expulsion, in order to retake the city, the engineer, being questioned by the general, declared he would take the place in fifteen days, on pain of losing his head; and in four days after this declaration the Austrians retired. This anecdote I learned from a worthy gentleman of this country, who had it from the engineer's own mouth. Perhaps it was the will of heaven. You see how favourably providence has interposed in behalf of the reigning empress of Russia, first in removing her husband; secondly in ordaining the assassination of prince Ivan, for which the perpetrators have been so liberally rewarded; it even seems determined to shorten the life of her own son, the only surviving rival from whom she had any thing to fear.[8]

The Genoese have now thrown themselves into the arms of France for protection: I know not whether it would not have been a greater mark of sagacity to cultivate the friendship of England, with which they carry on an advantageous commerce. While the English are masters of the Mediterranean, they will always have it in their power to do incredible damage all along the Riviera, to ruin the Genoese trade by sea, and even to annoy the capital; for notwithstanding all the pains they have taken to fortify the mole and the city, I am greatly deceived if it is not still exposed to the danger, not only of a bombardment, but even of a cannonade. I am even sanguine enough to think a resolute commander might, with a strong squadron, sail directly into the harbour, without sustaining much damage, notwithstanding all the cannon of the place, which are said to amount to near five hundred. I have seen a cannonade of above four hundred pieces of artillery, besides bombs and cohorns, maintained for many hours, without doing much mischief.[9]

During the last siege of Genoa, the French auxiliaries were obliged to wait at Monaco, until a gale of wind had driven the English squadron off the coast, and then they went along shore in small vessels at the imminent risque of being taken by the British cruisers. By land I apprehend their march would be altogether impracticable, if the king of Sardinia had any interest to oppose it. He might either guard the passes, or break up the road in twenty different places, so as to render it altogether impassable. Here it may not be amiss to observe, that when Don Philip[10] advanced from Nice with his army to Genoa, he was obliged to march so close to the shore, that in above fifty different places, the English ships might have rendered the road altogether impassable. The path, which runs generally along the face of a precipice washed by the sea, is so narrow that two men on horseback can hardly pass each other; and the road itself so rugged, slippery, and dangerous, that the troopers were obliged to dismount, and lead their horses one by one. On the other hand, baron de Leutrum,[11] who was at the head of a large body of Piedmontese troops, had it in his power to block up the passes of the mountains, and even to destroy this road in such a manner, that the enemy could not possibly advance. Why these precautions were not taken, I do not pretend to explain: neither can I tell you wherefore the prince of Monaco, who is a subject and partizan of France, was indulged with a neutrality for his town, which served as a refreshing-place, a safe port, and an intermediate post for the French succours sent from Marseilles to Genoa. This I will only venture to affirm, that the success and advantage of great alliances are often sacrificed to low, partial, selfish, and sordid considerations. The town of Monaco is commanded by every heighth in its neighbourhood; and might be laid in ashes by a bomb-ketch in four hours by sea.

I was fortunate enough to be recommended to a lady in Genoa, who treated us with great politeness and hospitality. She introduced me to an *abbate*,[12] a man of letters, whose conversation was extremely agreeable. He already knew me by reputation, and offered to make me known to some of the first persons in the republic, with whom he lived in intimacy. The lady is one of the most intelligent and best-bred persons I have known in any country. We assisted at her conversazione, which was numerous. She pressed us to pass the winter at Genoa; and indeed I was almost persuaded: but I had attachments at Nice, from which I could not easily disengage myself.

The few days we stayed at Genoa were employed in visiting the most remarkable churches and palaces. In some of the churches, particularly that of the *Annunciata*, I found a profusion of ornaments, which had more magnificence than taste. There is a great number of pictures; but very few of them are capital pieces. I had heard much of the *Ponte Carignano*, which did not at all answer my expectation. It is a bridge that unites two eminences which form the higher part of the city, and the houses in the bottom below do not rise so high as the springing of its arches. There is nothing at all curious in its construction, nor any way remarkable, except the heighth of the piers from which the arches are sprung. Hard by the bridge there is an elegant church,[13] from the top of which you have a very rich and extensive prospect of the city, the sea and the adjacent country, which looks like a continent of groves and villas. The only remarkable circumstance about the cathedral,[14] which is Gothic and gloomy, is the chapel where the pretended bones of John the Baptist are deposited, and in which thirty silver lamps are continually burning. I had a curiosity to see the palaces of Durazzo and Doria, but it required more trouble to procure admission than I was willing to give myself: as for the arsenal, and the rostrum of an ancient galley which was found by accident in dragging the harbour, I postponed seeing them till my return.

Having here provided myself with letters of credit for Florence and Rome, I hired the same boat which had brought us hither, to carry us forward to Lerici, which is a small town about half way between Genoa and Leghorn, where travellers, who are tired of the sea, take post-chaises to continue their route by land to Pisa and Florence. I payed three loui'dores for this voyage of about fifty miles; though I might have had a felucca for less money. When you land on the wharf at Genoa, you are plied by the felucca men just as you are plied by the watermen at Hungerford-stairs[15] in London. They are always ready to set off at a minute's warning for Lerici, Leghorn, Nice, Antibes, Marseilles, and every part of the Riviera.

The wind being still unfavourable, though the weather was delightful, we rowed along shore, passing by several pretty towns, villages, and a vast number of *cassines*, or little white houses, scattered among woods of olive trees, that cover the hills; and these are the habitations of the velvet and damask weavers. Turning Capo Fino we entered a bay, where stand the towns of Porto Fino, Lavagna, and Sestri di Levante, at which last we took up our night's lodging. The house was tolerable, and we had no great reason to complain of the beds: but, the weather being hot, there was a very offensive smell, which proceeded from some skins of beasts new killed, that were spread to dry on an out-house in the yard. Our landlord was a butcher, and had very much the looks of an assassin. His wife was a great masculine virago, who had all the air of having frequented the slaughter-house. Instead of being welcomed with looks of complaisance, we were admitted with a sort of gloomy condescension, which seemed to say, "We don't much like your company; but, however, you shall have a night's lodging in favour of the *patron of the gondola*, who is our acquaintance." In short, we had a very bad supper, miserably dressed, passed a very disagreeable night, and payed a very extravagant bill in the morning, without being thanked for our custom. I was very glad to get out of the house with my throat uncut.

Sestri di Levante is a little town pleasantly situated on the sea-side; but has not the conveniency of a harbour. The fish taken here is mostly carried to Genoa. This is likewise the market for their oil, and the paste called *macaroni*, of which they make a good quantity.

Next day, we skirted a very barren coast, consisting of almost perpendicular rocks, on the faces of which, however, we saw many peasants' houses and hanging terraces for vines, made by dint of incredible labour. In the afternoon, we entered by the Porto di Venere into the bay, or gulf of Spetia or Spezza, which was the Portus Lunæ of the ancients. This bay, at the mouth of which lies the island Palmaria, forms a most noble and secure harbour, capacious enough to contain all the navies in Christendom. The entrance on one side is defended by a small fort built above the town of Porto

Venere, which is a very poor place. Farther in there is a battery of about twenty guns; and on the right hand, opposite to Porto Venere, is a block-house, founded on a rock in the sea. At the bottom of the bay is the town of Spetia on the left, and on the right that of Lerici, defended by a castle of very little strength or consequence. The whole bay is surrounded with plantations of olives and oranges, and makes a very delightful appearance. In case of a war, this would be an admirable station for a British squadron, as it lies so near Genoa and Leghorn; and has a double entrance, by means of which the cruisers could sail in and out continually, which way soever the wind might chance to sit. I am sure the fortifications would give very little disturbance.

At the post-house in Lerici, the accommodation is intolerable. We were almost poisoned at supper. I found the place where I was to lie so close and confined, that I could not breathe in it, and therefore lay all night in an outward room upon four chairs, with a leathern portmanteau for my pillow. For this entertainment I payed very near a loui'dore. Such bad accommodation is the less excusable, as the fellow has a great deal of business, this being a great thoroughfare for travellers going into Italy, or returning from thence.

I might have saved some money by prosecuting my voyage directly by sea to Leghorn: but, by this time, we were all heartily tired of the water: the business then was to travel by land to Florence, by the way of Pisa, which is seven posts distant from Lerici. Those who have not their own carriage must either hire chaises to perform the whole journey, or travel by way of *cambiatura*, which is that of changing the chaises every post, as the custom is in England. In this case the great inconvenience arises from your being obliged to shift your baggage every post. The chaise or *calesse* of this country, is a wretched machine with two wheels, as uneasy as a common cart, being indeed no other than what we should call in England a very ill-contrived one-horse chair, narrow, naked, shattered and shabby. For this vehicle and two horses you pay at the rate of eight *paoli* a stage, or four shillings sterling; and the postilion expects two *paoli* for his gratification: so that every eight miles cost about five shillings, and four only, if you travel in your own carriage, as in that case you pay no more than at the rate of three *paoli* a horse.[16]

About three miles from Lerici, we crossed the Magra, which appeared as a rivulet almost dry, and in half a mile farther arrived at Sarzana, a small town at the extremity of the Genoese territories, where we changed horses. Then entering the principalities of Massa and Carrara, belonging to the duke of Modena,[17] we passed Lavenza, which seems to be a decayed fort with a small garrison, and dined at Massa, which is an agreeable little town, where the old dutchess of Modena resides. Notwithstanding all the expedition we could make, it was dark before we passed the Cerchio, which is an inconsiderable stream in the neighbourhood of Pisa, where we arrived about eight in the evening.

The country from Sarzana to the frontiers of Tuscany is a narrow plain, bounded on the right by the sea, and on the left by the Appenine mountains. It is well cultivated and inclosed, consisting of meadow-ground, corn fields, plantations of olives; and the trees that form the hedge-rows serve as so many props to the vines, which are twisted round them, and continued from one to another. After entering the dominions of Tuscany, we travelled through a noble forest of oak trees of a considerable extent, which would have appeared much more agreeable, had we not been benighted and apprehensive of robbers. The last post but one in this day's journey, is at the little town of Viareggio, a kind of sea-port on the Mediterranean, belonging to Lucca. The roads are indifferent, and the accommodation is execrable. I was glad to find myself housed in a very good inn at Pisa, where I promised myself a good night's rest, and was not disappointed. I heartily wish you the same pleasure, and am very sincerely

Yours.

# LETTER XXVII.

*Nice, January* 28, 1765.

DEAR SIR,

Pisa is a fine old city that strikes you with the same veneration you would feel at sight of an antient temple which bears the marks of decay, without being absolutely delapidated. The houses are well built, the streets open, straight, and well paved; the shops well furnished; and the markets well supplied: there are some elegant palaces, designed by great masters. The churches are built with taste, and tolerably ornamented. There is a beautiful wharf of free-stone on each side of the river Arno, which runs through the city, and three bridges thrown over it, of which that in the middle is of marble, a pretty piece of architecture: but the number of inhabitants is very inconsiderable; and this very circumstance gives it an air of majestic solitude, which is far from being unpleasant to a man of a contemplative turn of mind. For my part, I cannot bear the tumult of a populous commercial city; and the solitude that reigns in Pisa would with me be a strong motive to choose it as a place of residence.[1] Not that this would be the only inducement for living at Pisa. Here is some good company, and even a few men of taste and learning. The people in general are counted sociable and polite; and there is great plenty of provisions, at a very reasonable rate. At some distance from the more frequented parts of the city, a man may hire a large house for thirty crowns a year: but near the center, you cannot have good lodgings, ready furnished, for less than a *scudo* (about five shillings) a day. The air in summer is reckoned unwholesome by the exhalations arising from stagnant water in the neighbourhood of the city, which stands in the midst of a fertile plain, low and marshy: yet these marshes have been considerably drained; and the air is much meliorated. As for the Arno, it is no longer navigated by vessels of any burthen. The university of Pisa is very much decayed; and except the little business occasioned by the emperor's gallies, which are built in this town,[*2] I know of no commerce it carries on: perhaps the

* This is a mistake—no gallies have been built here for a great many years; and the dock is now converted into stables for the grand duke's horse guards.

214

inhabitants live on the produce of the country, which consists of corn, wine, and cattle. They are supplied with excellent water for drinking, by an aqueduct consisting of above a thousand arches, begun by Cosmo,[3] and finished by Ferdinand I.[4] grand-dukes of Tuscany; it conveys the water from the mountains at the distance of four miles. This noble city, formerly the capital of a flourishing and powerful republic, which contained above one hundred and fifty thousand inhabitants within its walls, is now so desolate that grass grows in the open streets; and the number of its people do not exceed sixteen thousand.

You need not doubt but I visited the Campanile, or hanging-tower, which is a beautiful cylinder of eight stories, each adorned with a round of columns, rising one above another. It stands by the cathedral, and inclines so far on one side from the perpendicular, that in dropping a plummet from the top, which is one hundred and eighty-eight feet high, it falls sixteen feet from the base. For my part, I should never have dreamed that this inclination proceeded from any other cause, than an accidental subsidence of the foundation on this side, if some connoisseurs had not taken great pains to prove it was done on purpose by the architect. Any person who has eyes may see that the pillars on that side are considerably sunk; and this is the case with the very threshold of the door by which you enter. I think it would have been a very preposterous ambition in the architects, to shew how far they could deviate from the perpendicular in this construction; because in that particular any common mason could have rivalled them;* and if they really intended it as a specimen of their art, they should have shortened the pilasters on that side, so as to exhibit them intire, without the appearance of sinking. These leaning towers are not unfrequent in Italy; there is one at Bologna, another at Venice, a third betwixt Venice and Ferrara, and a fourth at Ravenna; and the inclination in all of them has been supposed owing to the foundations giving way on one side only.

* All the world knows that a building with such inclination, may be carried up till a line drawn from the centre of gravity, falls without the circumference of the base.

In the cathedral, which is a large Gothic* pile, there is a great number of massy pillars of porphyry, granite, jasper, giullo, and verde antico, together with some good pictures and statues: but the greatest curiosity is that of the brass gates, designed and executed by John of Bologna,[8] representing, embossed in different compartments, the history of the Old and New Testament. I was so charmed with this work, that I could have stood a whole day to examine and admire it. In the Baptisterium, which stands opposite to this front, there are some beautiful marbles, particularly the font, and a pulpit, supported by the statues of different animals.

Between the cathedral and this building, about one hundred paces on one side, is the famous burying-ground, called *Campo Santo*, from its being covered with earth brought from Jerusalem. It is an oblong square, surrounded by a very high wall, and always kept shut. Within-side there is a spacious corridore round the whole space, which is a noble walk for a contemplative philosopher. It is paved chiefly with flat grave-stones: the walls are painted in fresco by Ghiotto, Giottino, Stefano, Bennoti, Buffalmaco,[9] and some others of his cotemporaries and disciples, who flourished immediately after the restoration of painting. The subjects are taken from the Bible. Though the manner is dry, the drawing incorrect, the design generally lame, and the colouring unnatural; yet there is merit in the expression: and the whole remains as a curious monument of the efforts made by this noble art immediately after her revival.† Here are some deceptions in perspective equally ingenious and pleasing; particularly the figures of certain animals, which exhibit exactly the same appearance, from whatever different points

---

*This edifice is not absolutely Gothic. It was built in the twelfth century after the design of a Greek architect from Constaninople[5] where by that time the art was much degenerated. The pillars of *granite* are mostly from the islands of *Elba* and *Giglia* on the coast of *Tuscany*, where those quarries were worked by the antient Romans. The *giullo*, and *verde antico*,[6] are very beautifull species of marble, yellow and green; the first, antiently called *marmor numidicum*, came from *Africa*; the other was found (according to *Strabo*) on the *mons Taygetus* in *Lacedemonia*:[7] but, at present, neither the one, nor the other is to be had except among the ruins of antiquity.
†The history of *Job* by *Giotto* is much admired.[10]

of view they are seen. One division of the burying-ground consists of a particular compost, which in nine days consumes the dead bodies to the bones: in all probability, it is no other than common earth mixed with quick-lime. At one corner of the corridore, there are the pictures of three bodies represented in the three different stages of putrefaction which they undergo when laid in this composition. At the end of the three first days, the body is bloated and swelled, and the features are enlarged and distorted to such a degree, as fills the spectator with horror. At the sixth day, the swelling is subsided, and all the muscular flesh hangs loosened from the bones: at the ninth, nothing but the skeleton remains. There is a small neat chapel at one end of the *Campo Santo*, with some tombs, on one of which is a beautiful bust by Buona Roti.*[11] At the other end of the corridore, there is a range of antient sepulchral stones ornamented with basso relievo, brought hither from different parts by the *Pisan* fleets, in the course of their expeditions. I was struck with the figure of a woman lying dead on a tomb-stone, covered with a piece of thin drapery, so delicately cut as to shew all the flexures of the attitude, and even all the swellings and sinuosities of the muscles. Instead of stone, it looks like a sheet of wet linen.†

---

*Here is a sumptuous *cenotaph* erected by pope Gregory XIII.[12] to the memory of his brother *Giovanni Buoncampagni*. It is called the *Monumentum Gregorianum*, of a violet coloured marble from *Seravezza* in this neighbourhood, adorned with a couple of columns of *touchstone*,[13] and two beautifull, spherical plates of alabaster.

†One of these antiquities representing the hunting of *Meleager*,[14] was converted into a coffin for the countess *Beatrice*,[15] mother of the famous countess *Mathilda*. It is now fixed to the outside of the church wall just by one of the doors, and is a very elegant piece of sculpture. Near the same place is a fine pillar of porphyry supporting the figure of a lyon and a kind of urn which seems to be a *sarcophagus*, though an inscription round the base, declares it is a *talentum* in which the antient *Pisans* measured the *census* or tax which they payed to *Augustus:* but in what metal or specie this census was payed, we are left to divine. There are likewise in the *Campo Santo* two antique Latin edicts of the *Pisan* Senate injoining the citizens to go into mourning for the death of *Caius* and *Lucius Caesar* the sons of *Agrippa*, and heirs declared of the emperor.[16] Fronting this cemetery on the other side of the Piazza of the Dome, is a large, elegant hospital in which the sick are conveniently and comfortably lodged, entertained and attended.

For four zechines I hired a return-coach and four from Pisa to Florence. This road, which lies along the Arno, is very good; and the country is delightful, variegated with hill and vale, wood and water, meadows and corn-fields, planted and inclosed like the counties of Middlesex and Hampshire; with this difference, however, that all the trees in this tract were covered with vines, and the ripe clusters black and white, hung down from every bough in the most luxuriant and romantic abundance. The vines in this country are not planted in rows, and propped with sticks, as in France and the county of Nice, but twine around the hedge-row trees, which they almost quite cover with their foliage and fruit. The branches of the vine are extended from tree to tree, exhibiting beautiful festoons of real leaves, tendrils, and swelling clusters a foot long. By this œconomy the ground of the inclosure is spared for corn, grass, or any other production. The trees commonly planted for the purpose of sustaining the vines, are maple, elm, and aller,[17] with which last the banks of the Arno abound.* This river, which is very inconsiderable with respect to the quantity of water, would be a charming pastoral stream, if it was transparent; but it is always muddy and discoloured. About ten or a dozen miles below Florence, there are some marble quarries on the side of it, from whence the blocks are conveyed in boats, when there is water enough in the river to float them, that is, after heavy rains, or the melting of the snow upon the mountains of Umbria, being part of the Appenines, from whence it takes its rise.

Florence is a noble city, that still retains all the marks of a majestic capital, such as piazzas, palaces, fountains, bridges, statues, and arcades. I need not tell you that the churches here are magnificent, and adorned not only with pillars of oriental granite, porphyry, jasper, verde antico, and other precious stones; but also with capital pieces of painting by the most eminent masters. Several of these churches, however, stand without fronts, for want of money to complete the plans. It may also appear superfluous to mention my having viewed

---

* It would have been still more for the advantage of the country and the prospect, if instead of these they had planted fruit trees for this purpose.

the famous gallery of antiquities, the chapel of St. Lorenzo, the palace of Pitti, the cathedral, the baptisterium, the *Ponte de Trinita*, with its statues, the triumphal arch, and every thing which is commonly visited in this metropolis. But all these objects having been circumstantially described by twenty different authors of travels, I shall not trouble you with a repetition of trite observations.

That part of the city which stands on each side of the river, makes a very elegant appearance, to which the four bridges and the stone-quay between them, contribute in a great measure. I lodged at the widow Vanini's, an English house delightfully situated in this quarter. The landlady, who is herself a native of England, we found very obliging. The lodging-rooms are comfortable; and the entertainment is good and reasonable.[18] There is a considerable number of fashionable people at Florence, and many of them in good circumstances. They affect a gaiety in their dress, equipage, and conversation; but stand very much on their punctilio with strangers; and will not, without great reluctance, admit into their assemblies any lady of another country, whose noblesse is not ascertained by a title. This reserve is in some measure excusable among a people who are extremely ignorant of foreign customs, and who know that in their own country, every person, even the most insignificant, who has any pretensions to family, either inherits, or assumes the title of *principe*, *conte*, or *marchese*.

With all their pride, however, the nobles of Florence are humble enough to enter into partnership with shop-keepers, and even to sell wine by retail. It is an undoubted fact, that in every palace or great house in this city, there is a little window fronting the street, provided with an iron-knocker, and over it hangs an empty flask, by way of sign-post. Thither you send your servant to buy a bottle of wine. He knocks at the little wicket, which is opened immediately by a domestic, who supplies him with what he wants, and receives the money like the waiter of any other cabaret. It is pretty extraordinary, that it should not be deemed a disparagement in a nobleman to sell half a pound of figs, or a palm[19] of ribbon or tape, or to take money for a flask of sour wine; and yet be counted infamous to match his daughter in the family of a person who has distinguished himself in any one of the learned professions.

Though Florence be tolerably populous, there seems to be very little trade of any kind in it: but the inhabitants flatter themselves with the prospect of reaping great advantage from the residence of one of the arch-dukes, for whose reception they are now repairing the palace of Pitti.[20] I know not what the revenues of Tuscany may amount to, since the succession of the princes of Lorraine; but, under the last dukes of the Medici family, they were said to produce two millions of crowns, equal to five hundred thousand pounds sterling. These arose from a very heavy tax upon land and houses, the portions of maidens, and suits at law, besides the duties upon traffick, a severe gabelle upon the necessaries of life, and a toll upon every eatable entered into this capital. If we may believe Leti, the grand duke was then able to raise and maintain an army of forty thousand infantry, and three thousand horse; with twelve gallies, two galeasses, and twenty ships of war.[21] I question if Tuscany can maintain at present above one half of such an armament. He that now commands the emperor's navy, consisting of a few frigates, is an Englishman, called Acton, who was heretofore captain of a ship in our East India company's service. He has lately embraced the catholic religion, and been created admiral of Tuscany.[22]

There is a tolerable opera in Florence for the entertainment of the best company, though they do not seem very attentive to the musick. Italy is certainly the native country of this art; and yet, I do not find the people in general either more musically inclined, or better provided with ears than their neighbours. Here is also a wretched troop of comedians for the bourgeois, and lower class of people: but what seems most to suit the taste of all ranks, is the exhibition of church pageantry. I had occasion to see a procession, where all the noblesse of the city attended in their coaches, which filled the whole length of the great street called the *Corso*. It was the anniversary of a charitable institution[23] in favour of poor maidens, a certain number of whom are portioned every year. About two hundred of these virgins walked in procession, two and two together, cloathed in violet-coloured wide gowns, with white veils on their heads, and made a very classical appearance. They were preceded and followed by an irregular mob of penitents in sack-cloth, with lighted tapers, and monks carrying crucifixes, bawling and bellowing the litanies: but the great object was a figure of the Virgin Mary, as big as the life, standing within a gilt frame, dressed in a gold stuff, with a large hoop, a great quantity of false jewels, her face painted and patched, and her hair frizzled and curled in the very extremity of the fashion. Very little regard had been paid to the image of our Saviour on the cross; but when his lady-mother appeared on the shoulders of three or four lusty friars, the whole populace fell upon their knees in the dirt. This extraordinary veneration paid to the Virgin, must have been derived originally from the French, who pique themselves on their gallantry to the fair sex.

Amidst all the scenery of the Roman catholic religion, I have never yet seen any of the spectators affected at heart, or discover the least signs of fanaticism. The very disciplinants, who scourge themselves in the Holy-week, are generally peasants or parties hired for the purpose. Those of the confrairies, who have an ambition to distinguish themselves on such occasions, take care to secure their backs from the smart, by means of secret armour, either women's boddice, or quilted jackets. The confrairies are fraternities of devotees, who inlist themselves under the banners of particular saints. On days of procession they appear in a body dressed as penitents and masked, and distinguished by crosses on their habits. There is scarce an individual, whether noble or plebeian, who does not belong to one of these associations, which may be compared to the Free-Masons, Gregoreans, and Antigallicans[24] of England.

Just without one of the gates of Florence, there is a triumphal arch erected on occasion of the late emperor's making his public entry, when he succeeded to the dukedom of Tuscany: and here in the summer evenings, the quality resort to take the air in their coaches. Every carriage stops, and forms a little separate conversazione. The ladies sit within, and the cicisbei[25] stand on the foot-boards, on each side of the coach, entertaining them with their discourse. It would be no unpleasant inquiry to trace this sort of gallantry to its original, and investigate all its progress. The Italians, having been accused of jealousy, were resolved to wipe off the reproach, and, seeking to avoid it for the future, have run into the other extreme. I know it is generally supposed that the custom of choosing cicisbei, was calculated to prevent the extinction of families, which would otherwise often happen in consequence of marriages founded upon interest, without any mutual affection in the contracting parties. How far this political consideration may have weighed against the jealous and vindictive temper of the Italians, I will not pretend to judge: but, certain it is, every married lady in this country has her cicisbeo, or servente, who attends her every where, and on all occasions; and upon whose privileges the husband dares not encroach, without incurring the censure and ridicule of the whole community. For my part, I would rather be condemned for life to the gallies, than exercise the office of a cicisbeo, exposed to the intolerable caprices and dangerous resentment of an Italian virago. I pretend not to judge of the national character, from my own observation: but, if the portraits drawn by Goldoni[26] in his Comedies are taken from nature, I would not hesitate to pronounce the Italian women the most haughty, insolent, capricious and revengeful females on the face of the earth. Indeed, their resentments are so cruelly implacable, and contain such a mixture of perfidy, that, in my opinion, they are very unfit subjects for comedy, whose province it is, rather to ridicule folly than to stigmatize such atrocious vice.

You have often heard it said, that the purity of the Italian is to be found in the *lingua Toscana*, and *bocca Romana*. Certain it is, the pronunciation of the Tuscans is disagreeably guttural: the letters C and G they pronounce with an aspiration, which hurts the ear of an Englishman; and is, I think, rather rougher than that of the X, in Spanish. It sounds as if the speaker had lost his palate. I really imagined the first man I heard speak in Pisa, had met with that misfortune in the course of his amours.

One of the greatest curiosities you meet with in Italy, is the Improvisatore;[27] such is the name given to certain individuals, who have the surprising talent of reciting verses extempore, on any subject you propose. Mr. Corvesi, my landlord,[28] has a son, a Franciscan friar, who is a great genius in this way. When the subject is given, his brother tunes his violin to accompany him, and he begins to rehearse in recitative, with wonderful fluency and precision. Thus he will, at a minute's warning, recite two or three hundred verses, well turned, and well adapted, and generally mingled with an elegant compliment to the company. The Italians are so fond of poetry, that many of them have the best part of Ariosto, Tasso, and Petrarch, by heart; and these are the great sources from which the Improvisatori draw their rhimes, cadence, and turns of expression. But, lest you should think there is neither rhime nor reason in protracting this tedious epistle, I shall conclude it with the old burden of my song, that I am always

Your affectionate humble servant.

DEAR SIR,

Your entertaining letter of the fifth of last month, was a very charitable and a very agreeable donation: but your suspicion is groundless. I assure you, upon my honour, I have no share whatever in any of the disputes which agitate the public: nor do I know any thing of your political transactions, except what I casually see in one of your newspapers, with the perusal of which I am sometimes favoured by our consul at Villefranche. You insist upon my being more particular in my remarks on what I saw at Florence, and I shall obey the injunction. The famous gallery which contains the antiquities, is the third story of a noble stone-edifice, built in the form of the Greek Π, the upper part fronting the river Arno, and one of the legs adjoining to the ducal-palace, where the courts of justice are held.[1] As the house of Medici had for some centuries resided in the palace of Pitti, situated on the other side of the river, a full mile from these tribunals, the architect Vasari,[2] who planned the new edifice, at the same time contrived a corridore, or covered passage, extending from the palace of Pitti along one of the bridges, to the gallery of curiosities, through which the grand-duke passed unseen, when he was disposed either to amuse himself with his antiquities, or to assist at his courts of judicature: but there is nothing very extraordinary either in the contrivance or execution of this corridore.

If I resided in Florence I would give something extraordinary for permission to walk every day in the gallery, which I should much prefer to the Lycæum, the groves of Academus,[3] or any porch or philosophical alley in Athens or in Rome. Here by viewing the statues and busts ranged on each side, I should become acquainted with the faces of all the remarkable personages, male and female, of antiquity, and even be able to trace their different characters from the expression of their features. This collection is a most excellent commentary upon the Roman historians, particularly Suetonius[4] and Dion Cassius.[5] There was one circumstance that struck me in viewing the busts of Caracalla,[6] both here and in the Capitol at Rome; that was a certain ferocity in the eyes, which seemed to contradict the sweetness of the other features, and remarkably justified the epithet *Caracuyl*, by which he was distinguished by the antient inhabitants of North-Britain. In the language of the Highlanders *caracuyl* signifies *cruel eye*, as we are given to understand by the ingenious editor of Fingal, who seems to think that Caracalla is no other than the Celtic word, adapted to the pronunciation of the Romans: but the truth is, Caracalla was the name of a Gaulish vestment, which this prince affected to wear; and hence he derived that surname.[7] The Caracuyl of the Britons, is the same as the *ὑπόδρα ἰδώ᾽ν*[8] of the Greeks, which Homer has so often applied to his Scolding Heroes. I like the Bacchanalian, chiefly for the fine drapery. The wind, occasioned by her motion, seems to have swelled and raised it from the parts of the body which it covers. There is another gay Bacchanalian, in the attitude of dancing, crowned with ivy, holding in her right hand a bunch of grapes, and in her left the thyrsus.[9] The head of the celebrated Flora is very beautiful: the groupe of Cupid and Psyche, however, did not give me all the pleasure I expected from it.

Of all the marbles that appear in the open gallery, the following are those I most admire. Leda with the Swan; as for Jupiter, in this transformation, he has much the appearance of a goose. I have not seen any thing tamer: but the sculptor has admirably shewn his art in representing Leda's hand partly hid among the feathers, which are so lightly touched off, that the very shape of the fingers are seen underneath. The statue of a youth, supposed to be Ganymede,[10] is compared by the connoisseurs to the celebrated Venus, and as far as I can judge, not without reason: it is, however, rather agreeable than striking, and will please a connoisseur much more than a common spectator. I know not whether it is my regard to the faculty that inhances the value of the noted Æsculapius,[11] who appears with a venerable beard of delicate workmanship. He is larger than the life, cloathed in a magnificent pallium,[12] his left arm resting on a knotted staff, round which the snake is twined, according to Ovid:

*Hunc modo serpentem baculum qui nexibus ambit*

*Perspice*——[13]

Behold the snake his mystic rod intwine.

He has in his hand the *fascia herbarum*, and the *crepidæ*[14] on his feet. There is a wild-boar represented lying on one side, which I admire as a master-piece. The savageness of his appearance is finely contrasted with the ease and indolence of the attitude. Were I to meet with a living boar lying with the same expression, I should be tempted to stroke his bristles. Here is an elegant bust of Antinous, the favourite of Adrian;[15] and a beautiful head of Alexander the Great, turned on one side, with an expression of languishment and anxiety in his countenance. The virtuosi are not agreed about the circumstance in which he is represented; whether fainting with the loss of blood which he suffered in his adventure at Oxydrace;[16] or languishing with the fever contracted by bathing in the Cydnus,[17] or finally complaining to his father Jove, that there were no other worlds for him to conquer.[18] The kneeling Narcissus is a striking figure, and the expression admirable. The two Bacchi are perfectly well executed; but (to my shame be it spoken) I prefer to the antique that which is the work of Michael Angelo Buonaroti, concerning which the story is told which you well know. The artist having been blamed by some pretended connoisseurs, for not imitating the manner of the ancients, is said to have privately finished this Bacchus, and buried it, after having broke off an arm, which he kept as a voucher. The statue, being dug up by accident, was allowed by the best judges, to be a perfect antique; upon which Buonaroti produced the arm, and claimed his own work. *Bianchi* looks upon this as a fable; but owns that Vasari tells such another of a child cut in marble by the same artist, which being carried to Rome, and kept for some time under ground, was dug up as an antique, and sold for a great deal of money.[19] I was likewise attracted by the Morpheus in touchstone, which is described by Addison,[20] who, by the bye, notwithstanding all his taste, has been convicted by Bianchi of several gross blunders in his account of this gallery.

With respect to the famous Venus Pontia, commonly called *de Medicis*, which was found at Tivoli, and is kept in a separate apartment called the *Tribuna*, I believe I ought to be intirely silent, or at least conceal my real sentiments, which will otherwise appear equally absurd and presumptuous. It must be want of taste that prevents my feeling that enthusiastic admiration with which others are inspired at sight of this statue: a statue which in reputation equals that of Cupid by Praxiteles,[21] which brought such a concourse of strangers of old to the little town of Thespiæ.[22] I cannot help thinking that there is no beauty in the features of Venus; and that the attitude is aukward and out of character.[23] It is a bad plea to urge that the antients and we differ in the ideas of beauty. We know the contrary, from their medals, busts, and historians. Without all doubt, the limbs and proportions of this statue are elegantly formed, and accurately designed, according to the nicest rules of symmetry and proportion; and the back parts especially are executed so happily, as to excite the admiration of the most indifferent spectator. One cannot help thinking it is the very Venus of *Cnidos* by Praxiteles, which Lucian describes. "Hercle quanta dorsi concinnitas! ut exuberantes lumbi amplexantes manus implent! quam scite circumductæ clunium pulpæ in se rotundantur, neque tenues nimis ipsis ossibus adstrictæ, neque in immensam effusæ pinguedinem!" "Heavens! what a beautifull back! the loins, with what exuberance they fill the grasp! how finely are the swelling buttocks rounded, neither too thinly cleaving to the bone, nor effused into a huge mass of flabby consistence!"[24] That the statue thus described was not the *Venus de Medicis*, would appear from the Greek inscription on the base, *ΚΛΕΟΜΕΝΗΣ ΑΠΟΛΛΟΔΟΡΟΥ ΑΘΗΝΑΙΟΣ ΕΠΩΕΣΕΝ*. *Cleomenes filius Apollodori fecit*; did we not know that this inscription is counted spurious, and that instead of *ΕΠΩΕΣΕΝ*, it should be *ΕΠΟΙΗΣΕ*. This, however, is but a frivolous objection, as we have seen many inscriptions undoubtedly antique, in which the orthography is false, either from the ignorance or carelessness of the sculptor. Others suppose, not without reason, that this statue is a representation of the famous Phryne, the courtesan of Athens, who at the celebration of the Eleusinian games, exhibited herself coming out of the bath, naked, to the eyes of the whole Athenian people.[25] I was much pleased with the dancing faun; and still better with the Lotti, or wrestlers, the attitudes of which are beautifully contrived to shew the different turns of the limbs, and the swelling of the muscles: but, what pleased me best of all the statues in the Tribuna was the Arrotino, commonly called the Whetter, and generally supposed to represent a slave, who in the act of whetting a knife, overhears the conspiracy of Cataline.[26] You know he is represented on one knee; and certain it is, I never saw such an expression of anxious attention, as appears in his countenance. But it is not mingled with any marks of surprise, such as could not fail to lay hold on a man who overhears by accident a conspiracy against the state. The marquis de Maffei[27] has justly observed that Sallust, in his very circumstantial detail of that conspiracy, makes no mention of any such discovery. Neither does it appear, that the figure is in the act of whetting, the stone which he holds in one hand being rough and unequal, no ways resembling a whetstone. Other alledge it represents Milico, the freedman of Scævinus, who conspired against the life of Nero, and gave his poignard to be whetted to Milico, who presented it to the emperor, with an account of the conspiracy:[28] but the attitude and expression will by no means admit of this interpretation. *Bianchi*, who shews the gallery,* thinks the statue represents the augur Attius Navius,[29] who cut a stone with a knife, at the command of Tarquinius Priscus. This conjecture seems to be confirmed by a medallion of Antoninus Pius, inserted by Vaillant[30] among his Numismata Prestantiora, on which is delineated nearly such a figure as this in question, with the following legend, "Attius Navius genuflexus ante Tarquinium Priscum cotem cultro discidit." He owns indeed that in the statue, the augur is not distinguished either by his habit or emblems; and he might have added, neither is the stone a cotes.[31] For my own part, I think neither of these three opinions is satisfactory, though the last is very ingenious. Perhaps the figure alludes to a private incident, which never was recorded in any history.[32] Among the great

---

* This antiquarian is now imprisoned for life, for having robbed the gallery and then set it on fire.

number of pictures in this Tribuna, I was most charmed with the Venus by Titian, which has a sweetness of expression and tenderness of colouring, not to be described. In this apartment, they reckon three hundred pieces, the greatest part by the best masters, particularly by Raphael, in the three manners by which he distinguished himself at different periods of his life. As for the celebrated statue of the hermaphrodite, which we find in another room, I give the sculptor credit for his ingenuity in mingling the sexes in the composition; but it is, at best, no other than a monster in nature, which I never had any pleasure in viewing: nor, indeed, do I think there was much talent required in representing a figure with the head and breasts of a woman, and all the other parts of the body masculine. There is such a profusion of curiosities in this celebrated musæum; statues, busts, pictures, medals, tables inlaid in the way of marquetry, cabinets adorned with precious stones, jewels of all sorts, mathematical instruments, antient arms and military machines, that the imagination is bewildered; and a stranger of a visionary turn, would be apt to fancy himself in a palace of the fairies, raised and adorned by the power of inchantment.

In one of the detached apartments, I saw the antependium of the altar, designed for the famous chapel of St. Lorenzo. It is a curious piece of architecture, inlaid with coloured marble and precious stones, so as to represent an infinite variety of natural objects. It is adorned with some crystal pillars, with capitals of beaten gold. The second story of the building is occupied by a great number of artists employed in this very curious work of marquetry, representing figures with gems and different kinds of coloured marble, for the use of the emperor. The Italians call it *pietre commesse*, a sort of inlaying with stones, analogous to the fineering of cabinets in wood. It is peculiar to Florence, and seems to be still more curious than the Mosaic work, which the Romans have brought to great perfection.

The cathedral of Florence is a great Gothic building, encrusted on the outside with marble; it is remarkable for nothing but its cupola, which is said to have been copied by the architect of St. Peter's at Rome, and for its size, which is

much greater than that of any other church in Christendom.*
The baptistery, which stands by it, was an antient temple,
said to be dedicated to Mars. There are some good statues of
marble within; and one or two of bronze on the outside of the
doors; but it is chiefly celebrated for the embossed work of its
brass gates, by Lorenzo Ghiberti,[35] which Buonaroti used to
say, deserved to be made the gates of Paradise. I viewed them
with pleasure: but still I retained a greater veneration for
those of Pisa, which I had first admired: a preference which
either arises from want of taste, or from the charm of
novelty, by which the former were recommended to my
attention. Those who would have a particular detail of
every thing worth seeing at Florence, comprehending
churches, libraries, palaces, tombs, statues, pictures, fountains, bridges, &c. may consult Keysler, who is so laboriously
circumstantial in his descriptions, that I never could peruse
them, without suffering the headach, and recollecting the old
observation, That the German genius lies more in the back
than in the brain.[36]

I was much disappointed in the chapel of St. Lorenzo.
Notwithstanding the great profusion of granite, porphyry,
jasper, verde antico, lapis-lazuli, and other precious stones,
representing figures in the way of marquetry, I think the
whole has a gloomy effect. These *pietre commesse* are better
calculated for cabinets, than for ornaments to great buildings,
which ought to be large masses proportioned to the greatness
of the edifice. The compartments are so small, that they
produce no effect in giving the first impression when one
enters the place; except to give an air of littleness to the
whole, just as if a grand saloon was covered with pictures
painted in miniature. If they have as little regard to propor-

---

* In this cathedral is the tomb of *Johannes Acutus Anglus*, which a man
would naturally interpret *John Sharp*; but his name was really *Hawkwood*,
which the Italians have corrupted into *Acut*. He was a celebrated general or
*condottiere*, who arrived in Italy at the head of four thousand soldiers of
fortune, mostly Englishmen who had served with him in the army of King
Edward III., and were dismissed at the Peace of *Bretigny*.[33] *Hawkwood*
greatly distinguished himself in *Italy*, by his valour and conduct, and died a
very old man in the *Florentine* service. He was the son of a tanner in Essex,
and had been put apprentice to a taylor.[34]

tion and perspective, when they paint the dome, which is not yet finished, this chapel will, in my opinion, remain a monument of ill taste and extravagance.

The court of the palace of Pitti is formed by three sides of an elegant square, with arcades all round, like the palace of Holyrood house at Edinburgh; and the rustic work, which constitutes the lower part of the building, gives it an air of strength and magnificence. In this court, there is a fine fountain, in which the water trickles down from above; and here is also an admirable antique statue of Hercules, inscribed *ΑΥΣΙΠΠΟΥ ΕΡΓΟΝ*, the work of Lysippus.[37]

The apartments of this palace are generally small, and many of them dark. Among the paintings, the most remarkable is the Madonna de la Seggiola, by Raphael, counted one of the best coloured pieces of that great master. If I was allowed to find fault with the performance, I should pronounce it defective in dignity and sentiment. It is the expression of a peasant rather than of the mother of God. She exhibits the fondness and joy of a young woman towards her first-born son, without that rapture of admiration which we expect to find in the Virgin Mary, while she contemplates, in the fruit of her own womb, the Saviour of mankind. In other respects, it is a fine figure, gay, agreeable, and very expressive of maternal tenderness; and the *bambino* is extremely beautiful. There was an English painter employed in copying this picture, and what he had done was executed with great success. I am one of those who think it very possible to imitate the best pieces in such a manner, that even the connoisseurs shall not be able to distinguish the original from the copy. After all, I do not set up for a judge in these matters, and very likely I may incur the ridicule of the virtuosi for the remarks I have made: but I am used to speak my mind freely on all subjects that fall under the cognizance of my senses; though I must as freely own, there is something more than common sense required to discover and distinguish the more delicate beauties of painting. I can safely say, however, that without any daubing at all, I am, very sincerely,

Your affectionate humble servant.

# LETTER XXIX.

*Nice, February 20, 1765.*

DEAR SIR,

Having seen all the curiosities of Florence, and hired a
good travelling coach for seven weeks, at the price of seven
zequines, something less than three guineas and a half, we set
out post for Rome, by the way of Sienna, where we lay the
first night. The country through which we passed is mountainous but agreeable. Of Sienna I can say nothing from my
own observation, but that we were indifferently lodged in a
house that stunk like a privy, and fared wretchedly at
supper. The city is large and well built: the inhabitants pique
themselves upon their politeness, and the purity of their
dialect. Certain it is, some strangers reside in this place on
purpose to learn the best pronunciation of the Italian tongue.
The Mosaic pavement of their duomo, or cathedral, has been
much admired; as well as the history of Æneas Sylvius,
afterwards pope Pius II.[1] painted on the walls of the library,
partly by Pietro Perugino,[2] and partly by his pupil Raphael
D'Urbino.

Next day, at Buon Convento, where the emperor Henry
VII.[3] was poisoned by a friar with the sacramental wafer, I
refused to give money to the hostler, who in revenge put two
young unbroke stone-horses[4] in the traces next to the coach,
which became so unruly, that before we had gone a quarter
of a mile, they and the postilion were rolling in the dust. In
this situation they made such efforts to disengage themselves,
and kicked with such violence, that I imagined the carriage
and all our trunks would have been beaten in pieces. We
leaped out of the coach, however, without sustaining any
personal damage, except the fright; nor was any hurt done to
the vehicle. But the horses were terribly bruised, and almost
strangled, before they could be disengaged. Exasperated at
the villany of the hostler, I resolved to make a complaint to
the *uffiziale* or magistrate of the place. I found him wrapped
in an old, greasy, ragged, great-coat, sitting in a wretched
apartment, without either glass, paper, or boards in the
windows; and there was no sort of furniture but a couple of
broken chairs and a miserable truckle-bed. He looked pale,

232

and meagre, and had more the air of a half-starved prisoner than of a magistrate. Having heard my complaint, he came forth into a kind of outward room or bellfrey, and rung a great bell with his own hand. In consequence of this signal, the post-master came up stairs, and I suppose he was the first man in the place, for the *uffiziale* stood before him cap-in-hand, and with great marks of humble respect repeated the complaint I had made. This man assured me, with an air of conscious importance, that he himself had ordered the hostler to supply me with those very horses, which were the best in his stable; and that the misfortune which happened was owing to the misconduct of the fore-postilion, who did not keep the fore horses to a proper speed proportioned to the mettle of the other two. As he took the affair upon himself, and I perceived had an ascendancy over the magistrate, I contented myself with saying, I was certain the two horses had been put to the coach on purpose, either to hurt or frighten us; and that since I could not have justice here I would make a formal complaint to the British minister at Florence.[5] In passing through the street to the coach, which was by this time furnished with fresh horses, I met the hostler, and would have caned him heartily; but perceiving my intention, he took to his heels and vanished. Of all the people I have ever seen, the hostlers, postilions, and other fellows hanging about the post-houses in Italy, are the most greedy, impertinent, and provoking. Happy are those travellers who have phlegm enough to disregard their insolence and importunity: for this is not so disagreeable as their revenge is dangerous. An English gentleman at Florence told me, that one of those fellows, whom he had struck for his impertinence, flew at him with a long knife, and he could hardly keep him at sword's point. All of them wear such knives, and are very apt to use them on the slightest provocation. But their open attacks are not so formidable as their premeditated schemes of revenge; in the prosecution of which the Italians are equally treacherous and cruel.

This night we passed at a place called Radicofani, a village and fort, situated on the top of a very high mountain. The inn stands still lower than the town. It was built at the expence of the last grand-duke of Tuscany; is very large, very cold, and uncomfortable. One would imagine it was contrived for coolness, though situated so high, that even in the midst of summer, a traveller would be glad to have a fire in his chamber. But few, or none of them have fire-places, and there is not a bed with curtains or tester in the house. All the adjacent country is naked and barren. On the third day we entered the pope's territories, some parts of which are delightful. Having passed Aqua-Pendente, a beggarly town, situated on the top of a rock, from whence there is a romantic cascade of water, which gives it the name, we travelled along the side of the lake Bolsena, a beautiful piece of water about thirty miles in circuit, with two islands in the middle, the banks covered with noble plantations of oak and cypress. The town of Bolsena standing near the ruins of the antient Volsinium, which was the birth-place of Sejanus,[6] is a paultry village; and Montefiascone, famous for its wine, is a poor decayed town in this neighbourhood, situated on the side of a hill, which, according to the author of the Grand Tour,[7] the only directory I had along with me, is supposed to be the Soracte of the ancients. If we may believe Horace, Soracte was visible from Rome: for, in his ninth ode, addressed to Thaliarchus, he says,

> *Vides, ut alta stet nive candidum*
> *Soracte*——[8]

> You see how deeply wreath'd with snow,
> *Soracte* lifts his hoary head,

but, in order to see Montefiascone, his eye-sight must have penetrated through the Mons Cyminus, at the foot of which stands the city of Viterbo. Pliny tells us, that Soracte was not far from Rome, *haud procul ab urbe Roma*;[9] but Montefiascone is fifty miles from this city. And Desprez, in his notes upon Horace, says it is now called Monte S. Oreste.[10] Addison tells us he passed by it in the Campania.[11] I could not without indignation reflect upon the bigotry of Mathilda, who gave this fine country to the see of Rome, under the dominion of which no country was ever known to prosper.

About half way between Montefiascone and Viterbo, one

of our fore-wheels flew off, together with a large splinter of the axle-tree; and if one of the postilions had not by great accident been a remarkably ingenious fellow, we should have been put to the greatest inconvenience, as there was no town, or even house, within several miles. I mention this circumstance, by way of warning to other travellers, that they may provide themselves with a hammer and nails, a spare iron-pin or two, a large knife, and bladder of grease, to be used occasionally in case of such misfortune.

The mountain of Viterbo is covered with beautiful plantations and villas belonging to the Roman nobility, who come hither to make the *villegiatura*[12] in summer. Of the city of Viterbo I shall say nothing, but that it is the capital of that country which Mathilda gave to the Roman see. The place is well built, adorned with public fountains, and a great number of churches and convents; yet far from being populous, the whole number of inhabitants not exceeding fifteen thousand. The post-house is one of the worst inns I ever entered.

After having passed this mountain, the Cyminus of the antients, we skirted part of the lake, which is now called de Vico, and whose banks afford the most agreeable rural prospects of hill and vale, wood, glade and water, shade and sun-shine. A few other very inconsiderable places we passed, and descended into the Campania of Rome, which is almost a desert.[13] The view of this country, in its present situation, cannot but produce emotions of pity and indignation in the mind of every person who retains any idea of its antient cultivation and fertility. It is nothing but a naked withered down, desolate and dreary, almost without inclosure, cornfield, hedge, tree, shrub, house, hut, or habitation; exhibiting here and there the ruins of an antient castellum, tomb, or temple, and in some places the remains of a Roman via. I had heard much of these antient pavements, and was greatly disappointed when I saw them. The Via Cassia or Cymina is paved with broad, solid, flint-stones, which must have greatly incommoded the feet of horses that travelled upon it, as well as endangered the lives of the riders from the slipperiness of the pavement: besides, it is so narrow that two modern carriages could not pass one another upon it, without the most imminent hazard of being overturned. I am still of opinion that we excel the ancient Romans in understanding the conveniencies of life.

The Grand Tour says, that within four miles of Rome you see a tomb on the road-side, said to be that of Nero, with sculpture in basso relievo at both ends.[14] I did see such a thing more like a common grave-stone, than the tomb of an emperor. But we are informed by Suetonius,[15] that the dead body of Nero, who slew himself at the villa of his freedman, was by the care of his two nurses and his concubine Atta, removed to the sepulchre of the Gens Domitia, immediately within the Porta del Popolo, on your left hand as you enter Rome, precisely on the spot where now stands the church of S. Maria del Popolo. His tomb was even distinguished by an epitaph, which has been preserved by Gruterus.[16] Giacomo Alberici tells us very gravely in his History of the Church,[17] that a great number of devils, who guarded the bones of this wicked emperor, took possession, in the shape of black ravens, of a walnut-tree, which grew upon the spot; from whence they insulted every passenger, until pope Paschal II.[18] in consequence of a solemn fast and a revelation, went thither in procession with his court and cardinals, cut down the tree, burned it to ashes, which, with the bones of Nero, were thrown into the Tyber: then he consecrated an altar on the place, where afterwards the church was built. You may guess what I felt at first sight of the city of Rome, which, notwithstanding all the calamities it has undergone, still maintains an august and imperial appearance. It stands on the farther side of the Tyber, which we crossed at the Ponte Molle, formerly called Pons Milvius, about two miles from the gate by which we entered. This bridge was built by Æmilius Censor,[19] whose name it originally bore. It was the road by which so many heroes returned with conquest to their country; by which so many kings were led captive to Rome; and by which the ambassadors of so many kingdoms and states approached the seat of empire, to deprecate the wrath, to sollicit the friendship, or sue for the protection of the Roman people. It is likewise famous for the defeat and death of Maxentius,[20] who was here overcome by Constantine the Great. The space between the bridge and Porta del Popolo, on the right hand, which is now taken up with gardens and villas, was part of the antient Campus Martius, where the comitiæ[21] were held; and where the Roman people inured themselves to all manner of exercises: it was adorned with porticos, temples, theatres, baths, circi, basilicæ, obelisks, columns, statues, and groves. Authors differ in their opinions about the extent of it; but as they all agree that it contained the Pantheon, the Circus Agonis, now the Piazza Navona, the Bustum and Mausoleum Augusti, great part of the modern city must be built upon the antient Campus Martius. The highway that leads from the bridge to the city, is part of the Via Flaminia, which extended as far as Rimini; and is well paved, like a modern street. Nothing of the antient bridge remains but the piles; nor is there any thing in the structure of this, or of the other five Roman bridges over the Tyber, that deserves attention. I have not seen any bridge in France or Italy, comparable to that of Westminster, either in beauty, magnificence, or solidity; and when the bridge at Black-Friars is finished, it will be such a monument of architecture as all the world cannot parallel.[22] As for the Tyber, it is, in comparison with the Thames, no more than an inconsiderable stream, foul, deep, and rapid. It is navigable by small boats, barks, and lighters; and, for the conveniency of loading and unloading them, there is a handsome quay by the new custom-house, at the Porto di Ripetta, provided with stairs of each side, and adorned with an elegant fountain, that yields abundance of excellent water.

We are told that the bed of this river has been considerably raised by the rubbish of old Rome, and this is the reason usually given for its being so apt to overflow its banks. A citizen of Rome told me, that a friend of his lately digging to lay the foundation of a new house in the lower part of the city, near the bank of the river, discovered the pavement of an antient street, at the depth of thirty-nine feet from the present surface of the earth. He therefore concluded that modern Rome is near forty feet higher in this place, than the site of the antient city, and that the bed of the river is raised in proportion; but this is altogether incredible. Had the bed of the Tyber been antiently forty feet lower at Rome, than it is at present, there must have been a fall or cataract in it immediately above this tract, as it is not pretended that the bed of it is raised in any part above the city; otherwise such an elevation would have obstructed its course, and then it would have overflowed the whole Campania. There is nothing extraordinary in its present overflowings: they frequently happened of old, and did great mischief to the antient city. Appian, Dio, and other historians, describe an inundation of the Tyber immediately after the death of Julius Cæsar, which inundation was occasioned by the sudden melting of a great quantity of snow upon the Appenines. This calamity is recorded by Horace in his ode to Augustus.

> Vidimus flavum Tiberim retortis
> Littore Etrusco violenter undis,
> Ire dejectum monumenta regis,
>   Templaque Vestæ:
> Iliæ dum se nimium querenti,
> Jactat ultorem; vagus et sinistrâ
> Labitur ripâ, Jove non probante
>   Uxorius Amnis.[23]

> "We saw, push'd backward to his native Source,
> The yellow Tiber roll his rapid Course,
> With impious Ruin threatning Vesta's Fane,
> And awful Monument's of Numa's Reign;
> With Grief and Rage while Ilia's Bosom glows,
> Boastful, for her Revenge, his Waters rose,
> But now, th' uxorious River glides away,
> So Jove commands, smooth-winding to the Sea."[24]

Livy expressly says, "*ita abundavit Tiberis, ut Ludi Apollinares, circo inundato, extra portam Collinam ad ædem Erycinae Veneris parati sint*"——[25] "There was such an inundation of the *Tyber* that, the *Circus* being overflowed, the *Ludi Apollinares* were exhibited without the gate *Collina*, hard by the temple of *Venus Erycina*." To this custom of transferring the *Ludi Apollinares* to another place when the Tyber had overflowed the *Circus Maximus*, Ovid alludes in his Fasti.

> Altera gramineo spectabis equiria campo
> Quem Tiberis curvis in latus urget aquis.
> Qui tamen ejecta si forte tenebitur unda,
> Cælius accipiet pulverulentus equos.[26]

## LETTER XXIX.

Another race thy view shall entertain,
Where bending Tyber skirts the grassy plain;
Or, should his vagrant stream that plain o'erflow,
The *Cælian* hill the dusty course will shew.

The Porta del Popolo (formerly, Flaminia,) by which we
entered Rome, is an elegant piece of architecture, adorned
with marble columns and statues, executed after the design of
Buonaroti. Within side you find yourself in a noble piazza,
from whence three of the principal streets of Rome are
detached. It is adorned with the famous Ægyptian obelisk,
brought hither from the Circus Maximus, and set up by the
architect Dominico Fontana[27] in the pontificate of Sixtus V.[28]
Here is likewise a beautiful fountain designed by the same
artist; and at the beginning of the two principal streets, are
two very elegant churches fronting each other. Such an
august entrance cannot fail to impress the stranger with a
sublime idea of this venerable city.

Having given our names at the gate, we repaired to the
dogana, or custom-house, where our trunks and carriage
were searched; and here we were surrounded by a number of
servitori de piazza, offering their services with the most
disagreeable importunity. Though I told them several times I
had no occasion for any, three of them took possession of the
coach, one mounting before and two of them behind; and
thus we proceeded to the Piazza d'Espagna, where the person
lived to whose house I was directed. Strangers that come to
Rome seldom put up at public inns, but go directly to
lodging houses, of which there is great plenty in this quarter. The Piazza d'Espagna is open, airy, and pleasantly
situated in a high part of the city immediately under the
Colla Pinciana, and adorned with two fine fountains. Here
most of the English reside: the apartments are generally
commodious and well furnished; and the lodgers are well
supplied with provisions and all necessaries of life. But, if I
studied œconomy, I would choose another part of the town
than the Piazza d'Espagna, which is, besides, at a great
distance from the antiquities. For a decent first floor and two
bed-chambers on the second, I payed no more than a scudo
(five shillings) per day. Our table was plentifully furnished

by the landlord for two and thirty pauls, being equal to sixteen shillings. I hired a town-coach at the rate of fourteen pauls, or seven shillings a day; and a servitore di piazza for three pauls, or eighteen-pence. The coachman has also an allowance of two pauls a day. The provisions at Rome are reasonable and good; the vitella mongana,[29] however, which is the most delicate veal I ever tasted, is very dear, being sold for two pauls, or a shilling, the pound. Here are the rich wines of Montepulciano, Montefiascone, and Monte di Dragone; but what we commonly drink at meals is that of Orvieto, a small white wine, of an agreeable flavour. Strangers are generally advised to employ an antiquarian to instruct them in all the curiosities of Rome; and this is a necessary expence, when a person wants to become a connoisseur in painting, statuary, and architecture. For my own part I had no such ambition. I longed to view the remains of antiquity by which this metropolis is distinguished; and to contemplate the originals of many pictures and statues, which I had admired in prints and descriptions. I therefore chose a servant, who was recommended to me as a sober intelligent fellow, acquainted with these matters: at the same time I furnished myself with maps and plans of antient and modern Rome, together with the little manual, called, *Itinerario istruttivo per ritrovare con facilita tutte le magnificenze di Roma e di alcune citta', e castelli suburbani.*[30] But I found still more satisfaction in perusing the book in three volumes, intitled, *Roma antica, e moderna,*[31] which contains a description of every thing remarkable in and about the city, illustrated with a great number of copper-plates, and many curious historical annotations. This directory cost me a zequine; but a hundred zequines will not purchase all the books and prints which have been published at Rome on these subjects. Of these the most celebrated are the plates of Piranesi,[32] who is not only an ingenious architect and engraver, but also a learned antiquarian; though he is apt to run riot in his conjectures; and with regard to the arts of antient Rome, has broached some doctrines, which he will find it very difficult to maintain. Our young gentlemen who go to Rome will do well to be upon their guard against a set of sharpers, (some of them of our own country,) who deal in pictures and antiques, and very often impose upon the uninformed stranger, by selling him trash, as the productions of the most celebrated artists. The English are more than any other foreigners exposed to this imposition. They are supposed to have more money to throw away; and therefore a greater number of snares are layed for them. This opinion of their superior wealth they take a pride in confirming, by launching out into all manner of unnecessary expence: but, what is still more dangerous, the moment they set foot in Italy, they are seized with the ambition of becoming connoisseurs in painting, musick, statuary, and architecture; and the adventurers of this country do not fail to flatter this weakness for their own advantage. I have seen in different parts of Italy, a number of raw boys, whom Britain seemed to have poured forth on purpose to bring her national character into contempt: ignorant, petulant, rash, and profligate, without any knowledge or experience of their own, without any director to improve their understanding, or superintend their conduct. One engages in play with an infamous gamester, and is stripped perhaps in the very first partie: another is poxed and pillaged by an antiquated cantatrice:[33] a third is bubbled by a knavish antiquarian; and a fourth is laid under contribution by a dealer in pictures. Some turn fiddlers, and pretend to compose: but all of them talk familiarly of the arts, and return finished connoisseurs and coxcombs, to their own country. The most remarkable phænomenon of this kind, which I have seen, is a boy of seventy-two,[34] now actually travelling through Italy, for improvement, under the auspices of another boy of twenty-two. When you arrive at Rome, you receive cards from all your country-folks in that city: they expect to have the visit returned next day, when they give orders not to be at home; and you never speak to one another in the sequel. This is a refinement in hospitality and politeness, which the English have invented by the strength of their own genius, without any assistance either from France, Italy, or Lapland. No Englishman above the degree of a painter or cicerone[35] frequents any coffee-house at Rome; and as there are no public diversions, except in carnival-time, the only chance you have for seeing your compatriots, is either in visiting the curiosities, or at a conversazione. The Italians are

# LETTER XXIX.

very scrupulous in admitting foreigners, except those who are introduced as people of quality: but if there happens to be any English lady of fashion at Rome, she generally keeps an assembly, to which the British subjects resort. In my next, I shall communicate, without ceremony or affectation, what further remarks I have made at Rome, without any pretence, however, to the character of a connoisseur, which, without all doubt, would sit very aukwardly upon,

Dear Sir,

Your Friend and Servant.

## LETTER XXX.

*Nice, February 28, 1765.*

DEAR SIR,

Nothing can be more agreeable to the eyes of a stranger, especially in the heats of summer, than the great number of public fountains that appear in every part of Rome, embellished with all the ornaments of sculpture, and pouring forth prodigious quantities of cool, delicious water, brought in aqueducts from different lakes, rivers, and sources, at a considerable distance from the city. These works are the remains of the munificence and industry of the antient Romans, who were extremely delicate in the article of water: but, however, great applause is also due to those beneficent popes who have been at the expence of restoring and repairing those noble channels of health, pleasure, and convenience. This great plenty of water, nevertheless, has not induced the Romans to be cleanly. Their streets, and even their palaces, are disgraced with filth. The noble Piazza Navona is adorned with three or four fountains, one of which is perhaps the most magnificent in Europe, and all of them discharge vast streams of water: but, notwithstanding this provision, the piazza is almost as dirty as West Smithfield, where the cattle are sold in London. The corridores, arcades, and even stair-cases of their most elegant palaces, are depositories of nastiness, and indeed in summer smell as strong as spirit of hartshorn.[1] I have a great notion that their ancestors were not much more cleanly. If we consider that the city and suburbs of Rome, in the reign of Claudius,[2] contained about seven millions of inhabitants, a number equal at least to the sum total of all the souls in England; that great part of antient Rome was allotted to temples, porticos, basilicæ, theatres, thermæ, circi, public and private walks and gardens, where very few, if any, of this great number lodged; that by far the greatest part of those inhabitants were slaves and poor people, who did not enjoy the conveniencies of life; and that the use of linen was scarce known; we must naturally conclude they were strangely crouded together, and that in general they were a very frowzy generation. That they were crouded together appears from the height of their houses, which the poet Rutilius[3] compared to towers made for scaling heaven. In order to remedy this inconvenience, Augustus Cæsar published a decree, that for the future no houses should be built above seventy feet high, which, at a moderate computation, might make six stories. But what seems to prove, beyond all dispute, that the antient Romans were dirty creatures, are these two particulars. Vespasian[4] laid a tax upon urine and ordure, on pretence of being at a great expence in clearing the streets from such nusances; an imposition which amounted to about fourteen pence a year for every individual; and when Heliogabalus[5] ordered all the cobwebs of the city and suburbs to be collected, they were found to weigh ten thousand pounds. This was intended as a demonstration of the great number of inhabitants; but it was a proof of their dirt, rather than of their populosity. I might likewise add, the delicate custom of taking vomits at each other's houses, when they were invited to dinner, or supper, that they might prepare their stomachs for gormandizing; a beastly proof of their nastiness as well as gluttony. Horace, in his description of the banquet of Nasiedenus, says, when the canopy, under which they sat, fell down, it brought along with it as much dirt as is raised by a hard gale of wind in dry weather.

> ———"*trahentia pulveris atri,*
> *Quantum non aquilo Campanis excitat agris.*"[6]

"Such clouds of dust revolving in its train
As *Boreas*[7] whirls along the level plain."*

---

* The same author who lived like a man of fashion and may be supposed to have been as nice as others of the same rank, in his invitation to *Torquatus*, mentions as an inducement that he shall have a clean table cloth, and be served in pewter well scoured

> *—ne turpe toral, ne sordida mappa*
> *corruget nares,* ne non et cantharus, et lanx
> *ostendat tibi te–*[8]

"—no dirty towel shall your nose offend—
My pots and dishes all are scour'd so bright,
As to reflect your image to the sight—"

A little lower in the same epistle, he says
> *Sed nimis arcta premunt olidæ convivia capræ*[9]

"The crowded feast disgusting steams annoy—"

I might observe, that the streets were often encumbered with the putrifying carcasses of criminals, who had been dragged through them by the heels, and precipitated from the *Scalæ Gemoniæ*, or Tarpeian rock,[12] before they were thrown into the Tyber, which was the general receptacle of the *cloaca maxima*[13] and all the filth of Rome: besides, the bodies of all those who made away with themselves, without sufficient cause; of such as were condemned for sacrilege, or killed by thunder, were left unburned and unburied, to rot above ground.

I believe the moderns retain more of the customs of the antient Romans, than is generally imagined. When I first saw the infants at the *enfans trouvés*[14] in Paris, so swathed with bandages, that the very sight of them made my eyes water, I little dreamed, that the prescription of the antients could be pleaded for this custom, equally shocking and absurd: but in the Capitol at Rome, I met with the antique statue of a child swaddled exactly in the same manner; rolled up like an Ægyptian mummy from the feet. The circulation of the blood, in such a case, must be obstructed on the whole surface of the body; and nothing be at liberty but the head, which is the only part of the child that ought to be confined. Is it not surprising that common sense should not point out, even to the most ignorant, that those accursed bandages must heat the tender infant into a fever; must hinder the action of the muscles, and the play of the joints, so necessary to health and nutrition; and that while the refluent blood is obstructed

---

Indeed it could not well be otherwise, if we consider that three persons at least were wedged together upon one couch or *triclinium*,[10] in a hot climate where the perspiration naturally rank and copious, was increased by the heat of the bed, the mutual contact of their bodies and the exercise of eating and drinking to excess. They had also another filthy custom which still prevails among the modern Italians; I mean that of spitting and hawking incessantly, and defiling the floor with slops of every kind. This was so much the case in antient times that the floor of the dining room was generally covered with *scobs* or saw-dust to absorb what Seneca calls the *purgamenta et jactus cænuntium*,[11] "the excretions and discharges of the guests." The *scobs* became at length a point of luxury. *Heliogabalus* ordered his portico to be strewed in lieu of *scobs* with gold and silver dust, and lamented that he could not find amber enough for that purpose.

in the veins, which run on the surface of the body, the arteries, which lie deep, without the reach of compression, are continually pouring their contents into the head, where the blood meets with no resistance? The vessels of the brain are naturally lax, and the very sutures of the skull are yet unclosed. What are the consequences of this cruel swaddling? the limbs are wasted; the joints grow rickety; the brain is compressed, and a hydrocephalus, with a great head and sore eyes, ensues. I take this abominable practice to be one great cause of the bandy legs, diminutive bodies, and large heads, so frequent in the south of France, and in Italy.

I was no less surprised to find the modern fashion of curling the hair, borrowed in a great measure from the coxcombs and coquettes of antiquity. I saw a bust of Nero in the gallery at Florence, the hair represented in rows of buckles, like that of a French petit-maitre, conformable to the picture drawn of him by Suetonius. *Circa cultum adeo pudendum, ut comam semper in gradus formatam peregrinatione achaica, etiam pene verticem sumpserit.*[15] "So very finical in his dress, that he wore his hair in the Greek fashion, curled in rows almost to the crown of his head." I was very sorry however to find that this foppery came from Greece. As for Otho,[16] he wore a galericulum, or tour, on account of thin hair, *propter raritatem capillorum.*[17] He had no right to imitate the example of Julius Cæsar, who concealed his bald head with a wreath of laurel. But there is a bust in the Capitol of Julia Pia, the second wife of Septimius Severus,[18] with a moveable peruke, dressed exactly in the fashionable mode, with this difference, that there is no part of it frizzled; nor is there any appearance of pomatum and powder. These improvements the beau-monde have borrowed from the natives of the Cape of Good Hope.

Modern Rome does not cover more than one-third of the space within the walls; and those parts that were most frequented of old are now intirely abandoned. From the Capitol to the Coliseo, including the Forum Romanum and Boarium, there is nothing intire but one or two churches, built with the fragments of ancient edifices. You descend from the Capitol between the remaining pillars of two temples, the pedestals and part of the shafts sunk in the

rubbish: then passing through the triumphal arch of Septimius Severus, you proceed along the foot of Mons
Palatinus, which stands on your right hand, quite covered
with the ruins of the antient palace belonging to the Roman
emperors, and at the foot of it, there are some beautiful
detached pillars still standing. On the left you see the remains
of the *Templum Pacis*, which seems to have been the largest
and most magnificent of all the temples in Rome. It was built
and dedicated by the emperor Vespasian, who brought into it
all the treasure and precious vessels which he found in the
temple of Jerusalem. The columns of the portico he removed
from Nero's golden house, which he levelled with the
ground. This temple was likewise famous for its library,
mentioned by Aulus Gellius.[19] Farther on, is the arch of
Constantine on the right, a most noble piece of architecture,
almost entire; with the remains of the *Meta Sudans*[20] before it;
and fronting you, the noble ruins of that vast amphitheatre,
called the Colossæum, now Coliseo, which has been dismantled and dilapidated by the Gothic popes and princes of
modern Rome, to build and adorn their paultry palaces.
Behind the amphitheatre were the thermæ of the same
emperor Titus Vespasian. In the same quarter was the *Circus
Maximus*; and the whole space from hence on both sides, to
the walls of Rome, comprehending above twice as much
ground as the modern city, is almost covered with the
monuments of antiquity. I suppose there is more concealed
below ground than appears above. The miserable houses, and
even garden-walls of the peasants in this district, are built
with these precious materials, I mean shafts and capitals of
marble columns, heads, arms, legs, and mutilated trunks of
statues. What pity it is that among all the remains of
antiquity, at Rome, there is not one lodging-house remaining. I should be glad to know how the senators of Rome were
lodged. I want to be better informed touching the *cava ædium*,
the *focus*, the *ara deorum penatum*, the *conclavia*, *triclinia*, and
*cænationes*; the *atria* where the women resided, and employed
themselves in the woolen manufacture; the *prætoria*,[21] which
were so spacious as to become a nusance in the reign of
Augustus; and the *xysta*, which were shady walks between
two porticos, where the men exercised themselves in the

winter. I am disgusted by the modern taste of architecture, though I am no judge of the art. The churches and palaces of these days are crowded with petty ornaments, which distract the eye, and by breaking the design into a variety of little parts, destroy the effect of the whole. Every door and window has its separate ornaments, its moulding, frize, cornice, and tympanum;[22] then there is such an assemblage of useless festoons, pillars, pilasters, with their architraves, entablatures, and I know not what, that nothing great or uniform remains to fill the view; and we in vain look for that simplicity of grandeur, those large masses of light and shadow, and the inexpressible *ΕΥΣΥΝΟΠΤΟΝ*,[23] which characterise the edifices of the antients. A great edifice, to have its full effect, ought to be *isolé*, or detached from all others, with a large space around it: but the palaces of Rome, and indeed of all the other cities of Italy, which I have seen, are so engaged among other mean houses, that their beauty and magnificence are in a great measure concealed. Even those which face open streets and piazzas are only clear in front. The other apartments are darkened by the vicinity of ordinary houses; and their views are confined by dirty and disagreeable objects. Within the court there is generally a noble colonnade all round, and an open corridore above: but the stairs are usually narrow, steep, and high: the want of sash-windows, the dullness of their small glass lozenges, the dusty brick floors, and the crimson hangings laced with gold, contribute to give a gloomy air to their apartments; I might add to these causes, a number of pictures executed on melancholy subjects, antique mutilated statues, busts, basso relievos, urns, and sepulchral stones, with which their rooms are adorned. It must be owned, however, there are some exceptions to this general rule. The villa of Cardinal Alexander Albani[24] is light, gay, and airy; yet the rooms are too small, and too much decorated with carving and gilding, which is a kind of gingerbread work.[25] The apartments of one of the princes Borghese are furnished in the English taste; and in the *palazzo di Colonna Connestabile*, there is a saloon, or gallery, which, for the proportions, lights, furniture, and ornaments, is the most noble, elegant, and agreeable apartment I ever saw.

It is diverting to hear an Italian expatiate upon the greatness of modern Rome. He will tell you there are above three hundred palaces in the city; that there is scarce a Roman prince, whose revenue does not exceed two hundred thousand crowns; and that Rome produces not only the most learned men, but also the most refined politicians in the universe. To one of them talking in this strain, I replied, that instead of three hundred palaces, the number did not exceed fourscore; that I had been informed, on good authority, there were not six individuals in Rome who had so much as forty thousand crowns a year, about ten thousand pounds sterling; and that to say their princes were so rich, and their politicians so refined, was, in effect, a severe satire upon them, for not employing their wealth and their talents for the advantage of their country. I asked why their cardinals and princes did not invite and encourage industrious people to settle and cultivate the Campania of Rome, which is a desert? why they did not raise a subscription to drain the marshes in the neighbourhood of the city, and thus meliorate the air, which is rendered extremely unwholsome in the summer, by putrid exhalations from those morasses? I demanded of him, why they did not contribute their wealth, and exert their political refinements, in augmenting their forces by sea and land, for the defence of their country, introducing commerce and manufactures, and in giving some consequence to their state, which was no more than a mite in the political scale of Europe? I expressed a desire to know what became of all those sums of money, inasmuch as there was hardly any circulation of gold and silver in Rome, and the very bankers, on whom strangers have their credit, make interest to pay their tradesmen's bills with paper notes of the bank of Spirito Santo?[26] And now I am upon this subject, it may not be amiss to observe that I was strangely misled by all the books I consulted about the current coin of Italy.[27] In Tuscany, and the Ecclesiastical State, one sees nothing but zequines in gold, and pieces of two paoli, one paolo, and half a paolo, in silver. Besides these, there is a copper coin at Rome, called bajocco and mezzo bajocco. Ten bajocchi make a paolo: ten paoli make a scudo, which is an imaginary piece: two scudi make a zequine; and a French loui'dore is worth two zequines and two paoli.

Rome has nothing to fear from the catholic powers, who respect it with a superstitious veneration as the metropolitan seat of their religion: but the popes will do well to avoid misunderstandings with the maritime protestant states, especially the English, who being masters of the Mediterranean, and in possession of Minorca,[28] have it in their power at all times, to land a body of troops within four leagues of Rome, and to take the city, without opposition. Rome is surrounded with an old wall, but altogether incapable of defence. Or if it was, the circuit of the walls is so extensive, that it would require a garrison of twenty thousand men. The only appearance of a fortification in this city, is the castle of St. Angelo, situated on the further bank of the Tyber, to which there is access by a handsome bridge: but this castle, which was formerly the *moles Adriani*, could not hold out half a day against a battery of ten pieces of cannon properly directed. It was an expedient left to the invention of the modern Romans, to convert an ancient tomb into a citadel. It could only serve as a temporary retreat for the pope in times of popular commotion, and on other sudden emergencies; as it happened in the case of pope Clement VII.[29] when the troops of the emperor took the city by assault; and this only while he resided at the Vatican, from whence there is a covered gallery continued to the castle: it can never serve this purpose again, while the pontiff lives on Monte Cavallo, which is at the other end of the city. The castle of St. Angelo, howsoever ridiculous as a fortress, appears respectable as a noble monument of antiquity, and though standing in a low situation, is one of the first objects that strike the eye of a stranger approaching Rome. On the opposite side of the river, are the wretched remains of the Mausoleum Augusti, which was still more magnificent. Part of the walls is standing, and the terraces are converted into garden-ground. In viewing these ruins, I remembered Virgil's pathetic description of Marcellus,[30] who was here intombed.

> *Quantos ille virum, magnum mavortis ad urbem.*
> *Campus aget gemitus, vel que Tyberine, videbis*
> *Funera, cum tumulum preter labere recentem.*[31]

Along his banks what groans shall *Tyber* hear,

## LETTER XXX.

### When the fresh tomb and fun'ral pomp appear!

The beautiful poem of Ovid *de Consolatione ad Liviam*, written after the ashes of Augustus and his nephew Marcellus, of Germanicus,[32] Agrippa and Drusus,[33] were deposited in this mausoleum, concludes with these lines, which are extremely tender:

> *Claudite jam Parcæ nimium reserata sepulchra;*
> *Claudite, plus justo, jam domus ista patet!*[34]

Ah! shut these yawning tombs, ye sister Fates!
Too long unclos'd have stood those dreary gates!

What the author said of the monument, you will be tempted to say of this letter, which I shall therefore close in the old stile, assuring you that I ever am,

Yours most affectionately.

## LETTER XXXI.

*Nice, March 5, 1765.*

DEAR SIR,

In my last I gave you my opinion freely of the modern palaces of Italy. I shall now hazard my thoughts upon the gardens of this country, which the inhabitants extol with all the hyperboles of admiration and applause. I must acknowledge however, I have not seen the famous villas at Frascati and Tivoli, which are celebrated for their gardens and water-works. I intended to visit these places; but was prevented by an unexpected change of weather, which deterred me from going to the country. On the last day of September the mountains of Palestrina were covered with snow; and the air became so cold at Rome, that I was forced to put on my winter cloaths. This objection continued, till I found it necessary to set out on my return to Florence. But I have seen the gardens of the *Poggio Imperiale*, and the *Palazzo de Pitti* at Florence, and those of the Vatican, of the pope's palace on Monte Cavallo, of the Villa Ludovisia, Medicea, and Pinciana, at Rome; so that I think I have some right to judge of the Italian taste in gardening. Among those I have mentioned, that of the Villa Pinciana is the most remarkable, and the most extensive, including a space of three miles in circuit, hard by the walls of Rome, containing a variety of situations high and low, which favour all the natural embellishments one would expect to meet with in a garden, and exhibit a diversity of noble views of the city and adjacent country.

In a fine extensive garden or park, an Englishman expects to see a number of groves and glades, intermixed with an agreeable negligence, which seems to be the effect of nature and accident. He looks for shady walks encrusted with gravel; for open lawns covered with verdure as smooth as velvet, but much more lively and agreeable; for ponds, canals, basins, cascades, and running streams of water; for clumps of trees, woods, and wildernesses, cut into delightful alleys, perfumed with honey-suckle and sweet-briar, and resounding with the mingled melody of all the singing birds of heaven: he looks for plats of flowers in different parts to refresh the sense, and please the fancy; for arbours, grottos, hermitages, temples, and alcoves, to shelter him from the sun, and afford him means of contemplation and repose; and he expects to find the hedges, groves, and walks, and lawns kept with the utmost order and propriety. He who loves the beauties of simple nature, and the charms of neatness, will seek for them in vain amidst the groves of Italy. In the garden of the Villa Pinciana, there is a plantation of four hundred pines, which the Italians view with rapture and admiration: there is likewise a long walk of trees, extending from the garden-gate to the palace; and plenty of shade, with alleys and hedges in different parts of the ground: but the groves are neglected; the walks are laid with nothing but common mould or sand, black and dusty; the hedges are tall, thin and shabby; the trees stunted; the open ground, brown and parched, has scarce any appearance of verdure. The flat, regular alleys of evergreens are cut into fantastic figures; the flower gardens embellished with thin cyphers and flourished figures in box, while the flowers grow in rows of earthen-pots, and the ground appears as dusky as if it was covered with the cinders of a blacksmith's forge. The water, of which there is great plenty, instead of being collected in large pieces, or conveyed in little rivulets and streams to refresh the thirsty soil, or managed so as to form agreeable cascades, is squirted from fountains in different parts of the garden, through tubes little bigger than common glyster-pipes.[1] It must be owned indeed that the fountains have their merit in the way of sculpture and architecture; and that here is a great number of statues which merit attention: but they serve only to encumber the ground, and destroy that effect of rural simplicity, which our gardens are designed to produce. In a word, here we see a variety of walks and groves and fountains, a wood of four hundred pines, a paddock with a few meagre deer, a flower-garden, an aviary, a grotto, and a fish-pond; and in spite of all these particulars, it is, in my opinion, a very contemptible garden, when compared to that of Stowe in Buckinghamshire,[2] or even to those of Kensington and Richmond. The Italians understand, because they study, the excellencies of art; but they have no idea of the beauties of nature. This Villa Pinciana, which belongs to the Borghese family, would make a complete academy for painting and sculpture, especially for the study of antient marbles; for, exclusive of the statues and busts in the garden, and the vast collection in the different apartments, almost the whole outside of the house is covered with curious pieces in basso and alto relievo. The most masterly is that of Curtius[3] on horseback, leaping into the gulph or opening of the earth, which is said to have closed on receiving this sacrifice. Among the exhibitions of art within the house, I was much struck with a Bacchus, and the death of Meleager, represented on an antient sepulchre. There is also an admirable statue of Silenus,[4] with the infant Bacchus in his arms; a most beautiful gladiator; a curious Moor of black marble, with a shirt of white alabaster; a finely proportioned bull of black marble also, standing upon a table of alabaster; a black gipsey with a head, hands, and feet of brass; and the famous hermaphrodite, which vies with that of Florence: though the most curious circumstance of this article, is the mattrass executed and placed by Bernini,[5] with such art and dexterity, that to the view, it rivals the softness of wool, and seems to retain the marks of pressure, according to the figure of the superincumbent statue. Let us likewise own, for the honour of the moderns, that the same artist has produced two fine statues, which we find among the ornaments of this villa, namely, a David with his sling in the attitude of throwing the stone at the giant Goliah; and a Daphne changing into laurel at the approach of Apollo. On the base of this figure, are the two following elegant lines, written by pope Urban VIII.[6] in his younger years.

> *Quisquis amans sequitur fugitivæ gaudia formæ,*
> *Fronde manus implet, baccas vel carpit amaras.*

Who pants for fleeting Beauty, vain pursuit!
Shall barren leaves obtain, or bitter fruit.

I ought not to forget two exquisite antique statues of Venus, the weeping slave, and the youth pulling a thorn out of his foot.

I do not pretend to give a methodical detail of the curiosities of Rome: they have been already described by different authors, who were much better qualified than I am for the task: but you shall have what observations I made on the most remarkable objects, without method, just as they occur to my remembrance; and I protest the remarks are all my own: so that if they deserve any commendation, I claim all the merit; and if they are impertinent, I must be contented to bear all the blame.

The piazza of St. Peter's church is altogether sublime. The double colonnade on each side extending in a semi-circular sweep, the stupendous Ægyptian obelisk, the two fountains, the portico, and the admirable façade of the church, form such an assemblage of magnificent objects, as cannot fail to impress the mind with awe and admiration: but the church would have produced a still greater effect, had it been detached entirely from the buildings of the Vatican. It would then have been a master-piece of architecture, complete in all its parts, intire and perfect: whereas, at present, it is no more than a beautiful member attached to a vast undigested and irregular pile of building. As to the architecture of this famous temple, I shall say nothing; neither do I pretend to describe the internal ornaments. The great picture of Mosaic work, and that of St. Peter's bark tossed by the tempest, which appear over the gate of the church, though rude in comparison with modern pieces, are nevertheless great curiosities, when considered as the work of Giotto, who flourished in the beginning of the fourteenth century. His master was Cimabue,[7] who learned painting and architecture of the Grecian artists, who came from Constantinople, and first revived these arts in Italy. But, to return to St. Peter's, I was not at all pleased with the famous statue of the dead Christ in his mother's lap, by Michael Angelo. The figure of Christ is as much emaciated, as if he had died of a consumption: besides, there is something indelicate, not to say indecent, in the attitude and design of a man's body, stark naked, lying upon the knees of a woman.[8] Here are some good pictures, I should rather say copies of good pictures, done in Mosaic to great perfection; particularly a St. Sebastian by Domenichino,[9] and Michael the Archangel, from a painting of Guido Rheni.[10] I am extremely fond of all this artist's pieces. There is a tenderness and delicacy in his manner; and his figures are all exquisitely beautiful, though his expression is often erroneous, and his attitudes are always affected and unnatural. In this very piece the archangel has all the air of a French dancing-master; and I have seen a Madonna by the same hand, I think it is in the Palazzo di Barberini, in which, though the figures are enchanting, the Virgin is represented holding up the drapery of the Infant, with the ridiculous affectation of a singer on the stage of our Italian opera. The Mosaic work, though brought to a wonderful degree of improvement, and admirably calculated for churches, the dampness of which is pernicious to the colours of the pallet, I will not yet compare to the productions of the pencil. The glassyness (if I may be allowed the expression) of the surface, throws, in my opinion, a false light on some parts of the picture; and when you approach it, the joinings of the pieces look like so many cracks on painted canvas. Besides, this method is extremely tedious and expensive. I went to see the artists at work, in a house that stands near the church, where I was much pleased with the ingenuity of the process; and not a little surprized at the great number of different colours and tints, which are kept in separate drawers, marked with numbers as far as seventeen thousand. For a single head done in Mosaic, they asked me fifty zequines. But to return to the church. The altar of St. Peter's choir, notwithstanding all the ornaments which have been lavished upon it, is no more than a heap of puerile finery, better adapted to an Indian pagod, than to a temple built upon the principles of the Greek architecture. The four colossal figures that support the chair, are both clumsy and disproportioned. The drapery of statues, whether in brass or stone, when thrown into large masses, appears hard and unpleasant to the eye; and for that reason the antients always imitated wet linen, which exhibiting the shape of the limbs underneath, and hanging in a multiplicity of wet folds, gives an air of lightness, softness, and ductility to the whole.

These two statues weigh 116257 pounds, and as they sustain nothing but a chair, are out of all proportion, inasmuch as the supporters ought to be suitable to the things supported. Here are four giants holding up the old wooden chair of the apostle Peter, if we may believe the book *De Identitate Cathedræ Romanæ*,[11] Of the Identity of the Roman Chair. The implements of popish superstition; such as relicks of pretended saints, ill proportioned spires and bellfreys, and the nauseous repetition of the figure of the cross, which is in itself a very mean and disagreeable object, only fit for the prisons of condemned criminals, have contributed to introduce a vitious taste into the external architecture, as well as in the internal ornaments of our temples. All churches are built in the figure of a cross, which effectually prevents the eye from taking in the scope of the building, either without side or within; consequently robs the edifice of its proper effect. The palace of the Escurial[12] in Spain is laid out in the shape of a gridiron, because the convent was built in consequence of a vow to St. Laurence,[13] who was broiled like a barbecued pig. What pity it is, that the labours of painting should have been so much employed on the shocking subjects of the martyrology. Besides numberless pictures of the flagellation, crucifixion, and descent from the cross, we have Judith with the head of Holofernes, Herodias with the head of John the Baptist, Jael assassinating Sisera in his sleep, Peter writhing on the cross, Stephen battered with stones, Sebastian[14] stuck full of arrows, Laurence frying upon the coals, Bartholomew flaed alive,[15] and a hundred other pictures equally frightful, which can only serve to fill the mind with gloomy ideas, and encourage a spirit of religious fanaticism, which has always been attended with mischievous consequences to the community where it reigned.

The tribune of the great altar, consisting of four wreathed brass pillars, gilt, supporting a canopy, is doubtless very magnificent, if not over-charged with sculpture, fluting, foliage, festoons, and figures of boys and angels, which, with the hundred and twenty-two lamps of silver, continually burning below, serve rather to dazzle the eyes, and kindle the devotion of the ignorant vulgar, than to excite the admiration of a judicious observer.

There is nothing, I believe, in this famous structure, so worthy of applause, as the admirable symmetry and proportion of its parts. Notwithstanding all the carving, gilding, basso relievo, medallions, urns, statues, columns, and pictures with which it abounds, it does not, on the whole, appear over-crouded with ornaments. When you first enter, your eye is filled so equally and regularly, that nothing appears stupendous; and the church seems considerably smaller than it really is. The statues of children, that support the founts of holy water when observed from the door, seem to be of the natural size; but as you draw near, you perceive they are gigantic. In the same manner, the figures of the doves, with olive branches in their beaks, which are represented on the wall, appear to be within your reach; but as you approach them, they recede to a considerable height, as if they had flown upwards to avoid being taken.

I was much disappointed at sight of the Pantheon, which, after all that has been said of it, looks like a huge cockpit, open at top. The portico which Agrippa added to the building, is undoubtedly very noble, though, in my opinion, it corresponds but ill with the simplicity of the edifice. With all my veneration for the antients, I cannot see in what the beauty of the rotunda consists. It is no more than a plain unpierced cylinder, or circular wall, with two fillets and a cornice, having a vaulted roof or cupola, open in the centre. I mean the original building, without considering the vestibule of Agrippa. Within side it has much the air of a mausoleum. It was this appearance which, in all probability, suggested the thought to Boniface IV.[16] to transport hither eight and twenty cart-loads of old rotten bones, dug from different burying-places, and then dedicate it as a church to the blessed Virgin and all the holy martyrs. I am not one of those who think it is well lighted by the hole at the top, which is about nine and twenty feet in diameter, although the author of the Grand Tour calls it but nine.[17] The same author says, there is a descent of eleven steps to go into it; that it is a hundred and forty-four feet in heighth, and as many in breadth; that it was covered with copper, which, with the brass nails of the portico, pope Urban VIII. took away, and converted into the four wreathed pillars that support the canopy of the high altar in the church of St. Peter, &c.[18] The truth is, before the time of pope Alexander VII.[19] the earth was so raised as to cover part of the temple, and there was a descent of some steps into the porch: but that pontiff ordered the ground to be pared away to the very pedestal or base of the portico, which is now even with the street, so that there is no descent whatsoever. The height is two hundred palmi, and the breadth two hundred and eighteen; which, reckoning the palmi at nine inches, will bring the height to one hundred and fifty, and the breadth to one hundred and sixty-three feet six inches. It was not any covering of copper which pope Urban VIII. removed, but large brass beams, which supported the roof of the portico. They weighed 186392 pounds; and afforded metal enough not only for the pillars in St. Peter's church, but also for several pieces of artillery that are now in the castle of St. Angelo. What is more extraordinary, the gilding of those columns is said to have cost forty thousand golden crowns: sure money was never worse laid out. Urban VIII. likewise added two bellfrey towers to the rotunda; and I wonder he did not cover the central hole with glass, as it must be very inconvenient and disagreeable to those who go to church below, to be exposed to the rain in wet weather, which must also render it very damp and unwholesome. I visited it several times, and each time it looked more and more gloomy and sepulchral.

The magnificence of the Romans was not so conspicuous in their temples, as in their theatres, amphitheatres, circusses, naumachia,[20] aqueducts, triumphal arches, porticoes, basilicæ, but especially their thermæ, or bathing-places. A great number of their temples were small and inconsiderable; not one of them was comparable either for size or magnificence, to the modern church of St. Peter of the Vatican. The famous temple of Jupiter Capitolinus was neither half so long, nor half so broad: it was but two hundred feet in length, and one hundred and eighty-five in breadth; whereas the length of St. Peter's extends to six hundred and thirty-eight feet, and the breadth to above five hundred. It is very near twice as large as the temple of Jupiter Olympius in Greece, which was counted one of the seven wonders of the world. But I shall take another opportunity to explain myself further on the antiquities of this city; a subject, upon which I am disposed to be (perhaps impertinently) circumstantial. When I begin to run riot, you should check me with the freedom of a friend. The most distant hint will be sufficient to,

Dear Sir,

Yours assuredly.

# LETTER XXXII.

*Nice, March* 10, 1765.

DEAR SIR,

The Colossæum or amphitheatre built by Flavius Vespasian, is the most stupendous work of the kind which antiquity can produce. Near one half of the external circuit still remains, consisting of four tire of arcades, adorned with columns of four orders, Doric, Ionic, Corinthian, and Composite. The height and extent of it may be guessed from the number of spectators it contained, amounting to one hundred thousand; and yet, according to Fontana's mensuration, it could not contain above thirty-four thousand persons sitting, allowing a foot and an half for each person: for the circuit of the whole building did not exceed one thousand five hundred and sixty feet. The amphitheatre at Verona is one thousand two hundred and ninety feet in circumference; and that of Nismes, one thousand and eighty. The Colossæum was built by Vespasian, who employed thirty thousand Jewish slaves in the work; but finished and dedicated by his son Titus,[1] who, on the first day of its being opened, produced fifty thousand wild beasts, which were all killed in the arena. The Romans were undoubtedly a barbarous people, who delighted in horrible spectacles. They viewed with pleasure the dead bodies of criminals dragged through the streets, or thrown down the Scalæ Gemoniæ and Tarpeian rock, for their contemplation. Their rostra[2] were generally adorned with the heads of some remarkable citizens, like Temple-Bar,[3] at London. They even bore the sight of Tully's[4] head fixed upon that very rostrum where he had so often ravished their ears with all the charms of eloquence, in pleading the cause of innocence and public virtue. They took delight in seeing their fellow-creatures torn in pieces by wild beasts, in the amphitheatre. They shouted with applause when they saw a poor dwarf or slave killed by his adversary; but their transports were altogether extravagant, when the devoted captives were obliged to fight in troops, till one side was entirely butchered by the other. Nero produced four hundred senators, and six hundred of the equestrian order, as gladiators in the public arena: even the women fought with wild beasts, as well as with each other, and drenched the amphitheatres with their blood. Tacitus says, "*Sed fœminarum illustrium, senatorumque filiorum plures per arenam fœdati sunt.*"[5] "But many sons of senators, and even matrons of the first rank, exposed themselves in this vile exercise." The execrable custom of sacrificing captives or slaves at the tombs of their masters and great men, which is still preserved among the negroes of Africa, obtained also among the antients, Greeks as well as Romans. I could never, without horror and indignation, read that passage in the twenty-third book of the Iliad, which describes twelve valiant Trojan captives sacrificed by the inhuman Achilles at the tomb of his friend Patroclus.

> Δώδεκα μεν Τρώων μεγαθυμων υἔας εσθλοὺς
> Τοὺς ἅμα σοι πάντας πὐρ ἐσθίει.[6]

Twelve gen'rous *Trojans* slaughter'd in their bloom,
With thy lov'd coarse the fire shall now consume.

Even Virgil makes his pious hero sacrifice eight *Italian* youths to the *manes* of *Pallas*.[7] It is not at all clear to me, that a people is the more brave, the more they are accustomed to bloodshed in their public entertainments. True bravery is not savage but humane. Some of this sanguinary spirit is inherited by the inhabitants of a certain island that shall be nameless—but, mum for that. You will naturally suppose that the Coliseo was ruined by the barbarians who sacked the city of Rome: in effect, they robbed it of its ornaments and valuable materials; but it was reserved for the Goths and Vandals of modern Rome, to dismantle the edifice, and reduce it to its present ruinous condition. One part of it was demolished by pope Paul II.[8] that he might employ the stones of it in building the palace of St. Mark. It was afterwards dilapidated for the same purposes, by the cardinals Riarius[9] and Farnese, which last assumed the tiara under the name of Paul III.[10] Notwithstanding these injuries, there is enough standing to convey a very sublime idea of antient magnificence.

The Circi and Naumachia, if considered as buildings and artificial basins, are admirable; but if examined as areæ intended for horse and chariot-races, and artificial seas for exhibiting naval engagements, they seem to prove that the antient Romans were but indifferently skilled and exercised either in horsemanship or naval armaments. The inclosure of the emperor Caracalla's circus is still standing, and scarce affords breathing room for an English hunter. The Circus Maximus, by far the largest in Rome, was not so long as the Mall; and I will venture to affirm, that St. James's Park would make a much more ample and convenient scene for those diversions. I imagine an old Roman would be very much surprised to see an English race on the course at New-Market. The Circus Maximus was but three hundred yards in breadth. A good part of this was taken up by the spina,[11] or middle space, adorned with temples, statues, and two great obelisks; as well as by the euripus, or canal, made by order of Julius Cæsar, to contain crocodiles, and other aquatic animals, which were killed occasionally. This was so large, that Heliogabalus, having filled it with excellent wine, exhibited naval engagements in it, for the amusement of the people. It surrounded three sides of the square, so that the whole extent of the race did not much exceed an English mile; and when Probus[12] was at the expence of filling the plain of it with fir-trees, to form a wood for the chase of wild beasts, I question much if this forest was more extensive than the plantation in St. James's Park, on the south side of the canal: now I leave you to judge what ridicule a king of England would incur by converting this part of the park into a chace for any species of animals which are counted game in our country.

The Roman emperors seemed more disposed to elevate and surprize, than to conduct the public diversions according to the rules of reason and propriety. One would imagine, it was with this view they instituted their naumachia, or naval engagements, performed by half a dozen small gallies of a side in an artificial basin of fresh water. These gallies, I suppose, were not so large as common fishing-smacks, for they were moved by two, three, and four oars of a side, according to their different rates, biremes, triremes, and quadriremes. I know this is a knotty point not yet determined; and that some antiquarians believe the Roman gallies had different tires or decks of oars; but this is a notion very ill supported, and quite contrary to all the figures of them that are preserved on antient coins and medals. Suetonius in the reign of Domitian,[13] speaking of these naumachia, says, "*Edidit navales pugnas, pene justarum classium, effosso, et circumducto juxta Tyberim Lacu, atque inter maximas imbres prospectavit.*"[14] "He exhibited naval engagements of almost *intire fleets*, in an artificial lake formed for the purpose hard by the *Tyber*, and viewed them in the midst of excessive rains." This artificial lake was not larger than the piece of water in Hyde-Park; and yet the historian says, it was almost large enough for real or intire fleets. How would a British sailor relish an advertisement that a mock engagement between two squadrons of men of war would be exhibited on such a day in the Serpentine river?[15] or that the ships of the line taken from the enemy would be carried in procession from Hyde-Park-Corner to Tower-wharf? Certain it is, Lucullus,[16] in one of his triumphs, had one hundred and ten ships of war (*naves longas*) carried through the streets of Rome. Nothing can give a more contemptible idea of their naval power, than this testimony of their historians, who declare that their seamen or mariners were formed by exercising small row-boats in an inclosed pool of fresh water. Had they not the sea within a few miles of them, and the river Tyber running through their capital! even this would have been much more proper for exercising their watermen, than a pond of still-water, not much larger than a cold-bath. I do believe, in my conscience, that half a dozen English frigates would have been able to defeat both the contending fleets at the famous battle of Actium, which has been so much celebrated in the annals of antiquity, as an event that decided the fate of empire.

It would employ me a whole month to describe the thermæ or baths, the vast ruins of which are still to be seen within the walls of Rome, like the remains of so many separate citadels. The thermæ Dioclesianæ might be termed an august academy for the use and instruction of the Roman people. The pinacotheca of this building was a complete musæum of all the curiosities of art and nature; and there were public schools for all the sciences. If I may judge by my eye, however, the thermæ Antonianæ built by Caracalla, were still more extensive and magnificent; they contained cells sufficient for two thousand three hundred persons to bathe at one time, without being seen by one another. They were adorned with all the charms of painting, architecture, and sculpture. The pipes for conveying the water were of silver. Many of the lavacra[17] were of precious marble, illuminated by lamps of chrystal. Among the statues, were found the famous Toro, and Hercole Farnese.

Bathing was certainly necessary to health and cleanliness in a hot country like Italy, especially before the use of linen was known: but these purposes would have been much better answered by plunging into the Tyber, than by using the warm bath in the thermæ, which became altogether a point of luxury borrowed from the effeminate Asiatics, and tended to debilitate the fibres already too much relaxed by the heat of the climate. True it is, they had baths of cool water for the summer: but in general they used it milk-warm, and often perfumed: they likewise indulged in vapour-baths, in order to enjoy a pleasing relaxation, which they likewise improved with odoriferous ointments. The thermæ consisted of a great variety of parts and conveniences; the natationes, or swimming places; the portici, where people amused themselves in walking, conversing, and disputing together, as Cicero says, *In porticibus deambulantes disputabant;*[18] the basilicæ, where the bathers assembled, before they entered, and after they came out of the bath; the atria, or ample courts, adorned with noble colonnades of Numidian marble and oriental granite; the ephibia, where the young men inured themselves to wrestling and other exercises; the frigidaria, or places kept cool by a constant draught of air, promoted by the disposition and number of the windows; the calidaria, where the water was warmed for the baths; the platanones, or delightful groves of sycamore; the stadia, for the performances of the athletæ; the exedræ, or resting-places, provided with seats for those that were weary; the palestræ, where every one chose that exercise which pleased him best; the gymnasia, where poets, orators, and philosophers recited their works, and harangued for diversion; the eleotesia, where the fragrant oils and ointments were kept for the use of the bathers; and the conisteria, where the wrestlers were smeared with sand before they engaged. Of the thermæ in Rome, some were mercenary, and some opened gratis. Marcus Agrippa, when he was edile,[19] opened one hundred and seventy private baths, for the use of the people. In the public baths, where money was taken, each person paid a quadrans, about the value of our halfpenny, as Juvenal observes,

> "*Cædere Sylvano porcum, quadrante lavari.*"[20]

> "The victim pig to god *Sylvanus* slay,
> And for the public bath a farthing pay."

But after the hour of bathing was past, it sometimes cost a great deal more, according to Martial,

> "*Balnea post decimam, lasso centumque petuntur
> Quadrantes———*"[21]

> "The bathing hour is past; the waiter tir'd;
> An hundred farthings now will be requir'd."

Though there was no distinction in the places, between the first patrician and the lowest plebeian, yet the nobility used their own silver and gold plate, for washing, eating, and drinking in the bath, together with towels of the finest linen. They likewise made use of the instrument called strigil, which was a kind of flesh-brush; a custom to which Persius alludes in this line,

> "*I puer, et strigiles Crispini ad balnea defer.*"[22]

> "Here boy, this brush to *Crispin's* bagnio bear."

The common people contented themselves with sponges. The bathing time was from noon till the evening, when the Romans ate their principal meal. Notice was given by a bell, or some such instrument, when the baths were opened, as we learn from Juvenal,

> "*Redde Pilam, sonat Æs thermarum, ludere pergis?
> Virgine vis sola lotus abire domum.*"[23]

> "Leave off; the bath bell rings—what, still play on?
> Perhaps the maid in private rubs you down."

There were separate places for the two sexes; and indeed there were baths opened for the use of women only, at the expence of Agrippina, the mother of Nero, and some other matrons of the first quality. The use of bathing was become so habitual to the constitutions of the Romans, that Galen, in his book *De Sanitate tuenda*,[24] mentions a certain philosopher, who, if he intermitted but one day in his bathing, was certainly attacked with a fever. In order to preserve decorum in the baths, a set of laws and regulations were published, and the thermæ were put under the inspection of a censor, who was generally one of the first senators in Rome. Agrippa left his gardens and baths, which stood near the Pantheon, to the Roman people: among the statues that adorned them was that of a youth naked, as going into the bath, so elegantly formed by the hand of Lysippus, that Tiberius,[25] being struck with the beauty of it, ordered it to be transferred into his own palace: but the populace raised such a clamour against him, that he was fain to have it reconveyed to its former place. These noble baths were restored by Adrian, as we read in Spartian;[26] but at present no part of them remains.

With respect to the present state of the old aqueducts, I can give you very little satisfaction. I only saw the ruins of that which conveyed the acqua Claudia, near the Porta Maggiore, and the Piazza of the Lateran. You know there were fourteen of those antient aqueducts, some of which brought water to Rome from the distance of forty miles. The channels of them were large enough to admit a man armed on horseback; and therefore when Rome was besieged by the Goths, who had cut off the water, Belisarius[27] fortified them with works to prevent the enemy from entering the city by those conveyances. After that period, I suppose the antient aqueducts continued dry, and were suffered to run to ruins. Without all doubt, the Romans were greatly obliged to those benefactors, who raised such stupendous works for the benefit, as well as the embellishment of their city: but it might have been supplied with the same water through pipes at one hundredth part of the expence; and in that case the enemy would not have found it such an easy matter to cut it off. Those popes who have provided the modern city so plentifully with excellent water, are much to be commended for the care and expence they have bestowed in restoring the streams called acqua Virgine, acqua Felice, and acqua Paolina, which afford such abundance of water as would plentifully supply a much larger city than modern Rome.

It is no wonder that M. Agrippa, the son-in-law, friend, and favourite of Augustus, should at the same time have been the idol of the people, considering how surprisingly he exerted himself for the emolument, convenience, and pleasure of his fellow-citizens. It was he who first conducted this acqua Virgine to Rome: he formed seven hundred reservoirs in the city; erected one hundred and five fountains; one hundred and thirty *castella*, or conduits, which works he adorned with three hundred statues, and four hundred pillars of marble, in the space of one year. He also brought into Rome, the acqua Julia, and restored the aqueduct of the acqua Marzia, which had fallen to decay. I have already observed the great number of baths which he opened for the people, and the magnificent thermæ, with spacious gardens, which he bequeathed to them as a legacy. But these benefactions, great and munificent as they seem to be, were not the most important services he performed for the city of Rome. The common-sewers were first made by order of Tarquinius Priscus, not so much with a view to cleanliness, as by way of subterranean drains to the *Velabrum*,[28] and in order to carry off the stagnant water, which remained in the lower parts, after heavy rains. The different branches of these channels united at the Forum, from whence by the Cloaca Maxima, their contents were conveyed into the Tyber. This great cloaca was the work of Tarquinius Superbus. Other sewers were added by Marcus Cato, and Valerius Flaccus,[29] the censors. All these drains having been choaked up and ruinous, were cleared and restored by Marcus Agrippa, who likewise undermined the whole city with canals of the same kind, for carrying off the filth; he strengthened and enlarged the Cloaca Maxima, so as to make it capable of receiving a large cart loaded with hay; and directed seven streams of water into these subterranean passages, in order to keep them always clean and open. If, notwithstanding all these conveniences, Vespasian was put to great expence in removing the ordure from the public streets, we have certainly a right to conclude that the antient Romans were not more cleanly than the modern Italians.

After the mausolea of Augustus, and Adrian, which I have

already mentioned, the most remarkable antient sepulchres at Rome, are those of Caius Cestius, and Cecilia Metella.[30] The first, which stands by the Porta di S. Paolo, is a beautiful pyramid, one hundred and twenty feet high, still preserved intire, having a vaulted chamber within-side, adorned with some ancient painting, which is now almost effaced. The building is of brick, but cased with marble. This Caius Cestius had been consul, was very rich, and acted as one of the seven *Epulones*, who superintended the feasts of the gods, called *Lectisternia*,[31] and *Pervigilia*.[32] He bequeathed his whole fortune to his friend M. Agrippa, who was so generous as to give it up to the relations of the testator. The monument of Cecilia Metella, commonly called *Capo di Bove*, is without the walls on the Via Appia. This lady was daughter of Metellus Creticus, and wife to Crassus, who erected this noble monument to her memory. It consisted of two orders, or stories, the first of which was a square of hewn stone: the second was a circular tower, having a cornice, adorned with ox heads in basso relievo, a circumstance from which it takes the name of *Capo di Bove*. The ox was supposed to be a most grateful sacrifice to the gods. Pliny, speaking of bulls and oxen, says,

"*Hinc victimæ optimæ et laudatissima deorum placatio.*"[33]

"They were counted the best victims and most agreeable to appease the anger of the gods."

This tower was surmounted by a noble cupola or dome, enriched with all the ornaments of architecture. The door of the building was of brass; and within-side the ashes of Cecilia were deposited in a fluted marble urn, of curious workmanship, which is still kept in the Palazzo Farnese. At present the surface of the ground is raised so much as to cover the first order of the edifice: what we see is no more than the round tower, without the dome and its ornaments; and the following inscription still remains near the top, facing the Via Appia.

CÆCILIÆ
Q. CRETICI F.
METELLÆ
CRASSI.

## LETTER XXXII.

To Cæcilia Metella daughter of Q. Creticus wife of Crassus.

Now we are talking of sepulchral inscriptions, I shall conclude this letter with the copy of a very singular will, made by Favonius Jocundus, who died in Portugal, by which will the precise situation of the famous temple of Sylvanus is ascertained.

*"Jocundi.*

*Ego Gallus Favonius Jocundus P. Favoni F. qui bello contra Viriatum succubui, Jocundum et Prudentem filios, e me et Quintia Fabia conjuge mea ortos, et Bonorum Jocundi Patris mei, et eorum, quæ mihi ipsi acquisivi hæredes relinquo; hac tamen conditione, ut ab urbe Romana huc veniant, et ossa hic mea, intra quinquennium exportent, et via latina condant in sepulchro, jussu meo condito, et mea voluntate; in quo velim neminem mecum, neque servum, neque libertum inseri; et velim ossa quorumcumque sepulchro statim meo eruantur, et jura Romanorum serventur, in sepulchris ritu majorum retinendis, juxta voluntatem testatoris; et si secus fecerint, nisi legittimæ oriantur causæ, velim ea omnia, quæ filijs meis relinquo, pro reparando templo dei Sylvani,* quod sub Viminali monte est, *attribui; manesque mei a Pont. Max.; a flaminibus dialibus, qui in capitolio sunt, opem implorent, ad liberorum meorum impietatem ulciscendam; teneanturque sacerdotes dei Silvani, me in urbem referre, et sepulchro me meo condere. Volo quoque vernas qui domi meæ sunt, omnes a prætore urbano liberos, cum matribus dimitti, singulisque libram argenti puri, et vestem unam dari. In Lusitania. In agro VIII. Cal Quintilis, bello Viriatino."*

"I *Gallus Favonius Jocundus,* son of P. *Favonius,* dying in the war against *Viriatus,*[34] declare my sons *Jocundus* and *Prudens* by my wife *Quintia Fabia,* joint heirs of all my estate, real and personal; on condition, however, that they come hither within the term of five years from the date of this my last will, and transport my remains to *Rome,* to be deposited in my sepulchre built in the *via latina* by my own order and direction: and it is my will that neither slave nor freedman shall be interred with me in the said tomb; that if any such there be, they shall be removed; and the Roman Law obeyed, in preserving after the antient form, the sepulchre according to the will of the testator. If they act otherwise without just cause, it is my will that the whole estate which I now

269

bequeathe to my children, shall be applied to the reparation of the temple of the god *Sylvanus*, *at the foot of mount Viminalis*; and that my *manes** shall implore the assistance of the *Pontifex Maximus*, and the *Flaminis-diales* in the capitol, to avenge the impiety of my children, and the priests of *Sylvanus* shall engage to bring my remains to *Rome* and see them decently deposited in my own sepulchre. It is also my will that all my domestic slaves shall be declared free by the city *prætor*, and dismissed with their mothers, after having received each, a suit of cloaths, and a pound weight of pure silver, from my heirs and executors.

At my farm in *Lusitania*

July 25.      during the *Viriatin* war."

My paper scarce affords room to assure you that I am ever,

Dear Sir,

Your faithful, &c.

---

* The *manes* were an order of gods supposed to take cognizance of such injuries.

# LETTER XXXIII.

*Nice, March* 30, 1765.

DEAR SIR,

You must not imagine I saw one half of the valuable pictures and statues of Rome; there is such a vast number of both in this capital, that I might have spent a whole year in taking even a transient view of them; and, after all, some of them would have been overlooked. The most celebrated pieces, however, I have seen; and therefore my curiosity is satisfied. Perhaps, if I had the nice discernment and delicate sensibility of a true connoisseur, this superficial glimpse would have served only to whet my appetite, and to detain me the whole winter at Rome. In my progress through the Vatican, I was much pleased with the School of Athens, by Raphael, a piece which hath suffered from the dampness of the air. The four boys attending to the demonstration of a mathematician are admirably varied in the expression. Mr. Webb's criticism on this artist is certainly just. He was perhaps the best ethic painter that ever the world produced. No man ever expressed the sentiments so happily, in visage, attitude, and gesture: but he seems to have had too much phlegm to strike off the grand passions, or reach the sublime parts of painting.[1] He has the serenity of Virgil, but wants the fire of Homer. There is nothing in his Parnassus which struck me, but the ludicrous impropriety of Apollo's playing upon a fiddle, for the entertainment of the nine muses.*

The Last Judgment, by Buonaroti, in the chapel of Sixtus IV.[2] produced to my eye the same sort of confusion that perplexes my ear at a grand concert, consisting of a great variety of instruments: or rather, when a number of people are talking all at once. I was pleased with the strength of expression, exhibited in single figures, and separate groupes: but, the whole together is a mere mob, without subordination, keeping, or repose. A painter ought to avoid all subjects that require a multiplicity of groupes and figures; because it is

---

* Upon better information, I must retract this censure; in as much as I find there was really a musical instrument among the antients of this figure, as appears by a small statue in bronze to be still seen in the Florentine collection.

not in the power of that art to unite a great number in one point of view, so as to maintain that dependence which they ought to have upon one another. Michael Angelo, with all his skill in anatomy, his correctness of design, his grand composition, his fire, and force of expression, seems to have had very little idea of grace. One would imagine he had chosen his kings, heroes, cardinals, and prelates, from among the *facchini*[3] of Rome; that he really drew his Jesus on the Cross, from the agonies of some vulgar assassin expiring on the wheel; and that the originals of his Bambini, with their mothers, were literally found in a stable. In the Sala Regia, from whence the Sistian chapel is detached, we see, among other exploits of catholic heroes, a representation of the massacre of the protestants in Paris, Thoulouse, and other parts of France, on the eve of St. Bartholomew,[4] thus described in the *Descrizione di Roma*,[5] "Nella prima pittura, esprime Georgio Vasari l'istoria del Coligni, grand'amiraglio di Francia, che come capo de ribelli, e degl'Ugonotti, fu ucciso; e nell'altra vicina, la strage fatta in Parigi, e nel regno, de ribelli, e degl'Ugonotti." "In the first picture, George Vasari represents the history of Coligni,[6] high admiral of France, who was slain as head of the rebels and hugonots; and in another near it, the slaughter that was made of the rebels and hugonots in Paris and other parts of the kingdom." Thus the court of Rome hath employed their artists to celebrate and perpetuate, as a meritorious action, the most perfidious, cruel, and infamous massacre, that ever disgraced the annals of any nation.

I need not mention the two equestrian statues of Constantine the Great, and Charlemagne, which stand at opposite ends of the great portico of St. Peter's church; because there is nothing in them which particularly engaged my attention. The sleeping Cleopatra, as you enter the court of the Belvedere, in the Vatican, is much admired; but I was better pleased with the Apollo, which I take to be the most beautiful statue that ever was formed.[7] The Nile, which lies in the open court, surmounted with the little children, has infinite merit; but is much damaged, and altogether neglected. Whether it is the same described in Pliny, as having been placed by Vespasian in the Temple of Peace, I do not know.[8] The

sixteen children playing about it, denoted the swelling of the
Nile, which never rose above sixteen cubits. As for the
famous groupe of Laocoon, it surpassed my expectation. It
was not without reason that Buonaroti called it a portentous
work; and Pliny has done it no more than justice in saying it
is the most excellent piece that ever was cut in marble; and
yet the famous Fulvius Ursini[9] is of opinion that this is not
the same statue which Pliny described. His reasons, mentioned by Montfaucon, are these. The statues described by
Pliny were of one stone; but these are not. Antonioli, the
antiquary, has in his possession, pieces of Laocoon's snakes,
which were found in the ground, where the baths of Titus
actually stood, agreeable to Pliny, who says these statues
were placed in the buildings of Titus.[10] Be that as it may, the
work which we now see does honour to antiquity. As you
have seen innumerable copies and casts of it, in marble,
plaister, copper, lead, drawings, and prints, and read the
description of it in Keyslar,[11] and twenty other books of
travels, I shall say nothing more on the subject; but that
neither they nor I, nor any other person, could say too much
in its praise. It is not of one piece indeed. In that particular
Pliny himself might be mistaken. "*Opus omnibus et picturæ, et
statuariæ artis præponendum. Ex uno lapide eum et liberos
draconumque mirabiles nexus de consilii sententia fecere summi
artifices.*"[12] "A work preferable to all the other efforts of
painting and statuary. The most excellent artists joined their
talents in making the father and his sons, together with the
admirable twinings of the serpents, of one block." Buonaroti
discovered the joinings, though they were so artfully concealed as to be before invisible. This amazing groupe is the
work of three Rhodian sculptors, called Agesander, Polydore, and Athenodorus,[13] and was found in the thermæ of
Titus Vespasian, still supposing it to be the true antique. As
for the *torso*, or mutilated trunk of a statue, which is called the
School of Michael Angelo, I had not time to consider it
attentively; nor taste enough to perceive its beauties at first
sight. The famous horses on Monte Cavallo, before the
pope's palace, which are said to have been made in emulation,
by Phidias[14] and Praxiteles, I have seen, and likewise those in
the front of the Capitol, with the statues of Castor and

Pollux; but what pleased me infinitely more than all of them together, is the equestrian statue of Corinthian brass, standing in the middle of this Piazza (I mean at the Capitol) said to represent the emperor Marcus Aurelius. Others suppose it was intended for Lucius Verus;[15] a third set of antiquaries contend for Lucius Septimius Severus; and a fourth, for Constantine, because it stood in the Piazza of the Lateran palace, built by that emperor, from whence pope Paul III. caused it to be removed to the Capitol.[16] I considered the trophy of Marius as a very curious piece of sculpture, and admired the two sphinges at the bottom of the stairs leading to this Piazza, as the only good specimens of design, I had ever seen from Ægypt: for the two idols of that country, which stand in the ground-floor of the Musæum of the Capitol, and indeed all the Ægyptian statues in the Camera Ægyptiaca of this very building, are such monstrous misrepresentations of nature, that they never could have obtained a place among the statues of Rome, except as curiosities of foreign superstition, or on account of the materials, as they are generally of basaltes, porphyry, or oriental granite.

At the farther end of the court of this Musæum, fronting the entrance, is a handsome fountain, with the statue of a river-god reclining on his urn; this is no other than the famous Marforio, so called from its having been found in Martis Foro. It is remarkable only as being the conveyance of the answers to the satires which are found pasted upon Pasquin, another mutilated statue, standing at the corner of a street.[17]

The marble coffin, supposed to have contained the ashes of Alexander Severus,[18] which we find in one of these apartments, is a curious antique, valuable for its sculpture in basso relievo, especially for the figures on the cover, representing that emperor and his mother Julia Mammea.

I was sorry I had not time to consider the antient plan of Rome, disposed in six classes, on the stair-case of this Musæum, which was brought hither from a temple that stood in the Forum Boarium, now called Campo Vaccino.

It would be ridiculous in me to enter into a detail of the vast collection of marbles, basso relievos, inscriptions, urns, busts, and statues, which are placed in the upper apartments of this edifice. I saw them but once, and then I was struck with the following particulars. A bacchanalian drunk; a Jupiter and Leda, at least equal to that in the gallery at Florence; an old *præsica*, or hired mourner, very much resembling those wrinkled hags still employed in Ireland, and in the Highlands of Scotland, to sing the *coronach*[19] at funerals, in praise of the deceased; the famous Antinous, an elegant figure, which Poussin[20] studied as the canon or rule of symmetry; the two fauns; and above all the *mirmillone*, or dying gladiator; the attitude of the body, the expression of the countenance, the elegance of the limbs, and the swelling of the muscles, in this statue, are universally admired; but the execution of the back is incredibly delicate. The course of the muscles called *longissimi dorsi*, are so naturally marked and tenderly executed, that the marble actually emulates the softness of flesh; and you may count all the spines of the vertebræ, raising up the skin as in the living body; yet this statue, with all its merit, seems inferior to the celebrated dying gladiator of Ctesilas, as described by Pliny,[21] who says the expression of it was such, as appears altogether incredible. In the court, on the opposite side of the Capitol, there is an admirable statue of a lion devouring a horse, which was found by the gate of Ostia, near the pyramid of Caius Cestius; and here on the left hand, under a colonnade, is what they call the Columna Rostrata, erected in honour of Caius Duilius,[22] who first triumphed over the Carthaginians by sea. But this is a modern pillar, with the old inscription, which is so defaced as not to be legible. Among the pictures in the gallery and saloon above, what pleased me most was the Bacchus and Ariadne of Guido Rheni; and the wolf suckling Romulus and Remus, by Rubens. The court of the Palazzo Farnese is surrounded with antique statues, among which the most celebrated are, the Flora, with a most delicate drapery; the gladiator, with a dead boy over his shoulder; the Hercules, with the spoils of the Nemean lion; but that which the connoisseurs justly esteem above all the rest is the Hercules, by Glycon,[23] which you know as well as I do, by the great reputation it has acquired. This admirable statue having been found without the legs, these were supplied by Gulielmo de la Porta[24] so happily, that when afterwards the original limbs were discovered, Michael Angelo preferred those of the modern artist, both in grace and proportion; and they have been retained accordingly. In a little house, or shed, behind the court, is preserved the wonderful groupe of Dirce, commonly called the Toro Farnese, which was brought hither from the thermæ Caracallæ. There is such spirit, ferocity, and indignant resistance expressed in the bull, to whose horns Dirce is tied by the hair, that I have never seen any thing like it, either upon canvass, or in stone. The statues of the two brothers endeavouring to throw him into the sea are beautiful figures, finely contrasted; and the rope, which one of them holds in a sort of loose coil, is so surprisingly chizzelled, that one can hardly believe it is of stone. As for Dirce herself, she seems to be but a subaltern character; but there is a dog upon his hind legs barking at the bull, which is much admired. This amazing groupe was cut out of one stone, by Appollonius and Tauriscus,[25] two sculptors of Rhodes; and is mentioned by Pliny in the thirty-sixth book of his Natural History.[26] All the precious monuments of art, which have come down to us from antiquity, are the productions of Greek artists. The Romans had taste enough to admire the arts of Greece, as plainly appears by the great collections they made of their statues and pictures, as well as by adopting their architecture and musick: but I do not remember to have read of any Roman who made a great figure either as a painter or a statuary. It is not enough to say those professions were not honourable in Rome, because painting, sculpture, and musick, even rhetoric, physic, and philosophy, were practised and taught by slaves. The arts were always honoured and revered at Rome, even when the professors of them happened to be slaves by the accidents and iniquity of fortune. The business of painting and statuary was so profitable, that in a free republic, like that of Rome, they must have been greedily embraced by a great number of individuals: but, in all probability, the Roman soil produced no extraordinary genius for those arts. Like the English of this day, they made a figure in poetry, history, and ethics; but the excellence of painting, sculpture, architecture, and music, they never could attain. In the Palazzo Picchini, I saw three beautiful figures, the celebrated statues of Meleager, the boar, and dog; together with a wolf, of excellent workmanship. The celebrated statue of Moses, by Michael Angelo, in the church of St. Peter in Vincula, I beheld with pleasure; as well as that of Christ, by the same hand, in the church of S. Maria sopra Minerva. The right foot, covered with bronze, gilt, is much kissed by the devotees. I suppose it is looked upon as a specific[27] for the tooth-ache; for, I saw a cavalier, in years, and an old woman successively rub their gums upon it, with the appearance of the most painful perseverance.

You need not doubt but that I went to the church of St. Peter in Montorio, to view the celebrated transfiguration, by Raphael, which, if it was mine, I would cut in two parts. The three figures in the air attract the eye so strongly, that little or no attention is payed to those below on the mountain. I apprehend that the nature of the subject does not admit of that keeping and dependence, which ought to be maintained in the disposition of the lights and shadows in a picture. The groupes seem to be intirely independent of each other. The extraordinary merit of this piece, I imagine, consists, not only in the expression of divinity on the face of Christ; but also in the surprising lightness of the figure, that hovers like a beautiful exhalation in the air.[28] In the church of St. Luke, I was not at all struck by the picture of that saint, drawing the portrait of the Virgin Mary, although it is admired as one of the best pieces of Raphael. Indeed it made so little impression upon me, that I do not even remember the disposition of the figures. The altar-piece, by Andrea Sacchi,[29] in the church of St. Romauldus, would have more merit, if the figure of the saint himself had more consequence, and was represented in a stronger light. In the Palazzo Borghese, I chiefly admired the following pieces: a Venus with two nymphs; and another with Cupid, both by Titian: an excellent Roman Piety, by Leonardo da Vinci; and the celebrated Muse, by Dominechino, which is a fine, jolly, buxom figure. At the palace of Colonna Connestabile, I was charmed with the Herodias, by Guido Rheni; a young Christ; and a Madonna, by Raphael; and four landscapes, two by Claude Lorraine,[30] and the other two, by Salvator Rosa.[31] In the *palazetto*, or summer-house belonging to the Palazzo Rospigliosi, I had the satisfaction of contemplating the Aurora of Guido, the colours of which still remain in high perfection, notwith-standing the common report that the piece is spoiled by the dampness of the apartment. The print of this picture, by Freij,[32] with all its merit, conveys but an imperfect idea of the beauty of the original. In the Palazzo Barberini, there is a great collection of marbles and pictures: among the first, I was attracted by a beautiful statue of Venus; a sleeping faun, of curious workmanship; a charming Bacchus, lying on an antient sculpture, and the famous Narcissus. Of the pictures, what gave me most pleasure was the Magdalen of Guido, infinitely superior to that by Le Brun[33] in the church of the Carmelites at Paris; the Virgin, by Titian; a Madonna, by Raphael, but not comparable to that which is in the Palazzo de Pitti, at Florence; and the death of Germanicus, by Poussin, which I take to be one of the best pieces in this great collection. In the Palazzo Falconeri, there is a beautiful St. Cecilia, by Guercino;[34] a holy family, by Raphael; and a fine expressive figure of St. Peter weeping, by Dominechino. In the Palazzo Altieri, I admired a picture, by Carlo Maratti,[35] representing a saint calling down lightning from heaven to destroy blasphemers. It was the figure of the saint I admired, merely as a portrait. The execution of the other parts was tame enough: perhaps they were purposely kept down, in order to preserve the importance of the principal figure. I imagine Salvator Rosa would have made a different disposi-tion on the same subject: that amidst the darkness of a tempest, he would have illuminated the blasphemer with the flash of lightning by which he was destroyed: this would have thrown a dismal gleam upon his countenance, distorted by the horror of his situation as well as by the effects of the fire; and rendered the whole scene dreadfully picturesque. In the same palace, I saw the famous holy family, by Corregio, which he left unfinished, and no other artist would undertake to supply; for what reason I know not. Here too is a judgment of Paris, by Titian, which is reckoned a very valuable piece. In the Palazzo Odescalchi, there is a holy family, by Buonaroti, and another by Raphael, both counted excellent, though in very different stiles, extremely charac-teristic of those two great rival artists.

If I was silly enough to make a parade, I might mention

some hundreds more of marbles and pictures, which I really saw at Rome; and even eke out that number with a huge list of those I did not see: but, whatever vanity I may have, it has not taken this turn; and I assure you, upon my word and honour, I have described nothing but what actually fell under my own observation. As for my critical remarks, I am afraid you will think them too superficial and capricious to belong to any other person but

Your humble servant.

# LETTER XXXIV.

*Nice, April 2, 1765.*

DEAR SIR,

I have nothing to communicate touching the library of the Vatican, which, with respect to the apartments and their ornaments, is undoubtedly magnificent. The number of books it contains does not exceed forty thousand volumes, which are all concealed from the view, and locked up in presses: as for the manuscripts, I saw none but such as are commonly presented to strangers of our nation; some very old copies of Virgil and Terence; two or three Missals, curiously illuminated; the book De Septem Sacramentis written in Latin by Henry VIII. against Luther;[1] and some of that prince's love letters to Anne Boleyn. I likewise visited the Libreria Casanatense, belonging to the convent of the church called S. Maria Sopra Minerva. I had a recommendation to the principal librarian, a Dominican friar, who received me very politely, and regaled me with a sight of several curious MSS. of the classics.

Having satisfied my curiosity at Rome, I prepared for my departure, and as the road between Radicofani and Montefiascone is very stony and disagreeable, I asked the banker Barazzi,[2] if there was not a better way of returning to Florence, expressing a desire at the same time to see the cascade of Terni. He assured me that the road by Terni was forty miles shorter than the other, much more safe and easy, and accommodated with exceeding good auberges. Had I taken the trouble to cast my eyes upon the map, I must have seen, that the road by Terni, instead of being forty miles shorter, was much longer than the other: but this was not the only mistake of Signiore Barazzi. Great part of this way lies over steep mountains, or along the side of precipices, which render travelling in a carriage exceeding tedious, dreadful, and dangerous; and as for the public houses, they are in all respects the most execrable that ever I entered. I will venture to say that a common prisoner in the Marshalsea or King's-Bench[3] is more cleanly and commodiously lodged than we were in many places on this road. The houses are abominably nasty, and generally destitute of provision: when eatables were found, we were almost poisoned by their cookery: their beds were without curtains or bedstead, and their windows without glass; and for this sort of entertainment we payed as much as if we had been genteelly lodged, and sumptuously treated. I repeat it again; of all the people I ever knew, the Italians are the most villainously rapacious. The first day, having passed Civita Castellana, a small town standing on the top of a hill, we put up at what was called an excellent inn, where cardinals, prelates, and princes, often lodged. Being meagre day, there was nothing but bread, eggs, and anchovies, in the house. I went to bed without supper, and lay in a pallet, where I was half devoured by vermin. Next day, our road, in some places, lay along precipices, which over-hang the Nera or Nar, celebrated in antiquity for its white foam, and the sulphureous quality of its waters.

*Sulfureâ Nar albus aquâ, fontesque Velini.*[4]
Sulphureous *Nar*, and the *Velinian* streams.

It is a small, but rapid stream, which runs not far from hence, into the Tyber. Passing Utricoli, near the ruins of the ancient Ocriculum, and the romantic town of Narni, situated on the top of a mountain, in the neighbourhood of which is still seen standing one arch of the stupendous bridge built by Augustus Cæsar, we arrived at Terni, and hiring a couple of chaises before dinner, went to see the famous Cascata delle Marmore, which is at the distance of three miles. We ascended a steep mountain by a narrow road formed for a considerable way along the brink of a precipice, at the bottom of which brawls the furious river Nera, after having received the Velino. This last is the stream which, running from the Lago delle Marmore, forms the cascade by falling over a precipice about one hundred and sixty feet high. Such a body of water rushing down the mountain; the smoak, vapour, and thick white mist which it raises; the double rainbow which these particles continually exhibit while the sun shines; the deafening sound of the cataract; the vicinity of a great number of other stupendous rocks and precipices, with the dashing, boiling, and foaming of the two rivers below, produce altogether an object of tremendous sublimity: yet great part of its effect is lost, for want of a proper point of view, from which it might be contemplated. The cascade would appear much more astonishing, were it not in some measure eclipsed by the superior height of the neighbouring mountains. You have not a front perspective; but are obliged to view it obliquely on one side, standing upon the brink of a precipice, which cannot be approached without horror. This station might be rendered much more accessible, and altogether secure, for the expence of four or five zequines; and a small tax might be levied for the purpose from travellers by the aubergiste at Terni, who lets his calasses for half a zequine a piece to those that are curious to see this phænomenon. Besides the two postilions whom I payed for this excursion, at the rate of one stage in posting, there was a fellow who posted himself behind one of the chaises, by way of going to point out the different views of the cascade; and his demand amounted to four or five pauls. To give you an idea of the extortion of those villainous publicans, I must tell you that for a dinner and supper, which even hunger could not tempt us to eat, and a night's lodging in three truckle beds, I paid eighty pauls, amounting to forty shillings sterling. You ask me why I submitted to such imposition? I will tell you—I have more than once in my travels made a formal complaint of the exorbitancy of a publican, to the magistrate of the place; but I never received any satisfaction, and have lost abundance of time. Had I proceeded to manual correction, I should have alarmed and terrified the women: had I peremptorily refused to pay the sum total, the landlord, who was the post-master, would not have supplied me with horses to proceed on my journey. I tried the experiment at Muy in France, where I put myself into a violent passion, had abundance of trouble, was detained till it was almost night, and after all found myself obliged to submit, furnishing at the same time matter of infinite triumph to the mob, which had surrounded the coach, and interested themselves warmly in favour of their townsman. If some young patriot, in good health and spirits, would take the trouble as often as he is imposed upon by the road in travelling, to have recourse to the fountain-head, and prefer a regular complaint to the comptroller of the posts, either in France or Italy, he would have ample satisfaction, and do great service to the community. Terni is an agreeable town, pretty well built, and situated in a pleasant valley, between two branches of the river Nera, whence it was called by the antients, Interamna. Here is an agreeable piazza, where stands a church that was of old a heathen temple.[5] There are some valuable paintings in the church. The people are said to be very civil, and provisions to be extremely cheap. It was the birth-place of the emperor Tacitus,[6] as well as of the historian of the same name.[7] In our journey from hence to Spoleto, we passed over a high mountain, called from its height, Somma, where it was necessary to have two additional horses to the carriage, and the road winds along a precipice, which is equally dangerous and dreadful. We passed through part of Spoleto, the capital of Umbria, which is a pretty large city. Of this, however, I can give no other account from my own observation, but that I saw at a distance the famous Gothic aqueduct of brick: this is mentioned by Addison as a structure, which, for the height of its arches, is not equalled by any thing in Europe.[8] The road from hence to Foligno, where we lay, is kept in good order, and lies through a delightful plain, laid out into beautiful inclosures, abounding with wine, oil, corn, and cattle, and watered by the pastoral streams of the famous river Clitumnus,[9] which takes its rise in three or four separate rivulets issuing from a rock near the highway. On the right-hand, we saw several towns situated on rising grounds, and among the rest, that of Assisio, famous for the birth of St. Francis,[10] whose body, being here deposited, occasions a great concourse of pilgrims. We met a Roman princess going thither with a grand retinue, in consequence of a vow she had made for the re-establishment of her health. Foligno, the Fulginium of the antients, is a small town, not unpleasant, lying in the midst of mulberry plantations, vineyards, and corn-fields, and built on both sides of the little river Topino. In choosing our beds at the inn, I perceived one chamber locked, and desired it might be opened; upon which the cameriere declared with some reluctance, *"Bisogna dire a su' eccellenza; poco fa, che una bestia e morta in questa camera, e non e ancora lustrata."* "Your excellency must know that a filthy beast died lately in that chamber, and it is not yet purified and put in order." When I enquired what beast it was, he replied, *"Un' eretico Inglese,"* "An English heretick."[11] I suppose he would not have made so free with our country and religion, if he had not taken us for German catholics, as we afterwards learned from Mr. R——y.[12] Next day, we crossed the Tyber, over a handsome bridge, and in mounting the steep hill upon which the city of Perugia stands, our horses being exhausted, were dragged backwards by the weight of the carriage to the very edge of a precipice, where, happily for us, a man passing that way, placed a large stone behind one of the wheels, which stopped their motion, otherwise we should have been all dashed in pieces. We had another ugly hill to ascend within the city, which was more difficult and dangerous than the other: but the postilions and the other beasts made such efforts, that we mounted without the least stop, to the summit, where we found ourselves in a large piazza, where the horses are always changed. There being no relays at the post, we were obliged to stay the whole day and night at Perugia, which is a considerable city, built upon the acclivity of a hill, adorned with some elegant fountains, and several handsome churches, containing some valuable pictures by Guido, Raphael, and his master Pietro Perugino, who was a native of this place. The next stage is on the banks of the lake, which was the Thrasimene of the antients, a beautiful piece of water, above thirty miles in circumference, having three islands, abounding with excellent fish: upon a peninsula of it, there is a town and castle. It was in this neighbourhood where the consul Flaminius was totally defeated with great slaughter by Hannibal.[13] From Perugia to Florence, the posts are all double, and the road is so bad that we never could travel above eight and twenty miles a day. We were often obliged to quit the carriage, and walk up steep mountains; and the way in general was so unequal and stony, that we were jolted even to the danger of our lives. I never felt any sort of exercise or fatigue so intolerable; and I did not fail to bestow an hundred benedictions per diem upon the banker Barazzi, by whose advice we had taken this road; yet there was no remedy but patience. If the coach had not been incredibly strong, it must have been shattered to pieces. The fifth night we passed at a place called Camoccia, a miserable cabaret, where we were fain to cook our own supper, and lay in a musty chamber, which had never known a fire, and indeed had no fire-place, and where we ran the risque of being devoured by rats. Next day one of the irons of the coach gave way at Arezzo, where we were detained two hours before it could be accommodated. I might have taken this opportunity to view the remains of the antient Etruscan amphitheatre, and the temple of Hercules, described by the cavalier Lorenzo Guazzesi,[14] as standing in the neighbourhood of this place: but the blacksmith assured me his work would be finished in a few minutes; and as I had nothing so much at heart as the speedy accomplishment of this disagreeable journey, I chose to suppress my curiosity, rather than be the occasion of a moment's delay. But all the nights we had hitherto passed were comfortable in comparison to this, which we suffered at a small village, the name of which I do not remember. The house was dismal and dirty beyond all description; the bed-cloaths filthy enough to turn the stomach of a muleteer; and the victuals cooked in such a manner, that even a Hottentot could not have beheld them without loathing. We had sheets of our own, which were spread upon a mattrass, and here I took my repose wrapped in a great-coat, if that could be called repose which was interrupted by the innumerable stings of vermin. In the morning, I was seized with a dangerous fit of the hooping-cough, which terrified my wife, alarmed my people, and brought the whole community into the house. I had undergone just such another at Paris, about a year before. This forenoon, one of our coach wheels flew off in the neighbourhood of Ancisa, a small town, where we were detained above two hours by this accident; a delay which was productive of much disappointment, danger, vexation, and fatigue. There being no horses at the last post, we were obliged to wait until those which brought us thither were sufficiently refreshed to proceed. Understanding that all the gates of Florence are shut at six, except two that are kept open for the accommodation of travellers; and that to reach the nearest of these gates, it was necessary to pass the river Arno in a ferry-boat, which could not transport the carriage;

I determined to send my servant before with a light chaise to enter the nearest gate before it was shut, and provide a coach to come and take us up at the side of the river, where we should be obliged to pass in the boat: for I could not bear the thoughts of lying another night in a common cabaret. Here, however, another difficulty occurred. There was but one chaise, and a dragoon officer, in the imperial troops, insisted upon his having bespoke it for himself and his servant. A long dispute ensued, which had like to have produced a quarrel: but, at length, I accommodated matters, by telling the officer that he should have a place in it gratis, and his servant might ride a-horseback. He accepted the offer without hesitation; but, in the mean time, we set out in the coach before them, and having proceeded about a couple of miles, the road was so deep from a heavy rain, and the beasts were so fatigued, that they could not proceed. The postilions scourging the poor animals with great barbarity, they made an effort, and pulled the coach to the brink of a precipice, or rather a kind of hollow-way, which might be about seven or eight feet lower than the road. Here my wife and I leaped out, and stood under the rain up to the ancles in mud; while the postilions still exercising their whips, one of the fore-horses fairly tumbled down the descent, and hung by the neck, so that he was almost strangled before he could be disengaged from the traces, by the assistance of some foot travellers that happened to pass. While we remained in this dilemma, the chaise, with the officer and my servant, coming up, we exchanged places; my wife and I proceeded in the chaise, and left them with Miss C——[15] and Mr. R——, to follow in the coach. The road from hence to Florence is nothing but a succession of steep mountains, paved and conducted in such a manner, that one would imagine the design had been to render it impracticable by any sort of wheel-carriage. Notwithstanding all our endeavours, I found it would be impossible to enter Florence before the gates were shut. I flattered and threatened the driver by turns: but the fellow, who had been remarkably civil at first, grew sullen and impertinent. He told me I must not think of reaching Florence: that the boat would not take the carriage on board; and that from the other side, I must walk five miles before I should reach the gate that was open: but he would carry me to an excellent osteria, where I should be entertained and lodged like a prince. I was now convinced that he had lingered on purpose to serve this inn-keeper; and I took it for granted that what he told me of the distance between the ferry and the gate was a lie. It was eight o'clock when we arrived at his inn. I alighted with my wife to view the chambers, desiring he would not put up his horses. Finding it was a villainous house, we came forth, and, by this time, the horses were put up. I asked the fellow how he durst presume to contradict my orders, and commanded him to put them to the chaise. He asked in his turn if I was mad? If I thought I and the lady had strength and courage enough to walk five miles in the dark, through a road which we did not know, and which was broke up by a continued rain of two days? I told him he was an impertinent rascal, and as he still hesitated, I collared him with one hand, and shook my cane over his head with the other. It was the only weapon I had, either offensive or defensive; for I had left my sword, and musquetoon in the coach. At length the fellow obeyed, though with great reluctance, cracking many severe jokes upon us in the mean time, and being joined in his raillery by the inn-keeper, who had all the external marks of a ruffian. The house stood in a solitary situation, and not a soul appeared but these two miscreants, so that they might have murdered us without fear of detection. "You do not like the apartments? (said one) to be sure they were not fitted up for persons of your rank and quality!" "You will be glad of a worse chamber, (continued the other) before you get to bed." "If you walk to Florence to night, you will sleep so sound, that the fleas will not disturb you." "Take care you do not take up your night's lodging in the middle of the road, or in the ditch of the city-wall." I fired inwardly at these sarcasms, to which, however, I made no reply; and my wife was almost dead with fear. In the road from hence to the boat, we met with an ill-looking fellow, who offered his service to conduct us into the city, and such was our situation, that I was fain to accept his proposal, especially as we had two small boxes in the chaise by accident, containing some caps and laces belonging to my wife. I still hoped the postilion had exaggerated in the distance between the boat and the city gate, and was confirmed in this opinion by the ferryman, who said we had not above half a league to walk. Behold us then in this expedition; myself wrapped up in a very heavy great-coat, and my cane in my hand. I did not imagine I could have walked a couple of miles in this equipage, had my life been depending; my wife a delicate creature, who had scarce ever walked a mile in her life; and the ragamuffin before us with our boxes under his arm. The night was dark and wet; the road slippery and dirty; not a soul was seen, nor a sound was heard: all was silent, dreary, and horrible. I laid my account with a violent fit of illness from the cold I should infallibly catch, if I escaped assassination, the fears of which were the more troublesome as I had no weapon to defend our lives. While I laboured under the weight of my great-coat, which made the streams of sweat flow down my face and shoulders, I was plunged in the mud, up to the mid-leg at every step; and at the same time obliged to support my wife, who wept in silence, half dead with terror and fatigue. To crown our vexation, our conductor walked so fast, that he was often out of sight, and I imagined he had run away with the boxes. All I could do, on these occasions, was to hollow as loud as I could, and swear horribly that I would blow his brains out. I did not know but these oaths and menaces might keep other rogues in awe. In this manner did we travel three long miles, making almost an intire circuit of the city-wall, without seeing the face of a human creature, and at length reached the gate, where we were examined by the guard, and allowed to pass, after they had told us it was a long mile from thence to the house of Vanini, where we proposed to lodge. No matter, being now fairly within the city, I plucked up my spirits, and performed the rest of the journey with such ease, that I am persuaded, I could have walked at the same pace all night long, without being very much fatigued. It was near ten at night, when we entered the auberge in such a draggled and miserable condition, that Mrs. Vanini almost fainted at sight of us, on the supposition that we had met with some terrible disaster, and that the rest of the company were killed. My wife and I were immediately accommodated with dry stockings and shoes, a warm apartment, and a good supper, which I ate with great satisfaction, arising not only from our having happily survived the adventure, but also from a

conviction that my strength and constitution were wonderfully repaired: not but that I still expected a severe cold,
attended with a terrible fit of the asthma: but in this I was
luckily disappointed. I now for the first time drank to the
health of my physician Barazzi, fully persuaded that the
hardships and violent exercise I underwent by following his
advice, had greatly contributed to the re-establishment of my
health. In this particular, I imitate the gratitude of Tavernier,
who was radically cured of the gout by a Turkish aga in
Ægypt, who gave him the bastinado, because he would not
look at the head of the bashaw of Cairo, which the aga carried
in a bag, to be presented to the grand signior at Constantinople.[16]

I did not expect to see the rest of our company that night,
as I never doubted but they would stay with the coach at the
inn on the other side of the Arno: but at mid-night we were
joined by Miss C—— and Mr. R——, who had left the carriage
at the inn, under the auspices of the captain and my servant,
and followed our foot-steps by walking from the ferry-boat
to Florence, conducted by one of the boatmen. Mr. R——
seemed to be much ruffled and chagrined; but, as he did not
think proper to explain the cause, he had no right to expect
that I should give him satisfaction for some insult he had
received from my servant. They had been exposed to a
variety of disagreeable adventures from the impracticability
of the road. The coach had been several times in the most
imminent hazard of being lost with all our baggage; and at
one place, it was necessary to hire a dozen of oxen, and as
many men, to disengage it from the holes into which it had
run. It was in the confusion of these adventures, that the
captain and his valet, Mr. R—— and my servant, had like to
have gone all by the ears together. The peace was with
difficulty preserved by the interposition of Miss C——, who
suffered incredibly from cold and wet, terror, vexation, and
fatigue: yet happily no bad consequence ensued. The coach
and baggage were brought safely into Florence next morning, when all of us found ourselves well refreshed, and in
good spirits. I am afraid this is not the case with you, who
must by this time be quite jaded with this long epistle, which
shall therefore be closed without further ceremony by,

Yours always.

# LETTER XXXV.

Nice, March 20, 1765.

Dear Sir,

The season being far advanced, and the weather growing boisterous, I made but a short stay at Florence, and set out for Pisa, with full resolution to take the nearest road to Lerici, where we proposed to hire a felucca for Genoa. I had a great desire to see Leghorn and Lucca; but the dread of a winter's voyage by sea in an open boat effectually restrained my curiosity. To avoid the trouble of having our baggage shifted every post, I hired two chaises to Pisa for a couple of zequines, and there we arrived in safety about seven in the evening, though not without fear of the consequence, as the calesses were quite open, and it rained all the way. I must own I was so sick of the wretched accommodation one meets with in every part of Italy, except the great cities, so averse to the sea at this season, and so fond of the city of Pisa, that I should certainly have stayed here the winter, had not I been separated from my books and papers, as well as from other conveniencies and connexions which I had at Nice; and foreseen that the thoughts of performing the same disagreeable voyage in the spring would imbitter my whole winter's enjoyment. I again hired two calesses for Lerici, proposing to lie at Sarzana, three miles short of that place, where we were told we should find comfortable lodging, and to embark next day without halting. When we departed in the morning, it rained very hard, and the Cerchio, which the chaises had formerly passed, almost without wetting the wheels, was now swelled to a mighty river, broad and deep and rapid. It was with great difficulty I could persuade my wife to enter the boat; for it blew a storm, and she had seen it in coming over from the other side hurried down a considerable way by the rapidity of the current, notwithstanding all the efforts of the watermen. Near two hours were spent in transporting us with our chaises. The road between this and Pietra Santa was rendered almost impassable. When we arrived at Massa, it began to grow dark, and the post-master assured us that the road to Sarzana was overflowed in such a manner as not to be passed even in the day-time, without imminent danger. We therefore took up our lodging for the night at this house, which was in all respects one of the worst we had yet entered. Next day, we found the Magra as large and violent as the Cerchio: however, we passed it without any accident, and in the afternoon arrived at Lerici. There we were immediately besieged by a number of patrons of feluccas, from among whom I chose a Spaniard, partly because he looked like an honest man, and produced an ample certificate, signed by an English gentleman; and partly, because he was not an Italian; for, by this time, I had imbibed a strong prejudice against the common people of that country. We embarked in the morning before day, with a gale that made us run the lee-gunwale in the water; but when we pretended to turn the point of Porto Venere, we found the wind full in our teeth, and were obliged to return to our quarters, where we had been shamefully fleeced by the landlord, who, nevertheless, was not such an exorbitant knave as the post-master, whose house I would advise all travellers to avoid. Here, indeed, I had occasion to see an instance of prudence and œconomy, which I should certainly imitate, if ever I had occasion to travel this way by myself. An Englishman, who had hired a felucca from Antibes to Leghorn, was put in here by stress of weather; but being aware of the extortion of inn-keepers, and the bad accommodation in their houses, he slept on board on his own mattrasses; and there likewise he had all his conveniencies for eating. He sent his servant on shore occasionally to buy provision, and see it cooked according to his direction in some public house; and had his meals regularly in the felucca. This evening he came ashore to stretch his legs, and took a solitary walk on the beach, avoiding us with great care, although he knew we were English: his valet, who was abundantly communicative, told my servant, that in coming through France, his master had travelled three days in company with two other English gentlemen, whom he met upon the road, and in all that time he never spoke a word to either: yet in other respects, he was a good man, mild, charitable, and humane. This is a character truly British. At five o'clock in the morning we put to sea again, and though the wind was contrary, made shift to reach the town of Sestri di Levante, where we were most graciously received by the publican butcher and his family. The house was in much better order than before; the people were much more obliging; we passed a very tolerable night, and had a very reasonable bill to pay in the morning. I cannot account for this favourable change any other way, than by ascribing it to the effects of a terrible storm, which had two days before torn up a great number of their olive-trees by the roots, and done such damage as terrified them into humility and submission. Next day, the water being delightful, we arrived by one o'clock in the afternoon at Genoa. Here I made another bargain with out patron Antonio, to carry us to Nice. He had been hitherto remarkably obliging, and seemingly modest. He spoke Latin fluently, and was tinctured with the sciences. I began to imagine he was a person of a good family, who had met with misfortunes in life, and respected him accordingly: but I afterwards found him mercenary, mean, and rapacious. The wind being still contrary, when we departed from Genoa, we could get no further than Finale, where we lodged in a very dismal habitation, which was recommended to us as the best auberge in the place. What rendered it the more uncomfortable, the night was cold, and there was not a fire-place in the house, except in the kitchen. The beds (if they deserved that name) were so shockingly nasty, that we could not have used them, had not a friend of Mr. R——[1] supplied us with mattrasses, sheets, and coverlets; for our own sheets were on board the felucca, which was anchored at a distance from the shore. Our fare was equally wretched: the master of the house was a surly assassin, and his cameriere or waiter, stark-staring mad. Our situation was at the same time shocking and ridiculous. Mr. R—— quarrelled over night with the master, who swore in broken French to my man, that he had a good mind to poinard that impertinent Piedmontese. In the morning before day, Mr. R——, coming into my chamber, gave me to understand that he had been insulted by the landlord, who demanded six and thirty livres for our supper and lodging. Incensed at the rascal's presumption, I assured him I would make him take half the money, and a good beating into the bargain. He replied, that he would have saved me the trouble of beating him, had not the cameriere, who was a very sensible fellow, assured him the padrone was out of his senses, and if roughly handled, might commit some extravagance. Though I was exceedingly ruffled, I could not help laughing at the mad cameriere's palming himself upon R——y, as a sensible fellow, and transferring the charge of madness upon his master, who seemed to be much more knave than fool. While Mr. R—— went to mass, I desired the cameriere to bid his master bring the bill, and to tell him that if it was not reasonable, I would carry him before the commandant. In the mean time I armed myself with my sword in one hand and my cane in the other. The inn-keeper immediately entered, pale and staring, and when I demanded his bill, he told me, with a profound reverence, that he should be satisfied with whatever I myself thought proper to give. Suprised at this moderation, I asked if he should be content with twelve livres, and he answered, "Contentissimo," with another prostration. Then he made an apology for the bad accommodation of his house, and complained, that the reproaches of the other gentleman, whom he was pleased to call my major-duomo, had almost turned his brain. When he quitted the room, his cameriere, laying hold of his master's last words, pointed to his own forehead, and said, he had informed the gentleman over-night that his patron was mad. This day we were by a high wind in the afternoon, driven for shelter into Porto Mauritio, where we found the post-house even worse than that of Finale; and what rendered it more shocking was a girl quite covered with the confluent small-pox, who lay in a room through which it was necessary to pass to the other chambers, and who smelled so strong as to perfume the whole house. We were but fifteen miles from St. Remo, where I knew the auberge was tolerable, and thither I resolved to travel by land. I accordingly ordered five mules to travel post, and a very ridiculous cavalcade we formed, the women being obliged to use common saddles; for in this country even the ladies sit astride. The road lay along one continued precipice, and was so difficult, that the beasts never could exceed a walking pace. In some places we were obliged to alight. Seven hours were spent in travelling fifteen short miles: at length we arrived at our old lodgings in St. Remo, which we found white-washed, and in great order. We supped pretty comfortably; slept well; and had no reason to complain of imposition in paying the bill. This was not the case in the article of the mules, for which I was obliged to pay fifty livres, according to the regulation of the posts. The post-master, who came along with us, had the effrontery to tell me, that if I had hired the mules to carry me and my company to St. Remo, in the way of common travelling, they would have cost me but fifteen livres; but as I demanded post-horses, I must submit to the regulations. This is a distinction the more absurd, as the road is of such a nature as renders it impossible to travel faster in one way than in another; nor indeed is there the least difference either in the carriage or convenience, between travelling post and journey riding. A publican might with the same reason charge me three livres a pound for whiting, and if questioned about the imposition, reply, that if I had asked for fish I should have had the very same whiting for the fifth part of the money: but that he made a wide difference between selling it as fish, and selling it as whiting. Our felucca came round from Porto Mauritio in the night, and embarking next morning, we arrived at Nice about four in the afternoon.

Thus have I given you a circumstantial detail of my Italian expedition, during which I was exposed to a great number of hardships, which I thought my weakened constitution could not have bore; as well as to violent fits of passion, chequered, however, with transports of a more agreeable nature; insomuch that I may say I was for two months continually agitated either in mind or body, and very often in both at the same time. As my disorder at first arose from a sedentary life, producing a relaxation of the fibres, which naturally brought on a listlessness, indolence, and dejection of the spirits, I am convinced that this hard exercise of mind and body, co-operated with the change of air and objects, to brace up the relaxed constitution, and promote a more vigorous circula-tion of the juices, which had long languished even almost to stagnation. For some years, I had been as subject to colds as a delicate woman new delivered. If I ventured to go abroad when there was the least moisture either in the air, or upon the ground, I was sure to be laid up a fortnight with a cough and asthma. But, in this journey, I suffered cold and rain, and stood, and walked in the wet, heated myself with exercise, and sweated violently, without feeling the least disorder; but, on the contrary, felt myself growing stronger every day in the midst of these excesses. Since my return to Nice, it has rained the best part of two months, to the astonishment of all the people in the country; yet during all that time I have enjoyed good health and spirits. On Christmas-Eve, I went to the cathedral at mid-night, to hear high mass celebrated by the new bishop of Nice,[2] in pontificalibus,[3] and stood near two hours uncovered in a cold gallery, without having any cause in the sequel to repent of my curiosity. In a word, I am now so well that I no longer despair of seeing you and the rest of my friends in England; a pleasure which is eagerly desired by

> Dear Sir,
> Your affectionate humble Servant.

# LETTER XXXVI.

DEAR SIR,

You ask whether I think the French people are more taxed than the English; but I apprehend, the question would be more apropos if you asked whether the French taxes are more insupportable than the English; for, in comparing burthens, we ought always to consider the strength of the shoulders that bear them. I know no better way of estimating the strength, than by examining the face of the country, and observing the appearance of the common people, who constitute the bulk of every nation. When I, therefore, see the country of England smiling with cultivation; the grounds exhibiting all the perfection of agriculture, parcelled out into beautiful inclosures, corn-fields, hay and pasture, woodland and common; when I see her meadows well stocked with black cattle; her downs covered with sheep; when I view her teams of horses and oxen, large and strong, fat and sleek; when I see her farm-houses the habitations of plenty, cleanliness, and convenience; and her peasants well fed, well lodged, well cloathed, tall and stout, and hale and jolly; I cannot help concluding that the people are well able to bear those impositions which the public necessities have rendered necessary. On the other hand, when I perceive such signs of poverty, misery, and dirt, among the commonalty of France, their unfenced fields dug up in despair, without the intervention of meadow or fallow ground, without cattle to furnish manure, without horses to execute the plans of agriculture; their farm-houses mean, their furniture wretched, their apparel beggarly; themselves and their beasts the images of famine; I cannot help thinking they groan under oppression, either from their landlords, or their government; probably from both.

The principal impositions of the French government are these: first, the taille, payed by all the commons, except those that are privileged: secondly, the capitation, from which no persons, (not even the nobles) are excepted: thirdly, the tenths and twentieths, called Dixiêmes and Vingtiêmes, which every body pays. This tax was originally levied as an occasional aid in times of war, and other emergencies; but by degrees is become a standing revenue even in time of peace. All the money arising from these impositions goes directly to the king's treasury; and must undoubtedly amount to a very great sum. Besides these, he has the revenue of the farms,[1] consisting of the droits d'aydes, or excise on wine, brandy, &c.; of the custom-house duties; of the gabelle, comprehending that most oppressive obligation on individuals to take a certain quantity of salt at the price which the farmers shall please to fix; of the exclusive privilege to sell tobacco; of the droits de controlle, insinuation, centième denier, franchiefs, aubeine,[2] echange et contre-echange arising from the acts of voluntary jurisdiction, as well as certain law-suits. These farms are said to bring into the king's coffers above one hundred and twenty millions of livres yearly, amounting to near five millions sterling: but the poor people are said to pay about a third more than this sum, which the farmers retain to enrich themselves, and bribe the great for their protection; which protection of the great is the true reason why this most iniquitous, oppressive, and absurd method of levying money is not laid aside. Over and above those articles I have mentioned, the French king draws considerable sums from his clergy, under the denomination of dons gratuits, or free-gifts; as well as from the subsidies given by the pays d'etats,[3] such as Provence, Languedoc, and Bretagne, which are exempted from the taille. The whole revenue of the French king amounts to between twelve and thirteen millions sterling. These are great resources for the king: but they will always keep the people miserable, and effectually prevent them from making such improvements as might turn their lands to the best advantage. But besides being eased in the article of taxes, there is something else required to make them exert themselves for the benefit of their country. They must be free in their persons, secure in their property, indulged with reasonable leases, and effectually protected by law from the insolence and oppression of their superiors.

Great as the French king's resources may appear, they are hardly sufficient to defray the enormous expence of his government. About two millions sterling per annum of his revenue are said to be anticipated for paying the interest of the public debts; and the rest is found inadequate to the charge of a prodigious standing army, a double frontier of fortified towns, and the extravagant appointments of ambassadors, generals, governors, intendants, commandants, and other officers of the crown, all of whom affect a pomp, which is equally ridiculous and prodigal. A French general in the field is always attended by thirty or forty cooks; and thinks it is incumbent upon him, for the glory of France, to give a hundred dishes every day at his table. When don Philip, and the marechal duke de Belleisle, had their quarters at Nice, there were fifty scullions constantly employed in the great square in plucking poultry. This absurd luxury infects their whole army. Even the commissaries keep open table; and nothing is seen but prodigality and profusion. The king of Sardinia proceeds upon another plan. His troops are better cloathed, better payed, and better fed than those of France. The commandant of Nice has about four hundred a year of appointments, which enable him to live decently, and even to entertain strangers. On the other hand, the commandant of Antibes, which is in all respects more inconsiderable than Nice, has from the French king above five times the sum to support the glory of his monarch, which all the sensible part of mankind treat with ridicule and contempt. But the finances of France are so ill managed, that many of their commandants, and other officers, have not been able to draw their appointments these two years. In vain they complain and remonstrate. When they grow troublesome they are removed. How then must they support the glory of France? how, but by oppressing the poor people. The treasurer makes use of their money for his own benefit. The king knows it; he knows his officers thus defrauded, fleece and oppress his people: but he thinks proper to wink at these abuses. That government may be said to be weak and tottering which finds itself obliged to connive at such proceedings. The king of France, in order to give strength and stability to his administration, ought to have sense to adopt a sage plan of œconomy, and vigour of mind sufficient to execute it in all its parts, with the most rigorous exactness. He ought to have courage enough to find fault, and even to punish the delinquents, of what quality soever they may be: and the first act of reformation ought to be a total abolition of all the farms. There are, undoubtedly, many marks of relaxation in the reins of the French government, and, in all probability, the subjects of France will be the first to take advantage of it. There is at present a violent fermentation of different principles among them, which under the reign of a very weak prince, or during a long minority, may produce a great change in the constitution. In proportion to the progress of reason and philosophy, which have made great advances in this kingdom, superstition loses ground; antient prejudices give way; a spirit of freedom takes the ascendant.[4] All the learned laity of France detest the hierarchy as a plan of despotism, founded on imposture and usurpation. The protestants, who are very numerous in the southern parts, abhor it with all the rancour of religious fanaticism. Many of the commons, enriched by commerce and manufacture, grow impatient of those odious distinctions, which exclude them from the honours and privileges due to their importance in the commonwealth; and all the parliaments, or tribunals of justice in the kingdom, seem bent upon asserting their rights and independence in the face of the king's prerogative, and even at the expence of his power and authority. Should any prince therefore be seduced by evil counsellors, or misled by his own bigotry, to take some arbitrary step, that may be extremely disagreeable to all those communities, without having spirit to exert the violence of his power for the support of his measures, he will become equally detested and despised; and the influence of the commons will insensibly encroach upon the pretensions of the crown. But if in the time of a minority, the power of the government should be divided among different competitors for the regency, the parliaments and people will find it still more easy to acquire and ascertain the liberty at which they aspire, because they will have the balance of power in their hands, and be able to make either scale preponderate. I could say a great deal more upon this subject; and I have some remarks to make relating to the methods which might be taken in case of a fresh rupture with France, for making a vigorous impression on that kingdom. But these I must defer till another occasion, having neither room nor leisure at present to add any thing, but that I am, with great truth,

Dear Sir,

Your very humble Servant.

# LETTER XXXVII.

*Nice, April 2, 1765.*

DEAR DOCTOR,

As I have now passed a second winter at Nice, I think myself qualified to make some further remarks on this climate. During the heats of last summer, I flattered myself with the prospect of the fine weather I should enjoy in the winter; but neither I, nor any person in this country, could foresee the rainy weather that prevailed from the middle of November, till the twentieth of March. In this short period of four months, we have had fifty-six days of rain, which I take to be a greater quantity than generally falls during the six worst months of the year in the county of Middlesex, especially as it was, for the most part, a heavy, continued rain. The south winds generally predominate in the wet season at Nice: but this winter the rain was accompanied with every wind that blows, except the south; though the most frequent were those that came from the east and north quarters. Notwithstanding these great rains, such as were never known before at Nice in the memory of man, the intermediate days of fair weather were delightful, and the ground seemed perfectly dry. The air itself was perfectly free from moisture. Though I live upon a ground floor, surrounded on three sides by a garden, I could not perceive the least damp, either on the floors, or the furniture; neither was I much incommoded by the asthma, which used always to harrass me most in wet weather. In a word, I passed the winter here much more comfortably than I expected. About the vernal equinox,[1] however, I caught a violent cold, which was attended with a difficulty of breathing; and as the sun advances towards the tropic, I find myself still more subject to rheums. As the heat increases, the humours of the body are rarefied, and, of consequence, the pores of the skin are opened; while the east wind sweeping over the Alps and Appenines, covered with snow, continues surprisingly sharp and penetrating. Even the people of the country, who enjoy good health, are afraid of exposing themselves to the air at this season, the intemperature of which may last till the middle of May, when all the snow on the mountains will probably be melted: then the air will become mild and balmy, till, in the progress of summer, it grows disagreeably hot, and the strong evaporation from the sea makes it so saline, as to be unhealthy for those who have a scorbutical habit. When the sea-breeze is high, this evaporation is so great as to cover the surface of the body with a kind of volatile brine, as I plainly perceived last summer. I am more and more convinced that this climate is unfavourable for the scurvy. Were I obliged to pass my life in it, I would endeavour to find a country retreat among the mountains, at some distance from the sea, where I might enjoy a cool air, free from this impregnation, unmolested by those flies, gnats, and other vermin, which render the lower parts almost uninhabitable. To this place I would retire in the month of June, and there continue till the beginning of October, when I would return to my habitation in Nice, where the winter is remarkably mild and agreeable. In March and April, however, I would not advise a valetudinarian to go forth, without taking precaution against the cold. An agreeable summer retreat may be found on the other side of the Var, at, or near the town of Grasse, which is pleasantly situated on the ascent of a hill in Provence, about seven English miles from Nice. This place is famous for its pomatum, gloves, wash-balls,[2] perfumes, and toilette-boxes, lined with bergamot.[3] I am told it affords good lodging, and is well supplied with provisions.

We are now preparing for our journey to England, from the exercise of which I promise myself much benefit: a journey extremely agreeable, not only on that account, but also because it will restore me to the company of my friends, and remove me from a place where I leave nothing but the air, which I can possibly regret. The only friendships I have contracted at Nice are with strangers, who, like myself, only sojourn here for a season. I now find, by experience, it is great folly to buy furniture, unless one is resolved to settle here for some years. The Nissards assured me, with great confidence, that I should always be able to sell it for a very little loss; whereas I find myself obliged to part with it for about one-third of what it cost. I have sent for a coach to Aix, and as soon as it arrives, shall take my departure; so that the next letter you receive from me will be dated at some place on the road. I purpose to take Antibes, Toulon, Marseilles, Aix, Avignon, and Orange, in my way: places which I have not yet seen; and where, perhaps, I shall find something for your amusement, which will always be a consideration of some weight with,

Dear Sir,

Yours,

303

# LETTER XXXVIII.

## To Dr. S—— at *Nice*.[1]

*Turin, March* 18, 1765.

DEAR SIR,

Turin is about thirty leagues from Nice, the greater part of the way lying over frightful mountains covered with snow. The difficulty of the road, however, reaches no farther than Coni,[2] from whence there is an open highway through a fine plain country, as far as the capital of Piedmont, and the traveller is accommodated with chaise and horses to proceed either post, or by cambiatura, as in other parts of Italy. There are only two ways of performing the journey over the mountains from Nice; one is to ride a muleback, and the other to be carried in a chair. The former I chose, and set out with my servant on the seventh day of February at two in the afternoon. I was hardly clear of Nice, when it began to rain so hard that in less than an hour the mud was half a foot deep in many parts of the road. This was the only inconvenience we suffered, the way being in other respects practicable enough; for there is but one small hill to cross on this side of the village of L'Escarene, where we arrived about six in the evening. The ground in this neighbourhood is tolerably cultivated, and the mountains are planted to the tops with olive trees. The accommodation here is so very bad, that I had no inclination to be a bed longer than was absolutely necessary for refreshment; and therefore I proceeded on my journey at two in the morning, conducted by a guide, whom I hired for this purpose at the rate of three livres a day. Having ascended one side, and descended the other, of the mountain called Braus, which took up four hours, though the road is not bad, we at six reached the village of Sospello, which is agreeably situated in a small valley, surrounded by prodigious high and barren mountains. This little plain is pretty fertile, and being watered by a pleasant stream, forms a delightful contrast with the hideous rocks that surround it. Having reposed myself and my mules two hours at this place, we continued our journey over the second mountain, called Brovis, which is rather more considerable than the first, and

304

in four hours arrived at La Giandola, a tolerable inn situated betwixt the high road and a small river, about a gunshot from the town of Brieglie,[3] which we leave on the right. As we jogged along in the grey of the morning, I was a little startled at two figures which I saw before me, and began to put my pistols in order. It must be observed that these mountains are infested with *contrabandiers*, a set of smuggling peasants, very bold and desperate, who make a traffic of selling tobacco, salt, and other merchandize, which have not payed duty, and sometimes lay travellers under contribution. I did not doubt but there was a gang of these free-booters at hand; but as no more than two persons appeared, I resolved to let them know we were prepared for defence, and fired one of my pistols, in hope that the report of it, echoed from the surrounding rocks, would produce a proper effect: but, the mountains and roads being entirely covered with snow to a considerable depth, there was little or no reverberation, and the sound was not louder than that of a pop-gun, although the piece contained a good charge of powder. Nevertheless, it did not fail to engage the attention of the strangers, one of whom immediately wheeled to the left about, and being by this time very near me, gave me an opportunity of contemplating his whole person. He was very tall, meagre, and yellow, with a long hooked nose, and small twinkling eyes. His head was cased in a woollen night-cap, over which he wore a flapped hat; he had a silk handkerchief about his neck, and his mouth was furnished with a short wooden pipe, from which he discharged wreathing clouds of tobacco-smoke. He was wrapped in a kind of capot[4] of green bays, lined with wolf-skin, had a pair of monstrous boots, quilted on the inside with cotton, was almost covered with dirt, and rode a mule so low that his long legs hung dangling within six inches of the ground. This grotesque figure was so much more ludicrous than terrible, that I could not help laughing; when taking his pipe out of his mouth, he very politely accosted me by name. You may easily guess I was exceed-ingly surprised at such an address on the top of the mountain Brovis: but he forthwith put an end to it, by discovering himself to be the marquis M.[5] whom I had the honour to be acquainted with at Nice. After having rallied him upon his equipage, he gave me to understand he had set out from Nice the morning of the same day that I departed; that he was going to Turin, and that he had sent one of his servants before him to Coni with his baggage. Knowing him to be an agreeable companion, I was glad of this encounter, and we resolved to travel the rest of the way together. We dined at La Giandola, and in the afternoon rode along the little river Roida,[6] which runs in a bottom between frightful precipices, and in several places forms natural cascades, the noise of which had well-nigh deprived us of the sense of hearing; after a winding course among these mountains, it discharges itself into the Mediterranean at Ventimiglia, in the territory of Genoa. As the snow did not lie on these mountains, when we cracked our whips, there was such a repercussion of the sound as is altogether inconceivable. We passed by the village of Saorgio, situated on an eminence, where there is a small fortress which commands the whole pass, and in five hours arrived at our inn, on this side the Col de Tende, where we took up our quarters, but had very little reason to boast of our entertainment. Our greatest difficulty, however, consisted in pulling off the marquis's boots, which were of the kind called Seafarot,[7] by this time so loaded with dirt on the outside, and so swelled with the rain within, that he could neither drag them after him as he walked, nor disencumber his legs of them, without such violence as seemed almost sufficient to tear him limb from limb. In a word, we were obliged to tie a rope about his heel, and all the people in the house assisting to pull, the poor marquis was drawn from one end of the apartment to the other before the boot would give way: at last his legs were happily disengaged, and the machines carefully dried and stuffed for next day's journey.

We took our departure from hence at three in the morning, and at four, began to mount the Col de Tende, which is by far the highest mountain in the whole journey: it was now quite covered with snow, which at the top of it was near twenty feet thick. Half way up, there are quarters for a detachment of soldiers, posted here to prevent smuggling, and an inn called La Ca, which in the language of the country signifies *the house*. At this place, we hired six men to assist us in ascending the mountain, each of them provided with a kind of hough to break the ice, and make a sort of steps for the mules. When we were near the top, however, we were obliged to alight, and climb the mountain, supported each by two of those men, called Coulants, who walk upon the snow with great firmness and security. We were followed by the mules, and though they are very sure-footed animals, and were frost-shod for the occasion, they stumbled and fell very often; the ice being so hard that the sharp headed nails in their shoes could not penetrate. Having reached the top of this mountain, from whence there is no prospect but of other rocks and mountains, we prepared for descending on the other side by the Leze, which is an occasional sledge made of two pieces of wood, carried up by the Coulants for this purpose. I did not much relish this kind of carriage, especially as the mountain was very steep, and covered with such a thick fog that we could hardly see two or three yards before us. Nevertheless, our guides were so confident, and my companion, who had passed the same way on other occasions, was so secure, that I ventured to place myself on this machine, one of the coulants standing behind me, and the other sitting before, as the conductor, with his feet paddling among the snow, in order to moderate the velocity of its descent. Thus accommodated, we descended the mountain with such rapidity, that in an hour we reached Limon, which is the native place of almost all the muleteers who transport merchandize from Nice to Coni and Turin. Here we waited full two hours for the mules, which travelled with the servants by the common road. To each of the coulants we paid forty sols, which are nearly equal to two shillings sterling. Leaving Limon, we were in two hours quite disengaged from the gorges of the mountains, which are partly covered with wood and pasturage, though altogether inaccessible, except in summer; but from the foot of the Col de Tende, the road lies through a plain all the way to Turin. We took six hours to travel from the inn where we had lodged over the mountain to Limon, and five hours from thence to Coni. Here we found our baggage, which we had sent off by the carriers one day before we departed from Nice; and here we dismissed our guides, together with the mules. In winter, you have a mule for this whole journey at the rate of twenty livres; and the guides are payed at the rate of two livres a day, reckoning six days, three for the journey to Coni, and three for their return to Nice. We set out so early in the morning in order to avoid the inconveniencies and dangers that attend the passage of this mountain. The first of these arises from your meeting with long strings of loaded mules in a slippery road, the breadth of which does not exceed a foot and an half. As it is altogether impossible for two mules to pass each other in such a narrow path, the muleteers have made doublings or elbows in different parts, and when the troops of mules meet, the least numerous is obliged to turn off into one of these doublings, and there halt until the others are past. Travellers, in order to avoid this disagreeable delay, which is the more vexatious, considering the excessive cold, begin the ascent of the mountain early in the morning before the mules quit their inns. But the great danger of travelling here when the sun is up, proceeds from what they call the Valanches.[8] These are balls of snow detached from the mountains which over-top the road, either by the heat of the sun, or the humidity of the weather. A piece of snow thus loosened from the rock, though perhaps not above three or four feet in diameter, increases sometimes in its descent to such a degree, as to become two hundred paces in length, and rolls down with such rapidity, that the traveller is crushed to death before he can make three steps on the road. These dreadful heaps drag every thing along with them in their descent. They tear up huge trees by the roots, and if they chance to fall upon a house, demolish it to the foundation. Accidents of this nature seldom happen in the winter while the weather is dry; and yet scarce a year passes in which some mules and their drivers do not perish by the valanches. At Coni we found the countess C——[9] from Nice, who had made the same journey in a chair, carried by porters. This is no other than a common elbow-chair of wood, with a straw bottom, covered above with waxed cloth, to protect the traveller from the rain or snow, and provided with a foot-board upon which the feet rest. It is carried like a sedan-chair; and for this purpose six or eight porters are employed at the rate of three or four livres a head per day, according to the season, allowing three days for their return. Of these six men, two are between the poles carrying like common chairmen, and each of these is supported by the other two, one at each hand: but as those in the middle sustain the greatest burthen, they are relieved by the others in a regular rotation. In descending the mountain, they carry the poles on their shoulders, and in that case, four men are employed, one at each end.

At Coni, you may have a chaise to go with the same horses to Turin, for which you pay fifteen livres, and are a day and a half on the way. You may post it, however, in one day, and then the price is seven livres ten sols per post, and ten sols to the postilion. The method we took was that of cambiatura. This is a chaise with horses shifted at the same stages that are used in posting: but as it is supposed to move slower, we pay but five livres per post, and ten sols to the postilion. In order to quicken its pace, we gave ten sols extraordinary to each postilion, and for this gratification, he drove us even faster than the post. The chaises are like those of Italy, and will take on near two hundred weight of baggage.

Coni is situated between two small streams, and though neither very large nor populous, is considerable for the strength of its fortifications. It is honoured with the title of the Maiden-Fortress, because though several times besieged, it was never taken. The prince of Conti[10] invested it in the war of 1744; but he was obliged to raise the siege, after having given battle to the king of Sardinia. The place was gallantly defended by the baron Leutrum, a German protestant, the best general in the Sardinian service: but what contributed most to the miscarriage of the enemy, was a long tract of heavy rains, which destroyed all their works, and rendered their advances impracticable.

I need not tell you that Piedmont is one of the most fertile and agreeable countries in Europe, and this the most agreeable part of all Piedmont, though it now appeared to disadvantage from the rigorous season of the year: I shall only observe that we passed through Sabellian,[11] which is a considerable town, and arrived in the evening at Turin. We entered this fine city by the gate of Nice, and passing through the elegant Piazza di San Carlo, took up our quarters at the Bona Fama,[12] which stands at one corner of the great square, called La Piazza Castel.

# LETTER XXXVIII.

Were I even disposed to give a description of Turin, I should be obliged to postpone it till another opportunity, having no room at present to say any thing more, but that I am always

Yours.

# LETTER XXXIX.

*Aix en Provence, May 10, 1765.*

DEAR SIR,

I am thus far on my way to England. I had resolved to leave Nice, without having the least dispute with any one native of the place; but I found it impossible to keep this resolution. My landlord, Mr. C——,[1] a man of fashion, with whose family we had always lived in friendship, was so reasonable as to expect I should give him up the house and garden, though they were to be paid for till Michaelmas,[2] and peremptorily declared I should not be permitted to sub-let them to any other person. He had of his own accord assured me more than once that he would take my furniture off my hands, and trusting to this assurance, I had lost the opportunity of disposing it to advantage: but, when the time of my departure drew near, he refused to take it, at the same time insisting upon having the key of the house and garden, as well as on being paid the whole rent directly, though it would not be due till the middle of September. I was so exasperated at this treatment from a man whom I had cultivated with particular respect, that I determined to contest it at law: but the affair was accommodated by the mediation of a father of the Minims, a friend to both, and a merchant of Nice, who charged himself with the care of the house and furniture. A stranger must conduct himself with the utmost circumspection to be able to live among these people without being the dupe of imposition.

I had sent to Aix for a coach and four horses, which I hired at the rate of eighteen French livres a day, being equal to fifteen shillings and nine-pence sterling. The river Var was so swelled by the melting of the snow on the mountains, as to be impassable by any wheel-carriage; and, therefore, the coach remained at Antibes, to which we went by water, the distance being about nine or ten miles. This is the Antipolis of the antients, said to have been built, like Nice, by a colony from Marseilles. In all probability, however, it was later than the foundation of Nice, and took its name from its being situated directly opposite to that city. Pliny says it was famous for its tunny-fishery;[3] and to this circumstance

Martial alludes in the following lines:

> *"Antipolitani, fateor, sum filia thynni.*
> *Essem si Scombri non tibi missa forem."*[4]

> I'm spawn'd from *tunny* of *Antibes*, 'tis true.
> Right *scomber* had I been, I n'er had come to you.*

At present, it is the frontier of France towards Italy, pretty strongly fortified, and garrisoned by a battalion of soldiers. The town is small and inconsiderable; but the basin of the harbour is surrounded to seaward by a curious bulwark founded upon piles driven in the water, consisting of a wall, ramparts, casemates, and quay. Vessels lie very safe in this harbour; but there is not water at the entrance of it to admit of ships of any burthen. The shallows run so far off from the coast, that a ship of force cannot lie near enough to batter the town; but it was bombarded in the late war. Its chief strength by land consists in a small quadrangular fort detached from the body of the place, which, in a particular manner, commands the entrance of the harbour. The wall of the town built in the sea has embrasures and saliant angles, on which a great number of cannon may be mounted.

I think the adjacent country is much more pleasant than that on the side of Nice; and there is certainly no essential difference in the climate. The ground here is not so encumbered; it is laid out in agreeable inclosures, with intervals of open fields, and the mountains rise with an easy ascent at a much greater distance from the sea, than on the other side of the bay. Besides, here are charming rides along the beach, which is smooth and firm. When we passed in the last week of April, the corn was in the ear; the cherries were almost ripe; and the figs had begun to blacken. I had embarked my

---

* The famous pickle *garum*[5] was made from the *thynnus* or *tunny* as well as from the *scomber*, but that from the *scomber* was counted the most delicate. Commentators, however, are not agreed about the *scomber* or *scombrus*. Some suppose it was the *herring or sprat*; others believe it was the mackarel; after all, perhaps it was the *anchovy*, which I do not find distinguished by any other Latin name: for, the *encrasicolus*[6] is a Greek appellation altogether generical. Those who would be further informed about the *garum* and the *scomber*, may consult Cælius Apicius *de re coquinaria, cum notis variorum.*[7]

heavy baggage on board a London ship, which happened to be at Nice, ready to sail: as for our small trunks or portmanteaus, which we carried along with us, they were examined at Antibes; but the ceremony was performed very superficially, in consequence of tipping the searcher with half a crown, which is a wonderful conciliator at all the bureaus in this country.

We lay at Cannes, a neat village, charmingly situated on the beach of the Mediterranean, exactly opposite to the isles Marguerites, where state-prisoners are confined. As there are some good houses in this place, I would rather live here for the sake of the mild climate, than either at Antibes or Nice. Here you are not cooped up within walls, nor crouded with soldiers and people: but are already in the country, enjoy a fine air, and are well supplied with all sorts of fish.

The mountain of Esterelles, which in one of my former letters I described as a most romantic and noble plantation of ever-greens, trees, shrubs, and aromatic plants, is at present quite desolate. Last summer, some execrable villains set fire to the pines, when the wind was high. It continued burning for several months, and the conflagration extended above ten leagues, consuming an incredible quantity of timber. The ground is now naked on each side of the road, or occupied by the black trunks of the trees, which have been scorched without falling. They stand as so many monuments of the judgment of heaven, filling the mind with horror and compassion. I could hardly refrain from shedding tears at this dismal spectacle, when I recalled the idea of what it was about eighteen months ago.

As we stayed all night at Frejus, I had an opportunity of viewing the amphitheatre at leisure. As near as I can judge by the eye, it is of the same dimensions with that of Nismes; but shockingly dilapidated. The stone seats rising from the arena are still extant, and the cells under them, where the wild beasts were kept. There are likewise the remains of two galleries one over another; and two vomitoria or great gateways at opposite sides of the arena, which is now a fine green, with a road through the middle of it: but all the external architecture and the ornaments are demolished. The most intire part of the wall now constitutes part of a monastery, the monks of which, I am told, have helped to destroy the amphitheatre, by removing the stones for their own purposes of building. In the neighbourhood of this amphitheatre, which stands without the walls, are the vestiges of an old edifice, said to have been the palace where the imperator or president resided: for it was a Roman colony, much favoured by Julius Cæsar, who gave it the name of Forum Julii, and Civitas Forojuliensis. In all probability, it was he who built the amphitheatre, and brought hither the water ten leagues from the river of Ciagne,[8] by means of an aqueduct, some arcades of which are still standing on the other side of the town. A great number of statues were found in this place, together with antient inscriptions, which have been published by different authors. I need not tell you that Julius Agricola,[9] the father-in-law of Tacitus, the historian, was a native of Frejus, which is now a very poor inconsiderable place. From hence the country opens to the left, forming an extensive plain between the sea and the mountains, which are a continuation of the Alps, that stretches through Provence and Dauphiné. This plain, watered with pleasant streams, and varied with vineyards, corn-fields, and meadow-ground, afforded a most agreeable prospect to our eyes, which were accustomed to the sight of scorching sands, rugged rocks, and abrupt mountains in the neighbourhood of Nice. Although this has much the appearance of a corn-country, I am told it does not produce enough for the consumption of its inhabitants, who are obliged to have annual supplies from abroad, imported at Marseilles. A Frenchman, at an average, eats three times the quantity of bread that satisfies a native of England, and indeed it is undoubtedly the staff of his life. I am therefore surprized that the Provençaux do not convert part of their vineyards into corn-fields: for they may boast of their wine as they please; but that which is drank by the common people, not only here, but also in all the wine countries of France, is neither so strong, nourishing, nor (in my opinion) so pleasant to the taste as the small-beer of England. It must be owned that all the peasants who have wine for their ordinary drink, are of a diminutive size, in comparison of those who use milk, beer, or even water; and it is a constant observation, that when there is a scarcity of wine, the common people are always more healthy, than in those seasons when it abounds. The longer I live, the more I am convinced that wine, and all fermented liquors, are pernicious to the human constitution; and that for the preservation of health, and exhilaration of the spirits, there is no beverage comparable to simple water. Between Luc and Toulon, the country is delightfully parcelled out into inclosures. Here is plenty of rich pasturage for black cattle, and a greater number of pure streams and rivulets than I have observed in any other parts of France.

Toulon is a considerable place, even exclusive of the basin, docks, and arsenal, which indeed are such as justify the remark made by a stranger when he viewed them. "The king of France (said he) is greater at Toulon than at Versailles." The quay, the jetties, the docks, and magazines, are contrived and executed with precision, order, solidity, and magnificence. I counted fourteen ships of the line lying unrigged in the basin, besides the Tonant of eighty guns, which was in dock repairing, and a new frigate on the stocks.[10] I was credibly informed that in the last war, the king of France was so ill-served with cannon for his navy, that in every action there was scarce a ship which had not several pieces burst. These accidents did great damage, and discouraged the French mariners to such a degree, that they became more afraid of their own guns than of those of the English. There are now at Toulon above two thousand pieces of iron cannon unfit for service. This is an undeniable proof of the weakness and neglect of the French administration: but a more surprizing proof of their imbecility, is the state of the fortifications that defend the entrance of this very harbour. I have some reason to think that they trusted for its security entirely to our opinion that it must be inaccessible. Capt. E——, of one of our frigates, lately entered the harbour with a contrary wind, which by obliging him to tack, afforded an opportunity of sounding the whole breadth and length of the passage. He came in without a pilot, and made a pretence of buying cordage, or some other stores; but the French officers were much chagrined at the boldness of his enterprize. They alledged that he came for no other reason but to sound the channel; and that he had an engineer aboard, who made drawings of the land and the forts, their bearings and distances. In all probability, these suspicions were communicated to the ministry; for an order immediately arrived, that no stranger should be admitted into the docks and arsenal.[11]

Part of the road from hence to Marseilles lies through a vast mountain, which resembles that of Esterelles; but is not so well covered with wood, though it has the advantage of an agreeable stream running through the bottom.

I was much pleased with Marseilles, which is indeed a noble city, large, populous, and flourishing. The streets, of what is called the new town, are open, airy, and spacious; the houses well built, and even magnificent. The harbour is an oval basin, surrounded on every side either by the buildings or the land, so that the shipping lies perfectly secure; and here is generally an incredible number of vessels. On the city side, there is a semi-circular quay of free-stone, which extends thirteen hundred paces; and the space between this and the houses that front it, is continually filled with a surprising croud of people. The gallies, to the number of eight or nine, are moored with their sterns to one part of the wharf, and the slaves are permitted to work for their own benefit at their respective occupations, in little shops or booths, which they rent for a trifle. There you see tradesmen of all kinds sitting at work, chained by one foot, shoe-makers, taylors, silver-smiths, watch and clock-makers, barbers, stocking-weavers, jewellers, pattern-drawers, scriveners, booksellers, cutlers, and all manner of shop-keepers. They pay about two sols a day to the king for this indulgence; live well and look jolly; and can afford to sell their goods and labour much cheaper than other dealers and tradesmen. At night, however, they are obliged to lie aboard. Notwithstanding the great face of business at Marseilles, their trade is greatly on the decline; and their merchants are failing every day. This decay of commerce is in a great measure owing to the English, who, at the peace, poured in such a quantity of European merchandize into Martinique and Guadeloupe,[12] that when the merchants of Marseilles sent over their cargoes, they found the markets overstocked, and were obliged to sell for a considerable loss. Besides, the French colonists had such a stock of sugars, coffee, and other commodities lying by them during the war, that upon the first notice of peace, they shipped them off in great quantities for Marseilles. I am told that the produce of the islands is at present cheaper here than where it grows; and on the other hand the merchandize of this country sells for less money at Martinique than in Provence.

A single person, who travels in this country, may live at a reasonable rate in these towns, by eating at the public ordinaries: but I would advise all families that come hither to make any stay, to take furnished lodgings as soon as they can: for the expense of living at an hotel is enormous. I was obliged to pay at Marseilles four livres a head for every meal, and half that price for my servant, and was charged six livres a day besides for the apartment; so that our daily expence, including breakfast and a valet de place, amounted to two loui'dores. The same imposition prevails all over the south of France, though it is generally supposed to be the cheapest and most plentiful part of the kingdom. Without all doubt, it must be owing to the folly and extravagance of English travellers, who have allowed themselves to be fleeced without wincing, until this extortion is become authorized by custom. It is very disagreeable riding in the avenues of Marseilles, because you are confined in a dusty high road, crouded with carriages and beasts of burden, between two white walls, the reflection from which, while the sun shines, is intolerable. But in this neighbourhood there is a vast number of pleasant country-houses, called Bastides, said to amount to twelve thousand, some of which may be rented ready furnished at a very reasonable price. Marseilles is a gay city, and the inhabitants indulge themselves in a variety of amusements. They have assemblies, a concert spirituel, and a comedy. Here is also a spacious cours, or walk shaded with trees, to which in the evening there is a great resort of well-dressed people.

Marseilles being a free port, there is a bureau about half a league from the city on the road to Aix, where all carriages undergo examination; and if any thing contraband is found, the vehicle, baggage, and even the horses are confiscated. We escaped this disagreeable ceremony by the sagacity of our driver. Of his own accord, he declared at the bureau, that we had bought a pound of coffee and some sugar at Marseilles, and were ready to pay the duty, which amounted to about ten sols. They took the money, gave him a receipt, and let the carriage pass, without further question.

I proposed to stay one night only at Aix: but Mr. A——r,[13] who is here, had found such benefit from drinking the waters, that I was persuaded to make trial of them for eight or ten days. I have accordingly taken private lodgings, and drank them every morning at the fountain-head, not without finding considerable benefit. In my next, I shall say something further of these waters, though I am afraid they will not prove a source of much entertainment. It will be sufficient for me to find them contribute in any degree to the health of

Dear Sir,

Yours assuredly.

# LETTER XL.

DEAR DOCTOR,

I found three English families at Aix, with whom I could have passed my time very agreeably; but the society is now dissolved. Mr. S——re[1] and his lady left the place in a few days after we arrived. Mr. A——r and lady Betty[2] are gone to Geneva; and Mr. G——r[3] with his family remains at Aix. This gentleman, who laboured under a most dreadful nervous asthma, has obtained such relief from this climate, that he intends to stay another year in the place: and Mr. A—r found surprizing benefit from drinking the waters, for a scorbutical complaint. As I was incommoded by both these disorders, I could not but in justice to myself, try the united efforts of the air and the waters; especially as this consideration was re-inforced by the kind and pressing exhortations of Mr. A——r and lady Betty, which I could not in gratitude resist.

Aix, the capital of Provence, is a large city, watered by the small river Are. It was a Roman colony, said to be founded by Caius Sextus Calvinus,[4] above a century before the birth of Christ. From the source of mineral water here found, added to the consul's name, it was called Aquæ Sextiæ. It was here that Marius,[5] the conqueror of the Teutones, fixed his head-quarters, and embellished the place with temples, aqueducts, and thermæ, of which, however, nothing now remains. The city, as it now stands, is well built, though the streets in general are narrow, and kept in a very dirty condition. But it has a noble *cours* planted with double rows of tall trees, and adorned with three or four fine fountains, the middlemost of which discharges hot water supplied from the source of the baths. On each side there is a row of elegant houses, inhabited chiefly by the noblesse, of which there is here a considerable number. The parliament, which is held at Aix, brings hither a great resort of people; and as many of the inhabitants are persons of fashion, they are well bred, gay, and sociable. The duc de Villars,[6] who is governor of the province, resides on the spot, and keeps an open assembly, where strangers are admitted without reserve, and made very welcome, if they will engage in play, which is the sole occupation of the whole company. Some of our English people complain, that when they were presented to him, they met with a very cold reception. The French, as well as other foreigners, have no idea of a man of family and fashion, without the title of duke, count, marquis, or lord; and where an English gentleman is introduced by the simple expression of *monsieur tel*, Mr. Suchathing, they think he is some plebeian, unworthy of any particular attention.

Aix is situated in a bottom, almost surrounded by hills, which, however, do not screen it from the Bize, or north wind, that blows extremely sharp in the winter and spring, rendering the air almost insupportably cold, and very dangerous to those who have some kinds of pulmonary complaints, such as tubercules, abscesses, or spitting of blood. Lord H—,[7] who passed part of last winter in this place, afflicted with some of these symptoms, grew worse every day while he continued at Aix: but, he no sooner removed to Marseilles, than all his complaints abated; such a difference there is in the air of these two places, though the distance between them does not exceed ten or twelve miles. But the air of Marseilles, though much more mild than that of Aix in the winter, is not near so warm as the climate of Nice, where we find in plenty such flowers, fruit, and vegetables, even in the severest season, as will not grow and ripen, either at Marseilles or Toulon.

If the air of Aix is disagreeably cold in the winter, it is rendered quite insufferable in the summer, from excessive heat, occasioned by the reflexion from the rocks and mountains, which at the same time obstruct the circulation of air: for it must be observed, that the same mountains which serve as funnels and canals, to collect and discharge the keen blasts of winter, will provide screens to intercept intirely the faint breezes of summer. Aix, though pretty well provided with butcher's meat, is very ill supplied with pot-herbs; and they have no poultry but what comes at a vast distance from the Lionnois. They say their want of roots, cabbage, cauliflower, &c. is owing to a scarcity of water: but the truth is, they are very bad gardeners. Their oil is good and cheap: their wine is indifferent: but their chief care seems employed on the culture of silk, the staple of Provence, which is every where

shaded with plantations of mulberry trees, for the nourishment of the worms. Notwithstanding the boasted cheapness
of every article of housekeeping, in the south of France, I am
persuaded a family may live for less money at York,
Durham, Hereford, and in many other cities of England than
at Aix in Provence; keep a more plentiful table; and be much
more comfortably situated in all respects. I found lodging
and provision at Aix fifty per cent. dearer than at Montpellier, which is counted the dearest place in Languedoc.

The baths of Aix, so famous in antiquity, were quite
demolished by the irruptions of the Barbarians. The very
source of the water was lost, till the beginning of the present
century, (I think the year 1704), when it was discovered by
accident, in digging for the foundation of a house, at the foot
of a hill, just without the city wall. Near the same place was
found a small stone altar, with the figure of a Priapus,[8] and
some letters in capitals, which the antiquarians have differ-
ently interpreted. From this figure, it was supposed that the
waters were efficacious in cases of barrenness. It was a long
time, however, before any person would venture to use them
internally, as it did not appear that they had ever been drank
by the antients. On their re-appearance, they were chiefly
used for baths to horses, and other beasts which had the
mange, and other cutaneous eruptions. At length poor people
began to bathe in them for the same disorders, and received
such benefit from them, as attracted the attention of more
curious inquirers. A very superficial and imperfect analysis
was made and published, with a few remarkable histories of
the cures they had performed, by three different physicians of
those days;[9] and those little treatises, I suppose, encouraged
valetudinarians to drink them without ceremony. They were
found serviceable in the gout, the gravel, scurvy, dropsy,
palsy, indigestion, asthma, and consumption; and their fame
soon extended itself all over Languedoc, Gascony, Dauphiné,
and Provence. The magistrates, with a view to render them
more useful and commodious, have raised a plain building, in
which there are a couple of private baths, with a bed-chamber
adjoining to each, where individuals may use them both
internally and externally, for a moderate expence. These
baths are paved with marble, and supplied with water each

by a large brass cock, which you can turn at pleasure. At one end of this edifice, there is an octagon, open at top, having a bason, with a stone pillar in the middle, which discharges water from the same source, all round, by eight small brass cocks; and hither people of all ranks come of a morning, with their glasses, to drink the water, or wash their sores, or subject their contracted limbs to the stream. This last operation, called the *douche*, however, is more effectually undergone in the private bath, where the stream is much more powerful. The natural warmth of this water, as nearly as I can judge from recollection, is about the same degree of temperature with that in the Queen's Bath, at Bath in Somersetshire.[10] It is perfectly transparent, sparkling in the glass, light and agreeable to the taste, and may be drank without any preparation, to the quantity of three or four pints at a time. There are many people at Aix who swallow fourteen half pint glasses every morning, during the season, which is in the month of May, though it may be taken with equal benefit all the year round. It has no sensible operation but by urine, an effect which pure water would produce, if drank in the same quantity.

If we may believe those who have published their experiments, this water produces neither agitation, cloud, or change of colour, when mixed with acids, alkalies, tincture of galls, syrup of violets, or solution of silver. The residue, after boiling, evaporation, and filtration, affords a very small proportion of purging salt, and calcarious earth, which last ferments with strong acids. As I had neither hydrometer nor thermometer to ascertain the weight and warmth of this water; nor time to procure the proper utensils, to make the preparations, and repeat the experiments necessary to exhibit a complete analysis, I did not pretend to enter upon this process; but contented myself with drinking, bathing, and using the *douche*, which perfectly answered my expectation, having, in eight days, almost cured an ugly scorbutic tetter, which had for some time deprived me of the use of my right hand. I observed that the water, when used externally, left always a kind of oily appearance on the skin: that when we boiled it at home, in an earthen pot, the steams smelled like those of sulphur, and even affected my lungs in the same manner: but the bath itself smelled strong of a lime-kiln. The water, after standing all night in a bottle, yielded a remarkably vinous taste and odour, something analogous to that of dulcified spirit of nitre. Whether the active particles consist of a volatile vitriol, or a very fine petroleum, or a mixture of both, I shall not pretend to determine: but the best way I know of discovering whether it is really impregnated with a vitriolic principle, too subtil and fugitive for the usual operations of chymistry, is to place bottles, filled with wine, in the bath, or adjacent room, which wine, if there is really a volatile acid, in any considerable quantity, will be pricked[11] in eight and forty hours.

Having ordered our coach to be refitted, and provided with fresh horses, as well as with another postilion, in consequence of which improvements, I payed at the rate of a loui'dore *per diem* to Lyons and back again, we departed from Aix, and the second day of our journey passing the Durance in a boat, lay at Avignon. This river, the Druentia of the antients, is a considerable stream, extremely rapid, which descends from the mountains, and discharges itself in the Rhone. After violent rains it extends its channel, so as to be impassable, and often overflows the country to a great extent. In the middle of a plain, betwixt Orgon and this river, we met the coach in which we had travelled eighteen months before, from Lyons to Montpellier, conducted by our old driver Joseph, who no sooner recognized my servant at a distance, by his musquetoon, than he came running towards our carriage, and seizing my hand, even shed tears of joy. Joseph had been travelling through Spain, and was so imbrowned by the sun, that he might have passed for an Iroquois. I was much pleased with the marks of gratitude which the poor fellow expressed towards his benefactors. He had some private conversation with our *voiturier*, whose name was Claude, to whom he gave such a favourable character of us, as in all probability induced him to be wonderfully obliging during the whole journey.

You know Avignon is a large city belonging to the pope. It was the *Avenio Cavarum* of the antients, and changed masters several times, belonging successively to the Romans, Burgundians, Franks, the kingdom of Arles, the counts of

Provence, and the sovereigns of Naples. It was sold in the fourteenth century, by queen Jane I. of Naples,[12] to pope Clement VI.[13] for the sum of eighty thousand florins, and since that period has continued under the dominion of the see of Rome. Not but that when the duc de Crequi, the French ambassador, was insulted at Rome in the year 1662, the parliament of Provence passed an arret, declaring the city of Avignon, and the county Venaissin, part of the ancient domain of Provence; and therefore reunited it to the crown of France, which accordingly took possession; though it was afterwards restored to the Roman see at the peace of Pisa.[14] The pope, however, holds it by a precarious title, at the mercy of the French king, who may one day be induced to resume it, upon payment of the original purchase-money. As a succession of popes resided here for the space of seventy years, the city could not fail to be adorned with a great number of magnificent churches and convents, which are richly embellished with painting, sculpture, shrines, reliques, and tombs. Among the last, is that of the celebrated Laura, whom Petrarch has immortalized by his poetry,[15] and for whom Francis I. of France took the trouble to write an epitaph. Avignon is governed by a vice-legate from the pope, and the police of the city is regulated by the consuls. It is a large place, situated in a fruitful plain, surrounded by high walls built of hewn stone, which on the west side are washed by the Rhone. Here was a noble bridge over the river, but it is now in ruins. On the other side, a branch of the Sorgue runs through part of the city. This is the river anciently called Sulga, formed by the famous fountain of Vaucluse in this neighbourhood, where the poet Petrarch resided. It is a charming transparent stream, abounding with excellent trout and craw-fish. We passed over it on a stone bridge, in our way to Orange, the *Arausio Cavarum* of the Romans, still distinguished by some noble monuments of antiquity. These consist of a circus, an aqueduct, a temple, and a triumphal arch, which last was erected in honour of Caius Marius, and Luctatius Catulus,[16] after the great victory they obtained in this country over the Cimbri[17] and Teutones. It is a very magnificent edifice, adorned on all sides with trophies and battles in basso relievo. The ornaments of the architecture, and the sculpture, are wonderfully elegant for the time in which it was erected; and the whole is surprisingly well preserved, considering its great antiquity. It seems to me to be as entire and perfect as the arch of Septimius Severus at Rome. Next day we passed two very impetuous streams, the Drome and the Isere. The first, which very much resembles the Var, we forded: but the Isere we crossed in a boat, which as well as that upon the Durance, is managed by the traille, a moveable or running pulley, on a rope stretched between two wooden machines erected on the opposite sides of the river. The contrivance is simple and effectual, and the passage equally safe and expeditious. The boatman has nothing to do, but by means of a long massy rudder, to keep the head obliquely to the stream, the force of which pushes the boat along, the block to which it is fixed sliding upon the rope from one side to the other. All these rivers take their rise from the mountains, which are continued through Provence and Dauphiné, and fall into the Rhone: and all of them, when swelled by sudden rains, overflow the flat country. Although Dauphiné affords little or no oil, it produces excellent wines, particularly those of Hermitage and Cote-roti. The first of these is sold on the spot for three livres the bottle, and the other for two. The country likewise yields a considerable quantity of corn, and a good deal of grass. It is well watered with streams, and agreeably shaded with wood. The weather was pleasant, and we had a continued song of nightingales from Aix to Fontainbleau.

I cannot pretend to specify the antiquities of Vienne, antiently called Vienna Allobrogum. It was a Roman colony, and a considerable city, which the antients spared no pains and expence to embellish. It is still a large town, standing among several hills on the banks of the Rhone, though all its former splendor is eclipsed, its commerce decayed, and most of its antiquities are buried in ruins. The church of Notre Dame de la Vie was undoubtedly a temple. On the left of the road, as you enter it, by the gate of Avignon, there is a handsome obelisk, or rather pyramid, about thirty feet high, raised upon a vault supported by four pillars of the Tuscan order. It is certainly a Roman work, and Montfaucon supposes it to be a tomb, as he perceived an oblong stone jetting out from the middle of the vault, in which the ashes of the defunct were probably contained.[18] The story of Pontius Pilate, who is said to have ended his days in this place, is a fable. On the seventh day of our journey from Aix, we arrived at Lyons, where I shall take my leave of you for the present, being with great truth,

Yours, &c.

# LETTER XLI.

DEAR SIR,

I am at last in a situation to indulge my view with a sight of Britain, after an absence of two years; and indeed you cannot imagine what pleasure I feel while I survey the white cliffs of Dover, at this distance. Not that I am at all affected by the *nescia qua dulcedine natalis soli*, of Horace.[1] That seems to be a kind of fanaticism founded on the prejudices of education, which induces a Laplander to place the terrestial paradise among the snows of Norway, and a Swiss to prefer the barren mountains of *Uri* to the fruitful plains of Lombardy. I am attached to my country, because it is the land of liberty, cleanliness, and convenience: but I love it still more tenderly, as the scene of all my interesting connexions; as the habitation of my friends, for whose conversation, correspondence, and esteem, I wish alone to live.

Our journey hither from Lyons produced neither accident nor adventure worth notice; but abundance of little vexations, which may be termed the Plagues of Posting. At Lyons, where we stayed only a few days, I found a return-coach, which I hired to Paris for six loui'dores. It was a fine roomy carriage, elegantly furnished, and made for travelling, so strong and solid in all its parts, that there was no danger of its being shaken to pieces by the roughness of the road: but its weight and solidity occasioned so much friction between the wheels and the axle-tree, that we ran the risque of being set on fire three or four times a day. Upon a just comparison of all circumstances, posting is much more easy, convenient, and reasonable in England than in France. The English carriages, horses, harness, and roads are much better; and the postilions more obliging and alert. The reason is plain and obvious. If I am ill-used at the post-house in England, I can be accommodated elsewhere. The publicans on the road are sensible of this, and therefore they vie with each other in giving satisfaction to travellers. But in France, where the post is monopolized, the post-masters and postilions, knowing that the traveller depends intirely upon them, are the more negligent and remiss in their duty, as well as the more encouraged to insolence and imposition. Indeed the stranger seems to be left intirely at the mercy of those fellows, except in large towns, where he may have recourse to the magistrate or commanding officer. The post stands very often by itself in a lone country situation, or in a paultry village, where the post-master is the principal inhabitant; and in such a case, if you should be ill-treated, by being supplied with bad horses; if you should be delayed on frivolous pretences, in order to extort money; if the postilions should drive at a waggon pace, with a view to provoke your impatience; or should you in any shape be insulted by them or their masters; I know not any redress you can have, except by a formal complaint to the comptroller of the posts, who is generally one of the ministers of state, and pays little or no regard to any such representations. I know an English gentleman, the brother of an earl, who wrote a letter of complaint to the Duc de Villars, governor of Provence, against the post-master of Antibes, who had insulted and imposed upon him. The duke answered his letter, promising to take order that the grievance should be redressed; and never thought of it after. Another great inconvenience which attends posting in France, is that if you are retarded by any accident, you cannot in many parts of the kingdom find a lodging, without perhaps travelling two or three posts farther than you would choose to go, to the prejudice of your health, and even the hazard of your life; whereas, on any part of the post-road in England, you will meet with tolerable accommodation at every stage. Through the whole south of France, except in large cities, the inns are cold, damp, dark, dismal, and dirty; the landlords equally disobliging and rapacious; the servants aukward, sluttish, and slothful; and the postilions lazy, lounging, greedy, and impertinent. If you chide them for lingering, they will continue to delay you the longer: if you chastise them with sword, cane, cudgel, or horse-whip, they will either disappear entirely, and leave you without resource; or they will find means to take vengeance by overturning your carriage. The best method I know of travelling with any degree of comfort, is to allow yourself to become the dupe of imposition, and stimulate their endeavours by extraordinary gratifications. I laid down a resolution (and kept it) to give no more

than four and twenty sols per post between the two postilions; but I am now persuaded that for three-pence a post
more, I should have been much better served, and should
have performed the journey with much greater pleasure. We
met with no adventures upon the road worth reciting. The
first day we were retarded above two hours by the dutchess
D——lle, and her son the duc de R——f——t,[2] who, by virtue
of an order from the minister, had anticipated all the horses at
the post. They accosted my servant, and asked if his master
was a lord? He thought proper to answer in the affirmative;
upon which the duke declared that he must certainly be of
French extraction, inasmuch as he observed the lillies of
France in his arms on the coach. This young nobleman spoke
a little English. He asked whence we had come; and understanding we had been in Italy, desired to know whether the
man liked France or Italy best? Upon his giving France the
preference, he clapped him on the shoulder, and said he was a
lad of good taste. The dutchess asked if her son spoke English
well, and seemed mightily pleased when my man assured her
he did. They were much more free and condescending with
my servant than with myself; for, though we saluted them in
passing, and were even supposed to be persons of quality,
they did not open their lips, while we stood close by them at
the inn-door, till their horses were changed. They were going
to Geneva; and their equipage consisted of three coaches and
six, with five domestics a horseback. The dutchess was a tall,
thin, raw-boned woman, with her head close shaved. This
delay obliged us to lie two posts short of Macon, at a solitary
auberge called Maison Blanche, which had nothing white
about it, but the name. The Lionnois is one of the most
agreeable and best cultivated countries I ever beheld, diversified with hill, dale, wood, and water, laid out in extensive
corn-fields and rich meadows, well stocked with black cattle;
and adorned with a surprising number of towns, villages,
villas, and convents, generally situated on the brows of
gently swelling hills, so that they appear to the greatest
advantage. What contributes in a great measure to the beauty
of this, and the Maconnois, is the charming pastoral Soame,
which from the city of Chalons winds its silent course so
smooth and gentle, that one can scarce discern which way its

current flows. It is this placid appearance that tempts so many people to bathe in it at Lyons, where a good number of individuals are drowned every summer: whereas there is no instance of any persons thus perishing in the Rhone, the rapidity of it deterring every body from bathing in its stream. Next night we passed at Beaune, where we found nothing good but the wine, for which we paid forty sols the bottle. At Chalons our axle-tree took fire; an accident which detained us so long, that it was ten before we arrived at Auxerre, where we lay.[3] In all probability we must have lodged in the coach, had not we been content to take four horses, and pay for six, two posts successively. The alternative was, either to proceed with four on those terms, or stay till the other horses should come in and be refreshed. In such an emergency, I would advise the traveller to put up with the four, and he will find the postilions so much upon their mettle, that those stages will be performed sooner than the others in which you have the full complement.

There was an English gentleman laid up at Auxerre with a broken arm, to whom I sent my compliments, with offers of service; but his servant told my man that he did not choose to see any company, and had no occasion for my service. This sort of reserve seems peculiar to the English disposition. When two natives of any other country chance to meet abroad, they run into each other's embrace like old friends, even though they have never heard of one another till that moment; whereas two Englishmen in the same situation maintain a mutual reserve and diffidence, and keep without the sphere of each other's attraction, like two bodies endowed with a repulsive power. We only stopped to change horses at Dijon, the capital of Burgundy, which is a venerable old city; but we passed part of a day at Sens, and visited a manufacture of that stuff we call Manchester velvet,[4] which is here made and dyed to great perfection, under the direction of English workmen, who have been seduced from their own country. At Fontainbleau, we went to see the palace, or, as it is called, the castle, which though an irregular pile of building, affords a great deal of lodging, and contains some very noble apartments, particularly the hall of audience, with the king's and queen's chambers, upon which the ornaments of carving and gilding are lavished with profusion rather than propriety. Here are some rich parterres of flower-garden, and a noble orangerie, which however we did not greatly admire, after having lived among the natural orange groves of Italy. Hitherto we had enjoyed fine summer weather, and I found myself so well, that I imagined my health was intirely restored: but betwixt Fontainbleau and Paris, we were overtaken by a black storm of rain, sleet, and hail, which seemed to reinstate winter in all its rigour; for the cold weather continues to this day. There was no resisting this attack. I caught cold immediately; and this was reinforced at Paris, where I stayed but three days. The same man, (Pascal Sellier, rüe Guenegaud, fauxbourg St. Germain) who owned the coach that brought us from Lyons, supplied me with a returned berline to Boulogne, for six loui'dores, and we came hither by easy journeys. The first night we lodged at Breteuil, where we found an elegant inn, and very good accommodation. But the next we were forced to take up our quarters at the house where we had formerly passed a very disagreeable night at Abbeville. I am now in tolerable lodging, where I shall remain a few weeks, merely for the sake of a little repose; then I shall gladly tempt that invidious straight which still divides you from

Yours, &c.

FINIS.

of carving and gilding, are lavished with profusion rather than propriety, as are contrasted pictures of flowers, birds, and a noble menagerie, which, however, we did not greatly admire, after having lived, among the natural simpler glories of the Highlands, we has enjoyed fine summer weather, and I found myself as well that I imagined my health was thereby repaired: but by wixt Fontainbleau and Paris, we were over taken by a black storm of rain, sleet, and hail, which seemed to re-animate within us all its rancour, for the chill weather continues to this day. There was no refusing this attack: I caught cold immediately, and thus was reinforced at Paris, where I staid but three days. The same may (Diesel Seller) the Burgundy, Strasbourg, &c. Germain, who owned the coach, that brought us from Lyons, supplied me with a carriage for the road, so he [?]for six louis d'ors, and we came hither by easy journeys. The Basil inn we lodged at present no[?] but the next we were forced to walk up our quarters in one house, where we had tolerably passed a very disagreeable night at Abbeville. I got now to tolerable lodging, where I shall remain a few weeks, merely for the sake of a little repose, and I shall gladly forget that tedious stage in which I still think of you from

Yours, &c.

FINIS.

# A REGISTER OF THE WEATHER.[1]

Kept at Nice from November 1763 to March 1765.

THERMOMETERS used in keeping the following REGISTER.

One of mercury, constructed after the manner of Reaumur, having on the scale 10 degrees from ice to temperate, 20 degrees silk-worm heat, boiling-water 80 degrees. The excessive heat at Paris 1707, at 35 degrees.

One of spirit of wine, constructed by Chateauneuf, graduated in the same manner. The spirit in this Thermometer rises at Senegal to 38, in France very rarely to 30, and in Peru, under the line, very seldom above 25.

They were placed in the shade, in a room without a fire, in a southerly exposition; and the observations made between ten and eleven in the forenoon.

The town of Nice is situated in the bay of Antibes, latitude forty-three degrees, forty minutes north; east longitude from London, seven degrees, twenty-five minutes, æquidistant from Marseilles, Genoa, and Turin, that is about ninety English miles. The north wind blows over the maritime Alps, at the feet of which the town is situated; the south from Cape Bona, on the coast of Barbary, sweeping the islands of Sardinia and Corsica in its passage: the east from the Riviera of Genoa; and the west from Provence.

The town of Nice is wedged between a steep rock to the eastward, and the river Paglion, which washes the walls upon the west, and falls into the Mediterranean, within thirty yards of the corner bastion.

This river is but a scanty stream, fed chiefly by the melting of the snow upon the mountains. It is sometimes swelled to a great depth by sudden torrents: but in the summer it is usually dry.

The town of Nice is built of stone, and the streets are narrow. It is said to contain twelve thousand inhabitants, in which case they must be much crowded, for the place is but small. There is a bridge of three arches over the Paglion, which is the entrance from the side of Provence. Nice is surrounded on this side by a wall and rampart of no strength: on the other side, it is commanded by a high rock, on which appear the ruins of an old castle, which was once deemed impregnable. It was taken and dismantled by Marechal Catinat, in the reign of Victor Amadeus, father to the present king of Sardinia. To the eastward of this rock is the harbour of Nice, in which there is not depth of water sufficient for ships of any burthen. The hills begin to rise about a short mile from the north gate of the town. The Var falls into the sea about four miles to the westward; and is fordable at the village of St. Laurent, which stands on the French side near the mouth of the river. The space between the Var and Nice is a succession of agreeable eminences, adorned with a great number of white houses or cassines, surrounded by planta-tions of olives, vines, oranges, lemons, and citrons. The air of Nice is pure and penetrating, yet mild, generally dry, and elastic; and the sky is remarkably clear and serene. The well-water is mostly hard, but not unwholesome; and there are some springs both in the town and neighbourhood, which are surprizingly cool, limpid, and agreeable.

# REGISTER OF THE WEATHER.

### November 1763.

From the 23d to the end fair weather, wind northerly—Mornings frosty—Evenings sharp—Sun at noon, warm, sky serene.

### December.

First week, squalls and rain, wind southerly.
Fifth blew fresh, wind south-west.
From the 5th to the end of the month fair weather, wind shifting from north to east—Sun at noon warm—Mornings and evenings frosty and sharp, distant mountains covered with snow—Green-peas, and all sorts of sallad, pinks, roses, July flowers, ranunculas, anemonies, all the winter, blowing.

### January 1764.

First week rain and squalls, wind southerly.
Second week, weather cloudy, wind southerly.
Remaining part of the month fair weather, clear sky, wind north-east—Mornings and evenings sharp, snow on the distant hills, almond trees in blossom.

### February.

From the 1st to the 25th fine weather, clear sky, mild and warm in the day, wind easterly, sharp and piercing in the evening. Snow on the distant hills. Almonds, peaches, and apricots in blossom.

# REGISTER of the WEATHER.

| Day of the month. | Reaumur's thermom. merc. deg. above Ice. | Chateauneuf's ther. spirit deg. above Ice. | |
|---|---|---|---|
| Feb. | | | |
| 25 | 4 | 6 | Wind north-west, blows fresh, weather cold. |
| 26 | 4 | 6 | north-west, blows fresh, air sharp, fair weather. |
| 27 | 4 | 6 | east, weather cloudy—Evening, air sharp and frosty. |
| 28 | 4 | 6 | north, air cold, weather cloudy—Afternoon, wind south, mizzling rain. |
| 29 | 6 | 9 | north, air cold—Afternoon, wind south-east, mizzling rain—At night, heavy rain. |
| Mar. | | | |
| 1 | 2½ | 5½ | south-west, air sharp—Afternoon, wind south, blows fresh. |
| 2 | 1½ | 4 | south east, weather calm and cloudy. |
| 3 | 2 | 5 | north by west, weather raw and cloudy—Afternoon, rain—Much rain in the night. |
| 4 | 4 | 7 | south, weather calm and cloudy. |
| 5 | 6 | 9 | south-east, weather fair and calm. |
| 6 | 6 | 9 | east, weather fair and calm, air sharp. |
| 7 | 4½ | 6½ | east, weather cloudy, some rain, air cold, heavy rain in the night. |
| 8 | 1½ | 4 | north by east, rain and squalls, air cold and raw. |
| 9 | 1½ | 4 | north-west, weather cloudy and calm—Hail in the night. |
| 10 | 1½ | 4 | south-west, weather cloudy, gleams of sun-shine. |
| 11 | 1½ | 4 | north north-east, fair weather, clear sky—Afternoon, mercury and spirit rise. |

| | | | |
|---|---|---|---|
| 12 | 1½ | 4 | north-east, fair weather, clear sky, mercury and spirit rise two degrees at noon. |
| 13 | 1½ | 4 | north-east, fair weather, clear sky, mercury and spirit rise two degrees at noon. |
| 14 | 1½ | 4 | south-west, calm and cloudy—Afternoon, clear sky—Evening, gusts of wind at east. |
| 15 | 4½ | 7 | south-west, calm fair weather—Afternoon, mercury and spirit rise three degrees. |
| 16 | 4 | 6½ | east, calm fair weather, clear sky—Afternoon, mercury and spirit rise three degrees. |
| 17 | 5½ | 8 | north-north-west, calm fair weather, clear sky—At noon, the mercury and spirit rise two degrees. |
| 18 | 5½ | 8 | east, fair weather, clear sky, little wind—Afternoon, the mercury and spirit rise three degrees. |
| 19 | 7 | 10 | easterly, fair weather, clear sky, little wind—At noon, mercury and spirit rise two degrees. |
| 20 | 7 | 9 | south, south-east, rain, cloudy, calm. |
| 21 | 6 | 8 | north, cloudy mizzling rain, cold and raw, snow upon the distant hills. |
| 22 | 6½ | 9 | east, gleams of sun-shine. |
| 23 | 7 | 10 | south-west, fair weather, clear sky—Afternoon, cloudy—Heavy rain at night, some thunder, hills on each side of the Var covered with snow. |
| 24 | 5 | 7 | north, weather cloudy, and calm. |
| 25 | 5½ | 7½ | north, cloudy, gleams of sun-shine, calm. |
| 26 | 7 | 9½ | north-north-east, fair weather, sun warm. |
| 27 | 6½ | 8½ | north-north-east, fair weather—Afternoon, cloudy. |

## REGISTER of the WEATHER.

| Day of the month. | Reaumur's thermom. merc. deg. above Ice. | Chateauneuf's ther. spirit deg. above Ice. | |
|---|---|---|---|
| Mar. | | | |
| 28 | 9 | 11 | Wind easterly, a fresh breeze, fair weather—Afternoon, cloudy—Evening, some rain. |
| 29 | 8 | 10 | —— easterly, fair weather |
| | | | —— east, fair weather } remarkably clear sky, sun warm, mercury and spirit rise three degrees about noon. |
| | | | —— east, fair weather |
| Apr. | | | |
| 1 | 9 | 10½ | —— south-east, fair weather, eclipse of the sun, at 9 hour 25 min. ended at 12 hour 29 min. its breadth 9 digits, 46 min. |
| 2 | 9 | 11 | —— easterly, fair weather } remarkably clear sky, sun hot. |
| 3 | 9 | 10 | —— easterly, fair weather |
| 4 | 10 | 11½ | —— easterly, fair weather |
| 5 | 11 | 12 | —— easterly, fair weather. |
| 6 | 12 | 13 | —— easterly, fair weather—Afternoon, calm and cloudy—At five, wind south, a fresh breeze, sprinkling drops of rain. |
| 7 | 9½ | 11 | —— easterly, almost calm, rainy weather. |
| 8 | 8½ | 10 | —— easterly, almost calm, rain. |

| Day | | | |
|---|---|---|---|
| 9 | 8½ | 10½ | southerly, cloudy weather, showers—Afternoon heavy rain, mercury and spirit fell 2 degrees, snow upon the distant hills. |
| 10 | 7½ | 10 | southerly, fair weather—Afternoon, blows fresh, air cold—Heavy rain in the night, snow on the hills. |
| 11 | 7 | 9 | northerly, heavy showers in the morning—At noon, blows fresh, sky watery, snow on the hills. |
| 12 | 7 | 9 | north-west, blows fresh, fair weather, sky watery. |
| 13 | 10 | 11½ | easterly, fair weather. |
| 14 | 10 | 11½ | westerly, blows fresh, fair weather, air sharp. |
| 15 | 10¼ | 12 | easterly, blows fresh, fair weather, air sharp. |
| 16 | 10½ | 12 | easterly, fair weather, sky cloudy, little wind in the morning—At noon, squally, at south-south-west, blows hard at night. |
| 17 | 12 | 14 | south-west, blows fresh, fair weather, sky clear—At noon, calm—At five in the afternoon, sudden squalls, which continued at short intervals all night. |
| 18 | 12½ | 15 | westerly, blows fresh, clear sky, warm. |
| 19 | 12 | 13½ | westerly, blows fresh, clear sky, warm. |
| 20 | 12½ | 13½ | southerly, clear sky, warm, little wind—Orange harvest. |
| 21 | 11½ | 13 | south-east, fair weather, sky a little cloudy, air sharp. little wind. |
| 22 | 11 | 12½ | easterly, fair weather, air sharp, clear sky. |
| 23 | 9 | 10½ | easterly, fair weather, air sharp, clear sky. |
| 24 | 9½ | 11 | easterly, fair weather, air sharp, snow on the distant hills. |
| 25 | 9½ | 11 | easterly, fair weather—Wind rises like the sea breeze in Jamaica, about nine in the morning, and subsides about four or five in the afternoon. |
| 26 | 9½ | 11 | easterly, calm, cloudy—Ripe strawberries, wheat in the ear, rye seven or eight feet high. |

# REGISTER of the WEATHER.

| Day of the month. | Reaumur's thermom. merc. deg. above Ice. | Chateauneuf's ther. spirit deg. above Ice. | |
| --- | --- | --- | --- |
| Apr. 27 | 9 | 10½ | Wind northerly, blows fresh, air sharp—About noon sprinkling showers, dark, cloudy weather—Afternoon, fair weather, wind easterly, snow on the distant hills. |
| 28 | 8 | 10 | —— easterly, fair weather, air sharp——Strawberries in the market. |
| 29 | 9 | 11 | —— easterly, fair weather, air sharp, clear sky. |
| 30 | 8½ | 10½ | —— easterly, sky cloudy—Sprinkling rain at noon —Afternoon and evening, fair weather—Wheat in the ear. |
| May 1 | 9½ | 11 | —— easterly, fair weather, air warm, clear sky. |
| 2 | 10 | 11½ | —— easterly, fair mild weather, snow still upon the mountains, clear sky. |
| 3 | 10½ | 11½ | —— south-west, fair weather——The mercury in the thermometer at four in the afternoon, risen to 14—Clear sky—Ripe cherries. |
| 4 | 11 | 12 | —— south-west, fair weather, sun warm, clear sky—Orange and lemon trees covered with blossoms. |
| 5 | 11 | 13 | —— easterly, fair weather, clear sky, mercury continues to rise. |
| 6 | 12½ | 13 | —— easterly, fair weather, sun hot, clear sky—Some ripe figs. |
| 7 | 14 | 14 | —— easterly, fair weather, sun hot, clear sky. |
| 8 | 14 | 14 | —— easterly, fair weather, sun hot, clear sky. |
| 9 | 14½ | 15 | —— easterly, fair weather, sun hot, clear sky. |
| 10 | 14 | 14½ | —— south-east, cloudy weather, mizzling rain. |

| | | | |
|---|---|---|---|
| 11 | 13 | 13½ | —— easterly, fair weather, clear sky. |
| 12 | 13 | 13½ | —— easterly, fair weather, sky a little cloudy. |
| 13 | 13 | 13½ | —— easterly, fair weather, clear sky, sun hot. |
| 14 | 14 | 14¼ | —— easterly, fair weather, clear sky—Afternoon, cloudy, some drops of rain. |
| 15 | 14 | 14½ | —— easterly, sky cloudy. |
| 16 | 14½ | 14½ | —— easterly, sky cloudy—Afternoon, some drops of rain. |
| 17 | 13½ | 14 | —— easterly, rain all day—Heavy showers in the night. |
| 18 | 13½ | 14 | —— south-west, cloudy—Rain in the night. |
| 19 | 12 | 13 | —— easterly, cloudy. |
| 20 | 12 | 12½ | —— easterly, fair weather, sky cloudy, olive trees in blossom. |
| 21 | 12 | 12½ | —— easterly, fair weather, sky cloudy. |
| 22 | 13 | 13½ | —— easterly, fair weather, clear sky—Afternoon, the mercury rose to 16, spirit to 17. |
| 23 | 14 | 15 | —— easterly, fair weather, clear sky, sun hot. |
| 24 | 15½ | 16 | —— easterly, fair weather, clear sky, sun hot. |
| 25 | 16 | 16½ | —— easterly, fair weather, clear sky, sun hot—Plump shower at seven in the evening. |
| 26 | 17 | 17 | —— easterly, fair weather, clear sky, sun hot. |
| 27 | 17 | 17½ | —— easterly, fair weather, clear sky, sun hot—In the afternoon, the mercury and spirit up at 20 degrees, being the heat of silk worms. |
| 28 | 17 | 17½ | —— easterly, fair weather, clear sky, sun hot—Afternoon, cloudy. |
| 29 | 17 | 17½ | —— easterly, fair weather—Evening, cloudy—Silk worms weaving. |
| 30 | 17 | 17½ | —— easterly, fair weather, sun hot. |
| 31 | 17 | 17 | —— easterly, fair weather—At noon, a little rain. |

## REGISTER of the WEATHER.

| Day of the month. | Reaumur's thermom. merc. deg. above Ice. | Chateau-neuf's ther. spirit deg. above Ice. | |
|---|---|---|---|
| June | | | |
| 1 | 16 | 16¼ | Wind easterly, fair weather—Afternoon, wind southerly, a fresh gale. |
| 2 | 15½ | 16 | —— easterly, fair weather—Season for winding the cocons of silk. |
| 3 | 15 | 15 | —— easterly, plump shower at four in the morning—Forenoon, fair weather. |
| 4 | 15¼ | 15½ | —— easterly, fair weather—Evening, cloudy. |
| 5 | 15 | 15¼ | —— southerly, sky cloudy—Afternoon, sprinkling rain. |
| 6 | 14¾ | 15 | —— easterly, fair weather. |
| 7 | 13½ | 14 | —— easterly, fair weather. |
| 8 | 14 | 14½ | —— easterly, fair weather. |
| 9 | 14¾ | 15 | —— easterly, fair weather—Pears and plumbs in the market. |
| 10 | 15½ | 16 | —— easterly, fair weather. |
| 11 | 16¼ | 16½ | —— easterly, fair weather. |
| 12 | 17 | 17 | —— easterly, fair weather—Corn ripe. |
| 13 | 17 | 17 | —— easterly, fair weather, sun hot, ⎫ |
| 14 | 19 | 19 | —— easterly, fair weather, sun hot, ⎬ refreshing breezes. |
| 15 | 19½ | 19 | —— easterly, fair weather, sun hot, ⎭ |
| 16 | 18½ | 18½ | —— easterly, fair weather, sun hot—Ripe figs and apricots. |
| 17 | 18 | 18 | —— easterly, fair weather, sun hot. |
| 18 | 19½ | 19 | —— easterly, fair weather, sun hot, vermin troublesome. |
| 19 | 19¾ | 19 | —— easterly, fair weather, sun hot—Removed to a country house within half a league of Nice. |

| | | | |
|---|---|---|---|
| 20 | 20 | 20 | — easterly, fair weather, the two thermometers in the shade, the front of the house, exposed to the east and south-east. |
| 21 | 21 | 21 | — easterly, sky cloudy, sun hot. |
| 22 | 23 | 23¼ | — easterly, fair weather, sun hot. |
| 23 | 23½ | 23¾ | — easterly, fair weather, great heat. |
| 24 | 23½ | 23¾ | — easterly, fair weather, sun hot. |
| 25 | 23 | 22 | — easterly, weather a little cloudy, sun hot, refreshing breeze. |
| 26 | 22 | 21 | — easterly, fair weather, refreshing breeze. |
| 27 | 22½ | 21 | — easterly, fair weather, refreshing breeze. |
| 28 | 22¾ | 21½ | — easterly, fair weather, refreshing breeze. |
| 29 | 24½ | 24 | — easterly, fresh gale—At three in the afternoon the mercury up at 29¾, the spirit at 29, heat excessive. |
| 30 | 22 | 21½ | — easterly, fair weather, sun very hot, returned to my house at Nice. |
| Jul. | | | |
| 1 | 21½ | 21 | — easterly, fair weather ⎫ |
| 2 | 22 | 21½ | — easterly, fair weather ⎬ warm. |
| 3 | 22½ | 21½ | — easterly, fair weather, sun hot—Afternoon, plump showers, mercury fallen to 18¾, spirit to 18—Rain in the night. |
| 4 | 19 | 19 | — northerly, cloudy—Evening, showers. |
| 5 | 18 | 18 | — easterly, fair weather—Season for the anchovy fishery. |
| 6 | 18 | 18 | — easterly, fair weather. |
| 7 | 19 | 19 | — easterly, fair weather. |
| 8 | 18½ | 18 | — easterly, fair weather—In the evening, sprinkling rain. |
| 9 | 19 | 18½ | — northerly, cloudy. |
| 10 | 19½ | 19 | — easterly, fair weather, sun hot—At night a little sprinkling rain. |

# REGISTER of the WEATHER.

| Day of the month. | Reaumur's thermom. merc. deg. above Ice. | Chateau-neuf's ther. spirit deg. above Ice. | |
|---|---|---|---|
| Jul. | | | |
| 11 | 20 | 19½ | Wind easterly, fair weather, sun hot. |
| 12 | 19 | 19 | —— easterly, fair weather, sun hot. |
| 13 | 20 | 19½ | —— south, fair weather, at noon mercury rose to 24½. |
| 14 | 21½ | 20½ | —— westerly, fair weather, sun hot—Ripe peaches, and apples. |
| 15 | 20 | 19½ | —— easterly, fair weather, sun hot. |
| 16 | 20 | 19½ | —— southerly, fair weather, sun hot. |
| 17 | 20 | 19½ | —— easterly, sun hot. |
| 18 | 19 | 18½ | —— easterly, fair weather, sun hot. |
| 19 | 20 | 19½ | —— easterly, sky a little cloudy. |
| 20 | 20 | 19½ | —— easterly, fair weather, sun hot. |
| 21 | 21 | 20½ | —— easterly, fair weather, sun very hot, ripe water melons from Antibes. |
| 22 | 22 | 21 | —— easterly, fair weather, very hot. |
| 23 | 22½ | 21½ | —— easterly, fair weather, very hot—Thunder in the night. |
| 24 | 22 | 21 | —— easterly, fair weather, refreshing breezes—At two in the afternoon the mercury rose to 26½. |
| 25 | 24 | 23 | —— easterly, fair weather, sun very hot. |
| 26 | 23 | 22 | —— easterly, fair weather, sun hot. |
| 27 | 21½ | 21 | —— easterly, fair weather—Afternoon, wind westerly. |
| 28 | 23 | 22 | —— easterly, fair weather, sun hot. |
| 29 | 22½ | 21½ | —— easterly, fair weather, sultry. |

| | | | |
|---|---|---|---|
| 30 | 23 | 22 | —— easterly, fair weather, sun very hot, ripe grapes.—The mercury rose at one to 26, the spirit to 25. |
| 31 | 23 | 22 | —— easterly, cloudy—Sprinkling showers at noon. |
| **Au.** | | | |
| 1 | 22 | 21 | —— easterly, fair weather—Some thunder in the afternoon. |
| 2 | 22½ | 22 | —— south-west, a fresh breeze, fair weather—Afternoon, wind increases, sultry hot, the mercury and spirit in the thermometer rise to 31. |
| 3 | 23 | 22 | —— easterly, fair weather, sun hot. |
| 4 | 22 | 21 | —— easterly, fair weather. |
| 5 | 21 | 20 | —— easterly, fair weather. |
| 6 | 21 | 20 | —— easterly, fair weather. |
| 7 | 21 | 20 | —— southerly, fair weather, a fresh breeze. |
| 8 | 21 | 20 | —— southerly, fresh breeze, cloudy weather—Hard gale in the night at south-west. |
| 9 | 22 | 21 | —— south-west, a fresh breeze. |
| 10 | 22 | 21 | —— easterly, fair weather, fresh breeze. |
| 11 | 21 | 20 | —— north-west, cloudy—Forenoon, mizzling rain—Squalls in the evening. |
| 12 | 21 | 20 | —— west, fair weather. |
| 13 | 21 | 20 | —— east, fair weather. |
| 14 | 21 | 20 | —— east, fair weather. |
| 15 | 20 | 19 | —— east, fair weather. |
| 16 | 20 | 19 | —— east, fair weather—noon, weather cloudy, wind north-west. |
| 17 | 20 | 19 | —— east, fair weather. |
| 18 | 20 | 19 | —— east, fair weather. |

345

# REGISTER of the WEATHER.

| Day of the month. | Reaumur's thermom. merc. deg. above Ice. | Chateauneuf's ther. spirit deg. above Ice. | |
|---|---|---|---|
| Au. | | | |
| 19 | 19 | 18 | Wind easterly, cloudy—At noon, a sudden squall, with a little rain, wind south-west, snow on the distant hills. |
| 20 | 19 | 18 | —— easterly, fair weather. |
| 21 | 18 | 18 | —— westerly, fair weather. |
| 22 | 19 | 19 | —— easterly, fair weather. |
| 23 | 19 | 19 | —— easterly, fair weather. |
| 24 | 19 | 18½ | —— easterly, fair weather, sun hot. |
| 25 | 19½ | 19 | —— easterly, fair weather—In the evening, close and cloudy. |
| 26 | 20 | 19½ | —— easterly, fair weather—Evening, cloudy. |
| 27 | 20 | 19½ | —— easterly, fair weather—Evening, close and cloudy. |
| 28 | 20½ | 20 | —— easterly, fair weather—Evening, cloudy. |
| 29 | 20½ | 20 | —— easterly, fair weather. |
| 30 | 21 | 20½ | —— easterly, fair weather, sun hot. |
| 31 | 21½ | 21 | —— easterly, fair weather, sun hot. |
| Sep. | | | |
| 1 | 21½ | 21 | —— easterly, fair weather, sun hot. |
| 2 | 21½ | 21 | —— easterly, fair weather, sun hot. |
| 3 | 22 | 21½ | —— easterly, fresh breeze, cloudy—Afternoon, sprinkling rain—In the night, thunder and lightning. |
| 4 | 21 | 20 | —— north-east—Morning, thunder showers—Forenoon, fair weather. |

| | | | |
|---|---|---|---|
| 5 | 22 | 21 | —— easterly—Morning, some clouds—Afternoon, wind westerly, cloudy. |
| 6 | 20½ | 20 | —— easterly, morning some clouds—Afternoon, fair weather. |
| 7 | 19 | 18 | —— easterly, fair weather, sun hot. |
| 8 | 20 | 19 | —— easterly, fair weather. |
| 9 | 19½ | 19 | —— easterly, fair weather. |
| 10 | 19 | 19 | —— southerly, fair weather—Afternoon, easterly wind, evening cloudy. |
| 11 | 20 | 19½ | —— easterly, fair weather. |
| 12 | 20½ | 20 | —— easterly, fair weather. |
| 13 | 21 | 20½ | —— easterly, fair weather. |
| 14 | 20 | 19 | —— easterly, cloudy—At noon, some rain, wind westerly—in the night, some rain and thunder. |
| 15 | 20 | 19 | —— southerly, fair weather. |
| 16 | 20 | 19 | —— westerly, fair weather. |
| 17 | 19 | 18 | —— westerly, very high—Afternoon, mercury 20, spirit of wine 19, rain. |
| 18 | 17 | 17 | —— easterly, fair weather. |
| 19 | 15½ | 15½ | —— easterly, cloudy. |
| 20 | 15 | 15 | —— southerly, fair weather. |
| 21 | 14½ | 15 | —— easterly, cloudy. |
| 22 | 15 | 15 | —— easterly, fair weather. |
| 23 | 15 | 15 | —— westerly, fair weather. |
| 24 | 15 | 15 | —— easterly, fair weather. |
| 25 | 15 | 15 | —— easterly, very high, fair weather. |
| 26 | 15 | 15 | —— easterly, fair weather. |
| 27 | 14 | 14½ | —— westerly, fair weather. |
| 28 | 15 | 15 | —— westerly, fair weather. |
| 29 | 13 | 13½ | —— westerly, rain. |
| 30 | 9 | 10 | —— easterly, fair weather, snow upon the mountains. |

# REGISTER of the WEATHER.

| Day of the month. | Reaumur's thermom. merc. deg. above Ice. | Chateau-neuf's ther. spirit deg. above Ice. | |
|---|---|---|---|
| Oct. | | | |
| 1 | 8 | 9½ | Wind easterly, fair weather—Afternoon, westerly wind, very high. |
| 2 | 9 | 10 | —— westerly, fair weather. |
| 3 | 11 | 11 | —— westerly, fair weather. |
| 4 | 12 | 12 | —— easterly, fair weather. |
| 5 | 11 | 13 | —— southerly, cloudy weather. |
| 6 | 13½ | 14 | —— easterly, fair weather. |
| 7 | 13½ | 14 | —— southerly, fair weather. |
| 8 | 13 | 14 | —— southerly, cloudy—Afternoon, small rain, vintage begun. |
| 9 | 15 | 15 | —— southerly, fair weather. |
| 10 | 15 | 15 | —— easterly, fair weather—Afternoon, cloudy, some drops of rain. |
| 11 | 14 | 14 | —— easterly, fair weather. |
| 12 | 15 | 15 | —— westerly, fair weather. |
| 13 | 14½ | 14 | —— westerly, cloudy—Afternoon, south wind—Night, rain, south wind, very high. |
| 14 | 13 | 14 | —— south, cloudy. |
| 15 | 12½ | 13 | —— southerly, rain. |
| 16 | 12 | 13 | —— westerly, cloudy. |
| 17 | 12 | 13 | —— westerly, cloudy. |
| 18 | 13 | 14 | —— easterly, fair weather. |
| 19 | 12 | 12½ | —— easterly, fair weather. |
| 20 | 12½ | 13 | —— easterly, fair weather. |

| | | | |
|---|---|---|---|
| 21 | 12¼ | 13 | —— easterly, fair weather. |
| 22 | 13½ | 14 | —— easterly, fair weather. |
| 23 | 12½ | 15 | —— westerly, fair weather—Afternoon, mercury 11½, heavy rain, northerly wind. |
| 24 | 8 | 9½ | —— northerly, cloudy. |
| 25 | 8 | 10 | —— northerly, clear sky, sharp air. |
| 26 | 10½ | 11½ | —— northerly, clear sky. |
| 27 | 7 | 8 | —— northerly, sky cloudy, air cold. |
| 28 | 5½ | 7 | —— north-east, sky cloudy, air cold. |
| 29 | 7½ | 9 | —— north-east, sky clear, air very sharp. |
| 30 | 5 | 7 | —— north, sky clear, air very sharp. |
| 31 | 5½ | 7½ | —— east, sky cloudy, air sharp, oil harvest begins. |
| Nov. | | | |
| 1 | 5 | 7 | —— north, sky cloudy, air cold. |
| 2 | 8 | 10 | —— north-east, fair weather, sun warm, |
| 3 | 10 | 11½ | —— north, fair weather, clear sky, sun warm, } little wind. |
| 4 | 10 | 11½ | —— north, fair weather, clear sky, sun warm, |
| 5 | 7½ | 9 | —— north, fair weather, sun warm. |
| 6 | 9 | 10½ | Little wind, east, fair weather, sun warm. |
| 7 | 7 | 9 | Wind west, blows fresh, sky cloudy. |
| 8 | 10 | 11½ | —— north, fair weather, sun warm. |
| 9 | 7 | 9 | —— east, cloudy in the forenoon—Afternoon, fair weather. |

| Day of the month. | Reaumur's thermom. merc. deg. above Ice. | Chateauneuf's ther. spirit deg. above Ice. | |
|---|---|---|---|
| Nov. | | | |
| 10 | 7 | 9 | Wind north, cloudy. |
| 11 | 7 | 9 | — east, fair weather. |
| 12 | 8½ | 10 | — east, cloudy. |
| 13 | 10 | 11½ | — east, fine weather—Squalls of wind at night. |
| 14 | 8 | 9½ | — north-east, fine weather. |
| 15 | 7 | 9 | — north, fair weather, afternoon cloudy. |
| 16 | 5½ | 7 | — north, mizzling rain—Heavy rain all night. |
| 17 | 4 | 6 | — north-west—Rain all day and in the night, snow on the mountains. |
| 18 | 5½ | 7 | — east, blows fresh, cloudy, with showers—Heavy rain in the night. |
| 19 | 6 | 8 | — north-west, cloudy, with showers—At night heavy rain. |
| 20 | 5½ | 7 | — north-west, cloudy, showers—Heavy rain in the night. |
| 21 | 5 | 7 | — north-west, cloudy. |
| 22 | 4½ | 5½ | — westerly, cloudy—Afternoon, fair weather—Evening overcast. |
| 23 | 4 | 5 | — westerly, cloudy—Afternoon and evening, rain. |
| 24 | 3 | 4½ | — easterly—Heavy rain all day and all night. |
| 25 | 3 | 4½ | — north, heavy rain all day, snow on the mountains. |
| 26 | 3½ | 5 | — north, showers, interspersed with gleams of sunshine—Heavy rain in the night. |
| 27 | 3½ | 5 | — easterly, heavy showers—Afternoon, fair weather. |
| 28 | 3½ | 5½ | — easterly, fair weather, clear sky. |
| 29 | 3½ | 5½ | — north-west, cloudy. |

| | | | |
|---|---|---|---|
| 30 | 2½ | 3½ | —— north, fair weather, clear sky. |
| Dec. | | | |
| 1 | 4 | 6 | —— east, fair weather, clear sky. |
| 2 | 2½ | 4 | —— north, fair weather, clear sky. |
| 3 | 3 | 5 | —— north, cloudy—Afternoon, fair weather, clear sky. |
| 4 | 3 | 4½ | —— north, fair weather, clear sky, air sharp. |
| 5 | 2½ | 4½ | —— north, fair weather, clear sky, air sharp. |
| 6 | 3 | 5 | —— north, cloudy, high wind in the night. |
| 7 | 3 | 5 | —— east, squalls and rain—Afternoon, windy. |
| 8 | 2½ | 4 | —— north-west, clear weather. |
| 9 | 3 | 5 | —— north, clear weather. |
| 10 | 3 | 5 | —— north, fair weather. |
| 11 | 2 | 5 | —— west, rain in the forenoon—Afternoon, fair weather. |
| 12 | 2½ | 4 | —— north, fair weather, air sharp. |
| 13 | 2½ | 5 | —— north, fair weather. |
| 14 | 2 | 5 | —— north, fair weather. |
| 15 | 2 | 5 | —— north-east, cloudy—Evening, some rain. |
| 16 | 2 | 5 | —— north-east, heavy rain and thunder at three in the morning—Forenoon cloudy. |
| 17 | 2 | 4½ | —— north-west, fair weather, air cold. |
| 18 | 2 | 3½ | —— north, fair weather, air cold. |
| 19 | 1½ | 4 | —— northerly, cloudy, air sharp. |
| 20 | 1 | 3½ | —— north-east, mizzling rain. |
| 21 | 1 | 3½ | —— north-west, mizzling rain. |
| 22 | ½ | 3½ | —— north-west, weather damp and cloudy. |

# REGISTER of the WEATHER.

| Day of the month. | Reaumur's thermom. merc. deg. above Ice. | Chateauneuf's ther. spirit deg. above Ice. | |
|---|---|---|---|
| Dec. | | | |
| 23 | 1 | 4 | Wind easterly, cloudy, damp weather—Rain in the night. |
| 24 | 1 | 4 | —— northerly, cloudy, damp weather. |
| 25 | 1½ | 5 | —— easterly, cloudy, damp weather—Heavy rain in the night. |
| 26 | 1½ | 5 | —— northerly, cloudy, damp weather—Heavy rain in the afternoon and evening. |
| 27 | 1½ | 4½ | —— northerly, fair weather. |
| 28 | 1½ | 4½ | —— northerly, cloudy. |
| 29 | 1½ | 4½ | —— northerly, cloudy—Mizzling rain in the evening. |
| 30 | 1¾ | 5 | —— easterly—Forenoon, fair weather—Afternoon, cloudy. |
| 31 | 2 | 5 | —— easterly, cloudy weather. |
| 1765 Jan. | | | |
| 1 | 2½ | 5½ | —— northerly, cloudy weather—Afternoon, mizzling rain. |
| 2 | 3 | 6 | —— easterly, cloudy weather—Rain at noon—Heavy rain all the afternoon and night. |
| 3 | 4 | 6 | —— south-east, cloudy—Heavy rain, with some thunder in the afternoon and evening. |
| 4 | 2½ | 5 | —— north, cloudy—Afternoon, fair weather. |
| 5 | 2 | 4½ | —— north, fair weather. |
| 6 | 2 | 4½ | —— north, cloudy—Afternoon, fair weather. |

352

| | | | |
|---|---|---|---|
| 7 | 2 | 5 | north, cloudy—Sprinkling shower at one in the afternoon. |
| 8 | 2½ | 5½ | north, heavy rain at four in the morning—Forenoon, cloudy—Mizzling rain at noon. |
| 9 | 2 | 5 | east, rain in the morning and forenoon. |
| 10 | 2½ | 5½ | east, cloudy weather—Gleams of sunshine in the afternoon. |
| 11 | 3 | 5½ | north-west, cloudy weather—Mizzling rain in the afternoon. |
| 12 | 2 | 5 | easterly, clear weather. |
| 13 | 3 | 5½ | easterly, cloudy, with gleams of sunshine. |
| 14 | 3 | 5½ | easterly, heavy rain, with squalls at three in the morning—Forenoon, cloudy—Afternoon and evening, heavy continued rain. |
| 15 | 2½ | 5 | easterly, fair weather. |
| 16 | 3 | 5½ | north, fair weather—At night, mizzling showers, } great fall of snow on the mountains. |
| 17 | 3 | 5½ | east, cloudy weather—Afternoon and evening, heavy rain, } |
| 18 | 3 | 5½ | north, cloudy weather, |
| 19 | 3 | 5½ | north, fair weather, |
| 20 | 3 | 5½ | north, fair weather, } air sharp. |
| 21 | 2½ | 5 | north, fair weather, |
| 22 | 3 | 5½ | easterly, blows fresh and cold, cloudy weather. |
| 23 | 2 | 4½ | northerly, heavy rain. |
| 24 | 2 | 4½ | northerly, cloudy weather—Afternoon, rain. |
| 25 | 1½ | 4 | east, rainy weather—Evening, fair. |
| 26 | 1½ | 4 | north-east, blows fresh, heavy rain. |
| 27 | 3 | 5 | easterly, fair weather. |
| 28 | 3 | 5 | north, fair weather in the forenoon—Cloudy in the afternoon. |

# REGISTER of the WEATHER.

| Day of the month. | Reaumur's thermom. merc. deg. above Ice. | Chateauneuf's ther. spirit deg. above Ice. | |
|---|---|---|---|
| Jan. | | | |
| 29 | 3 | 5½ | Wind north, fair weather. |
| 30 | 4 | 6 | —— east, fair weather. |
| 31 | 4 | 6 | —— east, cloudy—Afternoon, mizzling rain. |
| Feb. | | | |
| 1 | 3 | 5 | —— north-west, mizzling rain, full of snow on the neighbouring mountains. |
| 2 | 1½ | 4 | —— north, cloudy. |
| 3 | 1 | 3½ | —— easterly, cloudy and cold. |
| 4 | ½ | 3 | —— easterly, cloudy and cold—Afternoon, rain. |
| 5 | 0 | 2½ | —— north, morning squally, cloudy weather, mizzling rain. |
| 6 | 0 | 2½ | —— north, fair weather—Evening, rain, heavy rain in the night. |
| 7 | ½ | 3 | —— north, cloudy, with gleams of sunshine. |
| 8 | ½ | 3½ | —— north, fair weather. |
| 9 | 1 | 4 | —— north, cloudy—Afternoon, clear. |
| 10 | 1 | 4 | —— north, cloudy, a sprinkling rain. |
| 11 | ½ | 3½ | —— north-west, fair weather—Afternoon, cloudy. |
| 12 | 1½ | 4 | —— north-west, fair weather. |
| 13 | 1 | 3½ | —— north, fair weather. |
| 14 | 1 | 3½ | —— south-east, cloudy—Evening, sprinkling rain. |
| 15 | 0 | 3 | —— east, cloudy and cold—Snow on the neighbouring hills. |

| Date | | | |
|---|---|---|---|
| 16 | | 2 | — north, dark and cold, with some sleet—Snow in the neighbourhood of Nice. |
| 17 | 1 deg. bel. ice<br>3 | 0 | — north—Morning, clear weather, air cold—Afternoon, overcast, rain and sleet—Heavy rain in the night—Snow in the neighbourhood of Nice. |
| 18 | 3 | 0 | — north, cloudy, cold. |
| 19 | 2 | 2 | — north, cloudy, cold—Afternoon, evening, and night, heavy rain. |
| 20 | 2 | 2 | — northerly, heavy rain—Afternoon, fair. |
| 21 | 2 | 2 | — northerly, cloudy weather—Afternoon, clear. |
| 22 | 0 | 4 | — northerly, cloudy weather—Afternoon and night, heavy rain with some thunder. |
| 23 | 0 | 3½ | — northerly, cloudy |
| 24 | ½ | 3½ | — north-east, clear weather, ⎫ |
| 25 | 1 | 5 | — north-east, fine weather, ⎬ Evenings, fog on the mountains. |
| 26 | 2½ | 5½ | — north-east, fine weather, ⎭ |
| 27 | 3 | 6 | — easterly, fine weather—Afternoon, cloudy—Rain all night. |
| 28 | 3 | 5½ | — easterly, rain all day and all night, with some thunder. |
| Mar. | | | |
| 1 | 2 | 4½ | — southerly, rain. |
| 2 | 1½ | 4½ | — northerly, fair weather, air sharp. |
| 3 | 3 | 5½ | — north-east, fair weather, air sharp. |
| 4 | 2½ | 4½ | — north-east, fair weather, air sharp. |
| 5 | 3 | 5½ | — north-east, fair weather—A little rain in the night. |
| 6 | 3 | 5½ | — easterly, mizzling rain. |
| 7 | 3 | 5½ | — north-west, rain, and cloudy weather. |
| 8 | 3½ | 6 | — easterly, cloudy weather in the morning, clears up at noon. |

REGISTER of the WEATHER.

| Day of the month. | Reaumur's thermom. merc. deg. above Ice. | Chateauneuf's ther. spirit deg. above Ice. | |
|---|---|---|---|
| Mar. | | | |
| 9 | 4½ | 7 | Wind westerly, fair weather—Afternoon, showers—Heavy rain in the night. |
| 10 | 4 | 6 | —— north-west, heavy rain all day. |
| 11 | 3 | 5½ | —— north-west, blows fresh, clear weather. |
| 12 | 3½ | 6½ | —— north-west, blows fresh, cloudy—Rain in the night. |
| 13 | 4 | 6½ | —— southerly, rainy weather. |
| 14 | 4 | 6 | —— southerly, fair weather. |
| 15 | 5 | 7 | —— southerly, cloudy weather. |
| 16 | 5 | 7 | —— easterly, fair weather. |
| 17 | 6½ | 8½ | —— easterly, clouds and sunshine. |
| 18 | 7 | 9 | —— easterly, fair weather—Afternoon, overcast. |
| 19 | 7½ | 9½ | —— easterly, cloudy—Afternoon and evening, heavy rain. |
| 20 | 7 | 9 | —— easterly, cloudy—Afternoon, a little rain. |
| 21 | 7 | 9 | —— north-east, cloudy. |
| 22 | 7 | 9 | —— easterly, fair weather. |
| 23 | 7 | 9 | —— easterly, fair weather. |
| 24 | 8 | 10 | —— easterly, clouds and sunshine. |
| 25 | 8 | 10 | —— easterly, cloudy. |
| 26 | 8 | 10 | —— easterly, fair weather. |
| 27 | 8 | 10 | —— easterly, clouds and sunshine. |
| 28 | 8½ | 11 | —— easterly, fair weather. |
| 29 | 9½ | 11 | —— easterly, fair weather—Evening, high wind at west. |

| | | | |
|---|---|---|---|
| 30 | 9 | 11 | —— westerly, blows fresh. |
| 31 | 9 | 11 | —— northerly, fair weather, fresh breeze. |
| Apr. | | | |
| 1 | | | —— easterly, fair weather, air sharp. |
| 2 | | | —— easterly, fair weather, air sharp. |
| 3 | | | —— easterly, cloudy, air sharp. |
| 4 | | | —— easterly, fair weather, air sharp. |
| 5 | | | —— south-east, fair weather, air sharp. |
| 6 | | | —— south-east, fair weather, air sharp. |
| 7 | | | —— easterly, fair weather, air sharp. |
| 8 | | | —— south-east, fair weather, a fresh breeze, air cold. |
| 9 | | | —— easterly, fair weather. |
| 10 | | | —— easterly, fresh breeze, fair weather—Evening, high wind at south-west. |
| 11 | | | —— south-west, fresh breeze, fair weather. |
| 12 | | | —— southerly, fresh breeze, fair weather. |
| 13 | | | —— easterly, fair weather, air sharp. |
| 14 | | | —— easterly, cloudy weather. |
| 15 | | | —— easterly, fair weather. |
| 16 | | | —— easterly, fair weather. |
| 17 | | | —— easterly, cloudy and cold—Afternoon, sprinkling rain—A fall of snow in the night upon the mountains. |
| 18 | | | —— easterly, fair weather, air cold. |
| 19 | | | —— easterly, fair weather, air sharp. |
| 20 | | | —— easterly, showers. |
| 21 | | | —— easterly, sprinkling showers. |

## REGISTER of the WEATHER.

| Day of the month. | Reaumur's thermom. merc. deg. above Ice. | Chateau-neuf's ther. spirit deg. above Ice. | |
|---|---|---|---|
| **Apr.** | | | |
| 22 | | | Wind easterly, at five in the morning a storm of thunder, hail and heavy rain—A fall of snow on the mountains. |
| 23 | | | —— easterly, at four in the morning rain—Forenoon, cloudy. |
| 24 | | | —— easterly, rain in the morning—Forenoon, cloudy. |

FINIS.

# Notes

A few preliminary points should be made, explanatory to the critical notes:

(i) When quoting, no attempt has been made to normalize punctuation and spelling in the text of the originals; editorial interpolations are enclosed within square brackets.

(ii) Full details of works referred to within the notes by abbreviation, author, or short title will be found in the key below.

(iii) Unless otherwise stated, the place of publication is London.

(iv) Where possible, references to classical authors are from the Loeb editions.

(v) In cross-referencing, my practice is to quote the Letter number, followed by page reference, or Letter number followed by note number.

(vi) Biographical details are normally included in the note to the *earliest* reference in the *Travels*, which may be found through the Index at the end of the volume. Cross-references to persons referred to by initials (e.g. Mrs. B——) are given within the notes.

## ABBREVIATIONS

| | |
|---|---|
| *DNB* | *Dictionary of National Biography* |
| MS.(S.) | Manuscript(s) |
| *NQ* | *Notes and Queries* |
| *OED* | *Oxford English Dictionary* |
| P.R.O | Public Record Office, London |
| S.P. | State Papers |
| Adm. | Admiralty Papers |
| *Travels* | *Travels through France and Italy* |
| MS. edition | Smollett's personal copy of the *Travels* with his manuscript notes, now in the British Library |

## SHORT TITLES

*(a) Works of Smollett*

| | |
|---|---|
| *Continuation* | *Continuation of the Complete History of England*, 5 vols., 1760–5. |
| *Humphry Clinker* | *The Expedition of Humphry Clinker*, ed. Lewis M. Knapp, Oxford English Novels, Oxford, 1966. |

| | |
|---|---|
| *Launcelot Greaves* | *The Life and Adventures of Sir Launcelot Greaves*, ed. David Evans, Oxford English Novels, Oxford, 1973. |
| *Letters* | *The Letters of Tobias Smollett*, ed. Lewis M. Knapp, Oxford, 1970. |
| Oxford edition | *Travels through France and Italy*, ed. Frank Felsenstein, Oxford University Press, 1979. |
| *Peregrine Pickle* | *The Adventures of Peregrine Pickle*, ed. James L. Clifford, Oxford English Novels, Oxford, 1964. |
| *Roderick Random* | *The Adventures of Roderick Random*, ed. P.-G. Boucé, Oxford English Novels, Oxford, 1979. |
| Seccombe | *Travels through France and Italy*, ed. Thomas Seccombe, World's Classics edn., Oxford, 1907. |

## (b) Other Works

| | |
|---|---|
| Addison | Joseph Addison, *Remarks on Several Parts of Italy*, 4th edn., 1733. |
| Bianchi | Giuseppe Bianchi, *Ragguaglio delle Antichità e Rarità che si Conservano nella Galleria Mediceo-Imperiale di Firenze*, part 1 [no other parts published?], Florence, 1759. |
| Boswell | *Boswell on the Grand Tour: Italy, Corsica, and France 1765–1766*, ed. F. Brady and F.A. Pottle, 1955. |
| Büsching | Anton Friedrich Büsching, *A New System of Geography*, 6 vols., 1762. |
| Gibbon | Edward Gibbon, *Journey from Geneva to Rome*, ed. G. A. Bonnard, 1961. |
| Gioffredo | Pietro Gioffredo, *Nicaea Civitas*, in J. G. Graevius, *Thesaurus Antiquitatum et Historiarum Italiae*, vol. IX, part 6, Leyden, 1723. |
| Joliat | Eugène Joliat, *Smollett et la France*, Paris, 1935. |
| Kahrl | George M. Kahrl, *Tobias Smollett Traveler-Novelist*, University of Chicago Press, 1945. |
| Keysler | Johann Georg Keysler, *Travels through Germany, Bohemia, Hungary, Switzerland, Italy and Lorrain*, 3rd edn., 4 vols., 1760. |
| Knapp | Lewis M. Knapp, *Tobias Smollett Doctor of Men and Manners*, Princeton University Press, 1949. |
| Martz | Louis L. Martz, *The Later Career of Tobias Smollett*, Yale University Press, 1942. |
| Montfaucon | Bernard de Montfaucon, *The Travels of the Learned Father Montfaucon from Paris thro' Italy*, 1712. |

| Moore | John Moore, *A View of Society and Manners in Italy*, 2 vols., 1781. |
| Morgan | John Morgan, *The Journal of Dr. John Morgan of Philadelphia from the City of Rome to the City of London 1764*, printed for private circulation by J.B. Lippincott, Philadelphia, 1907. |
| Northall | John Northall, *Travels through Italy*, 1766. |
| Nugent (1749) | Thomas Nugent, *The Grand Tour*, 4 vols., 1749. |
| Nugent (1778) | Thomas Nugent, *The Grand Tour*, 3rd edn., 4 vols., 1778. |
| Pliny | Pliny, *Natural History*. |
| *Roma Antica* | *Roma Antica, e Moderna*, 3 vols., Rome 1750. |
| Sharp | Samuel Sharp, *Letters from Italy*, 2nd edn., 1767. |
| Smith | Sir James Edward Smith, *A Sketch of a Tour on the Continent*, 2nd edn., 3 vols., 1807. |
| Sterne, *A Sentimental Journey* | Laurence Sterne, *A Sentimental Journey through France and Italy*, ed. Gardner D. Stout, Jr., Berkeley, 1967. |
| Valette de Travessac | Valette de Travessac, *Abrégé de l'Histoire de la Ville de Nismes*, 4th edn., Avignon, 1760. |
| Watkins | Thomas Watkins, *Travels through Switzerland, Italy, Sicily . . . in the Years 1787, 1788, 1789*, 2nd edn., 2 vols., 1794. |

## LETTER I

1. *traduced by malice . . . a domestic calamity*. From May 1762, Smollett edited *The Briton*, a patriotic periodical in defence of Lord Bute's unpopular ministry, finally being dismissed by Bute in February 1763 since the paper aggravated widespread dissatisfaction. Smollett's "domestic calamity" was the death on 3 April, at the age of fifteen, of his only child Elizabeth (*Letters*, p.114).

2. *threatened all the horrors of civil dissension*. Presumably a general reference to the popular unrest at the time of Lord Bute's ministry and more particularly to the celebrated Wilkes affair. See Georges Rudé, *Wilkes and Liberty*, Oxford, 1962.

3. *a family of five persons*. With Smollett were his wife, Mrs. Anne Smollett, Miss Anne Curry (II, n.3), (probably) his niece, Miss Frances Lassells and the servant, Alexander Tolloush.

4. *Every landlord . . . forty shillings*. The ambassador was the duc de Nivernais (1716–98), who arrived in England in 1762 to negotiate the

peace. He was presented with a bill for £43 for one night at an inn in Canterbury. See Dodsley's *Annual Register*, v, 1762, p.104.

5. *berlins.* "A four-wheeled covered carriage, with a seat behind covered with a hood" (*OED*).

6. *Dover is commonly termed a den of thieves.* Cf. Matthew 21:13.

7. *Above five years ago, in my passage from Flushing to Dover.* Smollett's biographers make no mention of a trip abroad around 1758, though we know for certain that he "made a Tour thro' part of France, Flanders and Holland" in 1749 (*Letters*, p.12). Cf. a similar description in *Peregrine Pickle*, pp.189–90.

8. *One would imagine the French were still at war with the English.* The Seven Years War, 1756–63, had ended less than five months before Smollett left London.

9. *a gentleman of the faculty:* i.e. a doctor.

10. *Mrs. B——.* Identified as Mme. Ballantyne, the wife of a Scottish merchant, living at rue Coquelin, Boulogne.

## LETTER II

1. *chambre syndicale.* No records of the *chambre syndicale de la librairie* at Amiens are extant. Its purpose was to ensure that works prejudicial to the state and the Church were not allowed to enter or be published in France. However, the correspondence concerning Smollett's books which took place between the duc de Praslin (1712–85), and Lamoignon de Malesherbes (1721–94), Directeur de la Librairie, survives; see A. C. Hunter, *Revue de Littérature Comparée*, XI, 1931, pp.736–7; Joliat, pp.249–53; *Letters*, pp.115–20.

2. *Mons. B——.* Identified as Charles-Antoine-François Bouvier, a minor state official. A contemporary traveller, Philip Thicknesse, *Useful Hints to Those Who Make the Tour of France*, 1768, p.17, recounts, "as I passed through Boulogne, I saw the young gentleman who so kindly received, and hospitably entertained, Mr. S—— and his family. This young man, whose youth and good offices ought to have saved him from the Doctor's ridicule, is now pointed out to every English and *Bretesh* [a snub at Smollett's Scottish origin] traveller, as an object of contempt, because he was picked out as a subject of satire, for rendering every civility that lay in his power to the Doctor in the best manner he was able."

3. *miss C——.* Anne Curry, to whom Mrs. Smollett "acted as chaperon" (Seccombe, p.xviii), was a native of Newcastle. On 5 June 1769, Smollett was a witness to her marriage at Florence to George Renner, a merchant at Leghorn (Knapp, *passim*).

4. *the Enfans trouvés.* According to Louis Sébastien Mercier, *Tableau de Paris*, Amsterdam, 1788, XII, pp.84–5, between six and seven thousand

children were abandoned each year at the notorious *Hôpital des Enfants trouvés.*

5. *procureur du roy:* public prosecutor. *subdelegate of the intendance:* official responsible for government of a small locality under the *ancien régime.*

6. *the earl of H——.* Referred to in Letter III as "My lord H——d", Francis Seymour Conway, Earl of Hertford (1718–94), the English ambassador to the court of France, only arrived in Paris 20 October 1763. See Appendix.

7. *the duchess of D——.* Margaret Douglas (d. 1774), daughter of James Douglas of Mains, married in 1758, when she was aged about forty-three, Archibald, first Duke of Douglas. William Cole, *A Journal of my Journey to Paris in the Year 1765,* ed. F. G. Stokes, 1931, p.165, describes her as "a large ungainly Person of a Woman, who seemed to have a great Deal of Pride & little Breeding". For Smollett's relationship to Margaret Douglas, see *Letters,* p.116.

## LETTER III

1. *doctor C——.* Unidentified.

2. *Hippocrates . . . for the gout.* See *The Aphorisms of Hippocrates,* trans. Thomas Coar, 1822, v, p.129; cf. Smollett, *An Essay on the External Use of Water,* 1752, ed. Claude E. Jones, Baltimore, 1935, p.56.

3. *Celsus . . . natatio.* Celsus, *De Medecina,* IV, 10.4.

4. *the Ladrone islands:* nowadays the Mariana islands.

5. *lord H——d.* Hertford; see II, n. 6.

6. *Mr. N——lle.* Richard Neville Aldworth Neville (1717–93) became secretary to the embassy in Paris on 4 September 1762 (*DNB*).

7. *general Paterson.* Sir James Paterson (d. 1765), rose to Lieutenant-General, serving for forty-nine years in the King of Sardinia's forces. In 1752 he was made commandant of Nice, a position he held until retirement in 1763. Paterson died at Bath, 5 September 1765, and was buried in Scotland (Knapp, p.250 n.).

8. *duc d'Aumont.* Louis-Marie d'Aumont was governor of Boulogne from 1753 to 1782.

9. *bishop suffragan.* The eleventh bishop of Boulogne from 1742 to 1789 was François-Joseph-Gaston de Partz de Pressy, mentioned by local historians as a man of great piety and virtue.

10. *seneschal's court . . . bailiwick.* J. M. Thompson, *The French Revolution,* fourth edn., 1951, pp.126, 130, describes how France's "judicial system, based on feudal land-tenure, cut up the country into nearly five hundred *bailliages* and *sénéchaussées,* whose boundaries were so uncertain that more than eighteen hundred parishes did not know to what district they belonged, and no map could be relied upon to show them correctly . . .

The *bailliages* were the seats of a hateful seigneurial jurisdiction."

11. *echevins*. OED quotes *Travels* as earliest example in English and defines: "A municipal functionary in French and Belgian towns, corresponding nearly to an English alderman."

12. *prince de Cruy*. Emmanuel de Croy (1718–83), prince of Meurs and Solre, Commander of the French forces in N.E. France from 1757, became Lieutenant-General (1759) and Marshal of France (1782). The "paltry fort" which Smollett saw, called the Machicoulis, was constructed and came into use in 1758.

13. *father Græme*. Smollett may have made the acquaintance of this priest, Patrick Græme, in an earlier trip to France before 1751. In *Peregrine Pickle*, p. 194, the hero and Jolter, his tutor "proceeded without any accident as far as Boulogne, where they breakfasted and visited old father Graham, a Scottish gentleman of the governor's acquaintance, who had lived as a Capuchin in that place for the space of threescore years, and during that period conformed to all the austerities of the order with the most rigorous exactness; being equally remarkable for the frankness of his conversation, the humanity of his disposition, and the simplicity of his manners."

14. *pere Charles*. According to Kahrl, pp. 37–8, the original of père Charles may have been Frère Balthazar, the thieving priest in *Roderick Random*, p. 240, "a merry facetious fellow, who . . . loved good eating and drinking better than his rosary, and paid more adoration to a pretty girl than to the Virgin Mary, or St. Genevive."

## LETTER IV

1. *D. H——*. David Hume (1711–76), the historian and philosopher, accompanied the Earl of Hertford to Paris in 1763, as his secretary (*DNB*).

2. *the earl of H——*. Hertford; see II, n. 6.

3. *Meriton*. The master of the Boulogne packet boat, which sailed to and from London, was Henry Meriton.

4. *A very great degree . . . converted into ice*. *The Monthly Review*, XXXIV, 1766, p. 422, comments, "But unluckily for this project, the Doctor hath told us above, that water will not freeze until it has deposited all its salt. If therefore it be previously necessary to effect this deposition, to what purpose should we freeze it in order to render it potable?"
   See also *The Gentleman's Magazine*, XLIV, 1774, p. 464, which describes the experiment as "an Irishcism".

5. *the Dog-and-duck, in St. George's fields*. The Dog and Duck in Lambeth (on the site of the present Imperial War Museum) was frequented by the lower middle class as a place of amusement. Lacking the sophistication of the more fashionable Ranelagh and Vauxhall, it was reputed a haunt of thieves and low characters. The well of water, St. George's Spa, was famous for its remedial qualities.

6. *chalybeate:* impregnated with iron. Cf. *Humphry Clinker*, p.183.

7. *a zonic:* stratum, zone.

8. *king's evil:* scrofula.

9. *a company of contractors . . . Hastings in Sussex.* In 1762, a project was set up to supply London with fish by land carriage or "fish machines" direct from the sea ports. The scheme was not a financial success, although similar attempts in France proved viable. The company of contractors at Hastings may have been Grant & Co. See *A Plan for the Better Supplying this Metropolis with Plenty of Fish* [1760?], p.7; H. Higgs, *Bibliography of Economics 1751–1775*, Cambridge, 1935, no. 4296.

10. *corinths:* currants.

11. *Mrs. B——.* Ballantyne; see I, n. 10.

12. *a substantial burgher.* The master tanner, Louis-Marie Duburquoy was found guilty in 1759 of the mortal wounding in a tavern brawl of Blaise Piot and his wife, but he was later pardoned and released.

13. *A furious abbé . . . condemned to be broke.* A full account of the incident is given by Ate. d'Hauttefeuille and Ls. Bénard, *Histoire de Boulogne-Sur-Mer,* 2 vols., 1860, II, pp.27–9.

14. *capillaire.* "Syrup flavoured with orange-flower water" (*OED*).

15. *Baronius . . . in the Vatican.* See Caesar Baronius (1538–1607), cardinal and librarian of the Vatican, *Annales Ecclesiasticus*, editio novissima, 12 vols., Antwerp, 1596–1629, I, p.184.

16. *Tillemont . . . as a fable.* See Louis Sébastien Le Nain de Tillemont (1637–98), French ecclesiastical historian, *Mémoires pour Servir à l'Histoire Ecclésiastique des Six Premiers Siècles*, second edn., 16 vols., Paris, 1701–14, I, p.447.

17. *And here it may . . . with the piles.* For commentary on the origin of Veronica and the significance of the *haemorrhoïssa*, see Butler's *Lives of the Saints*, ed. Herbert Thurston, S. J. and Donald Attwater, 4 vols., 1956, III, pp.82–3. Smollett, of course, in ascribing to Veronica the patronage of those suffering from the piles, puns on the word "haemorrhoids".

18. *St. Fiacre.* fl. A.D. 670 (?). A patron saint of gardeners and of French cab-drivers, whose vehicles were named after him.

19. *Baugé.* Scottish troops, commanded by the Earl of Buchan, were employed by the French dauphin in the defeat of the English army under the Duke of Clarence at Baugé in 1421, at which Clarence was slain.

## LETTER V

1. *Mrs. B——.* Ballantyne; see I, n. 10.

2. *Capt. L——.* Unidentified.

3. *flat-bottomed boats . . . the war.* Early in 1759, intelligence reached London that the French were building flat-bottomed boats on the beach at Havre-de-Grâce (le Havre), apparently with the intention of a projected invasion of England. As a result, Rear-Admiral Rodney conducted a fierce bombardment of Havre. See David Spinney, *Rodney*, 1969, pp. 148–61.

4. *After all . . . diminished.* In 1745, an act was passed "for repealing the present inland duty of 4 shillings *per* pound on all tea sold in *Great Britain*, and for granting other inland duties in lieu thereof; and for better securing the duty upon tea, and other duties of excise . . ." (*Gentleman's Magazine*, xv, 1745, pp. 273, 331). The duty was cut to one shilling per pound and supplemented with a tax on the gross price of all teas. Smollett's suggestion of lowering the duties anticipates Pitt's reduction of the tea-duty from fifty per cent to twelve per cent in 1785.

5. *While I stayed at Hastings.* Smollett may have stayed at Hastings during the summer of 1762, when he visited Dover "with a View to bathe in the Sea" (*Letters*, p. 107). See Kahrl, p. 64 n.

6. *pier-glasses.* "A large tall mirror; orig. one fitted to fill up the pier or space between two windows, or over a chimney-piece" (*OED*).

7. *testers.* "A canopy over a bed, supported on the posts of the bedstead or suspended from the ceiling" (*OED*).

8. *even a native of Edinburgh would stop his nose.* The shortcomings of the sanitary system of Edinburgh were well known. See *Humphry Clinker*, p. 218.

9. *a child befouling . . . mal odore.* The quotation is from the play by Carlo Goldoni (1707–93), *La buona moglie*, 1749, I. iii., written in Venetian dialect.

10. *Legiboli.* See Smollett's *Continuation*, II, p. 271 footnote: "The name the natives give to that part of South Barbary, known to merchants and navigators by that of The Gum-Coast, and called in maps, The Sandy Desart of Sara, and sometimes Zara."

11. *Kamschatka.* The peninsula terminating N.E. Asia between the Bering Sea and Sea of Okhotsk, now part of the U.S.S.R. Smollett's source here is G. F. Müller, *Voyages from Asia to America*, trans. Thomas Jefferys, 1761, p. ix: "When they [the natives of Kamschatka] make a Feast, they pour Water upon some . . . Mushrooms, and boil them. They then drink the Liquor, which intoxicates them; the poorer Sort, who cannot afford to lay in a Store of these Mushrooms, post themselves, on these Occasions, round the Huts of the Rich, and watch the Opportunity of the Guests coming down to make Water, and then hold a Wooden Bowl to receive the Urin, which they drink off greedily, as having still some virtue of the Mushroom in it, and by this Way they also get drunk." See Kahrl, p. 89.

12. *Mr. B——.* Bouvier; see II, n. 2.

13. *Mons. L——y.* M. de Louvigny, whose ancestor Robert de Louvigny in

1629 held fief from the baroness d'Engoudsent.

14. *father K——* . . . *curate of the parish.* Patrick Kelcher became the resident priest of the parish of Saint-Nicholas in 1754.

15. *the picture of Don Quixote after he had lost his teeth.* In Smollett's translation of *Don Quixote*, 2 vols., 1755, the copperplate (vol. 1, plate 5, facing p. 106), designed by Francis Hayman, shows Sancho examining his master's mouth, after the attack on the herd of sheep, in which a stone from a shepherd's sling had removed a number of Quixote's "grinders".

16. *madame la marquise.* Jeanne Antoinette Poisson, marquise de Pompadour (1721–64) was the mistress of Louis XV from 1744.

17. *I told him* . . . *the taking of Mahon.* The siege of Minorca in 1756 and the capture of Mahon, a Pyrrhic victory by French forces under the command of the Maréchal duc de Richelieu (1696–1788), was the first battle of the Seven Years War. The island was returned to Britain in 1763 and held until 1783 when it again became Spanish.

18. *in the year 1749* . . . *into disgrace.* Cf. *Peregrine Pickle*, 1751, p.291. For Mme. de Maintenon, see VII, n. 7.

19. *By the bye* . . . *Malbrough.* "The old French song, '*Malbrouk s'en va-t-en guerre*' (Marlborough is off to the wars), is said to date from 1709, when the Duke of Marlborough was winning his battles in Flanders, but it did not become popular till it was applied to Charles Churchill, 3rd Duke of Marlborough, at the time of his failure against Cherbourg (1758), and was further popularized by its becoming a favourite of Marie Antoinette about 1780, and by its being introduced by Beaumarchais into *Le Mariage de Figaro* (1784)." (Brewer, *Dictionary of Phrase and Fable*, fifth revised ed., 1959, p.583.)

20. *fermiers generaux.* See XXXVI, n. 1.

21. *Sancho Panza* . . . *shaving him.* See Smollett's translation of *Don Quixote*, II, Bk. II, ch. 15, p.204: "they heard a number of people talking, and a great noise in the palace, and presently Sancho entered the hall in a fright tucked with a dishclout by way of bib, and followed by several boys, or rather scullions, and other small gentry, one of whom brought a tray full of water, which, by its colour and filth, appeared to be dish-washings, pursuing and persecuting the poor squire, and struggling to thrust it under his chin, while another, with the same earnestness, endeavoured to lather his beard."

22. *a miraculous image* . . . *at the expence of the sailors.* According to local tradition, following a supposed visitation in A.D. 636, a statue carved in wood of the Virgin Mary carrying the infant Jesus, was found in a small boat off Boulogne. Over the centuries the Virgin Mary of Boulogne became an object of veneration. At the time of Henry VIII the English are said to have removed the statue with other plunder, but when Boulogne was returned to France, Henri II, to the joy of the people of the town, obtained the restitution of the sacred image from Edward VI, or possibly

replaced it. The "miraculous image" disappeared during the French Revolution. Only one hand (made of metal) remains, which is today kept in the Cathedral of Notre Dame de Boulogne. See *Histoire de Boulogne-Sur-Mer*, 2 vols., 1860, I, pp.246, 278.

23. *poor Canadians . . . the English*. The French at St. John capitulated to the British force under Lieutenant-Colonel Lord Rollo in 1758.

24. *Mr. M——*. Identified elsewhere (*Letters*, p.121) by Smollett as "Mr. Mayne, an English Gentleman (now dead)".

25. *They are already sealed . . . he passes*. A.R., *The Curiosities of Paris, in Nine Letters*, 1757, p.18, note, comments that baggage was commonly examined and plumbed with "a little leaden Seal, which is tied near the Lock, and costs five Sols, or Two-pence Halfpenny English. Passavana is a Certificate of Examination."

26. *A——'s*. Possibly the Anderston Club in Glasgow, an academic dining club. See *The Quarterly Review*, CIII, 1858, p.82.

## LETTER VI

1. *prince of Condé*. Louis Joseph de Bourbon, eighth Prince of Condé (1736–1818).

2. *Tresors de St. Denis*. The treasures included the crown jewels of France.

3. *our friend Hamilton*. Perhaps Archibald Hamilton, Senior (1719–93), the printer of *The Critical Review*. See Knapp, pp.285, 330–1.

4. *Hotel de Montmorency*. See Knapp, p.251 n.: "In *The Gentleman's Guide in his Tour through France*, fourth edition (London, 1770), p.233, the Hotel Montmorency, on La Rue Mazarine, is listed among the best hotels. Some other hotels in the Quartier St. Germain Des Pres were more expensive."

5. *mantua-maker*: dressmaker.

6. *Lully*. Jean-Baptiste Lully (1639–87) was born in Florence, but was naturalized French in 1661. He became, in 1670, the joint-director of the French opera.

7. *I suspect . . . bills of mortality*. Abbé Antonini, *Mémorial de Paris, et de Ses Environs*, new ed., Paris, 1744, p.3, states that "On compte dans Paris huit à neuf cens mille Habitans". This figure is repeated by Nugent and other guides.

8. *They have set up . . . some improvements*. The penny-post was established in England in 1683, though in Paris a similar system had been attempted without success as early as 1653. However, in 1758, Piarron de Chamousset (1717–73) obtained the royal patent to set up a *petite poste*.

9. *the machine at this place for raising water*. See Thomas Pennant, *Tour on the Continent 1765*, ed. G. R. de Beer, 1948, p.30: "Two miles from hence is

the famous Machine of Marli that flings the water of the Seine into an aquaduct on the top of a high mountain. There are three machines for that purpose, the first and greatest in the river, the 2d on the middle on the hill, the 3d near the aquaduct. The aquaduct is above 100 feet high, built on arches, that conveys the water to Marli, whence it is kept in three large reservoirs."

10. *Jewish gaberdine.* "A loose upper garment of coarse material; a smock frock" (*OED*). The association of gaberdine with Jews is probably a reminiscence of Shakespeare's *Merchant of Venice*, I.iii. 112–13.

11. *our hats . . . the stage.* Cf. *Roderick Random*, pp.50, 277. The Oxford editor, P.-G. Boucé, notes that the part of Pistol (particularly in *2 Henry IV* ) "came to be strongly identified at the time with the actor Theophilus Cibber (1703–58)," an engraving of whom "complete with huge cocked hat and swaggering looks, may be seen in his pantomime, *The Harlot's Progress* (1733)."

12. *à la pigeon.* Philip Thicknesse uses a similar phrase: "a man who never learned to make a bow, performs it worse in a head of hair dressed *a L'aille de Pidgeon*, than in a *scratch* wig." (*Observations on the Customs and Manners of the French Nation*, 1766, p.9.)

13. *Wig-Middleton.* Unidentified.

### LETTER VII

1. *Mrs. M——.* Possibly Mrs. Catherine Macaulay (1733–91), the historian, and wife of Smollett's friend, Dr. George Macaulay (*c.*1716–66). In October 1765, shortly after their return to England, the Smolletts accompanied Dr. and Mrs. Macaulay to Bath (Knapp, p.260).

2. *When the Indian chiefs . . . cheeks and eye-lids.* Smollett's *Continuation*, v, pp.24–6 reports the visit in May 1762 of three Indian chiefs led by "Outacite, signifying Man-killer".

3. *fard.* "Paint (*esp.* white paint) for the face" (*OED*).

4. *Powder or meal . . . their scald heads.* It was a common belief that the Poles were peculiarly subject to a disease of the head, *plica polonica*, which causes the hair to become matted and agglutinated.

5. *buchu.* "The name given by the natives at the Cape of Good Hope to the plant formerly termed *Diosma crenata*; now assigned in Pharmacopœias to various species of *Barosma*" (*OED*).

6. *I have known . . . to a determination.* In *Peregrine Pickle*, p.205, Smollett describes a similar couple, with whom Peregrine, visiting Paris, becomes embroiled.

7. *Maintenon.* Françoise d'Aubigné Maintenon (1635–1719), mistress and afterwards second wife of Louis XIV; first married to the writer, Paul

# VIII

Scarron (d. 1660). *Sevigné.* Marie de Rabutin-Chantal (1626–96), the famous letter writer. *Scuderi.* Madeline de Scudéry (1607–1701), novelist, author of *Artamène* (1650) and *Clélie* (1656). *Dacier.* Anne Lefèvre (1651–1720), a leading contemporary classicist, and wife of André Dacier (1651–1722), critic and commentator, secretary of the French Academy. *Chatelet.* Gabrielle Émilie de Breteuil, marquise de Châtelet (1706–49), scientist, more famous perhaps as the mistress of Voltaire.

8. *Des Cartes.* René Descartes (1596–1650), the celebrated philosopher and mathematician. *Maupertuis.* Pierre Louis Moreau de (1698–1759), mathematician and astronomer, who led a geodetic expedition to Lapland. *Reaumur.* René Antoine Ferchault de Réaumur (1683–1757), celebrated naturalist and natural philosopher. As a scientist, he is principally remembered as the inventor of the Réaumur thermometer (used by Smollett for his register of the weather at Nice) and for his experiments with metals. He also wrote a natural history of insects. *Buffon.* Georges Louis Leclerc, comte de Buffon (1707–88), the famous naturalist, author of *Histoire Naturelle.*

9. *pomatum:* pomade.

10. *Count Saxe . . . head of hair.* See Maurice Saxe (1696–1750), Marshal of France, *Mes Rêveries* (1756), translated into English by Sir William Fawcett as *Reveries or Memoirs upon the Art of War*, 1757, pp.4–5: "In the field, the hair is a filthy ornament for a soldier, and after once the rainy season is set in, his head can hardly be ever dry . . . I would have a soldier wear his hair short, and be furnished with a small wig, either grey or black, and made of Spanish lamb-skin, which he should put on in bad weather: this wig will resemble the natural head of hair so well, as to render it almost impossible to distinguish the difference; will fit extremely well, when properly made; cost but about twenty pence, and last during his whole life: it will be also very warm; prevent colds and fluxes; and give quite a good air."

11. *decrotteur:* shoe black, boot-black.

12. *Considering . . . neighbours.* The humour of Smollett's unflattering analogy is reminiscent of Arbuthnot's characterisation of Louis XIV as Lewis Baboon (i.e. Bourbon) in *Law is a Bottomless-Pit*, 1712 (see *The History of John Bull*, ed. Alan W. Bower and Robert A. Erickson, Oxford, 1976).


## LETTER VIII

1. *Mr. M——.* According to Kahrl, p.105, who offers no supporting evidence, Dr. John Moore (1729–1802), father of the hero of Corunna and a close friend to Smollett.

2. *the manufacture for porcelain . . . at the village of St. Cloud.* Opened about 1695, the porcelain manufacture at Saint-Cloud was burnt down in 1773, and never rebuilt.

3. *the porcelain made at Chelsea.* The Chelsea Porcelain Works was established *c.* 1745, under the management of Nicholas Sprimont (d. 1771), a Frenchman. See Knapp, pp. 112, 218.

4. *Mr. Guastaldi, late minister from Genoa at London.* Giambattista Gastaldi was Genoese minister from 1741 to 1755.

5. *dutchess of Douglas.* See II, n. 7.

6. *an ordinary.* "An eating-house or tavern where public meals are provided at a fixed price; a dining-room in such a building" (*OED*).

7. *neats tongues:* ox-tongues.

8. *I pulled out the post-book.* This was the frequently republished *Liste générale des postes de France.*

9. *Joigne-ville:* apparently an error for Joigny.

10. *pompions:* pumpkins.

## LETTER IX

1. *the confluence of two large rivers.* The Rhône and the Saône.

2. *beca ficas:* "small migratory birds . . . much esteemed as dainties in the autumn, when they have fattened on figs and grapes: they are identified with the British Pettychaps and Blackcaps" (*OED*).

3. *grieves: une grive* is a thrush.

4. *Mandrin.* Louis Mandrin (1725–55), French popular hero, born in Dauphiné, became captain of the *contrebandiers,* successfully defying the king's troops for a number of years. In May 1755, he was captured by the French (who had illegally crossed the frontier) at the Château de Rochefort-en-Novalaise in Savoy. Taken to Valence, he was tried and condemned to be broken on the wheel. By the intervention of the Bishop of Valence, instead of being left to die, Mandrin was strangled immediately after receiving his punishment. A life of Mandrin, *Authentic Memoirs of the Remarkable Life and Surprising Exploits of Mandrin,* was translated into English in 1755. Smollett's account in the *Travels* accords with the traditional story in its basic details, although adding several unrecorded episodes.

5. *the famous bridge at St. Esprit . . . impetuosity of the river.* The bridge was begun in 1265, and built by the inhabitants of Saint-Saturnin, the town later assuming the name of the bridge. Three thousand feet in length, until the nineteenth century it was the longest bridge in Europe, spanning the Rhone on twenty-six arches.

6. *It is not comparable . . . solidity.* Westminster Bridge, which was demolished in favour of the present structure, 1854–62, was completed in 1750 after the design of the Swiss architect, Charles Labelye. Before this,

London Bridge was the only one to cross the Thames at London.

## LETTER X

1. *It rises . . . for the year 1718.* See Réaumur, "Essais de l'histoire des rivieres & des ruisseaux du royaume qui roulent des paillettes d'or", in *Histoire de l'Académie Royale des Sciences, Année M.DCCXVIII. Avec les Mémoires de Mathématique & de Phisique, pour la même Année,* 2nd edn., Paris, 1741, p.71. For Réaumur, see VII, n. 8.

2. *a pamphlet . . . antiquities.* Abbé Valette de Travessac, *Abrégé de l'Histoire de la Ville de Nismes,* 4th edn., Avignon, 1760, which Smollett used as the source of much of his information on Nîmes (see Martz, pp.82–3 and Oxford edition of the *Travels,* pp.xliii–xliv).

3. *Henry III. of France.* Succeeding his brother Charles IX in 1574, Henry III (1551–89) was deeply involved in the religious turmoil between the Catholic League and the Huguenots.

4. *croisards:* crusaders (obs.)

5. *Antoninus Pius.* The son of a consul (A.D. 86–161), he succeeded Hadrian as emperor in 138.

6. *in honour of Caius . . . Agrippa.* Marcus Vipsanius Agrippa (63–12 B.C.), the friend and colleague of the emperor Augustus (63 B.C.–A.D. 14), took as his third wife the emperor's daughter, Julia. Their two sons, Caius, born 20 B.C., and Lucius, born 17 B.C., were adopted by Augustus and, even as children, made consuls elect. Lucius died at Massilia (Marseilles) in A.D. 2 on his way to Spain, and Caius was mortally wounded in Armenia, A.D. 4.

7. *Cardinal Alberoni.* Giulio Alberoni (1664–1752), born in Parma, Italy, cardinal and first minister of Spain, 1715–19.

8. *Cheval Blanc. The Gentleman's Guide in His Tour through France,* Bristol, [1770?], p.71, recommends this as one of "the best inns". Boswell, pp.267, 269, who put up at the same inn, agrees with Smollett that it was "very dear".

9. *Mr. L——.* Unidentified.

10. *a gentleman from Chelsea.* From 1750 to 1763, Smollett lived at Monmouth House, Chelsea. See Knapp, pp.109–110.

11. *Irish regiment of Berwick.* A regiment of infantry was organized from the remnants of King James's army after the Peace of Ryswick (1697), and granted in 1698 to James Fitz-James, Duke of Berwick (1670–1734), natural son of James II and Arabella Churchill, sister of the Duke of Marlborough. Berwick was killed by a cannon-ball at Philipsburgh in 1734. The regiment retained his name until 1791, when it became the 88th Regiment of Infantry. See John Cornelius O'Callaghan, *History of the Irish Brigades in the Service of France,* Glasgow, 1870, pp.142–9.

12. *lieutenant colonel Teuts*. Identified as Lieutenant-Colonel Walter Tuite (P.R.O., S.P. 78/257, France 1763).

13. *The duke of Fitz-James*. Charles, duc de Fitz-James (1712–87), son of James Fitz-James, Duke of Berwick, followed his father's career in the army. In 1748, he was promoted to the rank of Lieutenant General, and in 1761 appointed Commandant of Languedoc, a post which he lost in 1763, following a bitter dispute with the *parlement* of Toulouse. He was raised, in 1775, to Marshal of France.

14. *the states of Provence*. By 1789 there existed in France but five Estates (i.e. assemblies composed of the clergy, nobility and commons), the largest of which was that of Languedoc.

15. *general P——n*. Paterson; see III, n. 7.

16. *Mr. B——d*. John Buckland (d. 1770), a native of London, came to Nice, *c*.1730. In 1748, he was Second Lieutenant in the King of Sardinia's galleys. The following year, he purchased a house at Villefranche, and in 1752 married Catherine Lauro, a native of that town. When he retired in 1762, he was appointed British vice-consul, a post he held until 1769. Buckland's will (1770) shows that he was converted to Catholicism. See Georges Doublet, "Un Ami de Smollett: John Buckland, Consul d'Angleterre à Nice", *L'Éclaireur du Dimanche*, no. 78, Nice, 7 May 1922, p.2; Doublet, *Les Anglais dans le Comté de Nice et en Provence Depuis le XVIII^{me} Siècle*, Musée Masséna, Nice, 1934, p.46.

17. *canal of Languedoc*. The canal of Languedoc (now known as the canal du Midi), linking the Atlantic with the Mediterranean, was completed under the auspices of Colbert in the reign of Louis XIV.

18. *Mr. Ray*. Alexander Ray, a Scotsman from East Lothian, acted as banker to many British travellers. Boswell, pp.267–9, calls him "a free, sensible, good-humoured man with a variety of agreeable knowledge." See also *The Correspondence of James Boswell and John Johnston of Grange*, ed. Ralph S. Walker, 1966, p.205; Sterne, *Letters*, pp.197–8.

### LETTER XI

1. *the Botanical Garden*. The "Jardin du Roy", begun at the end of the sixteenth century, was the first in Europe to specialize in medicinal plants.

2. *Dr. H——r*. Dr William Hunter (1718–83), the celebrated anatomist, obstetrician and collector, was a close friend of Smollett. Writing to Hunter from Boulogne, 11 July 1763 (*Letters*, p.116), Smollett asks if he "can be of any Service . . . in the way of picking up Books either at Paris, or Lyons, or Marseilles".

3. *Dr. Fitz-maurice*. In his letter to William Hunter, 6 February 1764 (*Letters*, p.120), Smollett states: "I had the advice of one Dr. Fitzmorrice, and [*sic*] honest irish Physician of the Place . . . ." Born in Ireland, Thomas

Fitz-Maurice became a doctor in the faculty of medicine in the University of Montpellier. He was naturalized French in 1757.

4. *professor F——*. Antoine Fizes (1690–1765) became professor of medicine in his native Montpellier in 1732, having previously held the chair of mathematics. Among other works, he was the author of *Specimen Medico-Chirugicum de Suppuratione in Partibus Mollibus*, Montpellier, 1742; *Opera Medica de Tumoribus, Suppuratione, Cataracta*, 2 parts, Montpellier, 1742. A life by Louis Estève, *La Vie et les Principes de M'. Fizes, Pour Servir à l'Histoire de la Médecine de Montpellier*, Amsterdam, 1765, appeared shortly after his death.

5. *Boerhaave*. Hermann Boerhaave (1668–1738), perhaps the most influential physician of his age, was born near Leyden, Holland, where he spent the whole of his professional life.

6. *Dr. Sm——ie*. Dr. William Smellie (1697–1763), the great obstetrician, died 5 March 1763, not long before Smollett's departure for the Continent. Smollett had helped Smellie to edit the manuscript of his *Treatise on the Theory and Practice of Midwifery*, 1751.

7. *Mrs. Mapp, the bone-setter*. William Hogarth pictured this grotesque Amazon in the engraving, *A Consultation of Physicians* (subtitled *The Company of Undertakers*), 1736. John Nichols and George Steevens, *The Genuine Works of Hogarth*, 2 vols., 1808, I, pp.91–2, describe her as "a famous masculine woman, who was called the Bone-Setter, or Shape-mistress . . . In most cases her success was rather owing to the strength of her arms, and the boldness of her undertakings, than to any knowledge of anatomy or skill in chirugical operations." Mrs. Mapp died in December 1737.

8. *trachæa arteria:* the windpipe.

9. *venesection:* phlebotomy or blood-letting.

10. *anomalous fever:* fever marked by irregularity of body temperature.

11. *febricula:* slight fever.

12. *Stimulated . . . happy effects*. Smollett's belief in the remedial qualities of bathing in sea water is brought out in his paper, *An Essay on the External Use of Water*, 1752; see Introduction, p.xi.

13. *On voit . . . une soupe*. In *Consultations Choisies de Plusieurs Medecins Célebres de l'Université de Montpellier Sur des Maladies Aigues et Chroniques*, 4 vols., Paris, 1748, which includes diagnoses of a variety of maladies, contributed by the leading figures of the Montpellier medical school, the similarity between sections of Consultation XXII, "*Sur une Phthisie pulmonaire*" (I, pp.157–66) and that presented to Smollett is apparent. Fizes seems to have ordered Smollett to follow the standard medical treatment at Montpellier for consumptive cases, without sufficient regard to the particular case. It is this neglect on Fizes's part which appears to have most annoyed Smollett. See Edouard Rist, "Une Consultation Médicale au

XVIII$^e$ Siècle", *Revue de Paris*, 63, Jan. 1956, pp.112–25.

14. *polypodium of the oak:* a type of fern.

15. *chalk of Briançon:* a variety of steatite (soapstone).

16. *antihecticum of poterius.* Described by R. James, M.D., *A Medicinal Dictionary*, 3 vols., 1743–45, I, as "a forcible penetrating Medicine", of service to a variety of disorders.

17. *balm of Canada:* a pale resin derived from the N. American species of the Balm of Gilead fir.

18. *pilulæ cynoglossæ:* preparation made from the root of hound's-tongue, traditionally used against catarrh.

19. *vomica:* purulent matter.

20. *Mr. O——d.* Richard Oswald (1705–84), a Scotsman, is described by Alexander Carlyle, *Anecdotes and Characters of the Times*, ed. James Kinsley, Oxford English Memoirs and Travels, 1973, p.45, as "a very Learned and Intelligent Merchant . . . [who] Establish'd himself at London, [and] acquir'd a Great fortune." During the Seven Years War he went to Germany as commissary-general to the forces of the Duke of Brunswick. He was the friend of Adam Smith, Benjamin Franklin, and Lord Shelburne. See Sterne, *Letters*, p.205; *DNB*.

21. *Mrs. St——e.* Elizabeth Sterne, *née* Lumley (1714–73) married Laurence Sterne in 1741. The Sternes, with their daughter Lydia, were at Montpellier from September 1763 to February 1764. See Sterne, *Letters*, pp.200–10.

22. *the scurvy is entirely an English disease.* Scurvy was so common among the English that it became known as *Morbus Anglicanus*. *OED* quotes "1742 Lond[on] & Country Brewer* I. (ed. 4) 17 Our British Malady the Scurvy". See also *Morbus Anglicanus Sanatus: or, a Remarkable Cure of an Inveterate Scurvy*, 1766, p.5.

## LETTER XII

1. *One was hanged . . . neighbourhood of Montauban.* François Rochette, a protestant minister at Montauban "was hanged as a self-convicted felon" in 1762 (*Continuation*, v, p.69).

2. *Frontignan:* a muscat wine, nowadays usually known as Frontignac. Nugent (1778), IV, p.36, recommends "*Frontignan*, excellent for a glass or two, especially with walnuts, two livres ten sols a bottle . . ."

3. *When I find . . . the character of his master.* Smollett's admiration for Jean-Baptiste Colbert (1619–83) appears in a long footnote to his edition of *The Works of M. de Voltaire*, 36 vols., 1761–9, VII, pp.89–90.

4. *Louvois.* François Michel Le Tellier, marquis de Louvois (1639–91), became minister of state for war in 1672. *Condé.* Louis de Bourbon,

prince de Condé (1621–86), the great French general. *Turenne*. Henri de la Tour d'Auvergne, vicomte de Turenne (1611–75), French general. *Luxemburg*. François Henri de Montmorency-Boutteville, duc de Luxembourg (1628–95) commanded the French invasion of Holland (1672). *Vendome*. Louis Joseph, duc de Vendôme (1654–1712), French general during the War of the Spanish Succession.

5. *revoke the edict of Nantz*. The Edict, signed at Nantes by Henry IV in 1598, gave religious freedom and the right of public worship to Protestant Huguenots. Louis XIV's revocation, 18 October 1685, deprived the Protestants of all religious and civil liberty, and led to persecutions.

6. *Tallard*. Camille d'Ostun, duc de Tallard (1652–1728), Marshal of France, taken prisoner by Marlborough at Blenheim (1704). *Villeroy*. François de Neufville, duc de Villeroi (1644–1730), Marshal of France, defeated by Marlborough at Ramillies in 1706. *Marsin*. Ferdinand, comte de Marsin (1656–1706), Marshal of France, participated with Tallard at Blenheim (1704), and was wounded before Turin, where he died in captivity.

7. *massacre the people of the Palatinate*. Louis XIV advanced claims to the Palatinate in the name of his sister-in-law, Elizabeth Charlotte, duchesse d'Orléans. In the invasion of 1688, the French committed appalling devastations.

8. *the buffoon Scarron*. Paul Scarron (1610–60), the comic poet and satirist, author of *Roman Comique* (1651–7) and *Enéide Travestie* (1648–53), which according to Voltaire, "could be received only as the work of a buffoon". (*The Works of M. de Voltaire*, ed. Smollett, Francklin, and others, 36 vols., 1761–9, IX, p.293).

9. *Without all doubt . . . le Grand*. Smollett's dislike of Louis XIV may be seen in a critical footnote in his translation of *The Works of M. de Voltaire*, ibid., VIII, p.162: "If greatness of soul consists in a love of pageantry, an ostentation of fastidious pomp, a prodigality of expence, an affectation of munificence, an insolence of ambition, and a haughty reserve of deportment; Lewis certainly deserved the appellation of Great. Qualities which are really heroic, we shall not find in the composition of his character."

10. *Mr. B——*. John Buckland; see X, n. 16.

11. *Buccaire*. Beaucaire.

12. *Cloacina*: goddess of sewers.

13. *This is a degree . . . North-Britain*. See V, n. 8.

14. *One of the English . . . his breath*. See N. Tindal, *The History of England by Mr. Rapin de Thoyras. Continued from the Revolution to the Accession of King George II*, 28 vols., 1728–47, XXVIII, pp.224–6: "In *September* [1723], four *English* Gentlemen were barbarously murdered in *France*. . . . About seven miles from *Calais* they were attacked by six ruffians well mounted, who stopped the postillions, came up to the chaises, and

demanded their money . . . when they had finished their search, they cried
*Tuez, Kill*; they first shot Mr. *Seabright* through the heart. Mr. *Davis* was
shot and stabbed in several places, and his skull cleft; they stabbed
*Spindelow* ["Mr. *Seabright*'s man"] in five places of his body, and left him
for dead, Mr. *Monpesson* at the same time received a shot which had laid
him sprawling on the ground. . . . Mr. *Monpesson*, who had lain as if he
had been dead, lifting up his head before the murderers were gone, one of
them came back to him and cut his throat; but he and *Spindelow* made a
shift with the help of some of the Country people to get back to *Calais*,
where Mr. *Monpesson* died 36 hours after, and *Spindelow*, recovering of his
wounds, returned to England."

15. *G——ow*. Glasgow, where Smollett studied from 1735 to 1739. See
Knapp, pp. 10–26.

16. *recolet:* a member of a branch of Franciscan friars (usually known as
Recollects), believing in detachment from worldly beings and recollection
in God.

17. *Monsieur Nadeau d'Etrueil.* The Governor of Guadeloupe when it fell to
the English under General Barrington in 1759, Nadeau d'Étreil was court-
martialled by the French in 1761 and imprisoned. In 1765, the court-
martial was reversed by Louis XV and D'Étreil was "re-instated in his
honours, reputation, and all other prerogatives" (*Gentleman's Magazine*,
XXXV, 1765, p.241). See also *Continuation*, III, pp. 140–60.

18. *The author of the Grand Tour . . . the right.* see Nugent (1749), IV, 174.

19. *Pharsalia of Lucan . . . swains.* Lucan, *Pharsalia*, I, ll.215–16. The
Rubicon formed part of the boundary between Italy and Cisalpine Gaul till
the time of Augustus, who extended Italy to the Var.
  These lines are quoted by Pietro Gioffredo (Petrus Jofredus), *Nicaea
Civitas*, Turin 1658 (republished J. G. Graevius, *Thesaurus Antiquitatum et
Historiarum Italiae*, IX, pt.6, Leyden, 1723, p.27), identified by Martz (pp.
83–5) as the source of Smollett's erudition in his descriptions of the
antiquities of the county of Nice. For details of Gioffredo (1629–92), see
*Nouvelle Biographie Universelle*. Martz is justified in suggesting that
"Smollett made very little use of the descriptive portions of Gioffredo's
work".

20. *Within the memory . . . Provence.* French invading forces crossed the Var
and occupied Nice in 1691, 1706, and 1744.

21. *Mr. M——e.* Mayne; see V, n. 23.

22. *count de V——n.* Probably Joseph Laurenti, comte de Venanson.

23. *the Piedmontese livre is about an English shilling.* For the Sardinian
currency, see XIX, p. 157 and note 1.

24. *Mr. B——d.* John Buckland; see X, n. 16.

25. *Mr. de Martines.* Unidentified.

26. *the Swiss regiment.* See XIII, n. 7.

27. *general P——.* Paterson; see III, n. 7.

28. *Mr. St. Pierre, junior.* Honoré Saint-Pierre (d. 1784) was the son of Antoine Saint-Pierre, a merchant of Seville established at Nice, who from 1749 was Spanish consul. Honoré was appointed consul for Naples in 1750, by Charles VII. In 1767, he married Sophie Moisson, a native of Saint-Tropez. In 1783, for the consideration of five thousand livres, the King of Sardinia granted him the title and estate of comte de Nieubourg. See Georges Doublet, "Un Prince Anglais en Meublé à Nice, durant la Season 1783–84", *L'Éclaireur du Dimanche*, no. 93, Nice, 22 August 1922, p.1; A. Demougeot, "Contribution à l'Étude de la Famille Saint-Pierre à Nice", *Nice Historique*, LX, 1957, pp.35–8.

29. *F——.* Antoine Fizes; see XI, n. 4.

30. *Brookes's Practice of Physic.* Richard Brookes M.D., *The General Practice of Physic*, 2 vols., 1751, contains descriptions of diseases, followed by prescriptions for their alleviation or cure.

## LETTER XIII

1. *This was the case in the year 1744.* In April 1744, during the War of the Austrian Succession, the French and Spanish armies crossed the Var and occupied Nice (which was unfortified) almost without resistance. There followed, however, a bloody battle near Villefranche, in which there was heavy loss on the side of the assailants, before the King of Sardinia's forces retreated to the sea, embarking on board the British ships, which carried them to safety. Nice remained under French occupation until the Treaty of Aix-la-Chapelle (1748).

2. *marechal Catinat.* Nicholas Catinat (1637–1712), Marshal of France, commanded French troops in Savoy aiding the Duke against the Calvinist group known as "Les Barbets des vallées vaudoises" (1686). In 1691, he bombarded and took Nice (the town remained in French hands until 1696), and, in 1693, decisively defeated the Savoyards at Marsaglia.

3. *Victor Amadeus, the father of his Sardinian majesty.* Victor Amadeus II (1666–1732), son of Charles Emmanuel II, married Anne Marie d'Orléans (1669–1728), a niece of Louis XIV, but in the War of the Grand Alliance fought on the side of Spain and Austria. In the War of the Spanish Succession, he allied himself with the French (1701), but changed sides two years later. By the Treaty of Utrecht (1713), he was made King of Sicily, though in compliance with the Quadruple Alliance (1718), he was obliged to accept Sardinia instead of Sicily (both islands being in Spanish hands), and in 1720, Victor Amadeus became King of Sardinia. In 1730, he abdicated in favour of his son, Charles Emmanuel III, who kept him under arrest when he attempted to revoke the abdication.

4. *It was afterwards . . . queen Anne's war.* During the War of the Spanish Succession, the Duke of Berwick (see X, n. 11) laid siege to Nice, which capitulated in January 1706 after a two months' resistance. By order of Louis XIV, the castle and fortifications were demolished. Under the terms of the Treaty of Utrecht (1713), Nice was again returned to Savoy.

5. *duke de Belleisle.* Charles Louis Auguste Fouquet, duc de Belle-Isle (1684–1761), Marshal of France, was captured by the English in 1745, but returned to command the French operations in Savoy, making his headquarters at Nice.

6. *tartanes:* small coasting vessels with single mast and bowsprit. *polacres:* ships with three masts, usually carrying square sails.

7. *a Swiss battalion . . . in his service.* The Swiss were traditionally the mercenaries of Europe, serving in the armies of many different nations. Gibbon, p.42, lists among others five Swiss regiments and one French regiment commanded by a Genevese officer, in the service of the King of Sardinia in 1764. The regiments were commonly named after their commanding officers. See also Emanuel May, *Histoire Militaire de la Suisse*, 8 vols., Lausanne, 1778.

8. *now called Cimia:* i.e. Cimiez.

9. *Ptolomy . . . Pliny.* See Ptolemy, *Geography*, III. i; Pliny, III. v. 47.

10. *præses:* president, governor.

11. *the count de Gubernatis.* Honoré Roger, comte de Gubernatis (d. 1774), was the first consul of Nice in 1747 and 1756. See J. Orestis di Castelnuovo, *La Noblesse Niçoise: Notes Historiques sur Soixante Familles*, 2 vols., Nice, 1912, I, pp.67–72.

12. *Valerian.* Roman Emperor from A.D. 253 to 260. *Gallienus.* Roman Emperor from A.D. 253 to 268, the son of Valerian, with whom he ruled jointly.

13. *This St. Pont . . . after his death.* St. Pontius, the son of Mark, a Roman senator, abjured idolatry in favour of the Christian faith. He was obliged to flee Rome, making his way to Cemenelion, where he was denounced to governor Claudius, and taken to the amphitheatre to be devoured by the bears, but (so the legend goes) instead of attacking him the beasts simply caressed him. When he refused to worship at the temple of Apollo, he was finally beheaded. See Robert Latouche, *Histoire de Nice*, 2 vols., Nice, 1951, I, pp.11–12.

14. *Charles V . . . king of Spain.* Charles V, Holy Roman Emperor and King (Charles I) of Spain (1500–58).

15. *Charles Emanuel I. duke of Savoy.* The son of Emmanuel Philibert and Margaret, daughter of Francis I of France, Charles Emmanuel (1562–1630) succeeded to the dukedom in 1580.

16. *lachrymatories:* vases intended to hold tears.

17. *Longobards*. A Germanic people, usually known today as Lombards, who invaded northern Italy in the sixth century.

18. *king Alboinus*. King of the Lombards from 563, he invaded northern Italy, taking Milan in 569; murdered in 572 at the instigation of his wife, Rosamund, after he had forced her to drink from a cup made from the skull of her father.

## LETTER XIV

1. *Mr. B——d*. John Buckland; see X, n. 16.

2. *the war of 1744*. See XIII, n.1.

3. *Sallee*: a Moroccan seaport frequently used by pirates.

4. *bottoms*: vessels.

5. *tilt*. "An awning over a boat" (*OED*).

6. *forçats*: galley-slaves.

7. *The king of Sardinia . . . Ville Franche*. The ships were the *Ascension* (renamed *San Carlo*) and the *Hermione* (renamed *San Vittorio*), purchased 1763–4. Both were of Spanish origin, captured during the war by the British. See Gibbon, p.41; idem, *Journal to January 28th 1763*, ed. D. M. Low, p.110; C. A. Gerbaix de Sonnaz, *I Savoiardi ed I Nissardi nella Marina da Guerra di Casa Savoia dal 1300 al 1860*, Turin, 1914, pp.32–3.

8. *Mr. A——*. Christopher Atkins (?–1791), joined the British Navy, *c*. 1747, and was promoted to Lieutenant in 1757. In 1763, he captained the *Hermione* to Villa Franca. See Gibbon, pp.11, 41.

9. *marquis de M——i*. Claude Allì, marquis de Maccarani, a knight of Malta, and a Lieutenant-Colonel in the King of Sardinia's army, captained one of the Savoyard gallies from 1752. He was appointed captain of the frigate *San Vittorio*, and in 1764 made at least two voyages to Sardinia. See Doublet, *Les Anglais dans le Comté de Nice et en Provence Depuis le XVIII^me Siècle*, Musée Masséna, Nice, 1934, p.50; Gerbaix de Sonnaz, op. cit., pp.31, 33; Augustus Hervey's *Journal*, ed. David Erskine, 1953, p.284.

10. *heaving down and careening*: turning a ship over on its side for cleaning, repairing, etc.

11. *Mr. P——n*. Paterson; see III, n. 7.

12. *He should therefore . . . averse to the English*. General Paterson was succeeded as commandant of Nice by a Savoyard, Giovanni Battista, comte de Nangis. He received his appointment 6 May 1763. See "Haute magistrature de la ville et du Comté de Nice", *Nice Historique*, 1904, p.52.

13. *It is not . . . port of Nice*. See *Itinerarium Antonini Augusti*, ed. G. Parthey and M. Pinder, Berlin, 1848, p.246. The *Itinerarium*, probably compiled in

the third century A.D., was the official list of roads in the Roman empire, giving the distance between towns.

14. *Portus Herculis Monæci*. Mentioned by Pliny: see XIII, n. 9.

15. *neque magnas, neque multas capit naves*. Strabo, *Geography*, IV. vi. 3.

16. *Ptolomy . . . Monæci Portus*. Ptolemy, *Geography*, III. i.

17. *Here I cannot help . . . statione Monæci*. Lucan, *Pharsalia*, I. ll.404–8.

18. *Hesperian*. "The land of the west, applied by the Greeks to Italy; by the Romans to Spain or regions beyond" (*OED*).

19. *Zephyr:* in classical mythology, the west wind. *Caurus*, the north-west wind.

20. *Charles II . . . Provence*. Charles the Lame (*c.* 1254–1309).

21. *Emanuel Philibert*. The son of Charles III of Savoy and Beatrice of Portugal, Emmanuel Philibert (1528–80) became Duke of Savoy in 1553.

22. *A——'s*. See V, n. 25.


## LETTER XV

1. *Mr. M——l*. Possibly George Macaulay: see VII, n. 1. Smollett's correspondent appears to be the same lady, Mrs. M——, to whom he addressed the earlier letter.

2. *Henry IV. of France*. Henry of Navarre (1553–1610) succeeded to the throne of France in 1589.

3. *punto*. Smollett puns here. *OED* defines a punto: 1. "A stroke or thrust with the point of the sword or foil." 2. "A small point of behaviour." i.e. punctilio.

4. *recontre:* a duel.

5. *in France, duels are forbid, on pain of death*. As early as 1566, an ordinance of Charles IX applied the death penalty to anyone taking part in a duel. Henry IV, under the influence of Sully, introduced several strong edicts against the practice, but their success in preventing duels was rather limited. A more recent edict of 1723 had, in vain, attempted a similar reform.

6. *pioneers:* obs. "One who digs a trench, pit, etc.; a digger, excavator . . ." (*OED*). Smollett's use of this word considerably postdates the last *OED* entry.

7. *the court of Lorrain*. Lorraine only became French in 1766 on the death of Stanislas Leszcynski, ex-King of Poland and father-in-law of Louis XV. In 1735, under the peace preliminaries of the War of the Polish Succession, Lorraine was granted to Stanislas, and ceded to him by the Austrians in 1738.

8. *Cornelius Nepos . . . that defect.* Cornelius Nepos (fl. first century B.C.), the author of *De Viris Illustribus*, does not recount this particular anecdote, which is from Plutarch's *Life of Themistocles*, XI. (Cornelius Nepos also wrote a life of Themistocles, which accounts for Smollett's error). The Spartan general was Eurybiades, and the incident took place shortly before the battle of Salamis, 480 B.C., in which the combined Greek fleet defeated the superior forces of the Persians under Xerxes.

9. *given to the surgeons.* The bodies of convicted assassins were given to the surgeons for dissection. See Hogarth, "The Reward of Cruelty", pl. IV, *The Four Stages of Cruelty*, 1751.

10. *spadassin:* bully, bravo.

11. *In the reign . . . trophy of his prowess.* George Villiers, second Duke of Buckingham (1628–1687) took the Countess of Shrewsbury (d. 1702) as his mistress, and forced her husband to a famous duel in January 1668. Shrewsbury died two months later from his wounds. It was generally believed that after the combat Buckingham made for Clieveden, where he lay with his mistress (see Alexander Pope, *Moral Essays*, epist. III, ll. 307–8), though this is evidently untrue as Clieveden was only built at a later date. See Pepys, *Diary*, 8 vols., ed. H. B. Wheatley, 1952, VII, pp. 265–6; Lady Burghclere, *George Villiers, Second Duke of Buckingham 1628–1687*, 1903, pp. 194–5.

12. *When the gallant earl of Ossory . . . other consequences.* Thomas, Earl of Ossory (1634–80) challenged Buckingham over the latter's remarks against his father, the Duke of Ormond, who had opposed the Irish Cattle bill (1666). Buckingham failed to appear at Chelsea Fields, the appointed venue, but sent a party with a warrant for Ossory's arrest. The following day, he complained to the Lords, with the result that Ossory was committed to the Tower and Buckingham to the custody of the Black Rod, until they had had a few days in which to cool down. See Pepys, op. cit., VI, pp. 37, 43; Burghclere, op. cit., p. 158.

## LETTER XVI

1. *Maximian.* Roman emperor from A.D. 286 to 305, the subordinate of Diocletian. He died in 310.

2. *Trumpilini.* The name survives in Val Trompia. *Camuni:* Val Camonica in the Rhaetian Alps. *Vennonetes:* according to Strabo, the most savage of the Rhaetian tribes, inhabiting the south side of the Alps near the sources of the Addua. *Isnarci:* usually Isarci, the inhabitants of the present day Val de Sarcho. *Breuni:* a Rhaetian tribe, who lived in the Tyrol not far from the Brenner, Val Bregna.

3. *an Italian manuscript.* Smollett found this manuscript, the work of an "Auctore Italo anonymo", in Gioffredo, pp. 44–7; see Martz, pp. 84–5.

4. *Pliny . . . lib. iii. cap. 20.* Pliny's *Natural History* is quoted by Gioffredo, p.47.

5. *Busching, in his Geography.* See Büsching, III, p.35. Smollett is credited to have written the article on the English translation of Büsching for *The Critical Review*, XII, 1761, pp.237–50 (L. L. Martz, "Tobias Smollett and the Universal History", *Modern Language Notes*, LVI, 1941, pp.1–14).

6. *Aulus Helvius.* Roman emperor from 1 January to 28 March A.D. 193, succeeded Commodus but was murdered by his troops.

7. *Commodus.* Roman emperor, A.D. 180–192, son of Marcus Aurelius.

8. *Didius Julianus.* Roman emperor, who bought his office of the prætorian guards, when they put up the empire for sale after the death of Pertinax. He was murdered, 1 June A.D. 193, and replaced by Severus.

9. *This was formerly . . . omnium bonorum.* The Latin extract originates from Sextius Aurelius Victor, *Epitome de Caesaribus*, 18, though culled by Smollett from Gioffredo, p.49.

10. *Diodorus Siculus . . . divertunt.":* Diodorus Siculus, *Bibliothecae Historicae*, V. 39.

11. *Troglodytæ:* cave-dwellers, inhabitants of the west coast of the Red Sea, along the shores of Upper Egypt and Ethiopia. See Pliny, VI. xxxiv–v.

12. *according to Ælian.* Claudius Aelianus, *De Natura Animalium*, VI. 10. (i); IX. 44.

13. *Sarmatæ:* a people of Asia, who lived on the north-east of the Sea of Azov, east of the Don, which separated them from the Scythians of Europe.

14. *Virgil, in his Georgics . . . terra.":* *Georgics*, III. ll.376–7.


## LETTER XVII

1. *Phocians.* Settlers from Phocaea, the Ionian city on the west coast of Asia Minor, placed a colony at Massilia (Marseilles), *c.* 600 B.C.

2. *Justin. Historiae Philipicae*, XLIII. iii.

3. *Polybius.* Not in Polybius' *History*; but referred to by Gioffredo, p.6.

4. *Tarquinius Priscus:* fifth King of Rome (sixth century B.C.).

5. *Salij:* a Ligurian people who lived west of the Var.

6. *Amadæus, surnamed the Red, duke of Savoy.* Amadeus VII (1360–91), the Red Count, succeeded his father, Amadeus VI, in 1383. He annexed the county of Nice to Savoy in 1388, with the connivance of the local House of Grimaldi.

7. *Vauban.* Sébastien Le Prestre, marquis de Vauban (1633–1707), the

military engineer, visited Nice in 1692–3, after it had fallen to Catinat, and again during its siege by Fitz-James (1705–6). R. Latouche, *Histoire de Nice*, 2 vols., Nice, 1951, I, p.57, reproduces part of Vauban's report of 1693, detailing plans for strengthening the town's fortifications.

8. *Francis I. of France*. King of France (1494–1547), succeeded Louis XII, 1515.

9. *pope Paul II*. Actually Paul III, Alexander Farnese (see XXXII, n. 10).

10. *Mezerai affirms . . . personal interview*. François Eudes de Mezerai (1610–83), the French historian, provides a splendid account of Farnese's machinations, in his *Histoire de France*, 3 vols., 1643–51, II, p.532.

11. *Ambrun:* i.e. Embrun.

12. *Here you may perceive . . . warmest affection*. Many British travellers to Italy in the eighteenth century expressed disgust or incredulity at the strange Italian custom of encouraging a married woman to be seen everywhere in the company of a *cavaliere servente*. Sharp, pp.73–5, condemns the notion that the habit is simply "an innocent kind of dangling fribble", and describes how "if you invite five ladies to dinner, you of course lay ten plates, as each for a certainty brings her Cicesbeo with her." The Earl of Orrery, *Letters from Italy in the Years 1754 and 1755*, ed. John Duncombe, 1773, p.114, considers that the cicisbeo has "many of the privileges of a husband, and all the virtues of an eunuch. He is an appendix to matrimony." See also Baretti, *An Account of the Manners and Customs of Italy*, 2nd edn., 2 vols., 1769, I, pp.101–3; Luigi Valmaggi, *I Cicisbei*, Turin, 1927; cf. XXVII, pp.221–2, for Smollett's further considerations on the subject.

13. *dean Swift's description of the Yahoos*. *Gulliver's Travels*, Bk. IV.

14. *porcheria:* dirtiness, obscenity, filth.

## LETTER XVIII

1. *Mr. B——*. Unidentified.

2. *beccaficas*. See IX, n. 2. *ortolans:* "a species of bunting . . . highly esteemed for its delicate flavour" (*OED*).

3. *Jamaica*. Smollett's familiarity with Jamaica was the result of his visit, *c.* 1742, during which he met his wife. See Knapp, p.38.

4. *presented with the trail:* served with its entrails.

5. *bonita:* the striped tunny.

6. *gurnard*. "Sea-fish with large head, mailed checks, and three free pectoral rays." (*OED*); cf. *Peregrine Pickle*, p.240.

7. *le loup:* type of bass, also known as the sea-wolf or sea-dace.

8. *moustel:* probably the musteline, "a subfamily of dogfishes or small sharks" (*OED*).

9. *the mustela of the antients:* mentioned by Pliny, IX. xxix. 63.

10. *vyvre, or . . . weaver:* i.e. weever, sting-fish.

11. *polype de mer:* octopus.

12. *ecrivisse de mer:* spiny lobster.

13. *Bollani . . . Keysler.* Keysler, III, pp.209–10, informs us that "Ballani or Ballari [are] found alive in large stones. The shell of this fish is thin, rough, and of an oblong figure: it is not unlike a date; hence they are called Dattili del Mare, or sea-dates. They are chiefly found in the shallows near Monte Comero or Conaro, about ten Italian miles from Ancona."

14. *murena:* a kind of eel, described by Pliny, IX. xxxix. 76, 77.

15. *Julius Cæsar . . . lamprey.* Cf. *Peregrine Pickle*, p.240.

16. *rup.* See Albanis de Beaumont, *An Historical and Picturesque Description of the County of Nice,* 1792, p.8: "The pound or weight of this province is equivalent to twelve ounces of France. There is also the rub [*sic*] which weighs twenty-five pounds: this is the weight for common purposes."

17. *garum.* See XXXIX, p.312.

18. *duc de St. Pierre.* Genovese Duca di S. Pietro e Marchese della Guardia: see *Dizionario Storico-Blasanico delle Famiglie Nobile e Notabili Italiane,* ed. G. B. Di Crollalanza, Pisa, 1886–90, I, p.465.


LETTER XIX

1. *Before I tell . . . six-pence sterling.* Sardinian currency at the time of Smollett, with English equivalent:

|  |  | s. | d. |
|---|---|---|---|
| GOLD. | A doppia di savoia = twenty-four livres Piedmontese, or | 24 | 0 |
|  | A mezzo doppia = twelve livres Piedmontese, | 12 | 0 |
| SILVER. | A scudo, or six livre piece, | 6 | 0 |
|  | A mezzo scudo, or three livre piece, | 3 | 0 |
|  | A quarto piece, or pezza di trenta soldi, | 1 | 6 |
| COPPER. |  |  |  |
| SILVERED. | A seven and a half sols piece, |  | 4½ |
|  | A two sols and a half piece, |  | 1½ |
| COPPER. | A one sol piece. |  |  |
|  | A piccalon, or the sixth part of a sol. |  |  |

2. *Martinmass:* the feast of St. Martin, 11 November.

3. *the monks . . . Paolo.* The order of Minims (the name of which is a term

of self-abasement) espoused the vows of poverty, chastity, obedience, and a continual Lent. It was instituted by St. Francis of Paula in 1453.

4. *betteraves:* i.e. beetroots. *chalot:* shallot, scallion.

5. *azerolles.* "The fruit of the Neapolitan Medlar, a species of hawthorn" (*OED*).

6. *a kind of small courge, or gourd:* probably courgette.

7. *badenjean . . . berengena:* aubergine, egg-plant.

8. *This fruit . . . mala insana.* Smollett makes the plausible suggestion that the Italian term for egg-plant, *melanzana*, derives from Latin, *mala insana*. (In English, "mad apple" is given by *OED* as an alternative name for the egg-plant). See also Angelico Prati, *Vocabularo Etimologico Italiano*, Turin, 1951, p.641.

9. *scarlets and hautboys:* types of strawberry. (See *OED*)

10. *bleeding hearts:* popular name for a variety of cherry.

11. *Frontignan.* See XII, n. 2.

12. *balderdash:* adulterate.

13. *cabaret:* tavern.

14. *quintal.* A hundred-weight (112 lbs.); the pound in Nice consisted but of twelve ounces.

15. *sarments:* (obs.) "a cutting of a tree" (*OED*).

16. *fascines:* long bundles of wooden sticks.


LETTER XX

1. *East-India company.* The East India Company, chartered by Queen Elizabeth I in 1600, held the monopoly of trade between England and India. By Robert Clive's victory over the Nabob Surajah Dowlah at Plassey in 1757, the Company had become the effectual ruler of Bengal.

2. *the Levant company.* In 1669, following the proposition of Colbert, Louis XIV ordered the establishment of the Compagnie Fermière du Levant, which operated from Marseilles.

3. *Here is likewise . . . every night.* In 1736, there were 223 Jews in Nice, comprising 43 families. Although prejudices existed, there appears to have been no persecution of the Jews, who set up a centre for Talmudic studies in the Nice ghetto. See Honel Meiss, *A Travers le Ghetto*, Nice, [1924].

4. *All Soul's Day:* 2 November.

5. *the corda or strappado: corda* is the Italian term for strappado.

6. *festi and profesti.* The gods were honoured on the *dies festi*, whereas the

*dies profesti* were ordinary working days. For further details of all these festivals, see William Smith, *A Dictionary of Greek and Roman Antiquities*, 3rd ed., 2 vols., 1890.

7. *agonales:* name for four festivals in the Roman calendar; that on 9 January was in honour of Liber, the Italian Bacchus. *carmentales:* in honour of the nymphs called Carmenta, regarded as goddesses foretelling fortunes of new-born children; celebrated on 11 and 15 January. *lupercales:* in honour of Lupercus, the Lycaean Pan, held not in March, but on 15 February, on the spot where Romulus and Remus were suckled by the wolf. *matronales:* festival representing the purity of old Roman life and the sanctity of marriage, celebrated by the Roman matrons on 1 March. *megalesia:* festival held annually in honour of Rhea, the mother of the gods, taking the form of ceremonial rites and games. *floralia:* in honour of Flora, instituted 238 B.C.; extended by degrees to six days, 28 April to 3 May. *matralia:* celebrated every year on 11 June, in honour of the Mater Matuta, goddess of the dawn of morning. *saturnalia:* held in mid-December, in honour of Saturn, during which work ceased, and was replaced by amusements and misrule. *robigalia:* celebrated on 25th April, instituted by Numa, in honour of the god Robigus. *venalia:* probably *vinalia*, the festival for the tasting of the new wine. *vertumnalia:* held on 12 August, in honour of Vertumnus, Roman god of the seasons. *fornacalia:* moveable festival, in honour of Fornax, goddess of furnaces, celebrated in order that the corn might be properly baked. *palilia:* held on 21 April, in honour of Pales, Roman god of shepherds. *laralia.* Special offerings were made to the Lares, gods of the household, at several times during the year. *latinæ.* The Latinæ was the name given to colonies founded after the destruction of the Latin League in 340 B.C. Their festivals were adopted by the Romans, in order to cement the alliance. *paganales.* The Italian pagi (cantons) had their tutelary deities and sanctuaries; various festivals were held in their honour (e.g. at the end of January to celebrate the end of seed-time). *sementinæ:* festival, fixed by the pontiffs, kept in seed-time at Rome for the purpose of praying to Tellus and Ceres for a good crop. *compitales:* celebrated once a year in honour of the Lares compitales, who presided over the various divisions of Rome, which were marked by the compita, or the points where two or more streets crossed each other. *imperativæ.* The feriæ imperativæ were held on certain emergencies at the command of the consuls, prætors, or a dictator. *novemdalia.* Whenever a rain of stones was believed to have happened, the anger of the gods was appeased by a festival lasting nine days.

8. *kalends, nones and ides.* In the Roman calendar, the kalends always denoted the first of the month; the nones were the seventh day of March, May, July, and October, and the fifth day of other months; the ides were on the fifteenth day of March, May, July, and October, and the thirteenth of all other months.

9. *dies alliensis:* a *dies nefastus*, or unlucky day, in memory of the defeat of the Romans by the Gauls and the Veii on the banks of the River Allia, north of Rome, in 390 B.C.

10. *as Lucan says . . . allia fastis.* Lucan, *Pharsalia*, VII. l.409.

11. *Now I am speaking . . . calendar condemn'd.* The source of Smollett's list of Roman festivals is *Roma Antica*, III, pp.103–5; see XXIX, n. 31. Martz, p.74 note, is justified in pointing out that "Smollett has derived some details here from another source".

### LETTER XXI

1. *fanal, or lanthorn:* lighthouse, beacon.

2. *feluccas:* small coasting vessels about the size of a common barge, propelled by oars or sails.

3. *tour du baton:* perquisites.

4. *Patois, from the Latin . . . his own country.* OED states that the origin of the term *patois* is unknown. Littré, *Dictionnaire de la Langue Française*, gives a not entirely satisfactory derivation through *patois*, which originates from low Latin *patriensis*, a native. Smollett's derivation, through *patavinitas*, stems from Gaius Asinius Pollio (76 B.C.–A.D. 4 or 5), who objected to the use made by Livy of the dialectical peculiarities of his native *Patavium* (Padua). Cf. *Letters*, p.123.

5. *Mr. Walpole . . . surnamed Cœur de Lion.* See Horace Walpole, *A Catalogue of Royal and Noble Authors*, 2nd edn. ("corrected and enlarged"), 2 vols., London, 1759, I, pp.6–8, which includes the poem "Reiz Rizard" (called by him "the King's sonnet"), the MS. of which he says may be found in the library of St. Lorenzo, Florence.

6. *Voltaire . . . the same language.* See *Essay Sur l'Histoire Générale*, 9 vols., n.p., 1758–1763, II, pp.171–2 (part of Ch. LXIX, "Mœurs & Usages, Arts, Sciences, vers les treiziéme & quatorziéme Siécles."). The same specimens of Provençal poetry may be found in the translation, co-edited by Smollett, Franklin, and others, of *The Works of M. de Voltaire*, 36 vols., 1761–9, III, pp.30–2.

7. *a canzon or hymn . . . lately printed at Nice.* The printed source of this hymn was probably a collection of "cansons", many of which were published in the Provence during the eighteenth century. G. Fumagalli, *Dictionnaire Geographique d'Italie pour Servir à l'Histoire de l'Imprimerie dans ce Pays*, Florence, 1905, p.262, states that Nice had a printing house from 1619.

### LETTER XXII

1. *hough:* i.e. hoe.

2. *Meliga . . . Indian corn:* i.e. maize.

3. *hasty-pudding.* "A pudding made of flour stirred in boiling milk or water to the consistency of a thick batter" (*OED*).

4. *pectoral.* "A medicine, food, or drink, good for affections of the chest" (*OED*).

5. *paillasses:* straw mattresses.

6. *catamenia:* menstruation.

7. *damascene:* damascene plum, a damson.

8. *wind up my bottom. OED* lists "the cocoon of a silkworm" as an obsolete meaning of "bottom" recording the use of this term to 1665. The idiomatic usage of the phrase "wind up one's bottom", signifying "to sum up, conclude", survived into the eighteenth century.

## LETTER XXIII

1. *frails:* "A kind of basket made of rushes, used for packing figs, raisins, etc." (*OED*).

## LETTER XXIV

1. *Ever since my arrival . . . state of my health.* Smollett suffered from this complaint for a number of years. See XL, p. 322; *Letters,* pp. 30, 132.

2. *tabes.* "Slow progressive emaciation of the body or its parts" (*OED*).

3. *Mr. Sch——z.* Schutz. Writing from Nice, 20 April 1767 (Fitzwilliam [Milton] Correspondence, Northamptonshire Record Office), the second Earl Fitzwilliam describes Mr. Schutz as "without exception the *best hearted* man I ever met with in my life. . . . He is the best advocate I know for this Climate, for this is the second time, that he has been brought to life again by the air of Nice, within these three years". Possibly George Frederick Schutz (1724–1802), groom to George III as Prince of Wales (*Horace Walpole's Correspondence,* ed W. S. Lewis, 1960, 20, p. 15n.). For details of the family of Schutz see Falconer Madan, *The Madan Family,* Oxford, 1933, pp. 65–8.

4. *sub Dio:* in the open air; cf. *Humphry Clinker,* pp. 89–90.

5. *Lebeche . . . Lybicus:* i.e. Libeccio, the Italian name for the south-west wind.

6. *Fahrenheit's thermometer:* named after Gabriel Daniel Fahrenheit (1686–1736), its inventor.

7. *the Sabine mountains:* the Roman Apennines, or Sibillini Mountains.

8. *july-flowers:* gillyflowers.

9. *peripneumonies:* inflammation of the lungs, i.e. pneumonia. *ardent fevers:* burning fevers.

10. *putrid fevers.* "A name for typhus fever" (*OED*). *exanthemata:* pustules, or eruptions. *erisipelatous:* febrile disease causing deep red colour on skin (commonly known as St. Anthony's fire). *miliary eruptions:* rash characterized by spots resembling millet-seeds.

11. *Rocabiliare:* i.e. Roquebillière.

12. *the curé.* The *curé* of Rocabiliare, who succeeded Jean-Baptiste Robaudi in 1756, was dom Delbecchi.


## LETTER XXV

1. *Dr. A——:* probably Dr. John Armstrong (1709–79), author of the poem, *The Art of Preserving Health* (1744). For his relationship with Smollett, see Lewis M. Knapp, "Dr. John Armstrong", *PMLA*, LIX, 1944, pp. 1019–58.

2. *But, as there is a road . . . Riviera of Genoa.* Until the construction at the time of Napoleon of the Corniche road, most British travellers to Italy followed the arduous route from Geneva over the Alps, via Chambéry and Mount Cenis, to Turin.

3. *Itinerarium of Antoninus.* See *Itinerarium Antonini Augusti*, ed. G. Parthey and M. Pinder, Berlin 1848, pp. 139–42, which lists the route of the Via Aurelia, "a Roma per Tusciam et Alpes maritimas Arelatum usque".

4. *Marcus Aurelius.* Marcus Aurelius Antoninus (A.D. 121–80), Roman emperor from A.D. 161, author of the famous *Meditations.*

5. *calash:* a type of light carriage.

6. *Miss C——.* Anne Curry; see II, n. 3.

7. *Mr. R——.* Unidentified. In the MS. edition of the *Travels*, there are two instances in which he is referred to as "R——i", emended by Smollett to "R——y". See Knapp, p. 257.

8. *The present prince . . . Grimaldi.* Honoré-Camille-Léonor Grimaldi (Honoratus III) became Prince of Monaco in 1733. His mother, Louise-Hippolyte Grimaldi (1697–1731), the heiress of Monaco, married in 1715, Jacques-François-Léonor de Goyon, Sire de Matignon and comte de Thorigny (1689–1751). In 1731, on the death of his father-in-law, Goyon became Prince of Monaco, but later gave the title to his eldest son.

9. *three small towns.* Monaco, Rocquebrune, and Menton. The last two are now part of France.

10. *This consists . . . in that kingdom.* Honoré Grimaldi (Honoratus II), Prince of Monaco, (1599–1662), placed himself under French protection when he drove the Spanish garrison from Monaco. When, in 1641, Spain

deprived the Grimaldis of possessions in the Kingdom of Naples and in the States of Milan, Louis XIII granted Honoratus the Duchy of Valentinois.

11. *hedge ale-house.* As an adjective in this context, "hedge" denotes "mean" or "inferior"; cf. *Roderick Random*, p.33.

12. *maestro di capella:* choir-master; sometimes, a composer.

13. *The people of St. Remo . . . diet of the empire.* In June 1753, the Genoese galleys, under the command of Agostino Pinelli, put an end to the revolt of St. Remo by bombarding the town. A garrison was left to keep order. The Diet of Ratisbon, in response to the appeal of the people of St. Remo, published an ineffectual treatise, *Memorie Risguardanti la Superiorità Imperiale Sopra le Città di Genova e di S. Remo,* 3 vols., Ratisbon, 1769 (French edn. 1768), claiming that on historical grounds the whole Riviera belonged to the Empire.

14. *Their dress . . . Georgia and Mingrelia.* Eugène Schuyler, "Smollett in Search of Health", *The Nation,* XLVIII, New York, 1889, p.425, suggests: "This supposed resemblance came probably from the fact that the women of the Riviera then generally covered their heads and shoulders with squares of cotton stuff, printed in bright colors, with Eastern designs; this garment is known as the *mezzaro,* and is still sometimes used in small villages on such occasions as the Christmas midnight mass. . . ." The former principality of Mingrelia, now forming part of N.W. Georgia, U.S.S.R., borders on the Black Sea.

15. *Finale is the capital . . . the year 1745.* The Genoese Republic, having purchased Finale from Charles VI of Austria in 1713, contested the action of his daughter, Maria Theresa, who, by the Treaty of Worms in 1743, ceded to the King of Sardinia all claims she had to the Marquisate of Finale. The Genoese, in possession of Finale, sued France and Spain for protection, and in 1745, Don Philip led the Spanish army into Italy, temporarily stripping the King of Sardinia of all his dominions. In response, the English fleet bombarded Finale, and in 1746, Genoa fell to the Austrians.

16. *St. Elmo:* patron saint of sailors; probably St. Erasmus (*c.* A.D. 303), a Syrian bishop, who died under the persecution of Diocletian.

17. *s——m——te:* sodomite.

18. *La Croix de Malthe. A Brief Account of the Roads of Italy,* 1775, p.19, recommends "at Genoa, the Cross of Malta. & S. Marta".

## LETTER XXVI

1. *Mr. R——.* Unidentified; see XXV, n. 7.

2. *fripier:* old-clothes-man.

3. *bank of St. George.* See Watkins, I, pp.251–2: "the celebrated *Bank of St. George,* established since the commencement of the fifteenth century . . . is

. . . managed exclusively by its own laws, and separate directors; its capital is immense, its credit universal, and the security as firm as the defenceless condition of Genoa will admit. In 1746 it supported the republic in its distress, by advancing 750,000 l. the whole of which . . . has been liquidated."

4. *the misfortunes . . . war of 1745.* Genoa capitulated before the advancing Austrian army in 1746, but the people, objecting to the heavy imposition and oppressive rule, suddenly revolted and threw out the enemy, slaughtering vast numbers of them.

5. *Nothing shews . . . in the field.* The Corsicans, under Genoese rule since the fifteenth century, revolted several times during the second quarter of the eighteenth century. With the return of Pasquale Paoli (1725–1807), whose father had been exiled to Naples, the rebels began to organize themselves, for a while taking over the island. In 1768, the Genoese, despairing of conquering Corsica, sold it to the French, who immediately invaded and overran the island, General Paoli escaping to England. See Boswell's *Account of Corsica*, 1768.

6. *True it is . . . share in the booty.* It was insinuated in various quarters that the marquis de Botta-Adorno (1688–1774), the Austrian general, was bribed by the Genoese to give up the city into their hands. Watkins, I, p. 271, tells us that Botta "suffered himself to be surprised and driven out of Genoa, by the populace,–perhaps by money." Far from being dropped from favour, Botta was later raised to Marshal of the Imperial army and appointed governor of Florence, a post he still held in 1764 when Smollett was there. See Gibbon, pp. 220–1, who gives an unflattering portrait of him.

7. *"There are mysteries . . . Horatio!":* A corruption of *Hamlet*, I. v. 167–8:
> There are more things in heaven and earth, Horatio,
> Than are dreamt of in your philosophy.

8. *You see how favourably . . . any thing to fear.* Tsar Peter III succeeded to the throne on the death of his aunt, Tsarina Elizabeth (1709–62). His wife, Catherine (1729–96) plotted "to establish an independent interest in favour of herself and her son, the grand duke Paul Petrowitz, whom his father had not yet nominated to the succession." (*Continuation*, v, p. 86.) The Tsar was deposed in June 1762 and died in prison after seven days, an "event, which was indeed the natural consequence of his deposition." (ibid. p. 89.) In 1764, Ivan VI, great-grandson of Peter the Great, supplanted as a child by Elizabeth and claimed by many to be the true successor to the Russian throne, was murdered in prison, where he had spent most of his life. Catherine's son, the unbalanced Paul, born in 1754, survived her to become Paul I, but was murdered in 1801.

9. *I have seen . . . mischief.* Smollett took part in the bombardment of Boca Chica during the ill-fated attack on Cartagena in 1741. See his "Account of the Expedition against Carthagene", in his *Compendium of Authentic and Entertaining Voyages*, second edn., 7 vols., 1766, v. p. 325; also *Roderick Random*, ch. XXXI–XXXIV.

10. *Don Philip.* Don Philip (1720–65), second son of Philip V of Spain and Elizabeth Farnese, married Louise-Elizabeth of France, daughter of Louis XV (1739). During the War of the Austrian Succession, he led several armies into Italy, occupying Nice (1744) and continuing the campaign into Piedmont. In 1745, he led the Spanish army along the coast to Genoa, but was less successful in northern Italy (1746). By the Treaty of Aix-la-Chapelle (1748), he was granted the duchy of Parma.

11. *baron de Leutrum.* Frederick de Leutrum (1692–1755), a German Protestant, naturalized Piedmontese, entered the Sardinian service in 1707. As governor of Coni (1744), he was responsible for the gallant defence of the town during a two month-long siege by the French and Spanish armies, under the prince de Conti and Don Philip. See Giuseppe De-Botazzi, *Barone Frederico Leutrum*, Turin, 1899, pp.76–116.

12. *abbate:* abbot; cleric.

13. *Hard by . . . an elegant church:* church of Santa Maria Carignano.

14. *the cathedral:* church of San Lorenzo.

15. *Hungerford-stairs:* on the Thames, below the Strand, and between Craven St. and Villiers St., now part of the Victoria Embankment.

16. *For this vehicle . . . three paoli a horse.* The cost of travelling *cambiatura* is confirmed by Northall, pp.22–3: "The expence of each post is eight pauls for a chaise, and three to the driver." The *paolo* or *paul* (sometimes called *julio*) was a coin of the Ecclesiastic State, worth about sixpence in Smollett's time.

17. *Then entering . . . duke of Modena.* In 1741, Hercule-Renaud d'Este (1727–1803), son and heir of Francis III, Duke of Modena, married Marie-Thérèse de Cibo (1725–1790), daughter and heiress of Alderano I, fourth Duke of Massa (1690–1731). As a consequence, Massa passed into the hands of the Dukes of Modena.


## LETTER XXVII

1. *the solitude . . . place of residence.* On his return to Italy in Autumn 1768, Smollett settled near Pisa, and passed two winters there. See Knapp, pp.279–87, and my own, "An Unrecorded Smollett Letter", *Ariel*, II, no. 4, 1971, pp.87–9.

2. *the emperor's gallies . . . in the town.* Smollett probably got his information from Keysler, I, pp.485–6, who describes the building of galleys as "the only particular advantage to artificers" in Pisa. When he settled in Pisa a few years later, he added the footnote as a correction in his MS. edition.

3. *Cosmo.* Cosimo I (1519–1574), first Medici Grand Duke of Tuscany, called the Great.

4. *Ferdinand I.* Ferdinand de' Medici (1549–1609), third Grand Duke.

5. *a Greek architect from Constantinople.* Buschetto, a Byzantine Greek, was the first architect of the duomo of Pisa, in the eleventh century.

6. *giullo:* i.e. giallo antico, a rich yellow marble. *verde antico.* "An ornamental variety of marble, consisting chiefly of serpentine mixed with calcite and dolomite" (*OED*).

7. *the other . . . Lacedemonia.* Mons Taygetus is the tallest mountain in the Peloponnese, immediately above ancient Sparta. Strabo, *Geography*, VIII. 5. 7. speaks of "Taenarius lapis".

8. *John of Bologna.* Giovanni Bologna, also known as Giambologna (1529–1608), the famous sculptor.

9. *Ghiotto . . . Buffalmaco.* Giotto (*c.* 1266–1336); Giottino (fl. mid-fourteenth century), sometimes identified with Giotto di Maestro Stefano; Stefano, probably Stefano Fiorentino (1301–50), a disciple of Giotto; Bennoti, probably Benozzo Gozzoli (*c.* 1420–97); Buffalmaco, Cristofani Buonamico (1262–*c.* 1351), a pupil of Andrea Tafi. Not all these artists are considered by modern art historians to have worked on the Campo Santo.

10. *The history of Job . . . admired.* Attributed to Giotto by Vasari; now thought to be the work of Taddeo Gaddi (d. 1366), who was the pupil of Giotto.

11. *Buona Roti.* Michelangelo Buonarroti (1475–1564).

12. *Pope Gregory XIII.* Gregory Boncampagni (1502–85), born in Bologna, became pope in 1572. His brother, Giovanni, a jurist, died in 1544. The cenotaph in his honour was the work of Bartolommeo Ammannati (1511–92).

13. *touchstone:* basanite; "a very smooth, fine-grained, black or dark-coloured variety of quartz or jasper" (*OED*).

14. *Meleager:* legendary Greek hero, who hunted and killed the Caly-donian boar.

15. *countess Beatrice.* Beatrice de Lorraine, Countess of Tuscany, governed Tuscany from the assassination of her husband, Boniface III, in 1052, to her death in 1076, when she was succeeded by Matilda (1046–1115).

16. *Caius and Lucius . . . the emperor.* See X, n. 6.

17. *aller:* (obs.) alder.

18. *I lodged . . . good and reasonable.* Vanini's is recommended by *The Gentleman's Guide in his Tour through Italy*, 1787, p.xxxii, as "a very good hotel". It was presumably run by the same Mary Vanini, who was a witness, with the Smolletts, to the marriage of Anne Curry and George Renner in 1769; Knapp, pp.283–4. Lady Anne Miller, *Letters from Italy*, 2nd edn., 2 vols., 1777, I, pp.362–3, gives a highly complimentary account of the household. See also *Humphry Clinker*, p.183.

19. *a palm.* Nugent (1749), III, p.65, notes: "A *Roman* palm, or a span and a

half, makes thirteen inches *English* measure."

20. *the inhabitants flatter . . . palace of Pitti.* Archduke Peter Leopold (1747–92), third son of Francis, Duke of Lorraine, and Maria Theresa of Hungary, married Marie-Louisa, daughter of Charles III of Spain in August 1764, and succeeded his father as Grand Duke of Tuscany in 1765. In 1790, on the death of his brother Joseph, he became Emperor Leopold II.

21. *If we may believe Leti . . . ships of war.* According to Gregorio Leti (1630–1701), the prolific Protestant historian, in his *L'Italia Regnante,* 4 vols., Valenza [actually Geneva], 1675–6, II, pp.294–303, the Grand Duke Cosimo III (1642–1723) possessed the most powerful army in Italy, including "nell' Arsenale di Pisa . . . 12 Galere, due Galeazze, due Gallioni, e vinti Vasselli di Guerra" (p.297).

22. *He that now commands . . . admiral of Tuscany.* Commodore John Acton (1704–66) was visited at Pisa by his relative, Edward Gibbon, the historian, who describes him in a letter, dated Rome, 9 October 1764, *Letters of Edward Gibbon,* ed. J. E. Norton, 3 vols., 1956, I, pp.183–4, as "in a most melancholy situation. Last winter he had a most violent attack of the Apoplexy; whilst in that situation he was persuaded either from motives of interest or devotion to change his religion in which he had been till then very steady. The immediate consequence of which imprudent step was the total neglect of all his English friends . . . I never saw a more lively picture of an unhappy man." See also Warren H. Smith, *Originals Abroad,* Yale, 1952, pp.115–25.

23. *the anniversary of a charitable institution.* Knapp, p.257, considers that this "was presumably the great annual procession of the Compagnia della Misericordia". For details of the latter, see *Enciclopedia Italiana.*

24. *Free-Masons.* Knapp, p.111, suggests that Smollett might have been a member of the Masonic group which met at the White Swan in Chelsea. See also, *Letters,* p.118. *Gregoreans.* "A society (often classed with the Freemasons), which existed in England in the eighteenth century" (*OED*). *Antigallicans:* opposed to the French, and, in consequence, to the Gallican church; see *NQ,* eleventh series, IV, 1911, pp.512–13.

25. *cicisbei.* See XVII, n. 12.

26. *Goldoni.* Carlo Goldoni (1707–93), the Venetian-born dramatist, creator of modern Italian comedy.

27. *Improvisatore. OED* quotes *Travels* as earliest example of the use of this word in English.

28. *Mr. Corvesi, my landlord.* Smollett's landlord at Nice; see XXXIX, n. 1.

## LETTER XXVIII

1. *The famous gallery . . . are held.* The comparison of the Uffizi Palace to a

Greek Π is made by Addison, p.236. Cf. Gibbon, p.130 and note; Watkins, I, p.297.

2. *Vasari*. Giorgio Vasari (1511–74), painter, architect, and author of *Le Vite de' più eccellenti Architetti, Pittori, e Scultori Italiani*, first published 1550.

3. *the Lycæum:* the garden with covered walks at Athens, where Aristotle taught his philosophy. *the groves of Academus:* a wood outside Athens, famous for its plane trees and olive plantations, where Plato taught.

4. *Suetonius*. Roman historian, fl. second century A.D., author of *The Lives of the Twelve Caesars*.

5. *Dion Cassius*. Roman historian (*c.* A.D. 150–235), the author of a history of Rome, written in Greek.

6. *Caracalla*. Marcus Aurelius Antoninus Caracalla (A.D. 186–217), Roman emperor from 211, succeeding his father Septimius Severus.

7. *In the language . . . that surname*. In 1762, James Macpherson (1736–96) had published *Fingal*, an ancient epic poem in six books, claiming it to be the work of Ossian, the legendary Gaelic poet. In the preface (p. viii), Macpherson asserts that "The Caracul of Fingal is no other than Caracalla, who, as the son of Severus, the Emperor of Rome, whose dominions were extended almost over the known world, was not without reason called in the poems of Ossian, *the Son of the King of the World*." Smollett's correction is just: *caracalla* was the name of a long tunic and hood worn by the Gauls, and adopted by the emperor, who as a result received the nickname by which he is usually known.

8. ὑπόδρα ἰδω`ν: threatening look; see Homer, *Iliad*, 1, l.148.

9. *thyrsus*. "A staff . . . tipped with an ornament like a pine-cone, . . . borne by Bacchus" (*OED*).

10. *Ganymede:* a beautiful youth, made immortal by Jupiter, to serve as his cup-bearer,

11. *Æsculapius*. Roman god of medicine and of healing.

12. *pallium:* kind of cloak or mantle, worn chiefly by the Greeks.

13. *Hunc modo . . . Perspice——*. Ovid, *Metamorphoses*, xv. ll.659–60.

14. *fascia herbarum:* fillet of medicinal herbs. *crepidæ:* type of sandal.

15. *Antinous, the favourite of Adrian:* a youth of extraordinary beauty, taken by the emperor Hadrian as his page; drowned in the Nile, *c.* A.D. 122.

16. *Oxydrace:* a great nation of the Punjab which resisted Alexander's advances, in battle with whom he was nearly killed.

17. *Cydnus:* river of Cilicia.

18. *a beautiful head of Alexander . . . to conquer*. The academic controversy over the bust of Alexander seems to have been brought to the attention of

visitors to the gallery. Addison, pp.237–8, who, like Smollett, admires the beauty of this work, thinks "the Sculptor had in his Thoughts the Conqueror's weeping for new Worlds, or some other the like Circumstance of his History." A later traveller, Moore, II, p.361, follows Smollett by listing the differences in opinion among the virtuosi "with regard to the circumstance in which the sculptor has intended to represent the hero" but concludes "how very uncertain a business this of a virtuoso is."

19. *Bianchi . . . great deal of money*. The curator of the museum, Giuseppe Bianchi, was the author of *Ragguaglio delle Antichità e Rarità che si Conservano nella Galleria Mediceo-Imperiale di Firenze*, part I, Florence, 1759, identified by Martz, pp.80–2, as the guide-book used by Smollett "to supplement his observations on the Uffizi Gallery". See also Introduction, p.xx.

20. *the Morpheus . . . described by Addison*. See Addison, pp.238–9: "Among the antique Figures there is a fine one of *Morpheus* in Touch-stone. . . . I at first took it for a *Cupid*, 'till I had taken notice that it had neither Bow nor Quiver . . .

'Tis probable they chose to represent the God of Sleep under the Figure of a Boy, contrary to all our modern Designers, because it is that Age, which has its Repose the least broken by Cares and Anxieties . . ."

21. *Praxiteles*. Greek sculptor, fl. fourth century B.C.

22. *Thespiæ*: an ancient town in Boeotia, situated at the foot of Mt. Helicon. The courtesan Phryne presented to Thespiæ, her native city, the celebrated statue of Cupid by Praxiteles.

23. *With respect to the famous Venus . . . out of character*. The veneration accorded the Venus de Medicis is typified by John, Earl of Orrery, *Letters from Italy in the Years 1754 and 1755*, 1773, pp.79–80: "beyond them all is the *Venus*. There I saw *artis summum opus*. Human power can go no further." Cf. *The Monthly Review*, XXXIV, 1766, pp.426–7, "we are unable to conceive any possible attitude more graceful and proper for a naked female"; and the *Journal Encyclopédique*, VI, 1 septembre 1766, p.91. It is important to remember that there were other travellers who agreed with Smollett, e.g. Keysler, II, p.20: "Amidst the admiration of all ages, . . . the Venus of Medicis has not escaped censure. Most connoisseurs agree that the head is rather too small in proportion to the other parts of the body, and particularly the hips; some find fault with the largeness of the nose; possibly the partition along the *vertebræ* of the back is a little too deep, considering the object is a soft plump female ..." See Introduction, pp.xv–xvi.

24. *"Hercle quanta dorsi . . . flabby consistence!"*: Pseudo-Lucian, *Affairs of the Heart*, 14 (Loeb edition, VIII, 1967). According to the Loeb editor, M. D. Macdonald, this dialogue was probably written by an imitator of Lucian, *c*. third century A.D.

25. *One cannot help . . . Athenian people*. Cf. Bianchi, pp.236–7, the source of much of Smollett's factual information.

26. *the conspiracy of Cataline*. Catiline's conspiracy, in 63 B.C., to establish himself as dictator was disclosed to Cicero by the mistress of one of the plotters, and Catiline was defeated in battle.

27. *The marquis de Maffei*. Smollett has in error taken Bianchi's reference to "Il Cavalier Maffei" (p.237) for Francesco Scipione, marquis de Maffei (1675–1755), the famous archaeologist and poet, whereas the allusion is to the little-known Italian archaeologist, Paolo Alessandro Maffei (1653–1716), "cav. dell' Ordine di S. Stefano e della Gvardia Pontificia", author of *Raccolta di Statue Antiche e Moderne*, Rome, 1704, which contains (p.42) a detailed description of the Arrotino.

28. *Others alledge . . . the conspiracy*. Milichus gave Nero the first information of Piso's conspiracy, A.D. 66, for which he was rewarded by the emperor with his freedom.

29. *Attius Navius:* a renowned augur, or soothsayer, supposed to have cut a whetstone with a razor, at the behest of Tarquin, 6th century B.C.

30. *Vaillant.* Jean Foy-Vaillant (1632–1706), French numismatist and historian, author of *Numismata Imperatorum Romanorum Praestantiora*, Paris, 1682, which ran through several editions.

31. *cotes:* whetstone (Latin: *cos, cotis*); not in *OED*.

32. *what pleased me best . . . in any history*. Other travellers also point out the different interpretations offered for this statue. See Gibbon, p.182; Moore, II, 363–4. Seccombe, p.lii, notes that the statue "is now described as 'A Scythian whetting his knife to flay Marsyas'". For the source of Smollett's description, see Bianchi, pp.237–8.

33. *the Peace of Bretigny:* known as the Great Peace of 1360, concluded by Edward III and the Black Prince with the King of France.

34. *In this cathedral . . . a taylor*. Northall, p.87, notes that Hawkwood "was a native of Sibble Hemingham, in Essex, and at first served as a common soldier in the wars of king Edward III. against France. He was knighted by that monarch for his bravery, and afterwards entered into the service of the Florentines, who conferred the greatest honours upon him when living, and buried him in the most pompous manner, in gratitude to his merit." The fresco to Hawkwood in the Duomo of Florence is the work of Paolo Uccello.

35. *Lorenzo Ghiberti*. Florentine sculptor (1378–1455).

36. *the old observation . . . the brain*. Possibly a combination by Smollett of two familiar proverbs, "That which is good for the *back* is bad for the head" (J. Ray, *A Compleat Collection of English Proverbs*, 1737, p.75); and "The German's wit is in his fingers" (G. L. Apperson, *English Proverbs and Proverbial Phrases*, 1929, p.245).

37. *Lysippus*. Greek sculptor, c. B.C. 370–324.

### LETTER XXIX

1. *Æneas Sylvius . . . Pius II.* Æneas Silvius de Piccolmini, (1405–64), born near Siena, became Pope in 1458.

2. *Pietro Perugino.* Pietro Vannucci (*c.* 1446–1523), called Perugino.

3. *Henry VII.* Henry of Luxemburg (*c.* 1275–1313) became Holy Roman Emperor in 1308. He is supposed to have been poisoned with a consecrated host, administered to him by Bernardo di Montepolitiano, a Dominican friar.

4. *stone-horses:* stallions.

5. *the British minister at Florence.* Sir Horace Mann (1701–86), minister from 1740, celebrated for his correspondence with Horace Walpole. See *DNB.*

6. *Sejanus.* Roman politican and conspirator (d. A.D. 31).

7. *according . . . the Grand Tour.* Nugent (1749), III, p.322.

8. *Vides . . . Soracte.* Horace, *Carmina*, I, ix, ll.1–2.

9. *Pliny tells us . . . urbe Roma.* Pliny, VII. ii. 19.

10. *And Desprez . . . Monte S. Oreste.* See Horace, *Opera*, ed. Ludovicus Desprez, 11th ed., 1752, p.25: "Hodie *Monte S. Oreste* vocatur".

11. *Addison . . . in the Campania.* See Addison, p.103: "In my way to *Rome*, seeing a high Hill standing by itself in the *Campania*, I did not question but it had a *Classic* Name, and upon Enquiry found it to be Mount *Soracte*. The *Italians* at present call it, because its name begins with an *S*, St. *Oreste.*"

12. *villegiatura.* "An early adaptation by Smollett of the Italian word for country retirement" (Seccombe, p.352).

13. *the Campania . . . a desert.* Many eighteenth-century travellers remark with horror the desolation of the once fertile Campania. Nugent (1749), III, p.62, cautions tourists to "lie thirty or forty miles short of *Rome*, if they cannot reach that city before night" on account of disease caused by "the serain or evening dew". Cf. Gibbon, p.235; Sharp, pp.49–50.

14. *The Grand Tour . . . both ends.* Nugent (1749), III, p.325.

15. *we are informed by Suetonius.* Lives of the Caesars, VI, "Nero", l.

16. *Gruterus.* Jean Gruter (1560–1672), author of *Inscriptiones Antiquæ.*

17. *Giacomo Alberici . . . History of the Church.* Alberici (d. 1610) was the author of *Compendio delle Grandezze dell'Illustre et Devotissima Chiesa di Santa Maria del Popolo di Roma*, Rome, 1600. Smollett seems to have thought that the "Compendio Istorico della Chiesa presente", referred to in *Roma Antica* (see XXIX, n. 31), was a general "History of the Church".

18. *pope Paschal II.* Paschal II (d. 1118) succeeded Urban II to the papacy in 1099.

19. *Æmilius Censor.* M. Æmilius Lepidus, censor in 179 B.C.

20. *Maxentius.* Roman emperor (d. A.D. 312), killed in battle against Constantine (c. 274–337), joint-emperor from 306, when the Milvian bridge broke under him and he was drowned in the Tiber.

21. *comitiæ:* assemblies of the Roman people.

22. *and when the bridge . . . parallel.* Old Black-Friars Bridge, begun in 1760, was completed in 1769, after the design of Robert Mylne (1734–1811), a Scotsman, with whom Smollett was probably acquainted; see F. Felsenstein, "An Unrecorded Smollett Letter", *Ariel*, II, no. 4, 1971, p.89; *Humphry Clinker*, p.87. See also IX, n. 6.

23. *Vidimus . . . Uxorius Amnis.* Horace, *Carmina*, I. ii, ll.13–20.

24. *We saw . . . to the Sea.* In his MS. edition of the *Travels*, Smollett gives directions to "insert the translation of these lines from Francis's version of ode II lib I." The translation incorporated here is from Philip Francis, *The Odes, Epodes, and Carmen Seculare of Horace*, 4 vols., Dublin, 1742, I.

25. *Livy . . . parati sint"*—Titus Livius, *Annales*, XXX, 38.10.

26. *Altera . . . equos.* Ovid, *Fasti*, III, ll.519–22.

27. *Dominico Fontana.* Italian architect (1543–1607). Fontana contributed to the building of St. Peter's, and was responsible for the Vatican Library and the Palace of Monte Cavallo.

28. *Sixtus V.* Felice Peretti (1521–90), Cardinal Montalto, Pope from 1585.

29. *vitella mongana:* sucking calf.

30. *the little manual . . . castelli suburbani.* Smollett refers here to Giuseppe Vasi's *Itinerario istruttivo diviso in otto stazioni o giornate per ritrovare con facilità tutte le antiche e moderne magnificenze di Roma . . . Con una breve digressione sopra alcune città e castelli suburbani*, Rome, stamp. di E. Pagliarini, 1763, which he used as the source for some of his information. For details on Vasi, see *Biografia degli Italiani Illustri . . . del Secolo XVIII*, 10 vols., Venice, 1834–45, VI, pp.124–6.

31. *Roma antica, e moderna.* The anonymous guide-book, *Roma Antica, e Moderna*, 3 vols., Rome, 1750, was Smollett's major source-book in his account of Rome. For the extent of Smollett's borrowings, see Martz, pp.73–80; Oxford edition, Appendix III.

32. *Piranesi.* Giovanni Battista Piranesi (1720–78), the Venetian architect, famous for his engravings and etchings of Rome, where he settled in 1744.

33. *cantatrice.* "A female professional singer" (*OED*).

34. *a boy of seventy-two.* Possibly William Hewett [Huet] (1693–1766/7) of Stretton, Leicestershire, an English eccentric of whom there is a detailed description in *Humphry Clinker*, pp.182–3. According to Smollett, Hewett, whose nickname was "Cavallo Bianco, from his appearing always

mounted on a pale horse, like Death in the Revelation", made the "Giro or circuit" of Italy twelve times in as many years.

35. *cicerone*: learned antiquarian; guide.


## LETTER XXX

1. *spirit of hartshorn*. "The aqueous solution of ammonia" (*OED*). Cf. *Humphry Clinker*, p.65.

2. *Claudius*. Tiberius Claudius Drusus Nero Germanicus (10 B.C.–A.D. 54), Roman emperor from A.D. 41.

3. *Rutilius*. Roman poet (fl. 5th century A.D.), author of the poem *De Reditu Suo*.

4. *Vespasian*. Titus Flavius Vespasianus (A.D. 9–79), emperor from A.D. 70.

5. *Heliogabalus*. Elagabalus (A.D. 205–22), emperor from 218; slain and succeeded by Alexander Severus.

6. *"trahentia . . . agris."*: Horace, *Satires*, II, VIII, ll.55–6.

7. *Boreas:* the north wind.

8. *ne turpe . . . tibi te*. Horace, *Epistles*, I, V, ll.22–4.

9. *Sed nimis . . . capræ:* ibid. l.29.

10. *triclinium:* couch running round three sides of the table; a table-couch.

11. *purgamenta . . . cænuntium*. See Lucius Annaeus Seneca, *Controversiarum*, IX, 2 (25), 4 (ed. H. J. Müller, Vienna, 1887), usually attributed nowadays to Seneca's father, M. Annaeus Seneca (d. A.D. 39).

12. *Scalæ Gemoniæ:* the flight of steps leading up the Capitoline on which the bodies of executed criminals were displayed. *Tarpeian rock:* the cliff from which convicted murderers were flung to their death.

13. *cloaca maxima:* the main sewer of ancient Rome, supposed to have been built by Tarquinius Superbus.

14. *enfans trouvés*. See II, n. 4.

15. *Circa cultum . . . sumpserit*. Suetonius, *Lives of the Caesars*, VI, "Nero", li.

16. *Otho*. Marcus Salvius Otho (A.D. 32–69), Roman emperor in 69, who killed himself after being defeated in battle by Vitellius.

17. *propter . . . capillorum*. Suetonius, op. cit., VII, "Otho", xii.

18. *Septimius Severus:* born A.D. 146, Roman emperor from 193 to 211.

19. *mentioned by Aulus Gellius*. Aulus Gellius, *Attic Nights*, V.xxi.9; XVI.viii.2.

20. *Meta Sudans:* a large fountain just south-west of the Colosseum, said to have been built by Domitian in A.D. 96.

21. *cava ædium:* the inner court of Roman houses. *focus:* house (lit. hearth) *ara deorum penatum:* altar of the household gods. *conclavia:* rooms. *cænationes:* dining-rooms. *atria:* forecourts, entrance rooms, where it was customary for the housewife and her maidens to sit spinning. *prætoria:* country mansions.

22. *tympanum.* "The vertical recessed face of a pediment, often adorned with sculpture" (*OED*).

23. *EYΣYNOΠTON.* The term eludes translation into English. It may be understood to mean "easily taken in at a glance; harmony in perspective".

24. *cardinal Alexander Albani:* cardinal and patron of the arts (1692–1779). His villa Albani, built *c.* 1760 (now known as Villa Torlonia), contained a celebrated collection of antiquities.

25. *a kind of gingerbread work.* "Orig. applied by sailors to the carved and gilded decorations of a ship; hence to architectural or other ornament of a gaudy and tasteless kind" (*OED*). Cf. *Roderick Random,* p.9.

26 *I expressed . . . Spirito Santo?:* The system of paper money had been common in Rome for some time, notes being circulated by the papal banks of the Mount of Piety and Spirito Santo. In general, British travellers in the eighteenth century show little enthusiasm for the banknote, while conservatively clinging to the system of letters of credit.

27. *And now I am . . . coin of Italy.* The currency lists for the Italian states given in many travel guides of the period are for the most part conflicting and confusing; (see, for instance, Nugent (1749), III, pp.55–60; Büsching, III, pp.7–9.) Each state had its own monetary system, although the zechine (sequin) of gold was acceptable throughout Italy.

28. *in possession of Minorca.* See V, n. 17.

29. *Clement VII.* Giulio de' Medici, Pope from 1523 to 1534. In 1527, Charles V, Holy Roman Emperor, besieged and sacked Rome, holding Clement prisoner until he ransomed himself.

30. *Marcellus.* M. Claudius Marcellus (43–23 B.C.) was adopted by his uncle, Augustus, marrying the emperor's daughter Julia, but died soon after.

31. *Quantos ille . . . recentem.* Virgil, *Aeneid,* VI, ll.872–4.

32. *Germanicus.* Germanicus Caesar (15 B.C.–A.D. 19), son of Nero Claudius Drusus, distinguished himself as a general. He was the father of the emperor Caligula and of Agrippina, the mother of Nero.

33. *Drusus.* Nero Claudius Drusus (*c.*38–9 B.C.), the brother of Tiberius, who later became emperor. He played a significant part in the wars in Germany and Gaul.

34. *Claudite . . . ista patet!:* Ovid [?], *Consolatio ad Liviam,* ll.73–4.

### LETTER XXXI

1. *glyster-pipes.* "A tube or pipe for administering clysters [enemas]" (*OED*).

2. *Stowe in Buckinghamshire:* seat of Richard Grenville, Earl Temple (1711–79), who inherited the estate from his uncle, Sir Richard Temple, Viscount Cobham (1675–1749). See Pope, *Moral Essays*, IV, 65–70.

3. *Curtius:* semi-legendary Roman youth, who with his steed leaped fully armoured into a huge abyss.

4. *Silenus:* the drunken companion and nurse of Bacchus; god of springs and running water.

5. *Bernini.* Gianlorenzo Bernini (1598–1680), architect and sculptor.

6. *pope Urban VIII.* Maffeo Barberini (1568–1644), a Florentine, became Pope in 1623.

7. *Cimabue: c.* 1240–1302.

8. *I was not . . . of a woman.* Michelangelo's *Pietà* in St. Peter's does not appear to have been the object of enthusiastic veneration which more recent travellers have made it. Despite its fame, many Grand Tourists fail to mention the statue. Smith, I, p.366, even dismisses the work as "unpleasant in design, and stiff and hard in execution".

9. *Domenichino.* Domenico Zampieri (1581–1641), called Domenichino.

10. *Guido Rheni:* 1575–1642.

11. *the book . . . Romanæ.* The author of this book was Francesco Maria Febei (1616–80), Archbishop of Tarsus.

12. *palace of the Escurial:* the royal monastery, El Escorial, built by Philip II, completed in 1584.

13. *St. Laurence.* Probably of Spanish birth, Laurence was a deacon of Rome during the papacy of Sixtus II. In 258, he was martyred by broiling on a gridiron.

14. *Sebastian.* Christian martyr, shot to death with arrows, *c.* 288, a frequent subject of religious painting.

15. *Bartholomew flaed alive.* St. Bartholomew, one of the twelve apostles, is said to have spread the Gospel to Asia Minor and Armenia, where he was flayed alive.

16. *Boniface IV.* Pope from 615 to 619.

17. *I am not . . . calls it but nine.* A misprint in the 1st edition of Nugent (1749), III, p.257. In the 3rd edition (1778, III, p.278), this has been corrected.

18. *The same author . . . St. Peter, &c.* See Nugent (1749), III, p.258.

19. *pope Alexander VII*. Born Fabio Chigi (1599–1667) in Siena, Pope from 1655.

20. *naumachia:* places built for the exhibition of mock sea battles, probably similar in shape to amphitheatres.

## LETTER XXXII

1. *Titus*. Titus Flavius Sabinus Vespasianus (A.D. 40–81), emperor from 79. In 70, he was responsible for the capture of Jerusalem.

2. *rostra:* platforms or stands for public speaking.

3. *Temple-bar:* the old Fleet Street gateway into London built by Wren (1670), sometimes known as the City Golgotha.

4. *Tully:* i.e. Marcus Tullius Cicero (106–43 B.C.), the famous orator.

5. *Sed fæminarum . . . sunt*. Tacitus, *Annales*, XV, 32.

6. Δώδεκα, . . ἐσθίει. Homer, *Iliad*, XXIII, ll. 181–2.

7. *Even Virgil . . . Pallas*. Virgil, *Aeneid*, X, ll. 517–20. Pallas, the son of Evander, was killed in battle by Turnus.

8. *pope Paul II*. Pietro Barbo (1417–71), born Venice, Pope from 1464. The Palace of St. Mark (usually known today as Palazzo Venezia) was built for him, *c.* 1455. At Smollett's time, it was the residence of the Venetian ambassador.

9. *Riarius*. Raphael Galeotto (1451–1521), Italian cardinal.

10. *Farnese . . . Paul III*. Alexander Farnese (1468–1549), born in Tuscany, Pope from 1534.

11. *spina*. "The barrier running up the middle of a Roman circus" (*OED*).

12. *Probus*. M. Aurelius Probus, Roman emperor A.D. 276–82.

13. *Domitian*. T. Flavius Domitianus (A.D. 51–96), emperor from 81, younger son of Vespasian.

14. *Edidit navales . . . prospectavit*. Suetonius, *Lives of the Caesars*, VIII, "Domitian", iv.

15. *the Serpentine river*. By order of Queen Caroline, consort of George II, the string of ponds in Hyde Park had been made into one, the Serpentine, in 1730.

16. *Lucullus: c.* 110–57 B.C., conqueror of Mithridates; he amassed vast treasures in Asia and lived in great luxury.

17. *lavacra*. *OED* gives *lavacre*, "a bath or font", last recorded 1657.

18. *as Cicero . . . disputabant*. Smollett probably quotes from memory Cicero, *Academica*, I. 17, "disputabant inambulantes in Lycio".

19. *edile:* appointed magistrate, responsible for the care of public edifices. Agrippa (see X, n.6) was appointed aedile in 33 B.C.

20. *Cædere . . . lavari.* Juvenal, *Satires,* II. vi. 447.

21. *Balnea . . . Quadrantes.* Martial, *Epigrams,* x. lxx. 13–14.

22. *I puer . . . defer.* Persius Flaccus, Satire v. 126.

23. *Redde . . . abire domum.* Smollett, following *Roma Antica,* I, p.484, wrongly attributes this quotation to Juvenal. It is, in fact, from Martial, *Epigrams,* XIV. clxiii.

24. *Galen . . . Sanitate tuenda.* According to the author of *Roma Antica,* I, p.485, the reference is from Book v of Galen's work.

25. *Tiberius.* Claudius Nero Tiberius (42 B.C.–A.D. 37), Roman emperor from A.D. 14, succeeding Augustus.

26. *as we read in Spartian.* See Aelius Spartianus, "Life of Hadrian", XIX. 10, in *Scriptores Historiae Augustae.*

27. *Belisarius.* The great general of Justinian, Belisarius (d. A.D. 565) overthrew the Vandal kingdom in Africa (534), but in 563 he was accused of plotting against the emperor and disgraced.

28. *Velabrum:* part of the west slope of the Palatine, at one time a morass.

29. *Marcus Cato.* Marcus Porcius Cato (234–149 B.C.), frequently surnamed Censorius, consul in 195, and censor in 184. *Valerius Flaccus.* L. Valerius Flaccus (d. 180 B.C.), consul with Cato in 195.

30. *Caius Cestius:* probably the same Caius Cestius (d. 12 B.C.) who was prætor and a tribune of the people. *Cecilia Metella:* daughter of Caecilius Metellus Creticus, consul in 69 B.C., who fought in Crete. She married Crassus, son of M. Crassus, the triumvir.

31. *the seven Epulones . . . Lectisternia.* See Basil Kennett, *The Antiquities of Rome,* 6th edn., 1717, pp.83–4: "*The Epulones . . .* had their Name from a Custom which obtain'd among the *Romans,* in time of Publick Danger, of making a sumptuous Feast in their Temples to which they did, as it were, invite the Deities themselves. . . . These *Regalio's* they call'd *Epula,* or *Lectisternia;* the Care of which belong'd to the *Epulones.*"

32. *Pervigilia:* devotional vigils.

33. *Hinc victimæ . . . placatio.* Pliny, VIII. lxx. 183.

34. *Viriatus:* celebrated Lusitanian shepherd, who for several years defied one Roman army after another. In 141 B.C., he made peace with Fabius Servilianus, the Roman general, but the following year he was assassinated.

### LETTER XXXIII

1. *Mr. Webb's . . . parts of painting.* Smollett refers here to Daniel Webb's

405

*Inquiry into the Beauties of Painting*, 1760. *The Critical Review*, IX, 1760, pp.197–205, contains a critique of this work, possibly by Smollett: "Speaking of Raphael, he [Webb] seems to think he had nothing of the sublime in his genius. His calm, though fertile genius could better delineate the fine and delicate movements of the mind, which have in them more of sentiment than passion . . . Raphael then stands confest the prince of ethic painters." (p.205).

For Daniel Webb (1719–98), see *DNB*.

2. *Sixtus IV*. Francesco della Rovere (1414–84), Pope from 1471, commissioned Michelangelo to work in the Sistine Chapel (named after him).

3. *facchini:* porters.

4. *the eve of St. Bartholomew:* the slaughter of French Huguenots, ordered by Catherine de Medicis, mother and regent of Charles IX of France; the massacre began on St. Bartholomew's Day, 24 August 1572.

5. *Descrizione di Roma*. Martz, p.74, notes here that Smollett calls *Roma Antica* by its subtitle: "The third volume deals with Roman history and customs, and hence bears the title, *Descrizione Delli Riti, Guerre Piu' Celebri, e Famiglie Piu' Illustri Degl' Antichi Romani*."

6. *Coligni*. Gaspard de Coligny (1519–72), French admiral and leader of the Huguenots, murdered on St. Bartholomew's Eve.

7. *I was better pleased . . . was formed*. The Apollo Belvedere, supposed to be a replica of a bronze by Leochares, fourth century B.C., was admired by many travellers, e.g. Peter Beckford, *Familiar Letters from Italy*, 2 vols., 1805, II, p.272.

8. *Whether it is the same . . . not know*. See Pliny, XXXVI. xi. 58.

9. *Fulvius Ursini*. Fulvio Orsini (1529–1600), bibliophile and collector, curator of the Farnesian Library. See *Enciclopedia Italiana*.

10. *His reasons . . . buildings of Titus*. See Montfaucon, pp.141–2: "In the Days of Pope *Leo* X. [1506] was dug up . . . that noble Statue of *Laocoon*, with his Children and the Snakes winding about them, which is now to be seen in a Court-yard of the *Vatican* Palace call'd *Belvedere*. Almost all Men immediately declar'd it was the same that *Pliny* speaks of, lib. 26. cap. 5. . . . But bring back all the Course of the Argument from the Beginning, it may be question'd whether the Statue of *Laocoon*, which is now in being, be the same that *Pliny* speaks of. To which Effect we must give Ear to *Fulvius Ursinius* in his Notes newly publish'd upon *Bartholomew Marlianus*. *These Statues*, says he, *which if Pliny gives a true Account of Titus's House, were made of one single Stone, are not the same that were in Titus's House; for these are made of two Stones, as may be easily perceiv'd by a skilful Artist, and even by others. Besides Antoniolus, the Antiquary, has some Pieces in his House of Laocoon's Snakes, found elsewhere on that Mount, where is the truer Place of Titus's Baths; whence we may guess, that Laocoon, which is now in the Vatican*

*Gardens, is not the same* Pliny *mentions to have been in* Titus*'s Buildings*. This is the Opinion and Testimony of that Great Man *Fulvius*, which if it does not quite destroy, at least much weakens the contrary Opinion . . ."

11. *the description of it in Keyslar*. Keysler, II, pp.296–7: "Whether this piece consists of two or more blocks put together, according to the opinion of Michael Angelo when it was first found, is a question: and hence a doubt arises, whether it be that mentioned by Pliny, who describes the groupe of Laocoön, &c. as made out of one single block. Fulvius Ursinus, also speaks of two pieces of serpents dug up in the same place, which may with greater probability be supposed to be part of Pliny's Laocoön. Be that as it will, the Laocoön of the Vatican is really admirable, whether considered as an original or as an antique copy; it being unreasonable to suppose that the first was not the only one those artists made."

12. *Opus omnibus . . . artifices*. Pliny, XXXVI. iv. 37.

13. *Agesander, Polydore, and Athenodorus:* fl. Rhodes, second century B.C.

14. *Phidias*. Athenian sculptor, *c.* 490–432 B.C.

15. *Lucius Verus*. L. Aurelius Verus (A.D. 130–69), colleague and joint-emperor with Marcus Aurelius.

16. *what pleased me . . . to the Capitol*. The statue of Marcus Aurelius, which was brought to the Piazza del Campidoglio in 1538, owed its preservation in the Middle Ages to the belief that it represented the Christian emperor Constantine the Great.

17. *At the father end . . . corner of a street*. Pasquin, a mutilated Greek statue, was used by the wits of Renaissance Rome to affix epigrams and lampoons (hence "pasquinade", see *OED*). To Marforio were pasted the answers to these pasquinades.

18. *Alexander Severus*. M. Aurelius Alexander Severus (A.D. 205–35), son of Gessius Marcianus and Julia Mammea, and first cousin of Elagabalus, became emperor in 222.

19. *coronach:* a lament for the dead. Cf. *Humphry Clinker*, p.242.

20. *Poussin*. Nicolas Poussin (*c.* 1593–1665), French painter, lived in Rome between 1624 and 1640.

21. *the celebrated . . . by Pliny*. See Pliny, XXXIV. xix. 73. Ctesilas (or Cresilas) was an Athenian sculptor, a contemporary of Phidias.

22. *Caius Duilius*. Roman general, consul in 260 B.C., in which year he commanded the first Roman naval victory, defeating the Carthaginians. The Columna Rostrata, erected in Duilius' honour, was dug up in the sixteenth century in a mutilated form, and an attempt was made to restore it.

23. *Glycon*. Athenian sculptor, first century B.C.

24. *Gulielmo de la Porta:* sculptor (d. 1577), called Fra Guglielmo del Piombo.

25. *Apollonius and Tauriscus:* two brothers, who worked in Rhodes, *c.* 150 B.C.

26. *In a little house . . . Natural History.* The group commonly known as the Toro Farnese, represents Dirce, the sister of Antiope, who was tied to the horns of a savage bull by Amphion and Zethus, sons of Antiope, in revenge for Dirce's ill-treatment of their mother. The statue, now in Naples, was greatly admired by eighteenth-century visitors to Rome. It is considered to be a free copy (second or third century A.D.) of the lost original described by Pliny, XXXVI. iv. 34.

27. *specific. OED* quotes "1779 JOHNSON *Lett.* (1788) II.64, How did you light on your specifick for the tooth-ach?"

28. *You need not doubt . . . in the air.* See Introduction, pp.xv–xvi.

29. *Andrea Sacchi:* sometimes called Ouche (1599–1661). His painting of St. Romuald is now in the Vatican gallery.

30. *Claude Lorraine.* Claude Gellée or Lorraine (1600–82), French landscape-painter, worked for much of his life in Rome.

31. *Salvator Rosa:* 1615–73.

32. *Freij.* Jakob Johann Frey (1681–1752), Swiss engraver, who worked most of his life in Rome. His *Icones Variæ*, 1721–7, includes (plate 5) the "Aurora" of Guido, engraved on two sheets.

33. *Le Brun.* Charles Le Brun (1619–90). His *Magdalen Repentant* (now in the Louvre), painted for the Carmelite church, Rue Saint-Jacques, was considered in the eighteenth century his *chef d'œuvre.*

34. *Guercino.* Giovanni Francesco Barbieri (1591–1666), called Guercino.

35. *Carlo Maratti:* 1625–1713, pupil of Andrea Sacchi.

## LETTER XXXIV

1. *the book . . . against Luther.* Editions of Henry VIII's *Assertio Septem Sacramentorum* were printed in London and Rome in 1521.

2. *the banker Barazzi.* Francesco Barazzi acted as banker and agent in Rome for many English travellers, e.g. Edward Gibbon (*Letters*, ed. J. E. Norton, 3 vols., 1956, I, p.188), John Armstrong (*Miscellaneous Works of Tobias Smollett, M.D.,* 6 vols., Edinburgh, 1820, I, p.191), David Garrick, (*Letters*, ed. D. M. Little and G. M. Kahrl, 3 vols., 1963, I, p.397).

3. *Marshalsea:* prison in Southwark, demolished in 1849. *King's-Bench:* prison situated in St. George's Fields, about a mile to the south of the Thames, to which Smollett was sent (1760) after libelling Admiral Knowles in *The Critical Review*; see Knapp, pp.230–6; *Launcelot Greaves*, p.163.

4. *Sulfureâ Nar . . . Velini.* Virgil, *Aeneid*, VII, l.517.

5. *a church . . . temple:* chiesa di San Salvatore.

6. *the emperor Tacitus.* Marcus Claudius Tacitus (*c.* A.D. 200–76), Roman emperor 275 to 276, killed by his own soldiers.

7. *the historian of the same name.* Cornelius Tacitus (*c.* A.D. 55–117).

8. *I saw at a distance . . . in Europe.* See Addison, p.95: "At *Spoleto*, the next Town on the Road, are some Antiquities. The most remarkable is an Aqueduct of a *Gothic* Structure, that conveys the Water from Mount St. *Francis* to *Spoletto*, which is not to be equall'd for its height by any other in *Europe*. They reckon from the Foundation of the lowest Arch to the Top of it 230 yards."

9. *the famous river Clitumnus.* The waters of this river were supposed to have the virtue of making cattle white that drank from it. White oxen were particularly favoured by the Romans for sacrifices to the deities.

10. *St. Francis.* Giovanni Francesco Bernadone (*c.* 1181–1226), founder of the Franciscan order.

11. *In choosing our beds . . . heretick.":* Smollett recalls this experience in *Humphry Clinker,* p.47.

12. *Mr. R———y.* Unidentified; see XXV n. 7.

13. *It was in this neighbourhood . . . Hannibal.* In 217 B.C., having crossed the Apennines, Hannibal ambushed the Roman army under Gaius Flaminius in a narrow pass between the hills and Lake Trasimene. Fifteen thousand Roman soldiers, including Flaminius, were systematically wiped out.

14. *described by . . . Guazzesi.* Lorenzo Guazzesi (1708–64), a native of Arezzo, was the author of several archaeological works, including "Dissertazione intorno agli anfiteatri della Toscana e particolarmente dell' Aretino", published in *Scelta di Dissertazioni Cavate da' Piu'Celebri Autori,* II, part 2, Venice, 1751, pp.15–48, probably the work referred to by Smollett.

15. *Miss C———.* Anne Curry; see II, n. 3.

16. *In this particular . . . at Constantinople.* Smollett's allusion to Jean-Baptiste Tavernier (1605–89), the great French traveller, is somewhat confusing, suggesting that he is citing from memory. Tavernier gives two accounts of the incident referred to here, but neither of them accords in its details with Smollett. See *The Persian Travels,* I, p.8, included among *The Six Voyages,* trans. J[ohn]. P[hillips]., 1677; and "Description of the Grand Seignior's Seraglio", added to *Collection of Travels through Turkey into Persia, and the East-Indies,* 1684, pp.57–8.

LETTER XXXV

1. *Mr. R———.* Unidentified; see XXV, n. 7.

## XXXVI

2. *the new bishop of Nice*. Jacques-Thomas Astésan, a Dominican, was consecrated Bishop of Nice in Rome, 15 July 1764; he arrived in Nice on 8 October, and officiated at the Christmas service in the cathedral.

3. *in pontificalibus:* in ceremonial attire.

### LETTER XXXVI

1. *the farms*. In pre-Revolutionary France, financial companies, known as the *fermiers généraux* (Farmers General), purchased from the state the rights of gathering indirect taxes and regulating the method of collection.

2. *droits de controlle:* duty paid by goldsmiths and silversmiths for compulsory hallmarking; also stamp duty on notaries' deeds. *insinuation:* tax on donations and loans. *centième denier:* tax made payable on the transfer of hereditary offices. *franchiefs*. The *franc fief* was a tax levied on non-nobles in tenure of noble lands. *aubeine*. See II, pp.9–10.

3. *pays d'états*. For purposes of administration and finance, eighteenth-century France was divided up into *pays d'états* and *pays d'élections*. The *pays d'états* paid a lump sum to the king, receiving in return exemption from the *taille*, the right of self-taxation and a greater degree of self-administration.

4. *There is at present . . . takes the ascendant*. In 1795, a publication entitled *Wonderful Prophecies* contained (pp.55–60) a prophecy, claimed to have been written by "*the late Dr. Smollet, a few Months before his Death, to the Rev. Dr.\*\*\*, of \*\*\*, Northumberland*", in which the author foretells the coming of the French Revolution. Although the attribution of the prophecy should be viewed with suspicion, it is probable that whoever compiled it had read Smollett's account of pre-Revolutionary France.

### LETTER XXXVII

1. *the vernal equinox:* 20 March.

2. *wash-balls:* balls of soap.

3. *bergamot*. "A woven fabric of tapestry composed of a mixture of flock and hair, said to have been first produced at Bergamo in Italy" (*OED*). Smollett's use of this meaning of the word considerably pre-dates the earliest *OED* entry.

### LETTER XXXVIII

1. *Dr. S—— at Nice*. Almost certainly Smollett himself, to whom the original of this Letter seems to have been written by an anonymous friend, who made the trip from Nice to Turin. Despite the improvement in his health, it is doubtful whether Smollett was sufficiently strong for the

arduous journey over the mountains referred to by his biographers (e.g. Knapp, p.258). In addressing it to himself, Smollett seems to have intended the Letter to be interpreted *hors série*, and thus requiring extensive authorial revision before publication.

2. *Coni:* i.e. Cuneo.

3. *Brieglie:* i.e. Breil.

4. *capot.* "A long shaggy cloak or overcoat with a hood, worn by soldiers, sailors, travellers, etc." (*OED*).

5. *marquis M.* Unidentified.

6. *Roida:* i.e. Roya.

7. *Seafarot:* according to Seccombe, p.351, a kind of "jack-boots or wading boots".

8. *the Valanches:* i.e. avalanches.

9. *countess C——.* Unidentified.

10. *The prince of Conti.* Louis François de Bourbon, Prince de Conti (1717–76), commanded the French army in northern Italy, winning the battle of Coni in 1744, but failing to take the citadel. See XXVI, n. 11.

11. *Sabellian:* i.e. Savigliano.

12. *the Bona Fama.* John Morgan, p.182, also stayed at the "Inn, the bonnes femmes w'ch ye best in Turin, & most frequented by ye English." It was demolished in the second half of the nineteenth century, the Via Pietro Micca now passing over the site. See also Onorato Derossi, *Nuova Guida per la Città di Torino,* 1781, p.143.

## LETTER XXXIX

1. *Mr. C——.* Corvesi; Smollett displays both tact and cunning by refusing to identify his grasping Nissard landlord here, but revealing his name elsewhere (XXVII, p.222). Corvesi is almost certainly François Clément Corvesi, who was ennobled Comte de Gorbio in 1779. By profession a lawyer, Corvesi was appointed "avocat fiscal-général" for Nice in 1768. In 1791, he was ousted by the Revolution from the Presidency of the Senate of Nice, dying in Carmagnole in 1796.

In an article, "La Maison et le Cocaïer du Comte de Gorbio", *L'Éclaireur du Dimanche*, no. 166, Nice, 13 Jan. 1924, p.1, the local historian, Georges Doublet describes Corvesi's house, at no. 3, Rue de la Terrasse, Nice, (still standing and now used as municipal offices), which was presumably where Smollett lived during his eighteen months' residence in Nice.

2. *Michaelmas:* 29 September.

3. *Pliny . . . tunny-fishery.* Pliny, XXI. xliii. 94.

# XXXIX

4. *"Antipolitani . . . missa forem."*: Martial, *Epigrams*, XIII. ciii.

5. *garum*: a fish-sauce. Cf. *Peregrine Pickle*, pp.239–40.

6. *encrasicolus*: literally a small fish.

7. *Cælius Apicius . . . variorum*. Cælius Apicius (*c.* 14 B.C.–A.D. 37), a famous Roman gourmet, was the supposed author of a collection of recipes, entitled *Apicii Coelli de Opsoniis et Condimentis*. Kahrl, p.48 n., remarks that *de re coquinaria* is "a shortened title frequently used for the book".

8. *Ciagne:* i.e. Siagne.

9. *Julius Agricola*. Gnaeus Julius Agricola (A.D. 37–93), Roman general, governor of Britain from 77 to 84.

10. *I counted . . . on the stocks*. The strength of the French navy at Toulon was a subject of considerable interest to the English even in peacetime. A list of ships in Toulon, counted "by the Means of a Person . . . employ'd during the War" (P.R.O., S.P. 92/71, 3 March 1764) includes twenty ships of the line, naming among them "Le Tonant". Another list of 3 December 1764, mentions fifteen ships of the line, four frigates, six xebeques and three ships on the stocks, including "a Frigate, whose name nor force is not yet known".

11. *Capt. E—— . . . docks and arsenal*. The monthly lists noting the movements of His Majesty's Vessels (P.R.O., Adm. 8/40, 41) show that the frigate *Thames*, carrying thirty-two guns, commanded by Captain John Eliot, was on the Mediterranean station through 1764 and 1765. An examination of the ship's log (P.R.O., Adm. 51/982) reveals that the *Thames* entered Toulon harbour, Saturday 23 March 1765 and remained there until 8 April, less than a month before Smollett's visit to the town.

Captain Eliot (1741–69), the brother of Edward, Lord Eliot (as he was created in 1784), assumed command of the *Thames* in 1761. Later, he was to captain the *Prince of Orange*, stationed at Chatham. In 1766, he received the appointment of Governor of West Florida, a position he held until his death. See John Charnock, *Biographia Navalis*, 6 vols., 1794–8, VI, p.391; Gibbon, p.78.

12. *Martinique and Guadeloupe*. These two West Indian islands were taken by the English during the Seven Years War, but returned to France under the peace terms of 1763.

13. *Mr. A——r*. Henry Archer (1700–68) of Hale, Hants., younger brother of Thomas, first Lord Archer, Baron Umberslade, married in 1743 Lady Elizabeth Montagu (d. 1789), daughter of George, first Earl of Halifax. As a Member of Parliament, Archer represented Warwick on the family interest, but in 1765, illness forced him to ask to be excused attending the House, at which time he went abroad. See Gavin de Beer, unpublished *Catalogue of British Visitors to Switzerland*, deposited in the Bibliothèque Publique et Universitaire, Geneva; *NQ*, ninth series, XI, 1903, pp.313–14; Lewis Namier and John Brooke, *The House of Commons 1754–1790*, 3 vols., 1964, II, pp.26–7.

### LETTER XL

1. *Mr. S——re.* Unidentified.

2. *Mr. A——r and lady Betty.* See XXXIX, n. 13.

3. *Mr. G——r.* Charles Gore (1711–68), was Member of Parliament for Cricklade, 1730–41; for Hertfordshire, 1741–61; and for Tiverton, 1762–1768. In November 1764, he announced his intention of spending the winter of 1764–5 in the south of France (see Edwin S. Chalk, "Tiverton Letters and Papers, 1724–1843", *NQ*, CLXX, 1936, p.171; Lewis Namier and John Brooke, *The House of Commons 1754–1790*, 3 vols., 1964, II, pp.520–1).

4. *Caius Sextius Calvinus.* Roman consul in 124 B.C. He fought against the Salluvii, later founding the colony of Aquæ Sextiæ (Aix).

5. *Marius.* Caius Marius (157–86 B.C.), seven times consul, defeated the Teutones near Aquæ Sextiæ in 102.

6. *The duc de Villars.* Honoré Armand, duc de Villars (1702–20), son of the famous Marshal Villars, is supposed to have been an unsavoury character, who traded on his father's reputation, inheriting from him the governorship of Provence.

7. *Lord H——.* Unidentified.

8. *Priapus.* Greek god of fertility.

9. *A very superficial . . . of those days.* Two of these works were Louis Arnaud's *Traité des Eaux Minerales d'Aix en Provence*, Avignon, 1705, and Antoine Aucane-Emeric's *Analyse des Eaux Minerales de la Ville d'Aix en Provence*, Avignon, 1705. The third treatise may have been an earlier work by I. S. Pitton, *Les Eaux Chaudes de la Ville d'Aix*, Aix, 1678.

10. *the Queen's Bath, at Bath in Somersetshire.* Philip Thicknesse, *The Valetudinarian's Bath Guide*, 2nd edn., 1780, p.63, notes that "in the Queen's Bath, the heat is between ninety eight, and ninety nine."

11. *pricked:* turned (sour).

12. *queen Jane I. of Naples.* The daughter of Charles, Duke of Calabria and Marie de Valois, Jane I (1327–82), succeeded to the throne of Naples in 1343.

13. *pope Clement VI.* Pierre Roger (1291–1352), born near Limoges, Pope from 1342, refused to leave Avignon for Rome, purchasing Avignon for the papacy in 1348.

14. *Not but . . . peace of Pisa.* Duc Charles II de Créqui (1623–87), soldier and statesman, was appointed, in 1662, French ambassador at Rome. An attempt on his life by members of the papal guard created a serious diplomatic wrangle, in which Louis XIV seized the city of Avignon and the surrounding comtat Venaissin from the papacy, holding them until the Peace of Pisa (1664).

15. *Among the last . . . his poetry.* Francesco Petrarch (1304–74) first met Laura, the subject of his celebrated series of love-poems, in Avignon in 1327.

16. *Luctatius Catulus:* consul with Marius in 102 B.C. He died in 60 B.C.

17. *Cimbri:* a Celtic people, supposed to have originated from Chersonesus Cimbrica (Jutland); they were destroyed by Marius and Catulus in 101 B.C.

18. *On the left . . . were probably contained.* See Montfaucon, p.4: "Not far from the River side stands a Tomb, the like whereof I never saw elsewhere. On four square Pillars, to which are joyn'd as many Columns of the *Tuscan* Order, only one half of them jutting out, stands a cross Vault, about eighteen Foot high, which sustains a Pyramid of above thirty Foot in length. In the midst of the Vault sticks out an oblong Stone, about the heighth of a Man, in which perhaps the Ashes are laid up."

## LETTER XLI

1. *nescia qua dulcedine . . . Horace.* Smollett misquotes, not from Horace, but from Ovid's *Epistolae ex Ponto,* I. 3. 35.

2. *the dutchess D——lle . . . Duc de R——f——t.* The duchesse de la Rochefoucauld d'Anville (or d'Enville) and her son, Louis-Alexandre, duc de la Rochefoucauld d'Anville (1743–92) were on their way to Geneva, where they were expected by Voltaire (*Correspondence,* ed. Theodore Besterman, LVIII, Geneva, 1960, pp. 114–15).

3. *Next night . . . where we lay.* Seccombe, p.xxiii, notes some confusion here: "On his homeward journey he indicates that he travelled from Beaune to Châlons and so by way of Auxerre to Dijon. The right order is Châlons, Beaune, Dijon, Auxerre."

4. *Manchester velvet:* "1762. *Lond. Chron.* 18–20 Mar. XI. 266/2 Blue Manchester velvets, with gold cords . . . are generally the uniform of Bum-bailiffs [etc.]" (*OED*).

## A REGISTER OF THE WEATHER

1. *A REGISTER OF THE WEATHER.* Martz, p. 89, notes that in keeping a register of the weather, Smollett was influenced by the practice of Alexander Drummond, *Travels through Different Cities of Germany, Italy, Greece, and Several Parts of Asia,* 1754, which work he edited for publication. According to Francesco Cordasco, "Smollett's 'Register of the Weather' ", *NQ,* CXCIV, 1949, p. 163: "What had suggested the idea of a *register* to Drummond and Smollett alike was certainly the practice of supplying such extensive notices long common in magazines. *The London Magazine, The Universal Magazine* compiled such *registers* frequently, and *The Gentleman's*

*Magazine* regularly included in its pages such notices for antecedent years."
Scott B. Rice, "The Significance of Smollett's Weather Register", *NQ*,
CCXV, 1970, pp.94–5, has argued that "Smollett was complying with a
familiar travel book convention first instituted under the auspices of the
Royal Society" in their "Directions for Sea-Men, bound for far Voyages",
*Philosophical Transactions*, 1665–66.

# Appendix

The hitherto unpublished personal letter printed below, concerning the detention of his books at Boulogne, is referred to by Smollett in Letter II, p. 12. It was addressed to Lord Hertford, who forwarded it for action to Richard Aldworth Neville, the British resident at Paris, in whose papers it has come to light (P.R.O., 30/50, 52, fols. 47–8). Other known personal correspondence written during Smollett's sojourn abroad may be consulted in Knapp, *Letters*, pp. 115–24.

My Lord
It is not without Reluctance that I presume to trouble your Excellency; but I hope the peculiar nature of my Situation, will plead effectually in my Excuse.

About the latter End of last month, I arrived with my Family at Boulogne, in my way to Nice in Provence, where I propose to reside some time in hope of recovering my Health which is greatly impaired.

My Books have been stopped at the Custom-House of this Place, in order to be sent to Amiens to be examined by the *chambre syndicale*; and this Examination will not only put me to great Expence, but also retard my Journey which is so necessary to the Preservation of my Life.

Your Excellency will see by the inclosed List, that the Books (the greater Part of which are written by myself) cannot possibly contain any thing contrary to the Religion or state of France; and when it is considered that I am not a subject of this Kingdom, but a stranger travelling through it for the Benefit of my Health, it is to be hoped I shall be exempted from the mortification, Danger and Expence of any further Delay.

If your Excellency would have the Goodness to interpose with the ministry of France, that my Books may be examined on the spot, and restored immediately, I flatter myself there would be no great Difficulty in obtaining such a Concession in favour of Humanity, in favour of Letters, the Professors of which, France has always affected to treat with particular marks of Consideration.

My Lord, I beg leave to assert a double claim to your Excellency's Protection; as a Subject of great Britain; as a writer who have acquired some Degree of Reputation in the world of Literature. I likewise appeal to your Lordship's Beneficent Disposition, which is universally known and respected.

In full Confidence of reaping the Benefit of your good offices, I have the Honour to be

My Lord,
Your Excellency's most obed$^t$ serv$^t$
T$^s$. Smollett

Boulogne sur mer
chez le Sieur Bouvier
July 11. 1763

The list of books prepared by Smollett and enclosed with this letter was transmitted to the duc de Praslin (II, n. 1). It is now in the Archives des Affaires Étrangères at Paris (*Correspondance politique, Angleterre*, 451, pièce no. 14. p. 15, reprinted here from Joliat, pp. 251-2):

| | | |
|---|---|---|
| histoire vrselle ancienne et moderne | 58 | volumes |
| hist$^e$ Complette d'Ang$^{re}$ | 8 | — |
| Traduction des œuvres de Vol$^{re}$ | 25 | — |
| Romans de Smolett | 12 | — |
| Trad$^{on}$ de D$^n$ Quichotte | 4 | — |
| œuvres de Shakespear | 8 | — |
| Comedies de Congreve | 3 | — |
| Revüe critique | 12 | — |
| Magazin Brit$^e$ | 4 | — |

Sisteme complet de Geographie, grand in-fol°.
Quelques autres Livres d'amusement en Anglois, Comedies et brochures.
Homere, Sophocle, virgile, Horace, Juvenal, Tibulle.
D$^n$ Quichotte en Espagnol.
5 Dictionnaires Grec, Latin, français, Italien, Espagnol.

# Index

## i. Index of Persons

*This Index lists individuals mentioned in the* Travels. *Biographical details are usually to be found in a note to the text (see first page-reference)*

A—, Dr., *see* Armstrong
A—, Mr., *see* Atkins
Acton, Commodore John, 220
Adrian, *see* Hadrian
Aemilius Censor, *see* Lepidus
Agesander, 273
Agricola, Gnaeus Julius, 314
Agrippa, Marcus Vipsanius, 83, 217 n.
  251, 258, 265–8
Agrippina, 265
Albani, Alexander, 248
Alberoni, Giulio, 84
Alboinus, 123
Alexander the Great, 226
Alexander VII, Pope, 258
Amadeus VII, Duke of Savoy, 145
Antinous, 226
Antoninus Pius, 82, 228
Antonioli, antiquary, 273
Appollonius, 276
A—r, Mr., *see* Archer
Archer, Henry, 318, 319
Armstrong, Dr. John, probable
  identification for Dr. A—, 195
Ariosto, Ludovico, 223
Athenodorus, 273
Atkins, Christopher, 127
Atta, 236
Attius Navius, 228
Augustus, Roman Emperor, 81, 83–4,
  141–2, 217 n., 251, 267, 281
Aulus Helvius, 143 n.
Aumont, Louis-Marie, duc d', 15
Aurelius, Marcus, 196, 274

B—, Mr., at Geneva, 151
B—, Mrs., *see* Ballantyne
B—, Mons., *see* Bouvier
Ballantyne, Mrs., 8, 24, 30
Barazzi, Francesco, 280, 284, 289
Barberini, Maffeo, *see* Urban VIII
Barbo, Pietro, *see* Paul II

Bartholomew, Saint, 257
Beatrice de Lorraine, Countess of
  Tuscany, 217 n.
B—d, Mr., *see* Buckland
Belisarius, 266
Belleisle, Charles Louis Auguste
  Fouquet, duc de, 116, 298
Bennoti, painter, 216
Bernini, Gianlorenzo, 254
Berwick, James Fitz-James, Duke of, 86
Bianchi, Giuseppe, 226, 228
Boerhaave, Hermann, 88
Boleyn, Anne, 280
Bologna, Giovanni, 216
Boncampagni, Giovanni, 217 n.
Boncampagni, Gregory, *see* Gregory
  XIII
Boniface IV, Pope, 258
Bourbon, Louis François de, prince de
  Conti, 309
Bouvier, Charles-Antoine-
  François, 10–12, 35
Buckingham, George Villiers, Second
  Duke of, 137–8
Buckland, John, 87, 105, 113, 124, 224
Buffalmaco, Christofani Buonamico,
  216
Buffon, Georges Louis Leclerc, comte
  de, 56
Buonaroti, Michelangelo, 217, 226,
  230, 239, 255, 271–3, 276, 277, 278
Buoncampagni, *see* Boncampagni

C—, Countess, from Nice, 308
C—, Dr., 13
C—, Mr., Smollett's landlord at Nice,
  *see* Corvesi
C—, Miss, *see* Curry
Caesar, Caius, 85, 217 n.
Caesar, Julius, 15, 18, 142, 238, 262, 314
Caesar, Lucius, 85, 271 n.
Calvinus, Caius Sextius, 319

Caracalla, Marcus Aurelius Antoninus, 224–5, 262, 263
Cataline, Lucius Sergius, 228
Catherine, Empress of Russia, 208
Catinat, Nicholas 116, 334
Cato, Marcus Portius, 267
Catulus, Luctatius, 324
Cestius, Caius, 268, 275
Charlemagne, 18, 272
Charles II, King of the Sicilies and Count of Provence, 130
Charles V, Holy Roman Emperor, 121, 146
Charles Emmanuel I, Duke of Savoy, 126, 146
Chatelet, Gabrielle Émilie de Breteuil, 56
Chigi, Fabio, *see* Alexander VII
Cicero, Marcus Tullius, 260
Cimabue, Giovanni, 255
Claude, French *voiturier*, 323
Claudius, Roman Emperor, 18, 243
Clement VI, Pope, 324
Clement VII, Pope, 250
Colbert, Jean-Baptiste, 104
Coligni (Coligny), Gaspard de, 272
Commodus, 143 n.
Condé, Louis de Bourbon, prince de, 104
Condé, Louis Joseph de Bourbon, (eighth) prince de, 42
Constantine the Great, 236, 247, 272
Conti, see Bourbon
Conway, Francis Seymour, *see* Hertford
Correggio, Antonio, 278
Corvesi, François Clément, 222, 311
Cosimo I, Grand Duke of Tuscany, 215
Cosmo, *see* Cosimo
Créqui, Charles, duc de, 324
Croy, Emmanuel de, 17
Cruy, *see* Croy
Ctesilas, 275
Curry, Anne, 11, 198, 286, 289

D—, Duchess of, *see* Douglas
Dacier, Anne Lefevre, 56
Descartes, René, 56
Didius Julianus, 143 n.
D—lle, Duchess, *see* Rochefoucauld d'Anville
Domenichino, 255, 277, 278
Domitian, 263
Douglas, Margaret, Duchess of, 12, 64
Drusus, Nero Claudius, 251

Duilius, Caius, 275
Dutreil, *see* Etreil

E—, Capt., *see* Eliot
Edward III, King of England, 230 n.
Elagabalus, *see* Heliogabalus
Eliot, Captain John, 315
Emmanuel Philibert, Duke of Savoy, 130, 146
Este, Hercule-Renaud d', Duke of Modena, 213
Étreil, Nadeau d', 110

F—, Professor, *see* Fizes
Farnese, Alexander, *see* Paul III
Ferdinand I, Grand Duke of Tuscany, 215
Fitz-James, Charles, duc de, 86
Fitz-Maurice, Dr. Thomas, 88
Fizes, Antoine, 88–102, 114
Flaccus, Valerius, 267
Flaminius, Gaius, 284
Fontana, Dominico, 239, 260
Francis I, King of France, 146, 324
Francis, Saint, of Assisi, 283
Freij (Frey), Jakob Johann, 278

Gallienus, 121, 141
Germanicus Caesar, 251, 278
Ghiberti, Lorenzo, 230
Ghiotto, *see* Giotto
Giottino, 216
Giotto, 216, 255
Glycon, 275
Goldoni, Carlo, 33, 222
Gore, Charles, 319
G—r, Mr., *see* Gore
Graeme (or Graham), Father Patrick, 19
Gregory XIII, Pope, 217 n.
Grimaldi, Princes of Monaco, 122, 172, 199, 209
Guastaldi (Gastaldi), Giambattista, 64
Guazzesi, Lorenzo, 285
Gubernatis, Honoré Roger, comte de, 120, 122, 141
Guercino, Giovanni Francesco Barbieri, 278
Guido, *see* Reni

H—, D., *see* Hume
H—, Earl of, *see* Hertford
H—, Lord, 320
Hadrian, 83, 226, 266, 267

# Index

Hamilton, 'our friend', 42
Hannibal, 284
Hawkwood, John, 230 n.
Heliogabalus, 244, 245 n., 262
Henry III, King of France, 82
Henry IV, King of France, 131
Henry V, King of England, 28
Henry VII, Holy Roman Emperor, 232
Henry VIII, King of England, 39
Hertford, Francis Seymour Conway, first Earl of, 12, 14, 21
H—r, Dr., see Hunter
Hume, David, 21
Hunter, Dr. William, 88

Ivan, Prince, proclaimed Ivan VI, Emperor of Russia, 208

Jane I, Queen of Naples, 324
Jocundus, Gallus Favonius, 269–70
Joseph, muleteer, 73–8, 323

K—, Father, see Kelcher
Kelcher, Father Patrick, 35

L—, Capt., 30
L—, Mr., 86
Laurence, Saint, 257
Le Brun, Charles, 278
Lepidus, Aemilius, Censor, 236
Leutrum, Baron Frederick de, 209, 309
Livius, Titus, 174
Lorraine, Claude, 277
Louis XIV, King of France, 47, 103, 104–5
Louvigny, M. de, 35–8
Louvois, François Michel Le Tellier, marquis de, 104
Lucullus, 263
Lully, Jean-Baptiste, 45
Luther, Martin, 280
Luxemburg, François Henri de Montmorency-Boutteville, duc de, 104
L—y, Mons., see Louvigny
Lysippus, 231, 266

M., marquis, traveller to Turin, 305–6
M—, Mr., valetudinarian, see Mayne
M—, Mr., correspondent, 63
M—, Mrs., see Macaulay, Catherine
Macaulay, Catherine, possible identification for Mrs. M—, 52

Macaulay, Dr. George, possible identification for Mr. M—l, 131
Maccarani, Claude Alli, marquis de, 127
Macpherson, James, 225
Maffei, Francesco Scipione, marquis de, 228
Maintenon, Françoise d'Aubigné, 36, 56, 105
Mandrin, Louis, 76–8
Mapp, Mrs., 89
Maratti, Carlo, 278
Marcellus, Marcus Claudius, 250–1
Marius, Caius, 319, 324
Marlborough, John Churchill, first Duke of, 36
Marsin (Marchin), Ferdinand, comte de, 104
Martines, Mr. de, 113
Masculus, Marcus Aurelius, 120
Mathilda, Grand Countess of Tuscany, 217 n., 235
Maupertuis, Pierre Louis Moreau de, 56
Maxentius, 236
Maximian, 141
Mayne, Mr., 40, 113, 114
M—e, Mr., see Mayne
Medicis, Giulio de, see Clement VII
Meriton, Henry, 21
Metella, Cecilia, 268–9
M—i, marquis de, see Maccarani
Michelangelo, see Buonaroti
Milico (Milichus), 228
M—l, Mr., see Macaulay, George
Modena, Duke of, see Este
Molière, Jean-Baptiste Poquelin de, 45
Monaco, Prince of, see Grimaldi

Nadeau, see Étreil
Nero, 228, 236, 260, 265
Neville, Richard Neville Aldworth, 14
N—lle, Mr., see Neville

O—d, Mr., see Oswald
Orsini, see Ursini
Ossory, Thomas, Earl of, 137–8
Oswald, Richard, 101
Otho, Marcus Salvius, 246

Paoli, Pasquale, 207
Paschal II, Pope, 236
Paterson, General Sir James, 14–15, 87, 113, 128, 193 n.
Paul II, Pope, 261

# Index

Paul III, Pope, 261, 274
Peretti, Felice, *see* Sixtus V
Pertinax, *see* Aulus Helvius
Perugino, Pietro, 232, 284
Petrarch, Francesco, 223, 324
Phidias, 273
Philip, Don, 209, 298
Phryne, 227
Piccolmini, Aeneas Silvius de, *see* Pius II
Piranesi, Giovanni Battista, 240
Pius II, Pope, 232
P—n, General, *see* Paterson
Polydore, 273
Pontius, Saint, 121
Porta, Guglielmo de la, 275
Poussin, Nicolas, 275, 278
Praxiteles, 227, 273
Probus, Marcus Aurelius, 262

R—, Mr., 198, 200, 206, 284, 286, 289
Racine, Jean, 45
Raphael, 231, 232, 277, 278, 284
Ray, Alexander, 87, 105
Réaumur, René Antoine Ferchault de, 56, 333
Reni, Guido, 255, 275, 277, 278, 284
R—f—t, duc de, *see* Rochefoucauld d'Anville
Rheni, *see* Reni
Riarius, Raphael Galeotto, 261
Richard I, King of England, 175
Rochefoucauld d'Anville, Louis-Alexandre, duc de la, 329
Rochefoucauld d'Anville, duchesse de la, 329
Roger Pierre, *see* Clement VI
Rosa, Salvator, 278
Rovere, Francesco della, *see* Sixtus IV
Rubens, Peter Paul, 275
R—y. Mr., *see* R—

S—, Dr., at Nice, probably Smollett himself, 304
Sacchi, Andrea, 277
Saint-Pierre, Honoré, 113–14
Saxe, Maurice, 60
Scævinius, 228
Scarron, Paul, 105
Schutz, Mr., 188–9
Sch—z, Mr., *see* Schutz
Scuderi, Madeleine de, 56
Sebastian, Saint, 257
Sejanus, 234

Sellier, Pascal, 331
Severinus P. Aelius, 119–20
Severus, Lucius Septimius, 246, 274, 325
Severus, Marcus Aurelius Alexander, 274
Sevigné, Marie de Rabutin-Chantal, 56
Shrewsbury, Anna Maria Brudenell, Countess of, 137
Shrewsbury, Francis Talbot, eleventh Earl of, 137
Sixtus IV, Pope, 271
Sixtus V, Pope, 239
Smellie, Dr. William, 88
Sm—ie, Dr., *see* Smellie
Smollett, Mrs. Anne, 2–3, 8, 71, 198, 286, 287–8
S—re, Mr., 319
St—e, Mrs., *see* Sterne
Stefano, 216
Sterne, Mrs. Elizabeth, 101
St. Pierre, Genoves, duc de, 15

Tacitus, Cornelius 283, 314
Tacitus, Marcus Claudius, 283
Tallard, Camille d'Ostun, duc de, 104
Tarquinius Priscus, 145, 228, 267
Tarquinius Superbus, 267
Tasso, Torquato, 223
Tauriscus, 276
Tavernier, Jean-Baptiste, 289
Teuts, *see* Tuite
Tiberius, 266
Titian, 229, 277, 278
Titus, 260, 273
Tuite, Lieutenant Colonel Walter, 86
Tully, *see* Cicero
Turenne, Henri de la Tour d'Auvergne, vicomte de, 104

Urban VIII, Pope, 254, 258–9
Ursini (Orsini), Fulvius, 273

Valerian, 121
Vanini, Mary, 219, 288
Vasari, Giorgio, 224, 226, 272
Vauban, Sébastien Le Prestre, marquis de, 145
Venanson, Joseph Laurenti, comte de, 113
Vendôme, Louis Joseph, duc de, 104
Verus, Lucius Aurelius, 274
Vespasian, 244, 247, 260, 267, 272

# Index

Victor Amadeus II, King of Sardinia,
  116, 334
Villars, Honoré Armand, duc de, 319,
  328
Villeroi, François de Neufville, duc de,
  104

Viriatus, 269–70
V—n, count de, *see* Venanson

Wig-Middleton, 50

# ii. Index of Books cited by Smollett

Addison, Joseph, *Remarks on Several Parts of Italy*, 226, 234, 283
Aelian, *De Natura Animalium*, 144
Alberici, Giacomo, *Compendio delle Grandezze dell'Illustre e Devotissima Chiesa di Santa Maria del Popolo di Roma*, 236
Antoninus, *Itinerarium*, 129, 196
Apicius, Cælius, *De Re Coquinaria*, 312 n.
Appian *Roman History*, 238
Aulus Gellius, *Attic Nights*, 247

Baronius, Caesar, *Annales Ecclesiasticus*, 28
Bianchi, Giuseppe, *Ragguaglio delle Antichità e Rarità che si Conservano nella Galleria Mediceo-Imperiale di Firenze*, 226
Brookes, Richard, *The General Practice of Physic*, 114
Büsching, Anton Friedrich, *A New System of Geography*, 143

Celsus, *De Medecina*, 14
Cervantes, Miguel de, *Don Quixote*, 36, 37
Cicero, *Academica*, 264

Desprez, Ludovicus, *see* Horace
Dio, *see* Dion Cassius
Diodorus Siculus, *Bibliothecae Historicae*, 144
Dion Cassius, *Romaika*, 224, 238

Febei, Francesco Maria, *De Identitate Cathedræ Romanæ*, 256

Galen, *De Sanitate Tuenda*, 266
Goldoni, Carlo, *La Buona Moglie*, 33
Gruter(us), Jean, *Inscriptiones Antiquæ*, 236

Henry VIII, *Assertio Septem Sacramentorum*, 280
Hippocrates, *Aphorisms*, 14
Homer, *Iliad*, 225, 261
Horace, *Opera* (ed. Ludovicus Desprez) 234, 244, 327; (trans. P. Francis), 238

Justin, *Historiæ Philipicæ*, 145
Juvenal, *Satires*, 265

Keysler, Johann Georg, *Travels through Germany, Bohemia, Hungary, Switzerland, Italy and Lorrain*, 154 n., 230, 273

Leti, Gregorio, *l'Italia Regnante*, 220

Livy, *Annales*, 238
Lucan, *Pharsalia*, 111, 129–30, 170
Lucian [?], *Affairs of the Heart*, 227

Maffei, Paolo Alessandro, *Raccolta di Statue Antiche e Moderne*, 228
Martial, *Epigrams*, 265, 312
Mezerai, François Eudes de, *Histoire de France*, 146
Montfaucon, Bernard de, *The Travels . . . from Paris thro' Italy*, 273, 325

Nepos, Cornelius, *Vitae Excellentium Imperatorum*, 135
Nugent, Thomas, *The Grand Tour*, 110–11, 234, 236, 258

Ovid, *Consolatio ad Liviam*, 251; *Epistolae ex Ponto*, 341; *Fasti*, 238–9;
    *Metamorphoses*, 225–6

Persius, *Satires*, 265
Pliny, *Natural History*, 119, 142–3, 234, 268, 272–3, 275, 276, 311
Polybius, *History*, 145
Ptolemy, *Geography*, 119, 129

Réaumur, René Antoine Ferchault de, "Essais de l'Histoire des
    Rivieres . . .", 79
*Roma Antica, e Moderna*, 240, 272
Rutilius, *De Reditu Suo*, 244

Sallust, *De Catilinæ Coniuratione*, 228
Saxe, Maurice, *Mes Rêveries*, 60
Seneca, *Controversiarum*, 245 n.
Shakespeare, William, *Hamlet*, 208; *2 Henry IV* (Pistol), 49
Spartian, *Scriptores Historiae Augustae*, 266
Strabo, *Geography*, 129, 216 n.
Suetonius, *The Lives of the Twelve Caesars*, 224, 236, 246, 263

Tacitus, *Annales*, 261
Tillemont, Louis Sébastien le Nain de, *Mémoires pour Servir à l'Histoire
    Ecclesiastique des Six Premiers Siècles*, 28
Travessac, Abbé Antoine Valette de, *Abrégé de l'Histoire de la Ville de
    Nismes*, 80, 84

Vaillant, Jean Foy, *Numismata Imperatorum Romanorum Praestantiora*, 228
Valette, *see* Travessac
Vasi, Giuseppe, *Itinerario Istruttivo . . . di Roma*, 240
Virgil, *Aeneid*, 250–1, 261, 281; *Georgics*, 144
Voltaire, François-Marie Arouet, *Essay sur l'Histoire Générale*, 175

Walpole, Horace, *A Catalogue of Royal and Noble Authors*, 175
Webb, Daniel, *Inquiry into the Beauties of Painting*, 271